Russian Television Today

The most important stories in Russia have traditionally been those of literature; today that function is fulfilled by TV drama. This book examines the role of dramatized narratives in Russian television, demonstrating how they grapple with key questions of both national identity and recent history. *Russian Television Today* shows how visual drama succeeds in offering some answers or consolation, laying claim to a window on past generations and showing Russian viewers what might be salvageable from the Soviet experience. Just as President Putin uses that experience to hone a fresh understanding of what it means to "be" Russian, so TV's heroes and heroines frequently express themselves with a related, soothing simplicity. Extending and complicating any such harmonies, this book then turns to other important developments: the manufacturing of new "national" on-screen characters and their peculiar relationship to both classic or Soviet literature and Latin-American soaps – all filtered through the enduring emphases of love, fidelity, humor, and irony. Since, however, those filters are often designed to block an unpleasant actuality, this book also pays considerable attention to the pressing problem of domestic crime and its troubled representation on screen – either as Mafia or police adventures.

Overall, *Russian Television Today* provides a detailed account of critical social and aesthetic issues in Russia's primetime visual media, all the way from historical epics to the recent, more profitable emphases of situation comedy and reality shows.

David MacFadyen is Professor in the Department of Slavic Languages and Literatures at the University of California, Los Angeles, USA. He is the author of numerous books on many aspects of Russian literature and culture, including the poetry of Joseph Brodsky, classic Soviet prose, popular song across the twentieth century, comedic cinema, and animated film.

Routledge Contemporary Russia and Eastern Europe Series

1 Liberal Nationalism in Central Europe
Stefan Auer

2 Civil-Military Relations in Russia and Eastern Europe
David J. Betz

3 The Extreme Nationalist Threat in Russia
The Growing Influence of Western Rightist Ideas
Thomas Parland

4 Economic Development in Tatarstan
Global Markets and a Russian Region
Leo McCann

5 Adapting to Russia's New Labour Market
Gender and Employment Strategy
Edited by Sarah Ashwin

6 Building Democracy and Civil Society East of the Elbe
Essays in Honour of Edmund Mokrzycki
Edited by Sven Eliaeson

7 The Telengits of Southern Siberia
Landscape, Religion and Knowledge in Motion
Agnieszka Halemba

8 The Development of Capitalism in Russia
Simon Clarke

9 Russian Television Today
Primetime Drama and Comedy
David MacFadyen

Russian Television Today

Primetime drama and comedy

David MacFadyen

LONDON AND NEW YORK

First published 2008
by Routledge
2 Park Square, Milton Park, Abingdon, Oxon, OX14 4RN

Simultaneously published in the USA and Canada
by Routledge
711 Third Avenue, New York, NY 10017

Routledge is an imprint of the Taylor & Francis Group, an informa business

First issued in paperback 2011

© 2008 David MacFadyen

Typeset in Goudy by Taylor & Francis Books

All rights reserved. No part of this book may be reprinted or
reproduced or utilized in any form or by any electronic, mechanical, or
other means, now known or hereafter invented, including
photocopying and recording, or in any information storage or retrieval
system, without permission in writing from the publishers.

British Library Cataloguing in Publication Data
A catalogue record for this book is available from the British Library

Library of Congress Cataloging in Publication Data
MacFadyen, David, 1964-

Russian television today : primetime drama and comedy / David
MacFadyen.

p. cm. – (Routledge contemporary Russia and Eastern Europe series)
Includes bibliographical references and index.
ISBN-13: 978-0-415-42462-2 (hardback : alk. paper) 1. Television
broadcasting–Russia (Federation)–History. 2. Television programs–
Russia (Federation)–History. I. Title.
PN1992.3.R8M33 2007
791.450947–dc22

2006036315

ISBN10: 0-415-42462-3 (hbk)
ISBN10: 0-415-49176-2 (pbk)
ISBN10: 0-203-96165-X (ebk)

ISBN13: 978-0-415-42462-2 (hbk)
ISBN13: 978-0-415-49176-1 (pbk)
ISBN13: 978-0-203-96165-0 (ebk)

For the editors of Kinokultura, with gratitude

Contents

	Introduction: sweeping statements and broad horizons	1
1	Action heroes: Don Quixote or James Bond?	9
2	Adaptations: TV drama vs. literary prestige	32
3	Soaps: the influence of Latin America	64
4	Costume drama: "life as it really is"	84
5	Melodrama: little people in the big city	103
6	Heroines: airports, planes, and wedding trains	126
7	Comedy: nervous giggling and its serious object	149
8	Law and order: making sense of *something*	168
9	Criminal series: Soviet traditions come home	187
10	Conclusion: fighting the good fight	209
	Filmography	215
	Notes	226
	Index	241

Introduction
Sweeping statements and broad horizons

> Counter-revolutions always follow revolutions. They, in turn, are followed by a search for people guilty of revolutionary excess – and their punishment. Russian history is full of such examples.
> (President Vladimir Putin, 2001)

The most important and popular stories in Russia have traditionally been those of literature; that function is currently being fulfilled by TV drama. In prior decades, socialist media repeatedly boasted to the outside world that nobody reads more than Soviet citizens; nowadays, however, opinion polls reveal with equal frequency that more than half of Russia's public has read little or no literature in recent memory. Elderly arbiters of Slavic culture hang their heads and intone somewhat ominously that the printed page has lost its battle for cultural prominence. The nine chapters that follow, although cognizant of any such wretchedness, aim to paint a less miserable picture; they examine visual tales of artful, hopeful change that Russians are telling themselves in today's primetime. Televised yarns in fact often make considerable and respectful *use* of literature in order to reassess the nation's sad past and/or posit some happier future, at least for social microcosms such as friends, families, and starry-eyed lovers.

In addition, Russian television nowadays can *create* bestsellers. Popular TV series often become big, popular books. Long, peopled chronicles of love, laughter, and despicable intrigue work just as well on paper. They offer the consolation of a crystal ball and do so with huge profits. Weaving both in and out of literature, both with and without the printed page, televised dramas fill broadcasting schedules every evening all across Russia, from the Baltic to the Pacific.

As Putin suggests in the above epigraph, many TV stories display well-structured parallels with the grand narratives of social actuality. They borrow from history (from a shared, recognizable past) and then, willy-nilly, start to color its future. They reflect old views and create new ones. Television shows frequently cast a retrospective glance at Russia's history before debating the futures of their influential heroes; they do so by grappling with two key questions: "What really happened to us?" and, accordingly, "Why?"

Turning first to the prestige of a literary canon or the partisan influence of an equally canonized history, Russian primetime recurrently conjures sweeping statements in order to join the dots between exciting, engaging stories of two people and those of an entire "nation." Generalizations are used to connect the past to the present in an entertaining and feasible fashion.

Using historical or collective situations to comprehend and articulate a modern selfhood, television melodrama regularly subscribes to the undemanding, though comprehensive, Hegelianism that Putin notes – or it tries at least to posit some existential agency therein. The results may constitute examples of what he calls "common sense," but whenever headstrong presidents start employing the rhetoric of historical inevitability to predict, influence, or *correct* the status quo, matters are quickly complicated. This problem has certainly been exacerbated by Putin's media policy and the type of shows it has supported since the Kursk disaster, all in the name of displaying history's purported rationale. Russia's national television stations are today either state-owned or overseen by affiliated companies, so in many instances today's TV serials do reflect the Kremlin's views, though this is not always the case and we will examine closely any exceptions.

One Russian proverb holds that "all novelty is simply a well-forgotten past." Without a doubt, lots of TV dramas show us what is salvageable from the Soviet experience. Putin's manipulation of past traditions comes on the heels of some revisionist scholarship in the West that has reassessed the core tenets of Soviet culture. These new viewpoints are extremely useful in any broad, if not equally sweeping, assessments of how post-Soviet mores operate; i.e. assessments of what they continue to draw upon long after 1991. Mikhail Epstein has suggested, for example, that a reconsideration (if not dismissal) of history's received milestones can shed light upon several enduring, if not imposing, "Russo-Soviet topoi" that try to define the quiddity of Russianness. Clichés or not, political rhetoric and its TV audience value these kinds of generalizations very highly.

Paradoxically, such topoi often lie outside language, because here one senses some of the most important platitudes of Russian self-awareness, conceivable as an illogical, "indescribable 'inner world,' an expansive, authentic 'life force.'"[1] These ineffable vagaries might be a reasonable starting place for our examination of today's narrative tropes, but ultimately they just restate many of the abstractions underlying the clichés. The guilty party here is an often apophatic outline of what the Slavic soul is *not*: "'Western' rational articulation, precision, delimitation, reserve, calculation, reflection, or predictability."[2] Nationhood on today's TV is often invoked in a similarly fuzzy social sense, as communal existence beyond the historical lifespan of ideas like "commun-ism," and is thus habitually associated with loss, with something both unspeakable and absent. It was something abused by the more avaricious, doctrinaire aspects of Soviet materialism and is now being manhandled by modern, corporate Russia. Today's body politic therefore overlaps with ways in which bodies of suffering or sympathy characterize themselves: an identity gained either through defeat or something born of nothing.

Soviet revisionism in a wide-ranging ecological context

In a recent essay concerning other elements of Soviet culture that endure in present-day Russian essentialism, Mikhail Epstein offers perhaps the grandest of all such negations. He begins by stating what it means to be "Russian" spatiotemporally, to be the product of a given land or legacy. When Russians speak of the country and history that have made them who they are, their idea of endless space often "swallows up" anything temporal, leading to a specific double entendre in his Russo-Soviet topoi. The sheer enormity of Russia inspires both a sense of nothingness (of a place too big to see) and some insistent awareness of great heroism required to do that magnitude justice – or save it in times of major conflict.

Given, in addition, that this enormity has for centuries been part and parcel of centralized imperial projects, the "provinces" are likewise seen as realms that may once have had their own center, but over time were beaten and annexed, leaving most of the nation as *nothing* in particular. Russians, as a result, do not feel at home in the unbounded, unpeopled place they call home:

> This void is terrifying. Nature, the proverb notwithstanding, does not abhor a vacuum, but humans do. In Russia, we all seem to suffer from a love–hate complex towards space. What is that celebrated [Gogolian] "fast driving" that "what Russian does not love?" [sic]. Is it a flight into space or *from* space? It is both. Having rushed into the void, people try as quickly as possible to hurl themselves out of its invisible surroundings, to prevail, to reach a firm boundary, a crowded refuge.[3]

And yet, in the context of another recent study by Katerina Clark, we are told that the same emptiness and grandeur have often been invoked as an ostensible, ever-*present* embodiment of some long, institutionalized and "extraordinary *time*."[4] Enormity and insignificance, presence and absence, are frequently bound together in popular memory; small compressed spaces and private timelines are bound to their possible dissolution in nothingness – or an incomprehensibility synonymous with magical stately presence.

Whenever this magic is challenged, as in 1917, immobile presence then contemplates its *own* absence, in this case its obsolescence at the hands of modernist progression. That which always "was or is," i.e. an antique essence beyond the ken of historians and cartographers, then stands face to face with that which "can, will or should be," i.e. socially desirable but not (yet) existent. Thomas Lahusen has synthesized these spiraling oppositions in twentieth-century Russian self-awareness as the competition between what is "now" or unchanging, and that which is "evolutionary."[5]

Elsewhere Epstein has suggested other ways in which stasis and growth, all and (maybe) nothing, might be involuntarily wedded by popular or generalized Russo-Soviet custom. "Circles of repetitive celebrations" went round and round as socialist culture enjoyed the demarcation of its achievements, month after month, to the point where it ended up going nowhere in particular. "Practically every day was the anniversary of something [magnificent], and the noise of the celebration died out, with each gala evening passing into a festive matinee."[6] These recurrences resulted from what he calls the synthetic, "serious eclecticism" of socialist realism, which would later metamorphose into a repeatedly "playful" eclecticism, a strange harbinger of postmodernism.[7]

Other scholarly work of late by Evgenii Dobrenko has asserted that socialist realism was indeed a great synthesizing force, over and over again, because it operated almost exclusively in the domain of mass taste and the most popular, accessible aesthetic possible. The reason for this choice, he claims, was that "Soviet power was a pragmatic of *pure* power, its strategy dictated by the logic of self-preservation, the logic of keeping power."[8] There was nothing it would not do or adopt as it yearned, like the hero of Fedor Gladkov's *Cement*, for "a world more boundless than it was for Spinoza." The willful involvement of Russian book-buyers or readers in this yearning simply amplified and extended it. Thus, adds Dobrenko, in socialist art:

> The consumer [of truly expansive/inclusive art] becomes a creator, and the creator a consumer. There is no end to creativity. It has no obstacles. It is actually popular and "organic." [As Aleksandr Fadeev said,] "Art cannot be considered real art if it does not become profoundly popular, necessary to the people and loved by them. The people do not want to smother anyone's artistic individuality. They stand behind an organic, great free and content-rich creativity."[9]

With this Spinozistic organicity there emerge additional contradictions. How, for example, can today's scholars or politicians, even, conflate conservative, Stalinist tales of Russia's "subdued nature" and the simultaneous fight for Gladkov's and Fadeev's sprawling ecology? This book will maintain that there is, in fact, no difference or inconsistency between a Leninist drive for everything and a growing proximity towards Epstein's nothingness. That same paradox is embodied by today's TV tales, by the engaging chronicles that state-sponsored television endorses, since they so often employ the Soviet past to reflect or model a post-Soviet future. Today's reconsideration of Soviet literary culture helps us reconsider and understand the most popular television, too.

It is sometimes said that Russian TV dramas (and news) have become "more apolitical" since 2003.[10] This popularized, eclectically middlebrow aesthetic and the avoidance of political extremism or experimentation have

Introduction 5

been included in other reassessments of socialist art. The first and perhaps most famous of these was Vera Dunham's study of middleclass cultural "mediation" after World War Two. Our own study concurs, but aims to move middleclass eclecticism away from cultural pragmatism and further in the direction of a risky, essentially socialist romanticism. A vertiginous, ecologically expansive romanticism was, it seems, always a key element of Soviet rhetoric, of its speeches and most conventional realist stories – the invocation of Epstein's tightly bound dyad: everything and/or nothing. This Spinozistic romanticism was dragged into Soviet storytelling from pre-revolutionary experience, and in television productions of today it remains of equal value to Russia's state-funded media, trying to reinstate a sweeping sense of national, post-Soviet pride. A vacuity is never far from today's omnipresent, calming rhetoric or cozy dramas, from the "small crowded refuges" of soap operas – and it may in fact be brought even closer by them.

TV's limited language, "surmounted" by nostalgia for the 1970s

Civic pride and patriotic television invoke profoundly social states; to that extent the following chapters are in agreement with Dobrenko whenever he brings myriad Soviet readers into the history of semantic negotiation. There is, however, good reason to take polite issue with Svetlana Boym's recent assertion that Soviet art and stories "manipulated the consciousness [of recipients], using the techniques that automatically secure emotional responses."[11] Similarly, one might question Epstein's contention that socialist art "used ideological force on the [public's] consciousness."[12] There was no automatic security in these processes, and TV now is having the same problems as socialist cinema and literature in "guiding" social consciousness. The quandaries faced nowadays by screenwriters and directors often begin with a difficult renegotiation of Russia's historically validated platitudes, the views of spatiotemporality suggested above.

Putin's narratives of socialist dignity *redux* are likewise made on the scale of Epstein's shibboleths, designed to fill an empty nation and/or voided nature. They work both verbally *and* visually, contemplating the ineffable or undoable, and in doing so they unavoidably bump up against their representational limitations. With regard to this issue, in my 2005 study of Russian animated film, *Yellow Crocodiles and Blue Oranges*, I showed how the screenplays of many Soviet cartoons, facing the same problem, grew *smaller* over time. Language considered its limits; notions of perfect interaction grew less wordy or effable and more musical or visual. In justifying this process as illustrative of what socialist art was often doing elsewhere (or Putin is today), that particular study also sketched the history of phenomenology in the USSR.

The argument was made that the most fundamental, ideal basis of desired socialist interaction, of everybody everywhere, was best investigated as an issue of consciousness, rather than quotidian, mappable reality. Phenomenology, after all, does not deny the existence of material phenomena that demarcate Soviet existence; it merely posits them as "phenomenal occurrences" of objects with acts of intending. Things exist as they occur to us, an aphoristic truism that leads us to admit, perhaps, the primacy of intuiting over the things we intuit. The workings and troubled reputation of phenomenology in Russia show us a path that dialectical materialism, from its idealist, Hegelian roots, could (and should) have taken to discover more about social consciousness and emotional, nationally social essences (which are pre- or *extra*-linguistic). What Soviet language wanted most of all, just like Gladkov's hero, was something that could not be said.

Following attention will therefore define the "politics" of socialist-inspired storytelling, its factional scheming as follows: Did it (or does it now through Putin) rely upon feasible, effable schemes or a phenomenological awareness beyond itself, an overcoming of the subject–object divide? Some kind of silent, apophatic *membership* with the void or uninhabited nature, especially if untilled and unspeakable geography outlines and *drives* the desires enacted on its playing field? I will contend that Soviet stories "then," just as Putinesque drama now, have done precisely that by drawing upon a deeply romantic consciousness, demarcating a yearning for something that never was (or never could "be" in its entirety). The empty object of desire was and remains not so much a lost past or borderless map, but an undoable, unutterable future.

In respectful contradistinction to recent reassessments of socialist realism, therefore, this study will not dissolve the significance of rhetoric wholly into outdoor social practices, nor stress its role in quotidian reality, but will attempt a return to the oratory *per se*, a reconsideration of its social function *within itself*. After all, if the stories examined in this book embody the search for undoable prospects, they also contain within themselves the seeds of their own demise, long before they become the social tools of other, disparate people for other purposes. Dogma and the stories thereof will be shown as *intentionality*, as endlessly pondered steps towards the ineffable, unmanageable ecological grandeur and emptiness of which Epstein and Lahusen speak. They intend doing a great deal. This task, if undertaken to the full, would be an encounter with the Real in the Lacanian sense and the construction of eternally wedded, social networks of verity in the Badiouian. It would be really social and truly real.

The perfect, organic union of Soviet cultural creator and consumer, of artist and reader, was supposed to be waist-deep in the endless "situation[s] of creativity itself" on the scale of Fadeev's "naturally popular" networks noted above. These goals of organic production are exactly the metaphors investigated by TV today. Their ontology originates in some vertiginous aspects of socialist art; yet if we turn on Moscow television, they are fashioning the most popular stories in the world's biggest country in four, eight, twelve episodes or more. It is on TV that the long, traditionally serialized

Russian narrative can now be found. Television picks up where a socialist reworking of Golden Age prose left off.

This study will pay much attention to the importance of literary adaptations. The relationship between verbal and visual narratives has been a troublesome aspect of Russian filmmaking since its inception, when silent adaptations of classic literature helped to allay directors' insecurity in the face of St. Petersburg's serious dramatic theater. We will examine ways in which early, visualized Soviet storytelling (then) and the status thereof (now) are interrelated; they both seek to mirror and manipulate more serious times. The two periods in greatest thematic demand for television now are Stalinism (such as the autumn 2006 series *His Wife* [*Ego zhena*])[13] and the much safer years under Brezhnev, which repeated Stalin's emphasis upon "cultured" and educated aesthetics. These periods uneasily interwove a zealous, self-assured patriotism and bureaucratic, self-satisfied security. Both are sought today.

In particular, the 1970s are affectionately, earnestly remembered. They were a fine age for filmmaking: between 1965 and 1980, Soviet citizens went to the movies on average twenty times each year.[14] Brezhnev's term in office likewise witnessed an explosion in television drama, driven frequently by adaptations of popular World War Two and spy stories. Not only did concern over brash Western culture lead to more "tasteful" adaptations of respectable Russian literature, but television became the venue of a warmed-over Stalinist contrariness, as noted by Stephen Hutchings. The Stagnation once gave birth to and now inspires small-screen stories along these same lines (written or filmed by that 1970s generation); it was a time of serious, significant TV:

> Under Brezhnev, television adaptations assumed greater importance. The televisual appearance of stock characters from the international literary canon like Sherlock Holmes, Tom Sawyer and the heroes of J.K. Jerome helped sate the mounting curiosity of ordinary Soviet people about all things Western. Such adaptations also complemented international policies of détente, promulgating cosy stereotypes of the eccentric English gentleman which enabled official culture to claim that it was 'fostering international understanding,' but at the same time, to ensure that progressive views of the iniquities of capitalism prevailed.[15]

Hutchings' observation comes in the introduction to a collection of articles dedicated to cinematic adaptations of Russian literature. This field will be of use to us in that we are examining the shift from the wholly linguistic to the mainly visual: "fidelity" to a serious, once-cherished original in the creation of patriotic myths is always important in the creation of dogmatic, political adaptations for TV.

All things considered, television drama is not the loss of literature but its next logical step, perhaps, beyond the promotional or political zeal of the

Soviet novelistic project. Film not only moves beyond the linear workings of metonymy, as already contended in the above animation monograph; it also breaks down the division between author and creator.[16] As a *collaborative* project, television and film enact a cherished dream of socialist culture: the organic positioning of author in (and wholly reflective of) Dobrenko's "life as it is." Television series today frequently give voice to a virtual, never-realized potential of socialist custom that in turn slips and slides away from the current administration. Born of a realist tradition, these tales of love, lust, and adventure embody several social states that are always desired, but never attained. They are – ultimately – excessive.

This striking elusiveness, so closely tied to the Stagnation and Putin's own youth of the 1970s, has led of late to TV films such as *December 32nd* (dir. Aleksandr Muratov, 2004). Three pensioners are magically made "thirty to forty" years younger, a wrinkled trio played by stars of Brezhnev's cinema: Andrei Miagkov, Armen Dzhigarkhanian, and Ada Rogovtseva. They relive a "wonderful" past but are eventually brought back to the present, where "happy faces around us" are only possible "if we're together." Both artistically and actually, this observation rings true for our study – though never for long. It gives voice to a spiraling ideal that may evanesce further with each passing year; a yearning towards other, absent people and places such that the credits of *December 32nd* dedicate the film "with love" to three icons of the Soviet 1970s – J.B. Priestley, Evgenii Shvarts, and Èl'dar Riazanov. Stable presidents and mentally unstable pensioners, it would appear, are looking for approval in the same places.

1 Action heroes
Don Quixote or James Bond?

Literature stays with us beyond the four walls of school. It will always be with us, opening more and more unique aspects of our nation's life. Literature introduces us to more and more creative aspects of the Soviet people.[1]

(From a Russian schoolbook of 1972)

A Russian Don Quixote, never at home

At the very start of the twenty-first century, within months of President Putin coming to power in Russia, a new television drama was broadcast, entitled *Rostov-Papa*. Far from the only fresh dramatic series on national television, it nonetheless epitomized a massively popular art form that had exploded over the last few years. *Rostov-Papa* embodied a type of social dreaming in ten short tales which interwove their isolated characters' lives across the embankments, streets, stairwells, offices, buses, and bedrooms of a southern port. This drama frames our initial discussion of action heroes, how much they cost to film and what (if anything) they should (or can) say. Language and lucre are very closely tied to nostalgic Russian TV's stories of taciturn gallantry.

The eighth story in *Rostov-Papa* was entitled *The New Don Quixote* (*Novyi Don-Khitot*), based upon a screenplay by Elena Gremina and director Kirill Serebrennikov. A retired high-school teacher of literature, Ktorov, spends his entire pension on paperback adventure stories, on pulp fiction that combines broad-shouldered Soviet machismo and modern, well-armed panache. Inspired by the need to undertake a similar task of honor and romantic excess, he adopts the name of the "Faithful One" (*Vernyi*) and goes in search of a long-lost student, Mariia, whom he once loved. Finding her proves to be difficult but he keeps looking, sometimes obsessively. Moving further and further from rational behavior, Ktorov grows nonetheless closer to a realization of his ideal, in that he is changing, improving, and undermining objective actuality by infusing it with passion. His reality is nothing without the unmanageably romantic.

Accompanied by the young and initially cynical drunkard Panas, Ktorov wanders through Rostov, bumping on occasion into other female students of the past, none of whom have become happy women in their adult lives. The one Mariia, meanwhile, eludes them. Ktorov and Panas scream at a Coca-Cola stand, blaming the "Americans" for stealing her, perhaps as the heroine of *West Side Story*. The two men even grab the microphone at a rally of lady communist pensioners, in the hope of finding social sympathy and more candidates of the right age amid a sea of home-sewn red banners. They are once again unlucky, however, especially when Ktorov's fervent, rambling speech about boundless love and charity is dismissed angrily by the ladies as the diversionary rhetoric of somebody "who's been bribed by the city administration." Passion, policy and avarice are all muddled up; they can all be equally pushy and sometimes occupy the same space.

As his search for ineffable perfection breaks down and becomes a loud, senseless screaming in the street, Ktorov is saved from arrest only by a middle-aged woman who suddenly announces herself as Mariia and promises to look after him in the mental hospital where she works. She tells the police that Ktorov had once assigned her, long ago, a series of school essays on "The Theme of Soviet Women in Soviet Literature," a task that left her with some of "life's happiest memories."

What, however, transpires is that "Mariia" is lying. In the months after her declaration to the police, she begins stealing the stories told or written by Ktorov in hospital. Mariia the doctor then publishes them under her own name and becomes a famous authoress, claiming that Ktorov and Panas are wholly fictitious. Outraged by this deceit when he sees Mariia interviewed on television, Panas storms the press conference of her book launch, proving that he does indeed exist. Yet even this episode ends up being published and dramatized over time in a pseudo-Latin, serialized TV version of the *whole* story, of how the doctor both acquired and vivified her "tragic detective" novels.

The dramatized TV-novella where Panas' messy tale concludes in melodramatic dialog and white nylon suits itself concludes a tight circle of adventures; pulp fiction and Latin passions both spawn and then return to the Russian TV-tale, skirting as they do so the expansive, heartfelt rhetoric of dreamy, failed feats, often those of Soviet citizens. All of these stories and styles have ended up on the small screen, resulting in something formless, a tasteless mess that is both true and false.

The ideal was and remains elsewhere. Ktorov had once told Panas to read Pushkin, Lermontov, Turgenev and Chekhov, because then "he'll understand everything." But he doesn't. Verity is too complex for the logical mind; only madness or a kitschy mélange of genres can hope to encapsulate it.

Figure 1.1 Rostov-Papa.

Tales of modern machismo, the delicate tedium of sanity or real life, classic literature, a Soviet social conscience, moneyed politics, and subversive fantasy are completely, utterly interwoven in ways that – just like the Soviet citizen Ktorov – aim for everything but end up with nothing in particular.

Long, verbose novels like the original *Don Quixote* have become long, slow TV series. They embody an overlap of personal passion and shared social dreaming that the greedy forces of modern Russia now make the domain of the mentally ill. Ktorov in real life called himself "The Faithful One"; now on-screen heroes rename him as "The Ideal One." They say he "wanted our town to be a town of eternal love." That sounds banal, unmanageable, and awfully reminiscent of social plans both socialist and pre-socialist. It fact it sounds silly enough for tens of millions of people, stuck in a mercilessly practical world, to take it just as seriously as Ktorov. In *Rostov-Papa* the hero takes this story of a ridiculously elusive ideal so seriously he dies for it.

The TV series as a genre aims to show today's Russian selfhood as unavoidably social, in this case through the open arms of ardor. The individual, when driven, is communal; the person *is* the polis, in this case the river town of Rostov. Here we see an overlap with the crisscrossing networks of recent films about passionate, peopled interaction such as *The Day of the Full Moon* (*Den' polnoluniia*, Karen Shakhnazarov, 1998), the French *Happenstance* (*Le Battement d'ailes du papillon*, Laurent Firode, 2000), or even the lighthearted British romantic comedy *Love Actually* (Richard Curtis, 2003). The story of our new Don Quixote maps itself neatly onto some social ideals of Western cinema, yet takes on a much more locally consequential form in reality, for the rhetoric of President Putin has employed similar metaphors since his inauguration in 2000. They speak of "Russia's [one] historical path," into "a free society of [countless] free people," dredged from dark Soviet waters to be buffed and burnished once again. Television often acts out what politics speaks of, what it would like to do but cannot do in actuality, for it remains a romantic, irrational excess. Its purview is so extensive it means nothing in particular.

The more cynical of Russia's journalists see Putin's talk of an extended, caring and "democratic" actuality, past or future, as purely normative.[2] In other words, his stories and promises might *create* a reality, at least a conscious one, if repeated often enough. Likewise, tales of individual fantasy reflect and can perhaps make consciousness into something factually social. We will investigate the stories of those like Ktorov, broadcast on TV stations increasingly controlled by politicians like Putin, in order to define the relationship between romance and reality.

Whose normality is coming to life on screen, though? The quixotic viewers' (as willing, expansive passion) or Putin's (as willful, progressive policy)? Are we watching the desired future of dreamers, succumbing to love, or the improved and roseate past of nostalgic pensioners, aggressively rebuilt by politicians? In a word, how Soviet are TV dramas in Russia today and which side of Epstein's Russianness do they show? The assumed essences that always exist ("here") or Lahusen's things that may – or may not – be (i.e. "nowhere")?

In her study of post-Soviet cinema and its search for a new, replacement male protagonist after 1991, Birgit Beumers discerned three main tendencies: the "escapist hero," the "war hero," and the "killer hero."[3] I would suggest that these three categories have nowadays to a large degree dovetailed; this creates even more confusion between self- and social definition in parallels between crime and warfare, say. Such combinations are designed to escape a corrupt reality and invoke somewhere better, fairer, and simpler. Our new man of La Mancha is a fine introductory model, but nonetheless he is presented with gentle irony. In many televised stories, the matters he embodies become deadly serious as the heroes fight for rectitude. One such example would be *The Maker of More Misery* (*Umnozhaiushchii pechal'*, 2005), which stars Aleksei Makarov; examined anon, this is a story based upon the "desolation" brought to Russia by those like oligarch Mikhail Khodorkovskii. Grimmer tales yet show a marriage of war, killing, and escaping in louder, larger forms, for example the TV/feature film *Hunter* (*Eger'*, 2004) with maverick action hero Igor' Lifanov and his "helpless" love interest, TV star Anna Bol'shova. On occasion cinema amplifies in a most telling way the type of TV stories with which these and other actors are associated. It stresses why action heroes *act*.

Aleksei Makarov, a Russian James Bond

> Russia's unity is strengthened by its inherent patriotism, its cultural traditions and shared historical memory. Today an interest in Russia's history is returning to art, theater and cinema. This is an interest in our roots, in what we all hold dear. I am convinced this is the start of a spiritual renaissance.
>
> (Putin, 2000)

Russia's president is well aware of TV and cinema's role in creating the nation he would like to see. At the end of 2003 he paid a visit to Mosfil'm studios, where he was asked about his attitude to TV series today and their displacement of earlier Brazilian and Mexican dramas. "Of course it's a good thing," he said. "People watch homemade series because they show *our* life. After all, how interesting can it possibly be to find out who got some Conchita or other pregnant?"[4] Television has lots of work to do at home if it hopes to satisfy the government's desire: serious and socially consequential work.

The success of TV drama in Russia has been such that feature film production regularly benefits from its sponsorship; on the big screen Russian viewers encounter examples of a dramatic extreme related to the lachrymose, open-armed melodrama of our Don Quixote: the well-armed action flick. Some notable examples or variations upon the theme since Putin's inauguration have been *Brother 2* (*Brat 2*, 2000), *The Sisters* (*Sestry*, 2002), *War* (*Voina*, 2002), *Bimmer* (*Bumer*, 2003) and *Company Nine* (*Deviataia rota*, 2005). In those action movies where irony is absent, one feels a direct influence of policy.

In addition, while state-run television shows itself primarily to a domestic audience, cinema, funded by that television, is seen around the world. A good illustration of recent international storytelling with one foot on the Duma's red carpet would be Evgenii Lavrent'ev's *Lichnyi nomer* (*Countdown*) of 2004, an action movie produced jointly by the Kremlin-run television station Channel One, a major oil company, and a national veteran's group. *Countdown* outlined its central theme as follows. This and all subsequent, indented plot summaries are from studios' promotional materials:

> Terrorists from the group 'Ansar Allah' have announced a Holy War against civilization. They have a plan to turn Rome, the Eternal City, into a city of eternal death. Yet the world will be saved by the courage and heroism of Agent Smolin, by the selflessness and professionalism of [American journalist] Catherine Stone, and the strength of spirit within Umar the Chechen. Helped by the joint action of Russian and Western Special Forces, all captives will be freed and the world saved from the threat of a monstrous act of terrorism ... This film is full of unique special effects, never before seen in world cinema; they will keep the viewer in suspense from the opening credits to the final scene.

As Russian cinema, thanks to television, muscles its way towards Western notions of cinematic success, the term "blockbuster" has started to appear in blurbs, interviews, and reviews, most noticeably regarding *Night Watch* (*Nochnoi dozor*, Timur Bekmambetov, 2004) and *Countdown*. Both films, say their makers and fans, construct big, bold narratives according to the scale and standards of Hollywood.[5] They have covered their production costs with TV's advertising revenues and domestic ticket sales, and have drawn more money than simultaneous US releases in Russia, at least initially.

Yet the expression "blockbuster" hides a less positive significance. As a term designated during World War Two for bombs large enough to level entire blocks of urban housing, it was subsequently adopted by post-war realtors to describe an insidious, yet no less loathsome, process. If the ethnic (i.e. white) composition of a city block could be "busted" by getting some non-white minorities to purchase a property or two, the average housing price would quickly fall, leaving rich pickings for predatory agents as squeamish white owners quickly sold up, often at a loss, and moved to less diverse areas of town.

A celebratory term, often used to designate a constructive, successful originality, is thus equally redolent of conflict, destruction, and avarice. Over and above the trumpeting of this movie's new, unheard-of budgetary scale, the most commonly published facts and figures surrounding *Countdown* concern how much stuff was blown up. Perhaps this is what is meant by "special effects, never before seen"? In a most satisfyingly Slavic way, the special effects on offer aren't actually that "special," i.e. virtual, since 150 kilograms of TNT were employed here, not to imitate exploding vehicles, but to detonate them in actuality. One helicopter, six armored cars, two trucks, and sixteen cars are destroyed over the course of 105 minutes; a small cost for saving the world, it must be said.

The two main areas in which *Countdown* lays claim to being a blockbuster are therefore financial and thematic. Both of these are then designed to fuel a third element of sweeping grandeur, a "new" sense of pride and self-definition as per presidential rhetoric. This movie was generously funded by state coffers (10 percent of its $7 million budget) and many newspapers reported that initial, closed screenings of the film were made to both Putin and Nikolai Patrushev, head of the FSB (the Federal Security Service of the Russian Federation). They both liked it very much. Aleksei Makarov, who plays the film's hero, Agent Aleksei Smolin, said that the movie was meant to earn new respect for the FSB, the army, and the police. These upright, uniformed figures "give us something to be proud of." Promotional phrasing from the distributor, Top Line, often echoed the same thinking.

On this issue of theme, the resulting, key dilemma is whether *Countdown* does or does not wish to be seen as original, i.e. whether it draws happily and overtly upon Western models such as *Die Hard* (John McTiernan, 1988), or is perhaps more intent upon forging a path into new, yet equally noisy territory. The answer is most evident in the film's last twenty seconds. As a final, all-encompassing aerial scene fades to black, replete with executive aircraft and billowing clouds, the following text appears before us:

> This story is based upon real events: the life of Russian SAS [Special Air Service] officer Aleksei Galkin. After being imprisoned by Chechens, he continued his army service and was awarded the medal "Hero of Russia." Today, together with Galkin, each and every one of us continues the battle with terrorism. A battle we must win!

Possible though it often is to forgive Russian drama its patriotic bent of late by reminding ourselves of similar flag-waving in American TV and cinema, these three sentences go far beyond the pale. As a result, what appears to be a very straightforward, knockabout action film suddenly and most willingly ushers in a crowd of ugly bystanders, shuffling in gray suits on the edge of the film set.

The finger-wagging of this audience-oriented riposte might remind us of similar closing generalizations from other adventure stories like *Zvezda* (*The Star*, N. Lebedev, 2002), in that both movies draw upon the dignity of past battle in the name of another, more recent "conflict." Both hope to take a past patriotism and reinstate it. The closing lines of *The Star* are as follows. They conclude the tragic bravery of army scouts, sacrificing their lives in 1944 near the Polish border in order to send a radio message to HQ – and thus avert a potentially devastating counterattack from several armored divisions of the German army:

> Only in 1964 were the scouts of the Soviet army awarded the Order of the Patriotic War: First Degree (Posthumous). And today, each spring in May, the souls of the fallen strive once more to reach the blossoming fields of their homeland from Polish, Czech, and German grassland. They strive to reach the nation for which they gave their lives.

In *Countdown*, the cost and pathos of a concrete military invasion have been conflated with, i.e. replaced by, the demonized, undemanding scapegoat of "international terrorism." Given the obvious use of physical, armed conflict as one way in which to make themes of Fascism and militant "Islam" look similar, there then emerges the issue of which style to adopt, since stories of anger *per se* are unlikely to sell many tickets.

When *Zvezda* was reviewed on the pages of *Variety*, some of its patriotic spectacle was attributed to plagiarism from Steven Spielberg's *Saving Private Ryan* (1998) and *Jurassic Park* (1993), even though most of the special effects are direct visualizations of phrasing in the base text, Èmmanuil Kazakevich's story of 1946.[6] Something Soviet and something Californian walked hand in hand, to both political and fiscal benefit. They recognized each other, yet remained distinct.

Countdown, however, is much more a tale of increased sameness, of homogenization. Middle Eastern terrorists, for example, are shown duping Chechen rebels, so that viewers may lump all anti-state terrorisms into one basket, dismissed tidily as the product of an angry Islam – and thus fall into the comforting arms of contemporary politicking, which allows President Bush to announce that all terrorists or their ideologies simply "hate freedom." Apparently it's that simple, so that everybody can agree.

Not only does this film embody a woeful number of policy-driven, American stereotypes in its attempts to be purportedly different, but, given the state funds with which it was made, it also spends too much time reflecting on Putin's career or plans within the G8. *Countdown* uses London as the home for an émigré arch-enemy Pokrovskii (i.e. TV mogul Boris Berezovskii), scheming with ill-gotten gains from his well-funded hideout. Neither Pokrovskii nor the Chechen rebels, shown in an awfully manipulative reworking of the Dubrovka and Beslan tragedies, is the real enemy, however. Though both oligarchs and rebels lie beyond the Russian mainland, the real problem is thankfully dressed up as a Bin Laden look-alike, just in case we missed the point.[7]

These "Arabs," using a Moscow circus siege to keep the FSB busy, plan to fly a container of plutonium over Rome, during the G8, and explode it, creating a dirty bomb of epic proportions. If the plane flies below 3,000 meters, it will detonate, thus repeating the dramatic tension of *Speed* (Jan de Bont, 1994). Putin's words and shady off-screen presence, employed on at least three occasions in the film, make it clear that the cargo plane will not be allowed to leave Russian airspace. Despite overt references to the risk of a "second Chernobyl" in the screenplay, the idea of destroying the people of Russia and Belarus to save Italians and a handful of foreign dignitaries does not appear to trouble anybody. Similar self-sacrifice is perhaps supposed to hark back to archetypes *à la Star*, but it smells very different. The *Daily Telegraph* on 19 July 2005 quoted a Top Line executive as saying *Countdown* was supposed to show "Russia as a country that's ready to become a part of Europe."

This film yearns in many directions, each of which moves further from anything that feels like home. And yet Evgenii Lavrent'ev keeps searching elsewhere, to absent periods and places, as the newspaper *Rossiiskaia gazeta* explained: "He's intent on creating a legend; a true legend based even upon the acts of real people, yet one capable of becoming national folklore."[8] Another newspaper tried to flesh out this portrait and its potential as object of national desire:

> In distinction from American superheroes, the hero Makarov does not have an athletic build, nor is he a great ladies' man. He doesn't utter high-flown speeches, nor does he stoop to aphoristic witticisms like *Hasta la vista, baby*! He's a simple man, who acts in given situations according to his own code of honor. He's distinguished by his free and creative thought processes, together with his professionalism. He's blessed with a classic Russian sense of humor; he's kind-hearted and charming in his own, slightly clumsy way.[9]

That all sounds very admirable, and indeed Makarov's potential as a future serial hero seems considerable: he already has almost twenty TV dramas to his name, shot between 1999 and 2006. Recent squabbling over how to portray the figure of the detective Fandorin in adaptations of Boris Akunin's stories also seems adequate testament to the desire and/or need for a new national champion. Films such as *The Bourne Supremacy* (Paul Greengrass, 2004) floundered in Russian cinemas, precisely because their depiction of Russians is less than flattering. What remains troubling, though, is not who Makarov's hero is (physically or emotionally), but what he is doing and for whom. The same can be said of this film as a whole. One of its producers, Sergei Gribkov, defined the goal of *Countdown* as the depiction of "both external and internal terrorism. People must see even those things that might be uncomfortable for them to think about."[10] If the complexities of international terrorism are boiled down to a simple opposition of good and bad, there's no real problem; heaven knows that James Bond hardly did justice to geopolitical intricacy in the past. When, however, a government starts funding "blockbu$ters" and is then pampered early on with its own closed screenings (no doubt of editorial consequence) one starts to feel anxious.

The rather irate, binary presentation of Gribkov's "uncomfortable truth" seems less like entertainment and more like the militaristic rant of Jack Nicholson in the closing scenes of *A Few Good Men* (Rob Reiner, 1992). *Countdown* knows very clearly what it wants to say, and does so with force in its closing on-screen text. What it does not know, however, is to whom it speaks, whether to Western, domestic, or governmental audiences, and therefore the issue of how becomes muddled. *Countdown*, in its casting, for example, makes a few strange nods in the direction of more liberal, Western motifs, such as a savvy, rugged female journalist (Louise Lombard) or a high-ranking black dignitary (John Amos), yet both these stereotypes look very misplaced on a Russian screen.

Likewise, although this thunderous, polished movie aspires to the label of blockbuster, it involves too much self-erasure in doing so. In attempting to embody the modern significance of blockbuster as success, size, and generic novelty, *Countdown* slips further away from home (today). It yearns for a past ethos and a foreign policy. There is so much pandering and so little self-respect in this film, in fact, that the older meaning of blockbuster comes to mind again, together with the type of "blackface" that once marked Gogol's own sad self-deprecation in the name of entertaining a purportedly greater audience.[11] Silly though it sounds, in visual or social terms, that logic leads us back to the pitiful self-mockery of perhaps the quintessential blockbusting, real-estate TV comedy, *The Jeffersons* (CBS, 1975–85). "Moving on up" won't be easy, but it would be nice to do it with self-respect, rather than epigonism.

Countdown is an extreme example of where state-run television is placing its faith and funds when it comes to action. International policy may dream of future gains on overseas screens, but much of what we see on television, as with Ktorov, revolves around saving a domestic cultural heritage that was until recently being lost. And many more people in Russia watch TV than go to the movies. Television heroes completely sympathize with their cinematic counterparts, but often act a little differently. They are quieter.

Cinema's action heroes blow things up; television puts them back together (and does so for less money)

In Episode Four of Dmitrii Mednov's *Side by Side with Love* (*Parallel'no liubvi*, 2004), an outrageously affluent businessman (and broad-shouldered gubernatorial candidate) is publicly embarrassed. He has been slowly falling in love with his female campaign advisor and this evening must face her mother across a small dinner table. An imposing matriarch (Lidiia Fedoseeva-Shukshina), she immediately takes him to task for knowing no literature, especially after he admits ignorance of Aleksei Tolstoi's *Road to Calvary* – the novel's heroines provide the names for both the advisor and her younger sister. Shukshina's harangue does not abate and so the butch businessman tries to defend himself. He fails, but this type of faultfinding is so familiar to the daughters that the youngest interrupts her mother in order to stop some tediously familiar phrasing:

> MOTHER: Have you read Dostoevskii?
> BUSINESSMAN: Yes, I have. Not much, though, 'cos I work a lot.
> MOTHER: Well, that's not much of an excuse, young man. You have to read the Russian classics. If all politicians and businessmen would read the Russian classics———
> DAUGHTER: " ... then we'd all live a lot better. Russian literature teaches people morality."

Although the daughter sighs at this tirade, the mother's point remains serious. It comes, to boot, from the real-life spouse of a famous Soviet writer. What is television, literature's nemesis, doing by telling people of action to read

Action heroes 19

Figure 1.2 Side by Side with Love.

literature? Ktorov spoke of its importance, but Panas found that the printed page somehow fell short of the ideals it sought to embody. And what exactly is being dragged from the nineteenth century, all the way through the Soviet experience, and then offered to the oligarchs of today? "Morality"?

The heroes of Soviet literature and cinema, in both historical and ideological senses, are often referenced seriously and ironically in Russian TV series. Television is remembering, quoting, and, in some senses, saving the literature that society's movers and shakers don't know very well. Yet TV does so by keeping people *away* from libraries and on their sofas. Romantically driven and melodramatic television series show this strange process best of all, with the kind of caring, cultured, and morally upstanding social bonds that allow producers and directors to rummage around in the past. These broadcasts can mine the metaphors of socialism (parenthood/brotherhood/family/love), thus keeping the "social" yet dumping the "ism." They show the bravery of kindness in a cruel society, and do so by leaning heavily on the structural workings of the narratives they most resemble: serialized novels of the nineteenth century. Pre-Soviet forms and heroic Soviet morals dovetail to counter the savagery of post-Soviet marketplace corruption.

This book, in mapping those morals, finds extended common ground with Elena Prokhorova's research on detective series in the Soviet Union under Brezhnev. A connection here with Prokhorova's work is possible since her study synthesizes (and then foreshadows) a productive overlap between socialist tradition and the start of the twenty-first century. One of her key tenets is that "Soviet television of the 1970s made Soviet narratives and icons polysemous."[12] My recent monographs on socialist song and prose classics concluded, in a comparable spirit, that their "Sovietness" came from what journalism or socialist academe said about them, rather than what they described in reality (that is, prior to policy's crude redefinition of their "true purpose"). Politicians frequently needed (polysemous or) apolitical adventure stories and pop songs, say, in order then to create telling, promotional metaphors of social cohesion. Those reworked metaphors could turn little love songs between two people into oratorical bombast applicable to 200 million. Stories of total forgiveness and acceptance (amid love, family, trusted friends, or nature) were things dogma needed and employed, yet could not enact – they were disproportionate.

This undoable, traumatic excess would (and will) not go away any time soon, since the Brezhnev years were calm and trouble-free (if we speak with Russian notions of relativity). For all the increased artistic constraints, daily life (jobs, state support systems, and communications) worked well. The grandeur of state spectacle both reflected this self-assured stability whilst growing in size in order to mask any possibly dissonant voices; in doing so high styles became muddled with the low. High culture was less tedious, and "mass" culture was less of a guilty pleasure, as with the Sherlock Holmes series. The 1970s are, therefore, a fruitful period for the nostalgic directors and viewers of today.

That decade's serene populism avoids generic obsolescence for yet another reason: criminal series of thirty years ago involved more than just crime. As Prokhorova notes in her forward-looking finale, many of the detective shows (and their heroes) that grew from the traditions of the 1970s were generically muddled, producing such re-fashionable combinations as the "police procedural/sitcom [or the] gangster saga/male melodrama." My aim is to investigate the nature and workings of these stubborn, ever-enjoyable mélanges. How do so many long, drawn-out stories wander back and forth between genres, decade after decade? What, in particular, can we say about the endurance of their romantically "impure" elements that ultimately provide the metaphors of cohesion or construction for TV's action heroes long after any criminal has stopped being subversive? This issue of endurance is, in part, closely tied to cash; accountants help to decide what makes a good hero.

As recently as 1999–2000 only 5 percent of nationally broadcast series were made domestically; today more than 100 new and different dramas appear per annum. In 2005, a total of 538 TV series, mini-series, and soap operas (old or new) were shown on Russian TV; eight years prior, that cumulative figure was 103.[13] One continuity discernible in this snowballing state of affairs is that criminal dramas still outnumber melodramas, yet what is central to those stories, as we see in *Parallel'no liubvi*, is "the crisis of the [modern Russian] family as an institution."[14] Love for one's nearest and dearest is still drawn upon by screenwriters left, right, and center. The business of showing families' breakdowns (or uncertain renewals) in an entertaining fashion commands a joint production budget of $300 million per annum.

This figure was reached with particular speed after the start of the new millennium. In 2001, the cost of shooting all TV serials nationwide had been $40 million; by 2003 that total had risen to $70 million – and thus doubled in twelve months alone. This escalation will not stop, either. Industry experts suggest that Russia's television networks could hypothetically support 6,000 hours of broadcast drama per annum; currently the massive output outlined in this introduction constitutes slightly more than 3,500 hours per annum. Not surprisingly, the market leaders amid all the hustle and bustle are the stations Channel One, Rossiia, and, in third place, NTV.[15] At present these stations give approximately 40 percent of their airtime to serials and movies.[16]

The rather lazy tendency to joke about Russians watching episodes of *Santa Barbara* in primetime is now very obsolete. Almost a decade ago, the cost of showing an episode of *Santa Barbara* fluctuated between $12,000 and $14,000. The advertising sales from initial broadcast and (limited) subsequent repeats could bring up to $50,000 in revenue. A handsome profit, by any standards, but everything changed in August 1998. The nation's government announced its intent to default on overseas debts and nationwide financial collapse ensued with alarming rapidity. Buying foreign serials was suddenly too expensive an enterprise, especially after Russia started to observe international copyright laws in 1994, yet herein lay the chance of a lifetime for Russian serial production.

Television heads in Moscow now saw that it cost the same to film one episode of a soap in Russia as it did to buy an episode of some US equivalent, but a homemade product could be repeated endlessly (outside of the restrictive repeat-viewing clauses in US contracts), sold to somebody else, turned into a cheaper sequel, or subsidized from the outset by product placement. It likewise became clear to Russian feature film studios that making one hour of television drama would cost them 50 percent less than sixty minutes of footage destined for the big screen. Suddenly it made sense to make TV, not purchase it. The cost of producing an episode today can vary greatly, however, at between $30,000 and $200,000 (sometimes more), so this story of geographical shifts from Los Angeles to Moscow will also be one of greatly varying quality as the ability to make socially conscientious TV goes head to head with the desire to make it cheaply.

Thus began the television series as we know it today. This book will examine the role of long, televised serial narratives and the ways they have – despite all accusations of being cheap, tawdry entertainment – not only done extremely well for themselves, but also adopted many aspects of the treasured literary tradition in Russia (which has, by all accounts, long been abandoned by today's excessively faddish novelists). If you want to experience classic Russian stories of socially active heroes, walk away from the library, go home, and turn on the TV. Over and above the issue of funding, there now arises the additional conundrum of how to transfer the written word to a visual medium. In other words, how much should heroes' words cost to film – and what should they look like when we do so?

Moving literature to television – and the gap in between

> We will strengthen the independence of the media, above all by ensuring they are not economically dependent.
>
> (Putin, 2005)

A central issue here, already touched upon in *Countdown*, is how action movies may be dangerously simplified when working primarily to political purpose, in the broadest sense, whenever a national form of storytelling might become nationalism and delineate two camps "for" or "against" Putin. Qualities central to the former camp, to a pro-governmental value system, would include support for powerful security services, a willingness to manipulate any (fleeting) endorsement of the US in Iraq, the "election" of local governors by the President himself, and a readiness to see further state control over TV, albeit – allegedly and ironically – without "the [1970s'] mellifluous tones of stagnation."[17] If television is going to be governmental, it ought (supposedly) to shy away from self-flattering narratives.

Here we can draw a parallel between engagingly presented stories in both literature and politics. Trade publications in the United States dealing with the successful, persuasive transferal of novels to the silver screen often stress a need to find the affective load lying beyond the limits of metonymy. Words can only say so much and longer scripts (or speeches) aren't necessarily more poignant than short ones. Something always remains unsaid after the last word. If literature, dogmatic or not, is to improve upon itself visually, the job must be done emotionally, i.e. invisibly:

We must dispense with stories that appeal only to the intellect, such as stories that involve the explanation of lofty themes, obscure principles, or pure debate. Don't confuse the word *debate* with *contest*. A debate is purely intellectual; a contest is emotional. We do not react emotionally to intellectual issues; we may think about them, but we don't feel them.[18]

An emotionally compelling tale, done visually, should appeal to the emotions – it should *reemploy already-familiar* feelings – in order to go beyond language and contemplate an enduring lack:

We have reality before our eyes well before language, and what language does is ... it digs a hole in it, it opens up visible/present reality toward the dimension of the immaterial unseen. When I simply see [or film] you, I simply see you – but it is only by *naming* you that I can indicate the abyss in you beyond what I see.[19]

Key, therefore, in the transfer of active, social words from page to screen is the issue of wordless remembering, of somehow redoing and augmenting a work that itself wished to evoke feelings felt before – thus making yesterday relevant today, maybe more so. If action stories like *Countdown* are busy with constant, appealing motion, then in melodramas such as *Side by Side with Love* what are "remembered and reenacted are the adventitious conjunctions [or 'contests'] of place and person which make deep feeling and fulfillment possible ... The whole sequence is suffused by the never-very-bitter sweetness of intense happiness and love lost and lovingly recollected."[20] Melodrama and its bathetic mechanisms are, likewise, immediately, inherently dependent upon the presence *and* absence of a "pleasure, predicated on a rhythm of possession, loss, and restitution."[21] Idea(l)s come *and* go; in fact, in order to come at all, they (like Mariia) must have "gone" at least once before. The similarity between this movement and nostalgic, patriotic politicking is clear.

In moving a jingoistic, stirring, or weepy story from page to screen, are we therefore simply adding to the intensity of emotional release, increasing the significance of emotions back and forth – and thus *retarding* the forward drive of any clearly progressive or partisan narrative? After all, "emotional responses are even more fundamental to our interest in and enjoyment of movies than our anticipation of what is going to happen next and our eventual satisfaction at seeing a story through."[22] So how straightforward can our stories be, even with presidential funding?

They are, in fact, frequently so aimless that they mean no one thing in particular, as we saw with the quixotic, chivalric adventures of Ktorov, and it is this issue of absence or a missing singularity that needs to be addressed first. It will help us to appreciate the enduring gap between literature and television, between high and low, good and bad, real and artificial that

Brezhnevian culture hoped to blur. Useful support here is available in some central tenets from Jacques Derrida, who once showed the Achilles heel of socialist culture by refusing the all-encompassing binary opposites that underlie so much political rhetoric, maintaining that finite intellect and vocabularies can never dovetail what *is* (i.e. total plenitude now) and what conceivably might be known or categorized (later).

The problem is language's inability to be either conclusive or constitutive of a singular originality. Emotions draw narratives repeatedly backwards; words expose their own pretensions towards plenitude. This issue is well captured in Derrida's notion of "originary delay." In saying or defining anything once (and for all), there has to be some implied "second" in order for a first to be counted. This second is a prerequisite for the first: "It permits the first to *be* first by its delayed arrival. The first, recognizable only after the second, is in this respect a third. Origin, then, is a kind of dress rehearsal ... The original, in that sense, is always a copy."[23] Once again, progress is frustrated and absolute assertions or verities are impossible. Complete, full meaning is always deferred, except at infinity, because each spoken original also contains a "trace" of absence, the present trace of an "absolute" past which never took place. That trace, which troubles even the phenomenological "presentism" I suggested earlier, resides in the gaps between all words or narrative units, and will certainly reappear whenever we talk about a genre like the TV series, which by its very nature is founded upon even more repetition.

Emptiness is constantly shown within presence, and the outside is shown within the inside. For Russians today this idea comes from a Frenchman whose "desolate, 'emptied' landscape" of thought after 1991 "promised nothing other than 'total surprise,' the possibility of the impossible."[24] As a philosopher who shied away from Freud's searches for full, "dictatorial" meaning, Derrida for Russian scholars has often demonstrated what his Slavic readers see as the presence of absence in storytelling, the dismantling of grand narratives as a multitude of linguistic speculations after the death of Soviet doctrine and its own binarisms.[25]

Close to the end of his life, Derrida published some related interviews on the subject of television. Here we find an explanation of a deconstructive attitude towards the moving image as a possible step beyond language and/or literature, its very constitution as "artifactuality." Derrida extends a new understanding of *différance* (of meaning's difference and deferral) to television's unions of stasis and movement (its social "events"), of both presence and absence. These ideas start to sound Badiouian, to put it mildly, whilst invoking the relationship of TV to the broadcasting of propriety and/or truth. Social truths, it transpires, do not lend themselves to any one "right or legal" representation, although TV does a better job than books and/or writing:

> The [televised] event is another name for that which, in the thing that happens, we can neither reduce nor deny (or simply deny). It is another name for experience itself, which is always experience of the other. The

event cannot be subsumed under any other concept, not even that of being. The "there is" [*il y a*] or the "that there is something rather than nothing" belongs, perhaps, to the experience of the event rather than to a thinking of being ... This is why a thinking of the event always opens a certain messianic space – as abstract, formal, and barren, as un-"religious" as it must be – and why this messianic dimension cannot be separated from justice, which I distinguish from law or right.[26]

The correlated philosophical ventures of Badiou push this impossible logic in search of veritable justice a tad further and reveal an extra resonance at the barren, messianic point where even the most active language stops, where the Real and "truth have no interest in interpretation. Instead, truth exposes the *gaps* in our understanding [of such things]."[27] Screenplays, especially those aspiring to singular assertiveness, expose an unutterable truth in their gaps, in their lack. Epstein's opposites, the Russian commonplaces of "all and naught," collapse into one another:

Oneness [i.e. everything] can only be presented adequately in terms of multiplicity ... Multiplicity rules out all relations between concepts and categories, including their non-relations. Deprived of all determination to the point where even its non-being is excluded from being, there is only one other "thing" that the concept of the one can possibly be: *nothing*. In other words, everything is also *nothing*, a gap, a lack, therefore, and a challenge.[28]

This is a procedure, not a state; it is *the* action story invoked by political tales of progress, development, and excessive changes that can never be *done in toto* by action heroes:

Since being is multiple, and truth *must be*, a truth shall be a multiple, thus a multiple-part of the situation of which it is the truth. As might be expected, it cannot be an already 'given or present' part. It shall stem from a singular procedure. In fact, this procedure can only be set into motion from the point of a supplement – something in excess of the situation, that is, an event. A truth is the infinite result of a risky supplementation. Every truth is post-eventful.[29]

Events are deviations from the usual; they are encountered in Lacan's divinely romantic but impossibly impractical dictate of revolution: *Ne pas céder sur son désir*. And, since in this philosophy of sweeping socialist materialism "there is no God, [it] also means: the One is [likewise] not. The multiple 'without-one' – every multiple being in turn nothing more than a multiple of multiples – is the law of being. The only stopping point is the void."[30]

Truth, a result of this eventful process, is what a subject helps to make or what he bears. A subject does not come *before* this process: "He is absolutely nonexistent in the situation 'before' the event. We might say the process of the truth *induces* a subject."[31] This, perhaps more than anything else, brings us to the endless events of the world, for "to exist is to be an element *of*."[32] Badiou calls here upon the "truth of Spinoza's substance, which is immediately expressed by an infinity of attributes."[33] This recourse to the unity of being allows him to claim – amazingly – that "Deleuzianism, the chaotic, desirous multiplicity of a Body without Organs, is fundamentally a Platonism with a different accentuation":

> In Deleuze, as in every great physicist of this kind, is a great power of speculative dreaming and something akin to a quivering tonality that is prophetic, *although without promise*. He said of Spinoza that he was the Christ of philosophy. To do Deleuze full justice, let us say that, of this Christ and his inflexible announcement of salvation by the All – a salvation that promises *nothing*, a salvation that is always *already there* – he was truly a most eminent apostle.[34]

This situation lies at the absolute core of organic Soviet culture and the daring, frequently hazardous stories under our investigation. Lunacharskii noted that "it was true" that apostolic Spinoza, after Hegel, "was *the* predecessor whom Soviet thought recognized."[35] This need to embrace and live as the philosopher was reiterated elsewhere, the need to see "him in his true light ... on the foundations of Marxism and Leninism."[36] One can also find quotes from Engels praising the "brilliance" of Spinoza, together with wise words from Lenin prompting the populace to study their thought processes through the harmonious, selfless plexus of nature.[37] This is the non-progressive, affective, all-embracing complexity of micropolitics found initially between two peoples and two faiths, all of which speak of an ecologically complex univocity that politics could only ever imagine. It is a plurality that *creates* subjectivity, so our book will be less a story of people initiating actions or events than multiple events making people. Thus the nature of bravery and (wordy) partisan action will change over the course of this study.

Action will operate between what Badiou has called natural and historical situations: a non-linear interplay of non-progressive multiplicities (quixotic audience sympathy in *Rostov-Papa*) and those beginning to move or develop in a given direction (the loud politics of *Countdown*). Verbose macropolitical institutions and reticent micropolitical individuals are part of the same exciting, bold process and (if honest or truthful) will enter this interplay with frequently mutual intent.

Initial post-Soviet storytelling on television

> In the last few years we have all discovered a lot of new things about our country. Quite a lot of it has been both frightening and heartless.[38]
> (From a Russian schoolbook of 1993)

At the time of openly admitted, blossoming multiplicity that we will first consider, at the twilight of the USSR, storytelling was trying to reinstate action. It was trying to be more eventful, rummaging around in "the shreds of a grandeur many had known at the time to be hollow, but [which] in time acquired density."[39] Television was a logical domain for such tales. By 1986, even, 93 percent of Russians had access to a TV set; in 1960 this had been possible for a mere 5 percent.[40] After perestroika, angry journalism on the small screen made manifest socialism's hollowness; in a profoundly deconstructive gesture, the "television of [Soviet] Potemkin villages" was dismantled.[41] What would take its place: more angry revisionism or mere escapism, something "uncomplicated and undemanding"?[42] In either case, the loss of calm control was already in the minds of many leading to a loss of quality, too.

Those factions of the viewing public unimpressed by either trash or cash denounced post-Soviet TV as a "terrorist and aggressor" who was "trying to oust" social responsibility and the prestigious singularity of literature.[43] Television certainly led to the kind of hostile activity that caused, most famously, the murder of journalist and chat-show host Vlad List'ev in 1995 amid dark tales of corruption and cupidity. This dangerous avarice, symbolized by ostentatious prizes for game shows and the moneyed, macho magazines that List'ev himself concocted, has led to today's epoch-mythologizing TV series like Aleksandr Buravskii's knockabout *Ice Age* (*Lednikovyi period*, 2002), set among the risks of mid-1990s corruption.

Yeltsin's *laissez-faire* stance towards these excesses – he rarely criticized the media – meant he was left largely in peace. Owners of the first post-Soviet media outlets, few in number but great in influence (being primarily politicians and financiers) thus posed as advocates of free speech – as long as it did not endanger their profit margins. A balance was maintained.

The 1990s' unsightly marriage of two tales (increasing wealth and social manipulation) under Yeltsin is perhaps best remembered by the public as a time when Latina actress and popular soap star Victoria Ruffo filmed advertisements for Russian investment scheme (and soon-to-be disgraced scandal) MMM. These advertisements involved average (though nonexistent) Russians comparing their average partners with the suave heroes and heroines of the Mexican hit TV drama *Simply Maria* – all in the presence of Ruffo herself as fairy godmother from afar, attempting to "convert the [Russian] viewer into a 'partner' by inducing the mimetic desire to invest":

> The [simple] Russian heroes [of the ads] got to meet the Mexicans who served as their inspiration; thus the Russian viewers watched as their stand-ins met the foreign movie star. When Maria walked into the apartment of [typical Russian] Marina Sergeevna, she entered the home of the viewer as well. After successfully domesticating the soap opera,

MMM bridged the distance between its own prosaic heroes and their exotic models. The Russian viewer was one step away from becoming a soap opera heroine herself.[44]

The story looked as if might come true, but it went tragically wrong, ruining the savings of 2 million people to the tune of over $1 billion. Ironically, it was mirrored almost simultaneously by deceptively high yields on the government-run short-term bond market. These were the type of unhappy endings Putin wanted to avoid, and their misery indeed allowed him both to pressure the owners of several channels and to consolidate political capital. Media giants, the potential backers of opposition parties, were gradually indicted for reasons of (supposed) social concern and common welfare. This new conservatism and re-nationalization of the media after 2000, perhaps as a result of Putin's KGB (Committee for State Security) service in East Germany, would lead to derisive parallels with Standartenfuhrer von Stirlitz, the central spy of the classic 1970s television series *The Seventeen Moments of Spring* (*Semnadtsat' mgnovenii vesny*).[45]

Controlling the businessmen who owned these stations or the audiences to whom their dramatic yarns were shown, however, was not easy. A telling example thereof is the recent history of the Ostankino TV Company, transferred in late 1994 into a closed joint-stock company and renamed ORT ("Russian Public Service Television"); the state held just over half of its shares. In 1998, broadcasting to almost every corner of Russia, it then became an open-stock company and financier Boris Berezovskii, working alongside the Kremlin, became the station's effective banker and chief editor due to his influence over voting procedures on the board.

After Putin's election, however, Berezovskii gradually became an opponent of the Kremlin and its media policies. He reportedly sold his shares (49 percent) to a series of investors overseen by "another Kremlin-connected Russian businessman," Roman Abramovich, familiar today as the London-based chairman of Chelsea Football Club. Meanwhile, ORT became known in 2002 as Channel One, the name by which it was already familiar to the Russian public. The station today has the largest number of viewers nationwide and remains very pro-Kremlin; Berezovskii, perhaps Putin's most vociferous critic and media-savvy opponent, left Russia in 2001, also for London, where he lives today in exile.

Rossiia, known previously as RTR, was initially created in 1990 by pro-Yeltsin factions in the struggle with Mikhail Gorbachev for media presence. It is wholly owned by the state, but until 1999 had trouble with anything resembling a nationwide network since it used myriad local stations (GTRKs) in order to boost its signal. These affiliates only employed Rossiia's programming as and when they saw fit. Thanks in part to a decree of February 2004 that made these troublesome local stations "re-transmitters" of Moscow-based programming, such predicaments were slowly eradicated by an increasingly centralized media system. Rossiia now reaches

99 percent of Russia's landmass and enjoys another 50 million viewers around the Commonwealth of Independent States (CIS) and Baltic nations. It is the flagship of Russia's State Television and Radio Company (VGTRK), an enormous media holding that includes other, smaller stations such as Kul'tura and Sport, together with eighty-nine other regional TV businesses, a host of radio companies, and several important on-line news portals.

Most evidently distinct from these processes of consolidation has been NTV, created in 1993 as an evening-only station by a banking consortium. NTV supported Yeltsin in the 1996 presidential campaign and enjoyed extended broadcasting rights as a consequence. Four years later, the station's founder and de facto owner, Vladimir Gusinskii, was felt to be unfairly disposed towards Moscow mayor Iurii Luzhkov, ex-prime minister Evegnii Primakov, and other, more liberal opponents of the Kremlin. Putin, nonetheless, won the presidency, and so NTV, having at times enjoyed a viewership of 100 million, faced serious problems. Between 1999 and 2001 it struggled to avoid paying big debts (reportedly over $1 billion) to a consortium led by Gazprom, a gas company close to Putin; these unpaid amounts were suddenly called in. A failed legal defense led to Gusinskii being imprisoned, and then he, as Berezovskii, also left Russia.

Coverage of the Kursk submarine disaster (2000) and the Dubrovka theater siege (2002) only served to worsen NTV's relationships with the Kremlin. Many of the station's leading journalists left to join TV6 or TVS, which for a short time remained the only independent voices on Russian national television, but both of these have since been silenced.

In order to avoid the further development of any political or ratings-related disasters, NTV has of late moved towards what many see as a more apolitical roster, perhaps in an attempt to mirror the success of STS – the nation's fastest-growing network. STS offers no news and refers to itself as "*Entertainment* Channel One," a jesting allusion to both the erstwhile shadow of ORT and a desire to scale the same heights – without the risk of over-politicking.[46]

The situation today is that Rossiia, just like Channel One, enjoys an approximate 25 percent market share, followed at some distance by NTV and STS (10–12 percent), while networks like Kul'tura (3–5 percent) or MTV Russia (1 percent) define the typical size of any remaining or consequential influence.[47] The feeling of belonging to some salvationary and commonly enjoyed fairytale, as promised by Ruffo, therefore hid a much more complex and Machiavellian series of events. Her words of active material gain revealed a series of lacks and losses. There is a commanding irony in the fact that Channel One under Berezovskii was instrumental in the political success of Yeltsin, the man who would one day designate Putin as his successor. Today Berezovskii remains abroad as Russia's second richest individual – yet is wanted by that same nation on charges of fraud and the abuse of office. Such are the reasons for his dark portrayal in

Countdown and the tales of action across much of what constitutes today's TV landscape.

Conclusion: the heroes of Russian TV (and its business practices) borrow from old worldviews they wish to outpace

Due to post-Soviet dilemmas of lack and loss, the theme of risky, hard-won membership (of regaining something) will occur repeatedly in the soapy operas of Russia's state-guided TV. This subject and the actions required to enact it are underwritten in part by drawing upon the melodramatic, peopled narratives already validated over and over by Russian culture, by large novels. The most famous pro-Putin organization among young people today, Moving Together (*Idushchie vmeste*) calls upon its members to read six classic novels a year and help reinstate the dramatic, often martial values of Soviet literature. Most famously, they also demanded the public destruction in 2002 of a new novel by writer Vladimir Sorokin, because it contained a homoerotic encounter between Stalin and Khrushchev.

If television is going to rectify these social failures and proffer an alternative, then we return to issues of how novelistic and cinematic legends can be collocated. Kamilla Elliott has recently suggested that some common ground between them always lies in "a parallel and overlapping dynamic ... drawing on a variety of art forms, including and especially theater."[48] She goes on to suggest in passing the relevance of Derrida's "blasting of the original/copy differential" for examining the genre.[49] It is our intention to take this prompt and to develop it as fully as possible, especially because visual, popular drama today is indeed so often multigeneric, just as Prokhorova noted of Brezhnevian shows. Television, having "outdone" linguistic metonymy, nonetheless has much to *learn* from prose – from the very traditions it has undermined.

Working with such grand or unwieldy terms as "the novel," though, some sweeping statements to match those of Mikhail Epstein *et al.* in our Introduction would help to demarcate clichés of novelistic enterprise as drawn upon in the popular imagination. What are the grand goals or metaphors of membership that Russian TV will try and take (back) from literature? Malcolm Jones gives us a good starting point:

> At the beginning of the nineteenth century, Russian culture experienced two irresistible imperatives (both exemplified in Pushkin's and Gogol's work): to grasp and represent in imaginative literature the full range of contemporary reality, exemplified in such concepts as the *narod* (the Russian people), the *rodina* ('motherland'), the vast primitive, anarchic Russian countryside, the history and the symbolism of her capital; and to understand their place in history. This latter quest sometimes embraced the idea of national historical mission, which at times, for example in Dostoevskii's hands, became messianic.[50]

Jones' reference here to the countryside is key, the fact that it was often landowners (Turgenev, Aksakov, and Tolstoi) who described it in idyllic terms, and the subsequent horrors of civil or world war or collectivization would do little to alter nature's moral significance. Despite the more doubting or cynical portraits painted by Saltykov-Shchedrin, Goncharov, or Bunin, say, the countryside was interwoven with anti-rationalist aspects of Orthodox Christianity (bolstered by negative attitudes towards Catholicism and Protestantism). It fostered an additional overlap with religion in that notions of self-realization in imitation of Christ were, at the start of the nineteenth century, interspersed with ideas from Rousseau. What Jostein Bortnes calls "ludic recombination" began; novelistic archetypes of Lazarus or Easter narratives (as in Dostoevskii, for example) began to merge repetition and variation: "Every human being, even a murderer, is a potential image of Christ."[51]

In characters such as Dostoevskii's Father Zosima, we witness the apophatic knowledge of potential divinity that linked natural man to a spiritual potential, "the negative way of knowing God through dissimilar similarities." Thus in the Russian novel of the nineteenth century, and even in the more radical, apocalyptic works of the early twentieth, "the idea of creativity as a repetition with variations on a single underlying pattern took the form of a continuous dialogue with the words of the Gospel about the true meaning of life."[52]

The material and the ideal (presence and absence) were often interwoven, whether in Gogol's fantastic realism or in more orthodox works. Whether one follows Pushkinian or Gogolian lines of development, though, doubts persisted in Russian prose over the reliability of ostensible existence, despite any later, Tolstoian faith in nature's continuity and structuring principles. The space between reality and something else, the gap between heroic words and the world, was often effected affectively:

> Many Western critics distinguish novels that *tell* readers what happens from novels that *show* them what happens; the Russian novelistic techniques let Tolstoi, Dostoevskii, and others go beyond both these practices and manipulate readers into experiencing for themselves what the characters in the novel are feeling and arguing.[53]

Consequently the issue at hand in Chapter 2 is how emotional, often maudlin Russian television and its heroes have dealt both with the cultural prestige of literature and its lacunae, with its imposing presence and inherent, heartfelt absence(s) so often *caused* by words.

2 Adaptations
TV drama vs. literary prestige

In the Soviet era when our education was atheistic, which Orthodox Christian values did that [post-World War Two] generation of schoolchildren learn from literature classes, from the works of Pushkin, Lermontov, Turgenev and Nekrasov ... or other Russian classics?[1]

(From a Russian schoolbook of 1999)

Introduction: *Zhivago* and *Karenina*, "they're all the same"

As the 2006 season began on Russian television, two tendencies made themselves especially manifest in lists of "Coming Attractions": an increase in adaptations of classic literature, building on the recent critical success of similar shows, together with several attempts to move beyond an eight-, ten-, or twelve-episode format. Size and stature underscored themselves as two goals of socially active TV drama; two desires to match the 120 episodes of 2003's costume drama *Poor Nastia* (investigated anon), which had been something of an aberration. It was heavily reliant upon foreign funds, and spawned no further shows on a similar scale. Now, however, it seemed that there was indeed sufficient money in the coffers of domestic channels to dream big. Some of these grand plans would materialize, while others would evanesce. Whenever "classic" projects came into being with difficulty, the slow work was often blamed not upon financial problems, but on the fact that large, serious books require long, serious schedules; the slower the filming, in fact, the better the book being filmed.

One good example of this logic came from popular actor Evgenii Mironov when discussing a forthcoming, enthusiastically promised adaptation of *The Brothers Karamazov*. Dostoevskii's novel, he said, "is the most important book in Russia. It has to be approached with a long-term plan; after all, scrambling up a hillside isn't the same as scaling Kilimanjaro."[2] This and other nineteenth-century works of literature had values beyond their age, for "every generation has its Karamazovs." Web forums inspired by announcement of the series conducted an angry debate over its possible benefit for a current generation – how its "wordiness" might hopefully overcome the more superficial workings of a primetime aesthetic.[3] Large literary adaptations would purportedly help children return to the books themselves, to libraries, but teachers from around Russia had seen little evidence of increased reading habits after such broadcasts. Television was not increasing anybody's historical awareness. Schoolchildren could not even recognize Czar Alexander in the profoundly non-literary, simply structured *Poor Nastia* – and boys remained stubborn viewers of gangster flicks.

One of the most interesting and representative of these adaptations was Aleksandr Proshkin's $4 million version of *Doctor Zhivago* that aired in May 2006. It suffered a multitude of sadly predictable problems en route to the screen. The most famous was a leak to Moscow's DVD pirates; the series was on sale in marketplaces and metro stations several months before its scheduled debut. Attempting to track down the guilty parties, Proshkin's investigators defined an amazing eighteen places in the production process where somebody "might" have stolen the footage. Some of Proshkin's problems involved too much money; others involved too little. Despite a handsome budget that attracted nimble-fingered criminals, he had in fact been obliged to save considerable money by using the outdoor, *fin-de-siècle* sets already seen in Karen Shakhnazarov's *A Rider Named Death* (2004) and Filipp Iankovskii's *State Counselor* (2005). The director could ill afford any other losses.

Several buildings along those cobbled streets were indeed irritatingly familiar, but the series as a whole can be considered a success. It is consistently aware of David Lean's imposing benchmark, and tries hard to match that standard, most evidently in the sweeping orchestral score by Èduard Artem'ev, himself best known for three Tarkovskii films and the Oscar-winning *Burned by the Sun* (1995). Artem'ev's music here underwrites a grand melancholy; Proshkin's visual evocation of this sad solitude is achieved with less snow than Lean's forerunner, but he makes frequent, striking use of smoke, dust, or incense to capture the encroachment of an equally ominous wasteland – the slow evanescing of a better age. In that same light, Vladimir Il'in and Oleg Iankovskii deserve special mention for exemplifying the stagy gestures of a fading, ineffectual intelligentsia (Gromeko) or the savagery of omnivorous commerce (Komarovskii).

This same savagery was the cause of Proshkin's woes. The series was based on an initial conception by Central Partnership in 2003 after reaching an agreement with Pasternak's relatives. It was ready for broadcasting at the end of 2005, but had been scared off the winter schedules by competition from two other shows discussed below, *The Master and Margarita* and *The Golden Calf*.[4] This delayed debut left many copies of the finished, printed film in semi-public realms, which gave the pirates lots of time to plunder them. Consequently *Zhivago*'s premiere, still overshadowed by these criminal intrusions, was rather strangely staggered; showings began in Belarus, where pirated copies had been less accessible. It captured almost 45 percent of all that nation's urban viewers, while Russian officials at NTV claimed, somewhat unconvincingly, that people who buy DVDs are not the same audience who watch television. Advertisers, "therefore," could still count on a sizeable market share in Moscow and beyond. The Russian press, however, felt no moral obligation to wait, and reviewed the DVDs well ahead of time, often using the illegal prints to do so.[5]

Initially there had been something excitingly unique about the bootlegs; the very first of them, with all eleven episodes squeezed onto one disk, had sold for 8,000 rubles ($300).[6] The picture quality was less than perfect. Not surprisingly, though, these production standards improved with time and demand. The pirates quickly created an elegant boxed set by March 2006 for sale at 800 rubles ($30) on the streets, further undermining any likelihood that shoppers would wait for a "quality," official version. In addition, mpeg4 files appeared all over the internet with equal haste. The major actors committed to the series' major roles were less than happy: Oleg Men'shikov, Chulpan Khamatova, Oleg Iankovskii, Andrei Panin, and Kirill Pirogov. Several newspapers spoke on their behalf, mourning the ruination of "the last, finest example of a novel in Russia – and therefore in the world."[7]

Similarly disturbing disrespect became part and parcel of filming Lermontov's *Hero of Our Time* in the same year. Here the complaints concerned any ability of a young, modern actor, Igor' Petrenko, to live up to the standards of Soviet dramaturgy (despite the absence of any full-length cinematic version of the novel in the Soviet canon). These curmudgeons lauded something absent, yet offered no constructive attitudes towards the *hic et nunc*.[8] The Moscow press, looking to bridge this gap, began by promoting Petrenko as the "Russian Alain Delon," a somewhat strange choice that underscored the problems of making Lermontov relevant after 126 years.[9]

In fact the title of Lermontov's tome had already recently been used to advertise a much more forceful action hero, played by Dmitrii Brusnikin in the 2003 crime series *Instructor*. This "newer" and more relevant man, Illarion Zabrodov, is a recently retired officer who looks forward to a quiet life restoring antique books. The world of twenty-first-century crime, however, brings him back into the fray as "an honorable soldier." Boys, girls, and retirees are unable to concentrate on their own books, because literary models demand too much of them.

> The hero of Lermontov's time, as the author himself wrote, embodied the sins of a generation. A hero of the twenty-first century, however, is made of virtues. He doesn't roam the country aimlessly, seducing women as he goes. A modern hero busies himself with something socially useful: he restores old books, teaches the younger generation martial arts or struggles against organized crime. Although ... on the subject of women ... we wouldn't say they're completely absent here!

On that score, perhaps, all heroes of all times *are* the same; the difference between our hero and Pechorin, however, is that ours doesn't leave women with a broken heart. He genuinely loves them.[10]

Even the canon's most self-assured heroes can lack staying power or importance for disrespectful Russian viewers. Sergei Solov'ev's simultaneously produced *Anna Karenina* provides another interesting example. The director had begun finance negotiations in the mid-1990s, but only a decade later did shooting the novel seem fiscally feasible. Suddenly both Channel One and Rossiia were bidding over the project. The former network won the auction, while Rossiia took its funds off to *The Master and Margarita*; NTV was busy with a reworking of Gogol's *Dead Souls*, discussed below. These ostentatious, old-world shows would average inordinately high production costs of more than $200,000 per episode.

When Solov'ev began filming *Karenina* with Sergei Bezrukov and Tat'iana Drubich in the main roles, a stately pace was imposed upon this project, too. It was shut down for several months for financial reasons, leading one major newspaper to ask whether the project, so famous on the big screen, would ever reach completion.[11] The fact that Solov'ev was planning to shoot both TV and feature versions at the same time did little to accelerate the timetable in anticipation of big profits; quite the opposite. The weight of the past (of prestige) was felt immediately – and it cost a lot.

Although Solov'ev declared an aversion to "lecturing" anybody with corrective, time-honored values, he nonetheless used a discussion of Dostoevskii to restate Proshkin's view that classic literature is unchanging. It is therefore worthy of long, slow or unavoidably expensive treatments. It deserves undying and well-funded respect (in which case it *does* lecture us with its value system). Proshkin gives voice to – but does not elucidate – an odd interface of prestigious stasis and change:

> You should film a classic novel just as Dostoevskii authored it, neither better nor worse; show what Dostoevskii has left in our heads, hearts and souls. After all, he wrote everything down; his manuscripts are in state archives. Their remnants linger in our individual consciousness and in society, too. They form a symbolic system in the lives of that society, in its members. That system changes, just as people do. It's important to show these changes instead of offering a literary primer for people who can't read ... or don't want to. That's why there can be 10, 20, or 30 TV adaptations of a given classic. The main thing is to avoid the attitude that "People'll never read the novel, but at least they'll watch our TV show."[12]

Solov'ev then offered an example from the memoirs of actor Viacheslav Tikhonov, famous for playing both Gestapo agent Stirlitz in 1973 and Prince Bolkonskii in the earlier, Oscar-winning movie *War and Peace*. When

Tikhonov asked a young girl which part of *War and Peace* she liked best, she replied: "The scene where Natasha dances with Stirlitz."

Solov'ev's quote and recalled jibe are both offered at the expensive of profiteering and politically driven cinema; nonetheless he embraces a parallel set of values that are no less grand. This paradox or muddled overlap is equally evident in viewer polls of late. In *Izvestiia* at the end of 2004, a quarter of Russians held that television lacks contemporary themes, while another quarter believed it should propagate positive values. This deadlock, however, was convincingly broken by the 51 percent of audience members who felt that *whatever* the theme, be it old, new, or "classic," TV drama today is a mere reflection of state sponsorship. This battle between respect for the past and progressive, Putinesque ideas that *draw* upon that past will be of enduring interest for this study. It throws up issues of realism *per se*, of fidelity to a linguistically embodied corpus, and, in turn, of the relation of that corpus to various simulacra.

The equally imposing presence of a twentieth-century canon: Solzhenitsyn

> Russian TV series today are a disaster. It's not because of the genre; there's nothing wrong with TV series in and of themselves. David Lynch made a masterpiece out of *Twin Peaks*. But these [literary adaptations] have to be taken seriously. We're dealing with works of art.
> (Iu. Grymov, 2004, on filming Liudmila Ulitskaia's renowned novel *Kukotskii's Case*)[13]

The paradoxes in Proshkin's rationale (respect for unchanging values *and* changing aesthetics) are felt market-wide. Cynical observers in the Russian press note that any TV adaptation will unavoidably be a compromise with the director's highfaluting intentions. The typical format nowadays is "an enlightening costume-drama added to a cheap soap opera." It characteristically involves several famous Soviet actors, together with some cheaper TV stars. Bulgakov can therefore be made funnier and Solzhenitsyn more exciting – and indeed they have to be, in order for any "timeless" classics to survive.

In many cases, these cookie-cutter literary adaptations star Sergei Bezrukov or Evgenii Mironov in leading roles, sometimes Oleg Men'shikov. Publishers then stick these actors' faces on new editions of the classic novel, thus upping sales (in the case of Bulgakov) to approximately 200 extra copies per week in any of Moscow's larger bookstores. Television's defenders in this tawdry process are few and far between; one of them has been Daniil Dondurei, editor of the journal *The Art of Cinema*:

> We shouldn't choose between different art forms; we should read books *and* watch TV. What happens afterwards is pretty insignificant. You can get to know the novel first, and then watch the screen version ... but

things usually happen the other way around. I know people who watched *The Master and Margarita*, for example, and then ran out to buy the book the very next day. TV or film adaptations of literature will never be a perfect copy. Watching a TV version, therefore, isn't enough to get a full idea of the book. Even so, Russian viewers really need this kind of cinema as a bulwark against all those criminal, anti-intellectual films. Over the last decade Russians have drowned in a sea of that stuff.[14]

Visual adaptations have justified themselves with greatest difficulty whenever a well-loved Soviet film version was still in the viewers' memories. This long, additional shadow was especially troublesome for Solov'ev. He had pondered filming *Karenina* for almost three decades, but heads at Goskino had always felt guilty discussing a new movie while director Aleksandr Zarkhi was still alive, the man responsible for the 1967 adaptation – itself the sixteenth, worldwide. Zarkhi died in 1997.

What "change" could be added to the novel's unchanging prestige? Solov'ev's defenders in 2006 justified his project by saying that Western versions of *Karenina* had always been essentially romantic, whereas Russian equivalents delved deeper into psychological, social, and political elements; Solov'ev would add something new.[15] Yet his main obstacle to filming this book was a *Russian, Soviet* film. Why add something psycho-political to a film that was "already" so? The fact that this project would be commissioned by Nikita Mikhalkov's "Tri Tè" studio led many to expect that elegantly clothed, patriotic principles would take center-stage. Bezrukov and Drubich would, in addition, help the director prove his assertion that "classic literature is inexhaustible and can be filmed eternally, even if others did so successfully before you."[16] This upsetting logic either ties the permanence of patriotism to profit, or it *lessens* the power of national intransience in the face of more powerful, shifting semiotic systems. Patriotism's signified ("us") has an increasing number of signifiers. "We" means nothing in particular.

These problems of inexhaustible, archetypal literature can be extended to prestigious novels of the Soviet period, too. Parallel to the problems discussed thus far ran versions of Solzhenitsyn's *The First Circle* (published in 1968) and *The Golden Calf* by Il'f and Petrov (1931). Speaking of her role in the Solzhenitsyn adaptation, mature actress Inna Churikova celebrated the book's "lofty, free spirit. These are true heroes of honor and conscience, the kind you just don't see nowadays ... Our film is very up to date, though, so maybe there's hope for mankind yet." The project likewise endlessly celebrated itself as noncommercial, while the actors advertised (immodestly) their willingly accepted modest wages. One of *The First Circle*'s key thespians, Dmitrii Pevtsov, had his head shaved completely for Episode Ten; the press noted how this would create difficulties in his daily work on the Moscow stage. The ethical importance of *The First Circle* made this haircut a justifiable, laudable forfeit.

Although Solzhenitsyn himself did not take part in the casting or any of the press conferences, he was – according to his wife – most pleased with the result of these sacrifices. She called *The First Circle* a "pleasant surprise," especially with its attention to detail, all the way from prison-scene locations to Stalinist crockery and even the prisoners' own post-war, strangely denim attire – of equally strange American origin.[17]

This series was masterminded by Gleb Panfilov, who, although he had directed Solzhenitsyn on the stage, was now responsible for showcasing Russia's first cinematic version of the novel.[18] It debuted on 29 January 2006 on Rossiia, when the station spoke on Panfilov's behalf, underscoring the seriousness of the task at hand:

> We're perfectly aware that over and above any ratings-related issues, we're obliged as a state TV channel to enlighten and educate people. Aleksandr Solzhenitsyn is a classic writer on the level of Tolstoi and Dostoevskii; his renown extends far beyond Russia's borders. His books were largely responsible for the way our country was both seen and understood by the world for several decades. Here in Russia there's a long-standing, paradoxical attitude to classic literature: it's respected, but nobody reads it. We hope that our adaptation will help many Russian viewers discover Solzhenitsyn; the direct participation of Solzhenitsyn himself has endowed our series with his novel's true spirit.[19]

When seen in the context of Solzhenitsyn's entire corpus, interwoven as the massive *Red Wheel*, the author himself defines that spirit as tales of how "Russians, tragically, have destroyed both their own past and future."[20] The series' producer, Maksim Panfilov, wanted to place at least some elements of helpful self-definition in this inescapable dourness and declared *The First Circle* a narrative of "how, in the hardest possible circumstances, an individual can choose a difficult, but worthy path. And win! That's a subject worthy of any age."[21] As the lead actor, Evgenii Mironov, put it:

> Who knew that Solzhenitsyn would stand up against everybody, against the State, the *entire* State – and win? Amazing! It sounds like something out of a fairytale, but it did happen, all the same, so things like this really can occur.[22]

Whatever its potential as a finger-wagging, teacherly tool, this series is an artistic success, especially in the light of *Meetings with Solzhenitsyn*, the author's own dull television show that was canceled in September 1995, due to poor ratings. His self-penned screenplay and off-screen narration for *The First Circle* do indeed accentuate Rossiia's respectful, serious intentions, despite the predominance of silly false beards and inflexible wigs – as on Stalin's head. The soundtrack was thankfully recorded live (i.e. not with additional dialogue recording [ADR]), save several re-recorded conversations that were initially whispered at insufficient volume. The use of Stalinist architecture's vacant, imposing walls and herringbone floors, so visible across Russia even today, likewise does much to grant the broadcasts a disconcerting contemporary relevance.

If one were looking for failings, however, they might paradoxically also come from Solzhenitsyn's hands-on approach, for *V kruge pervom* is a tad wordy. The author, in essence, took his favorite monologs or dialogs from the novel and then "dramatized" them, which results in an unnaturally marked frequency of aphorisms. This, however, does not detract from an extremely powerful storyline. The series stresses the dramatic deadlock between those men who actually *gain* a sense of mental and verbal freedom or relief from (finally) being incarcerated and the Soviet prison guards, who cannot ever *grant* their prisoners freedom, since they do not, in Solzhenitsyn's words, "have it" themselves. The vacant state is unable to grant significance to its subjects.

This problem of lack is impressively invoked at the start of each episode by the use of popular/political songs recorded between the Purges and the end of the 1940s. The decade is mapped with the strident jollity of ditties by Pokrass, Dunaevskii, Shvartsman, Lebedev-Kumach, and others, but the first and last episodes showcase the rousing "Russia" of 1947 by Novikov and Alymov. Essentially an obsequious celebration of Stalin as the "ancient knight and father of the Soviet people," this song nonetheless needs to draw upon something *greater* than the Kremlin and its residents in order to convey that mighty paternalism. Alymov's lyrics employ the "unfettered and beautiful land" that is Russia and then – in turn – one country is itself compared to the bigger sky, to the sun and "a *boundless*, blossoming expanse of *infinite* fields." This need for policy (something very specific) to draw first upon nature, followed by the immateriality of the heavens (nothing in particular) will return many times. The "nature" of a purportedly organic patriotism is less than clear; language runs around trying to pinpoint and then outpace it. This endless *glissage* of a spoken or sung nationalism is tied to *loss*, to boundless realms, or a pitiless, now-absent history (for which the nation itself has no "unchanging" signifiers).

Solzhenitsyn's televised investigation of this sad dilemma was nonetheless attractive; *The First Circle*'s debut was watched by a third of Russia's adult viewers. As we will see with *The Master and Margarita*, this show was also broadcast in a confident format: two episodes at a time, back to back, without advertisements.[23] Whether this was due to the book's classic status or a modish, star-studded cast remained a moot point.[24]

More weight from the recent past: Il'f and Petrov

Another disputable point or paradox was highlighted by the scheduling in 2006 of *The First Circle*; it clashed with the adaptation of Il'f and Petrov's *Golden Calf.* Any possible competition between them, however, was decided as the latter garnered an amazing number of negative reviews, even from the screenwriter, Il'ia Avramenko, and the actors. Avramenko called *The Golden Calf* a "cheap puppet show, devoid of talent."[25] Soviet classic actor Mikhail Svetin was not allowed to dub his own appearance in the series; he denounced the entire venture as "tedious," even if it starred one of the three great heroes of new Russian TV, known *en masse* as "MMM": Men'shikov (here in the role of Bender), Mironov, and/or Mashkov.[26] Worse still was the subsequent nomination of director Ul'iana Shilkina for the year's "anti-prize" *Abzats* in the category of "Weakest, Most Pointless TV Show."[27] The complete absence of close-ups, said some journalists, was an indication that the series had been filmed too rapidly, with no time to insert additional material.

These accusations, although common, are unjustified, even if some signs of penny-pinching appear in the frequent recourse to post-sync dialog. The series *does* include a large number of close-ups; only extreme proximity to faces and/or objects of vital, sustained interest is missing. Had these complaints not been made, most (if not all) viewers would have noticed no such lacunae. What does, however, seem unsuccessful is the attempt to reproduce a "wacky" aesthetic of the late 1920s. Footage is often accompanied by an accelerated piano score to evoke the lingering popularity of silent cinema; this, in turn, is joined early on by mock-silent footage from the Cruiser *Ochakov*. To this we can also add many black and white cartoon episodes that draw more upon animation styles of the early 1980s than anything from the New Economic Policy.

One might reasonably suggest that the press' negative attitudes came in part from the fact that Men'shikov was fighting a losing battle with viewers' fond memories of several Soviet actors in the role of Bender: Sergei Iurskii, Archil Gomiashvili, and Andrei Mironov, not to mention comedian and DJ Nikolai Fomenko in a 2005 TV musical version of *The Twelve Chairs* (dir. Maksim Papernik). In addition, further grumpiness was certainly voiced because this new edition had taken some considerable liberties with the text, such as the restoration of events excised from the familiar, Soviet redaction; one of these is the funeral of the poet Maiakovskii. The funeral scene is brief, virtually dialog-free, and essentially unobtrusive, even though it makes dramatic and swift use of approximately 200 extras and ten horses. Viewers did not treat this kind of disrespect kindly; amateur forums were on occasion heartless: "After fifteen minutes I realized that the series should be sold in drug stores – as a sleeping aid." Avramenko was so ashamed that he removed his name from the titles and credits: "I walk down the street with my head lowered." Nobody was laughing at the comedy. Men'shikov, according to the press, had depicted Bender as "somebody who didn't want to live under Soviet power ... and therefore was a sad, sometimes tragic philosopher."[28]

These bad reviews give some idea of television's downside for "bigger" movie stars. Many were not initially keen to jump on the bandwagon of serialized TV drama. Being typecast or stuck in one role for several years following the success of a given series concerned many artists and they often shied away from cut-rate television; even today most productions are filmed on video and fall short of the purportedly high benchmarks established by Soviet TV.[29] So how were thespians, especially the big stars, attracted to homemade television after Yeltsin, to work for the typical Russian viewership, 51 percent of whom are female, 49 percent male, and on average 38 years old?[30]

A pivotal figure in this objective was Aleksei Slapovskii, a self-acknowledged fan of *The Seventeen Moments of Spring*, who authored the screenplay for *Request Stop* (*Ostanovka po trebovaniiu*, dir. Dzhanik Faiziev, 2000 and 2001). Centered on a down-to-earth story of two modern couples, one hardworking yet somewhat naïve and the other fiscally brutal, the series was praised for building upon the Brezhnevian traditions of *Moscow Does Not Believe in Tears* (*Moskva slezam ne verit*, dir. Vladimir Men'shov, 1979), *Winter Cherry* (*Zimniaia vishnia*, dir. Igor' Maslennikov, 1985), and *The Irony of Fate* (*Ironiia sud'by*, dir. Èl'dar Riazanov, 1976). Of course, for all the praise, there would be a fair share of lingering discontent from some quarters. Killjoys claimed the show reflected (and enjoyed) a modern social dilemma, often bemoaned by Russian households – or at least by the husbands. Here we return to the problems faced by our action heroes. This is what happens when people do not respect literature's mores:

> In our society today an intellectual shift is taking place; it's probably connected to parallel shifts in the financial world. Men and women are swapping social roles. If aliens ever watched this TV series, they'd conclude that men on Earth are the weaker sex. These men trail after the main heroine and all want something from her: love, money, or a child. But she, being proud and independent, chooses the weakest of them all ... She courageously "adopts" the infantile hero and hopes to make a real man out of him. Anybody among you who wishes to repeat this exercise should be wished good luck and reminded of what happened to Frankenstein.[31]

Love stories could not be told as before because Russian families had changed too much, as had the place where they lived. Slapovskii deliberately wrote *Request Stop* to counter all the increasing "detective shows, action stories, and other nonsense." Instead, it would offer a new, respectful retro-tale based on human nature, rather than loud adventure.[32] Here, in this and related TV projects, there resided a different notion of community, the strains of an ahistorical patriotism that's "simple, like a lowing sound."[33] Yet despite these accusations of simplicity or sad, inverted binaries, it was occasionally asserted that the simple structural opposites of Mexican soap operas (be they ethical or gender-based) were actually instigating a desire among Russian viewers for something more *intricate*.

"People got tired of silly conflicts between some heroine – with her soul of sterile purity – and innumerable villains that surrounded her while they plotted in various wicked ways."[34] Love should, therefore, be somehow traditional, nationally specific, and complex at the same time.

If Slapovskii's "Russianness" could avoid cookie-cutter simplicity, it might find good company amid the claims of Valerii Todorovskii (TV drama chief at Rossiia) that visual episodic narratives are worthy inheritors of Chekhov's oeuvre – whilst feature films are more "Tolstoian." Agreement is heard at other TV stations today. Todorovskii's counterpart at Channel One, Dzhanik Faiziev, says today's TV drama is now made of compound or mixed genres – which is by no means a failing, for "human stories [thus] transpire." Neither life nor love is simple. Faiziev quotes the tragicomedy *Kramer versus Kramer* (Robert Benton, 1979) as a good benchmark for modern and multigeneric storytelling. Transferred to Russia, the resulting hero from such stories, say executives at STS, should be "strong, pleasant, attractive, and able to give people a good dose of optimism."[35] The classics, apparently, would help to solve this problem, too.

Standing on the shoulders of giants: *The Idiot* (dir. Vladimir Bortko, 2003)

The adaptation of Dostoevskii's *The Idiot* for Rossiia is perhaps the best example of this problematic bridge between literature and something local, newer, or simply "attractive."[36] The series' DVD box set of 2003 maintains that inside is the "first version of the novel in world cinema based on utmost fidelity to the original text." The producers, over and above their respect for the words of the original, also wanted to avoid any costume drama burdened by material objects – by an exacting fidelity to furniture or interiors of the period. Equally importantly, the series straddled two disparate periods of TV production. Conceived and constructed between 1999 and 2003, it was imagined during the heyday of Latin American serials but appeared during the renaissance of domestic shows. The "willful archaism" of *The Idiot* on TV is as much a deep bow of respect before the Brazilians as it is a nod towards Dostoevskii.

Here the issues of well-spoken status, cheapness, and profitable familiarity are all rolled together. Director Vladimir Bortko said: "You can call *The Idiot* a detective story – and probably a melodrama, too. It was written just like a soap opera for newspapers."[37] The newspaper *Russian News* (*Rossiiskie vesti*) likened the series to both Soviet detective dramas and the modern mystical show *Beyond the Wolves* (*Po tu storonu volkov*, dir. Vladimir Khotinenko, 2002; see p. 102) because it stresses love and other familial elements within its criminal plot. The same paper also maintained – simultaneously and in contradiction to Bortko – that the broadcasts are "an attempt to create a domestic show *different* from Latin American family sagas, with all their muddled relationships between relatives."[38] But how convincing was this claim to self-respecting socialist culture or the leather tomes of its libraries if foreign TV was a frequent point of reference (if only in order to outdo it)?

Elsewhere, the *Idiot* adaptation was called, more accurately, "a detective story of feelings" and this definition helps to clarify matters.³⁹ The series realizes certain affective and Brazilian elements that are novelistic:

> Like the [Latin-American] *telenovela*, *The Idiot* focuses on passions and suffering in the context of family relations and relies on criminal subplots. Similarly to *The Idiot, telenovelas* explore the combination of national and human values, often setting their narratives in a vaguely pre-industrial past. Staple fare in *telenovelas*, oppositions between demonic and spiritual men as well as loose and honest women also fashion the character structure for Dostoevskii's text. Finally, the *telenovela* is a highly theatrical genre relying on rigid camera work, long close-ups of the actors' faces, theatrical sets and incessant relationship-talk, all features central to the aesthetic organization of *The Idiot*.⁴⁰

In a land where nobody reads Tolstoi's novels any more, their structure and social intentions remain, working hard and finding much in common with Latin soaps.

Money aside, another reason that *The Idiot* borrowed from Brazil was that prior to the Russian TV renaissance domestic shows merely leaned on socialist clichés (or re-edited classics) in order to "console millions of people in the absence of new values and norms." If news broadcasts were designed to "explain that we're alive, then serials should explain *why* we're alive." New Brazilian soaps were already the logical heirs to the narrative structure, heroes, and ethical (depoliticized) tenets of the past; they could be made worthy of Viacheslav Tikhonov. They could one day be compared to "Stirlitz or the heroes of [Aleksei] Batalov and [Iurii] Nikulin."⁴¹

Classic serializations, both on Brazilian television or in nineteenth-century publishing houses, leave big gaps between segments and increase the audience's role in collaboratively creating meaning. Serialization turns a straightforward narrative into a better form of social glue. If extended over a long period of time, the punctuated storyline may start moving in the direction of a soap opera – where desire is never satisfied and nothing ever ends. Serials, however, do end (eventually) and therefore operate between coherence and diffusion, between satisfying a hope or desire and the more aimless business of desiring, pure and simple. The size of this fluctuating social group is, of course, often financially determined, just as is the length of a serialized novel.

This tension has certainly been evident in the history of American televised drama, where it becomes hard to distinguish between *bona fide*, theoretically endless soap operas and story arcs, which determine the themes of a series for one season and may – or may not – become the foundation of the following season's core narrative. This confusion began with the adoption of story arcs by the US show *Peyton Place* (1964–9), perhaps because the series was born of a feature film, itself an adapted novel. Any such confusion between endless and conclusive tales certainly fueled the major dramas of the 1980s like *Dallas*, *Dynasty*, and *Hill Street Blues*, but in essence even the busiest, most rambling soap operas are often neatly and conclusively distilled in the public's mind by a "supercouple" or tiny, central pair of protagonists, such as Bill Hayes and Susan Seaforth Hayes (they married in real life, also), who graced the cover of *Time* magazine on 12 January 1974.

The same logic can determine the size of social units being shown on screen, too – that is, the small character-clusters that in turn create groups of willing and empathetic viewers. Here again the stripped-down look of *The Idiot* comes into play. Scenes usually center on two or three people, being cheaper to shoot than outdoor, action-based footage:

> Although clearly economically determined, this interiority [on US television] enhances daytime's "women-centered" atmosphere since its dyadic structure and familiar setting necessitate a primarily emotional and interactive, rather than action-oriented narrative ... The sets are not hermeneutically crucial in themselves, as they are in cinema. Soaps focus on [how and] what characters say to one another, not where they say it.[42]

Elena Prokhorova has likewise suggested that earlier detective dramas of the 1970s were driven by maudlin dialog, not thunderous action.[43] The experience of watching today's retrospective, respectful, and emotional TV is often structured by cash *and* cultural mining; the whereabouts of that mine, however, seem unsure. So with all these wandering, homeless influences in the creation of emotional, classic melodramas – money (from advertising and profiteering), the Soviet tradition, Latin *telenovelas*, the big screen, and, last of all, the unassailable prestige of the Golden Age book, how is television now planning to make use of some *very* Soviet novels in the near future? The prestigious literary values sought by today's television are extracted from all manner of times and traditions, from the nineteenth century and from the darkest dogma of the twentieth, too.

Finding a home for the "perfect" Soviet text: *The Young Guard* (*Molodaia gvardiia*, dir. Sergei Lialin, in production 2006)

> How is the friendship of young Soviet people depicted in this novel? In what moments does it present itself strongest of all?[44]
>
> (From a Russian schoolbook under Brezhnev)

After 15 December 2004 and the legalization of Putin's desire to henceforth nominate regional governors, talk of Soviet grand narratives sounded louder than ever in the international press. Removing oligarchs, deputies, and now governors, Putin stepped forth as the lone teller of various tales designed to ward off extremes such as "terrorism" and "separatism." The newspaper *Komsomol'skaia Pravda* drew on parallels with allegedly similar policies in Russian history, all the way from Dmitrii Donskoi, Ivan the Terrible, and Boris Godunov en route to the Soviet experience. Discerning thus a fluctuation in Soviet history between totalitarian and democratic periods, the paper concluded that nostalgia has recently been greater for the former – for the "iron hands" of Stalin or Brezhnev; hence – it was suggested – the success of Putin's dogmatic yarns and any associated television series.[45]

Commenting upon this article, television presenter Mikhail Leont'ev insisted that "systematic corruption had eaten up" any positive aspects of communism, while liberal leader Irina Khakamada replied with marked sarcasm that Putin will soon offer Leont'ev cause for hope – by "reinstating the good old Soviet Union." Despite such disagreements, all contributors felt that the President's social and cultural policy indeed owes much to the "iron" half of the Soviet seesaw. Today's remakes of partisan Soviet epics would speak to this best of all. In doing so, they fix themselves accurately in time, in given historical events, but sometimes seem a tad unsure of the space(s) or nation they depict.

In the spring of 2005 Sergei Lialin began shooting a version of the archetypal Soviet novel *The Young Guard* by Aleksandr Fadeev (1946). The director was keen to maintain a distance from the book and a subsequent film version of 1948, since both are held in high regard to this day. Lialin's first respectful sidestep began with a decision to film in the Tula region:

> The story we're telling in this [six-part] series isn't based *entirely* on Fadeev's novel! It's simply based on some real events that took place during World War Two in the Ukrainian region of Krasnodon. The governing role of the Communist Party in the original film has been entirely removed, too; there was no such role [in real life]. Fadeev was forced to manufacture it. Our film is about the passion of some 16-year old boys and girls – who perish in the name of an ideal.

The series would thus be Soviet in the sense of a "time" called the Soviet Union, but not (all) the ideals that were foisted upon that chronotope from afar. Its power would come from principles, not policy – yet their ethical force, once divorced from bureaucratic procedure, becomes so vague that it can, sadly, be hijacked (or stolen *back*) by savvy spin doctors.

When asked precisely how it might be possible to use this television drama to redo something Soviet in a better, purer way, several actors from both the original and new films chipped in – including Inna Makarova and Vladimir Korenev:

> MAKAROVA: I can't say whether we need a new film version or not. The old film by Sergei Gerasimov was a work of genius – and I

was fortunate enough to act in it. But that movie was drenched in the smell of war: the sweat and blood of people defending their homeland. That period made the film for us. Today's times don't help this new version: we're living in a rotten age.

KORENEV: I like *The Young Guard* a lot. It's a patriotic book – and there aren't enough of those today. There's nothing bad in Fadeev's novel, though lots of people think otherwise.[46]

A brief background to the novel itself explains why this book was chosen – and why it results in this type of wrangling nowadays. Fadeev's story of tragically valiant effort expended on "making things right" tells of young partisans working against Nazi forces in an occupied Ukrainian town; in a rather impassioned manner, the young people attain both physical and philosophical maturity in their struggle for Soviet victory.

Under Stalin's prompting, though, a couple of articles in 1947 suggested that Fadeev had underplayed the guidance of the Party for these freedom fighters, and so the author was forced to increase socialist tenets and downplay the romance or violence. It was this newer text, which the author produced only with enormous effort, that continued to be printed in the Soviet Union. A few years after the painful reedit, an indicative assessment of the work appeared, saying that *Molodaia gvardiia* had inspired scholarly work around several key themes, in particular the "organizational role of the Party" that was always worthy of both high praise and cinematic attention.[47]

Perhaps the most persuasive indication that Fadeev's story always expressed something other than progressive ideologies is the context of his suicide, prompted both by the ravages of Stalinism and by the fact that he felt massive guilt at his own politicized behavior. The official coroner's report (and subsequently the press) blamed alcoholism alone, without stopping to admit what actually caused the drinking in the first place.[48] Two months before his death he had written in a letter of 16 March 1956: "We're not all the type of 'mechanical citizens' that Gor'kii once wrote about ... We feel or worry about [*perezhivaem*] everything that's tied up with the difficulties and failings of the people, of the State."[49] These are the contradictions inherent in discussions of the serial and its status as a sociopolitical remake.

Konstantin Fedin, in a letter to Fadeev of 26 September 1946, said in addition that his friend had tried in *Molodaia gvardiia* to capture both the real and the ideal, the "way life should be and the way it is, in its 'ideal' aspect."[50] Fedin conflates two things: the standard Soviet selection of myriad details for the purposes of a futural, progressive aesthetic, and his admission that there is something in life *already* that the author must then (after perceiving it) attempt in retrospect to capture. This is both realist exclusiveness – the choosing of details – and romantic, unrealizable inclusiveness.

Since this "ideal aspect" is, in the romantic sense, life "as it is" (totally), and Fadeev based his work upon real-life sources, the number of facts in the book can sometimes squeeze out the author altogether. At that point of a detailed, documented absolute there is no selection, no filtering, no "better" or marked information. Many real-life families in the villages of *Molodaia gvardiia* suffered malice and prejudice because their neighbors thought them the prototypes of Fadeev's *negative* characters:

> "I don't remember," said Fadeev, "in the history of literature a novelist who followed real-world events so closely" ... The facts of Krasnodon actually could have happened in any of hundreds of Soviet towns and villages ... That's why young people consider Fadeev's novel a book about themselves.[51]

They all see themselves because they see absolutely nobody in particular. They see everything because they see nothing.

Fadeev conducted much research into the archives and records of the young soldiers and their friends or families, which allowed him to say in the physical presence of his readers at conferences, "I did not idealize your young guards. That's the way they really were."[52] The most famous example of this reality comes at the very end of *Molodaia gvardiia*, when Fadeev simply offers a list of the real-life prototypes for his characters:

> I could have ended the novel with much pomp; I could have given it a conclusion of pathos or lyricism, and that would have left a deeper impression. But you see that I end it with a list of all the surnames of the participants in *Molodaia gvardiia* who were killed. I feel an internal obligation to at least in some way *list them all*, from respect and in their memory. So that's the way it'll stay.[53]

Here we see the far end of emotive socialist literature, which might be called the *true* realism and will be important to us throughout this book. All facts are potentially entertained, as a result of which all are unmarked, since there is no designation. Books on Fadeev's art continued to state that he had connected events "in his own way,"[54] but compared to the intentions of Muscovite policy-makers Fadeev makes markedly less selection. He accepts more phenomena and enters a state prior to specific intentionality. Soviet scholars noted that "Fadeev's metaphoric arsenal is modest,"[55] and indeed at the end of metaphoric intent – effected emotionally – total, endless change must surely be seen as no change, since there is no discernible stability relative to which it can be assessed. "Facts" remain in never-ending abundance. Selectiveness is no longer possible and so one is left with movement towards *all* the world's bare facts. This is the *bona fide* realism, but politics is not happy with it. Policy insists upon *limited* selectiveness, which depressed Fadeev so much that he shot himself. Television's ability to unnerve policy-makers with the "unlimiting" *modus operandi* of this novel remains today.

The relationship of details, of individuals, to an organic totality is clear in the text of *Molodaia gvardiia*. In some scenes there is a discernible, timelessly patriotic concern for the endless "country(side)" with explicitly personal origins:

> Since the war began Anatolii had made numerous speeches about the defense of the Soviet Union at Komsomol meetings but in none of them had he been able to convey his conception of his native land as something great and throbbing with life and song, something like Tais'ia Prokof'evna, his own mother, with her tall, plump figure, her kind rosy face and her beautiful old Cossack songs which he could remember her singing since he was a child. This conception of his country was always in his heart and it brought tears to his eyes when he heard his favorite songs or saw the trampled wheat or a burnt-out cottage.

A philosophy of song, dance and popular entertainment is, in fact, such a powerful, even universal, challenge to the restrictive notions of political oratory that during the war a suggestion is made to the Fascist invaders that a club be set up for *everybody*: "They may allow you to do it. They're stifled with boredom themselves." The recurring melodies thereof are so powerful they can even hope to overcome death when the partisans are taken to a coalmine shaft for their execution:

> They tortured Liuba Shevtsova until February 7th, endeavoring to obtain from her the code and the wireless transmitter. Before she was shot she managed to send her mother a brief note: 'Good-bye, Mama, your daughter Liuba is going away, into the damp ground.' As they led her out to be shot, she was singing one of her favorite songs: *On the wide streets and parks of Moscow* ... The SS *Rottenführer* who led her out to her execution wanted her to kneel and be shot in the nape of the neck, but Liuba refused to go down on her knees and received the bullet in her face.

Drawing on the past: the visual heritage of *The Young Guard*

> The soldiers of the Great Patriotic War are justly called the soldiers of freedom ... They fought for the right to live on their own land, to speak their native language and have their own statehood, culture and traditions.
>
> (Putin, 2005)

The line between social, national, and politicized memberships can be a fine one; hence the confusion over Putin's Sovietness in a land where Channel

One and Rossiia have access to 98 percent and 95 percent of the population, respectively. On 19 May 2005 a law was passed, overturning prior rulings of 2003 limiting the right of local governmental structures to establish mass media; the homogenization of television grew even more obvious, leading even to an increased frequency in certain set phrases used by the *vox populi* to describe Putin himself. The public began repeating what it heard on TV: "Honesty," "Decency," "Truthfulness," "Love and empathy for the people," among other idioms. Home is where the heart is, and someone was providing its name(s).

Given, in addition, that perhaps 70 percent of employees of the Russian media today graduated from Soviet universities or worked for erstwhile Soviet media, the cynicism of those upset by TV's purportedly "empathetic" pushiness does not abate:

> Not only are they [the television staff] familiar with propaganda techniques, but they don't want any changes – in either society or the media. They still consider it essential for Russian society to be dependent on a daily dosage of TV-delivered information. They believe the President's sovereignty can be long and problem-free in these circumstances alone.[56]

Even in quiet times, though, Putin would require some kind of opposition (be it real or rhetorical) in order to advertise a positive platform. Daniil Dondurei has suggested that ostensibly independent media like *Èkho Moskvy*, often critical of the president, actually bless him with an entity from which he can "defend the people." Without some kind of opposition "what could our State offer us? There's only one answer: an increase in bureaucracy. And you won't inspire anybody with that." Director of channel STS Aleksandr Rodnianskii likewise drew parallels between TV series like *A Policeman's Beat* (*Uchastok*), funded by Channel One and discussed on pp. 203–207, and the manipulation of events in Beslan. Both have been employed to tell simple, socially relevant yarns of opposing forces. These stories are resolved by a straight-shooting hero, political or literary, "who'll utter words of sympathy through gritted teeth" and embody a reliable bravado.[57]

This battleground between Good and Bad is mapped out across sympathy and empathy in places frequently beyond (or prior to) language and dogma. Politics therefore busies itself with what Dondurei terms the essentially "apolitical nature of the people." Hence the employment of patriotically tinted, feel-good terminology or serials, together with retro-concerts replete with Soviet pop songs, *à la* "Old Songs About What Matters" (*Starye pesni o glavnom*). Varnished, nationally transmitted retrospection might help to "distribute several social myths [of the past] that are suitable for an interpretation of the future, too. Myths that will let people discern domains of substance and significance, whether they're in serials, talk shows or game shows."[58]

Language, nevertheless, is unable to create lasting designations, as noted in the earlier, Derridean sections. So what about imagery? The 1948 film version of *The Young Guard* (dir. S. Gerasimov) is of importance here, too, offering a mode of enduringly pertinent visual representation. The film is as well known as the book, if not more so. It helps us to understand the cultural responsibility felt by today's television directors in the shadow of state subsidies or endorsement. In both this feature and the other biggest movies of the period, a visibly "harmonic" principle is evident, drawn from outside statecraft as an apolitically unifying force (of no fixed abode) to survive both late Stalinism and – very soon – the problems caused by his death. This visual style informs television today.

In the film we discover how important tight-knit, unplanned, and initially spontaneous groups are amid danger. Partisan boys and girls are presented to us in beautifully framed shots of little ensembles, modified with slow zooms towards the speaker at their center. Key matters of military resistance are discussed in equally modest, often silent isolation from the world: quiet farm offices or tiny bedrooms, for example. Aided by the dignity of Shostakovich's score, the poor lighting of rural southern housing also adds to the intensity of small crowded spaces, sometimes reduced even to the corner of a room. By the time, in fact, that these young people make private, fatal vows to battle the Germans, the illumination is limited to their faces alone. It is these diminutive arrangements that the film stresses, often amplified by music, in particular during a little social gathering hidden from the Germans, so Russian youths may play tangos to each other on the guitar, including the famous "Exhausted Sun" (*Utomlennoe solntse*).

The Young Guard marks the style of an age. It is not, however, an isolated example. Its social groupings, for example, are expanded a little in an ensemble work of the same year, *A Train Heads Eastwards* (*Poezd idet na Vostok*, dir. Iu. Raizman), which is based upon a railway journey from Moscow to Vladivostok beginning on Victory Day 1945. Unsuspecting strangers are thrown together; after a toast to military triumph, the first topic of general interest is an elderly lady's fidelity to her husband for forty years, plus a pensioner's visit to Lev Tolstoi as a little girl "to discover if there's happiness on earth." Gradually even the crabby passengers grow closer to one another, and after several days – as travel takes them into the land of endless, nameless forests and wide open rivers – talk turns to marriage or finding one's ideal partner. Nature and tales of Tolstoi teach them to take a risk, to hazard some social action. Bonds between figures grow to the point that when they are forced to be *apart* in separate carriages they start to dream about being together!

In the film version of *The Young Guard* and other hits of the mid-1940s, the visible or ineffable interactions of lovers and oceans, families and shipyards, people and time allow for a disappearing act by a pushy Soviet soloist into an organic choir. Music is often referenced as conduit for something ineffable, so if speakers or politicians find themselves striving for increasingly orchestral, baroque patterns of inexpressible empathy, for counterpoint more than dialectics, how can a director hope to depict or understand the accumulating wilderness this invokes? After all, even today across Russia's largest expanse of all, Siberia, "the primary issue is not just that of physical expanse, but the location of people within that space and what they are close to – or not close to (markets, communication routes and so on) ... Russia's huge size is not a strength. It is a disadvantage that has to be overcome."[59] It is this unmanageable, incommunicable size that leads to the varnished, fantastic insistence of today's TV news so redolent of prior decades: "Putin with the people, Putin with animals, Putin with children ... "[60] Time to redo the most famous Soviet fantasy of all.

Clarifying oddity and its relation to nationhood: *The Master and Margarita* (dir. Vladimir Bortko, 2005)

One recent attempt to show something fantastically Russian has been made with Vladimir Bortko's serial *The Master and Margarita*, based upon Mikhail Bulgakov's novel of devilish urban culture under Stalin. The director pulled in an amazing list of stars: Oleg Basilashvili, Sergei Bezrukov, Vladislav Galkin, Aleksandr Domogarov, Aleksandr Abdulov, Dmitrii Nagiev, Valentin Gaft, and others. This unusual array of TV idols would, Bortko told the actors, hopefully be matched by an equally unusual application of computer technology and thus the ability to depict mystical elements of the original book beyond real or ostensibly documented history. More than a third of eventual screen-time was indeed to some degree created digitally, allowing the crew of 100 technicians to make proud parallels with the wizardry of *Harry Potter* and declare the series "a million times harder to shoot than *The Idiot*."[61] Complexity often overshadowed pride, though, especially in the early stages, when the Russians had to recover from what they saw as unreasonable requests for $3 million in order to animate the feline figure of Begemot – even after a "special deal" was made for the impoverished Slavs.[62] Relief from hurt pride came when Bortko turned ultimately to the design firm that had handled the extremely flashy digital effects in Bekmambetov's *Night Watch*.[63]

Partly because of these concerns, ironically, the show was a disappointment. Loudly advertised on Rossiia in December 2005, it began its opening credits with a respectful, if not funereal, black and white photograph of Bulgakov. Indeed the Moscow scenes were likewise shot in sepia, with color saved primarily for the parallel biblical episodes. This decision led to some most unconvincing attempts to splice archive footage of the 1930s with the show itself. No commercials ran during the broadcast, at least for the first week. After that, with the need to make some cash, Rossiia's advertisements slowly regained their usual frequency.

For all the fuss, the special effects failed to impress. Not until Woland's appearance as stage magician was anything of consequence on offer, and our computerized cat proved on most occasions to be a small man in a furry costume. The budget for digital animation was unevenly distributed, sometimes at more than $500,000 per episode. This led to an extraordinarily grand and ostentatious ball sequence, yet the blue-screen episodes of Margarita airborne on a broomstick would hardly deserve a place on children's television.

Some of the actors, such as Sergei Bezrukov, nevertheless held that technology was actually of secondary importance in doing justice to literary works that ponder anything beyond the ostensible: filming it at all would be an achievement. The *Master and Margarita* story is legendary in Russian cinematography for failed, unfinished screen versions on the scale of Orson Welles' and Terry Gilliam's battles with *Don Quixote*. The early 1990s saw attempted several screen versions, followed by mythical rumors that Robert de Niro would play the character of Woland.[64] Stories are likewise told that both Igor' Talankin and Èl'dar Riazanov pondered the project before retreating. Even this time around Oleg Iankovskii had swiftly accepted – and then rejected – the role of Woland, leaving Oleg Basilashvili to take his place. This long and troubled history did not worry Bezrukov, though.

> Let's not be superstitious. It seems to me that if you approach Bulgakov with a real love [for his novel], you can film everything. It's another matter, however, if people come to the series as just another project to earn some money – or if they start making some screen version of great literature for the sake of their reputation. In those cases classic literature will punish you, mark my word. But if you work honestly, with your heart, soul and the desire to get people to read and watch a work of literature one more time, I reckon the book will surely "help" you. This author, after all, wanted to be remembered forever. Personally I think we're working towards an admirable goal. Once people see our version of *The Master and Margarita*, they'll be interested in other works by Bulgakov, too. That's what happened when Bortko did his version of Dostoevskii's *Idiot*. Honest people are forgiven a great deal [in their screen work]. If you're honest, if you start doing something with frankness and candor, that's the main thing.[65]

The Russian Orthodox Church, however, was unimpressed and maintained that Bezrukov's character of Yeshua (or Christ) had, as in the original novel, "replaced the true Christ with the figure of a helpless philosopher."[66] This "grounding" of the spiritual, though displeasing for some, is important for both Bulgakov's novel and Bortko's team. Not only does it address the matter of how to write or show the inexplicable, but, according to an equally Slavic logic, Bezrukov, when talking about his interpretation of a Christ-like figure, spoke to his peasant ancestry and "thus" a tendency to operate according to invisible intuition rather than via demonstrable intellect. This brings us back to some of the important formulae of Russian self-definition discussed in our Introduction:

> I am, after all, somebody of peasant ancestry and [only] a second-generation member of the intelligentsia – after my father. When I play in the role of Pushkin in the theater, for example, certain complications arise. Only intuition can tell me what's proper to depict, and what's not. That's what Vertinskii did with such genius – or Evstigneev in [the 1988 film version of Bulgakov's] *A Dog's Heart*. The way he played that role was an education in and of itself.[67]

Bezrukov's invocation of Aleksandr Vertinskii for an ideal and yet somehow Soviet aspect to his TV work is most important, especially because his depiction of Yeshua is quietly mannered and enacted alone, in strangely unpeopled scenes. Vertinskii, born in Kiev in 1889, became the father of cabaret performance in Russia, of an effete, decadent, and dramatized style of solo singing that epitomized, purportedly, the antithesis of socialist presentation. He indeed ran from the Soviet Union immediately after the Revolution, crossing the world via Paris, America, and China. Vertinskii became the darling of black-market record dealers in Russia and yet returned there in 1943 – under Stalin and during the events of Fadeev's *Molodaia gvardiia*. He came back more popular than he left, dying eventually and calmly in 1957 in a gorgeous hotel room of natural causes after a brilliant career on the stage and silver screen, recognized in no uncertain terms by the very regime he had fled (and had once scorned).

Where was the overlap and how does it help us understand Bezrukov's respectful invocation of a spiritual aspect of performance that owes so much to public enthusiasm in the Stalinist years when it was produced? One of the clearest explanations can be found in a song Vertinskii wrote on 19 January 1952, where the heartfelt, the metamorphic, the patriotic, and the religious interweave. Singing of his membership and career as a singer, as an individual made by the social, he intones:

> As a chimney sweep, spattered with black soot, and as a laborer, digging chalk from a hillside, I lived the strange life of my characters ... I just didn't manage to live my own. Changing roles and make-up with ease, dissolving in sadness and another's life, I lost my own life – but for that Seraphim will come at the hour of death for my soul!

The loss of one's subjectivity in processes of shared desire between many songs, people, and places dovetails with that of a Christological "divestiture." The Decadent becomes the divinely Soviet. The divine dissolution of self in the desire of others is a process prior to, part of, and yet *more than* policy. It intersects with the ardent goals of socialism, not its doctrinal aspects, but since socialist dogma unavoidably used the emotional power which existed *prior* to it, Vertinskii's songs and socialist ideology may sound on occasion very similar indeed. This is the spiritual (and yet profoundly materialist) similarity to which Bezrukov speaks. It also underlines the way in which he *shows* us the silent figure of Yeshua.

Nation as time rather than place: *The Icon Hunters* (dir. Sergei Popov, 2005) and *Esenin* (dir. Igor' Zaitsev, 2004)

An intuitive, proletarian, and ultimately "divine" role runs throughout socialist storytelling, even among those writers who stayed within the Union's borders and still found cause for disagreement with policy. It informs several other television series today, too, such as *The Icon Hunters* (*Okhotniki za ikonami*) of 2005. The drama takes place in a very distant, virtually anonymous Siberian village, "hidden from people and civilization in the deepest, most distant corners of the taiga." The host channel, Rossiia, described the series in greater detail:

> An artist known by his nickname of Begun ["Runner"] buys and sells rare icons. By pure chance he discovers that the extremely valuable Icon of the Radiant Eye is being housed in the church of a Siberian village called White Lake. Runner and his partner decide to leave for Siberia and steal the icon. They arrive from Moscow in the taiga village. Runner meets a young girl there, called Nezhdana, and falls in love with her. One of the locals, Eremei, finds out that Runner and Nezhdana have feelings for one another. He, too, loves her with all his heart and manages to discover the nasty plans of the Moscow visitors. By this time, Runner is already refusing to take part in the theft, but things are not that simple.[68]

In actual fact, the series was shot not far from Moscow, in Frianovo, and an entire faux village was required in order to capture the style of a more remote, dated locale. The people who then inhabited these "houses" were again from Frianovo, but only those with a "Slavic appearance" were hired for crowd scenes. The men were asked to wear beards and the women were given hair attachments so that the number of long braids increased significantly. Emphasizing this Christian, rustic constant in his visual narrative, director Sergei Popov chose a place that may sound deceptively urban but had, two decades earlier, actually seemed suitable for another cinematic competition between modern and rural values – Turgenev's *Fathers and Sons* in 1983. Nature was not always kind to the crew, though, despite their decision to stay close to Moscow; filming began on a day of minus 37° Celsius and the cameras simply refused to work.[69]

In a related extension of things documentary to the point of divinity, a local priest was hired as advisor. He corrected theological references in the screenplay and made sure everybody in the crowd scenes was crossing themselves properly: he noted actors doing so whilst wearing a hat or approaching icons in an incorrect manner, among other faults. This attention to detail stood the eight-episode series well, and talk soon began of a possible TÈFI award, Russia's equivalent of the Emmys.[70] The anachronistic mélange of its musical score seemed not to bother anybody: a combination of Brahms, the (now woefully hackneyed) folksong *Kalinka*, and in one urban scene the pop number "Beyond the Four Seas" (*Za chetyre moria*) by sensuous female quartet *Blestiashchie*.

What did cause more interest and concern was the use of religiously rustic themes in national entertainment. The show, said its supporters, might help to foster a belief in *something* at a time when social values were growing weaker with each passing year: "The series is simply brilliant ... Maybe we'll start thinking about a spiritual life now?! And start talking about 'icons,' not just 'wooden boards'?"[71] Faith could help actuality.

This issue of what constitutes the "actually, really national" became part of an interesting debate in the pages of tabloid newspapers, too, over whether key themes of the series were perhaps part and parcel of a lost, materialized Soviet heritage *à la* Bezrukov.

> Patriotism and 'stateliness' have reached unheard-of heights over the last few years. No matter what time it is, there's some TV serial or other going on about intrepid cops and filthy criminals. The public is nostalgic for the black-and-white world of the Soviet years, or so TV producers seem to think. In actual fact, though, viewers are getting *tired* of that world. The director of *Icon Hunters* understood as much, too.

> Sure he understood! So now he's offering us a story to watch that's all about a very, very decent, heroic criminal (Begun) and another, nasty one. What's the difference? ... Nowadays you can make a hero out of anybody. Remember [Mafia kingpin] Sasha Belyi from *The Brigade* [played by Bezrukov]? He has almost become a figure of national pride. It's all really simple. The main thing is that some soppy, sickly-sweet scenes are inserted at the right moments. And I personally think the director doesn't even care whether the end result looks convincing. But I'm a grown-up girl now and haven't believed in those Robin Hood figures for ages – the kind of people who behave appallingly towards others during the day and then cry into their pillows at night.[72]

Starring another one of the nasty, yet soppy heroes from *The Brigade* (Dmitrii Diuzhev), *The Icon Hunters* was indeed walking a thin, if not invisible, line between showing a most Soviet, "black-and-white world" and invoking aspects of a wholly materialist endeavor which somehow, taken to its extreme, could instigate an opposite state – in this case a divinely driven

Figure 2.1 Icon Hunters.

conman. The series dallies with these paradoxes as far as possible from the Big City; distance from the metropolis becomes a distance back in time. This is also, as with communication across modern Siberia, a distance from the definable. Begun (played by Andrei Smoliakov) says at one point: "Russia is inexhaustible. Everybody thinks that's she's a container of some sort, but she's ... she's *oh*, so big!" Later we're told that there must be mammoths walking somewhere, because something this big and everlasting is illogical. Begun and his partner (Diuzhev) find themselves walking around in circles, going nowhere: "These are *our* footsteps! We've been taken around in a full circle!" Siberia manipulates a human presence, not vice versa, hence the final scenes which show the establishment of a family back in modern Moscow; some kind of modest, doable, and effable social unit is realized, instead of arrogant ecological violence or greed.

This familial theme of small social groups is vital to the series, driven constantly from behind the scenes by Runner's son, scribbling pictures of the mythical ancient town Kitezh Grad. Something in the past will hold together and structure the broken present. When Runner, representative of that social breach, first enters the village where the icon is held, he pretends to be an ethnographer collecting songs. "Every village has its own songs," says an elder, "Why d'you want someone else's?" Runner's adopted role as preserver of national harmony falls flat. The settlement's "holy fool" likewise mocks on several occasions the word "civilization" when Runner's partner complains of the village's backwardness, an indication that – paradoxically – superior society is "here" (wherever that may be), not in Moscow. And indeed the series is replete with archaic turns of phrase that embody an older, bucolic concord in the extended family: "Peace to this house" or "Peace to you, stranger," and so forth.

The role of the unmappable countryside is vital in saving the better, belittled, and somehow heavenly aspects of the Soviet literary experience, as shown by the 2004 series *Esenin*. It stars precisely the actor who played our "Robin Hood" or inverted, honorable criminal in a morally muddled world, Sergei Bezrukov – our urbanized peasant and poet. The drama proposes a different, hypothesized version of Esenin's death in the form of a political detective story.[73] In developing this alternative, better version of Esenin's life and significance as a verbal craftsman, stolen back from dogmatic philologists, director Igor' Zaitsev wanted to avoid any direct or trite synonymy between the sad poet and suicide, too. Just as unpalatable was the related baggage of the poet's legendary "decadence, vulgarity, alcoholism, aimless womanizing and hooliganism." Zaitsev held that Esenin, through his excessive, worldly passions aimed for a notion of freedom that, although circumcised rhetorically by the Soviets, would never find acceptance in political reality: "Esenin wanted to be free, but in Soviet Russia that would turn out to be impossible. His fate was decided from the moment he chose himself 'political protection.'"

Esenin, the blue-eyed, blond champion of pristine, coniferous expanses, enacted Soviet promise better than those who turned dreams into legislation. He did so by investigating the relationship between verse and *paysage*; he was thus raised to the level of cultural icon, the unspeakable essence of something national – expressed today by cheap portraiture woven into even cheaper rugs.

58 *Russian television today*

Figure 2.2 Esenin.

Docudramas: *Brezhnev* (dir. Sergei Snezhkin, 2005) as a visual genesis and stable balance

> State stability built on a solid economic foundation is a blessing for Russia and for its people.
>
> (Putin, 2001)

Esenin would make a bad politician. The revolutionary and romantic inversions of his borderline Sovietness, although frequently and *necessarily* invoked on podia, are replaced with something much more restrained and manageable, termed by the *Washington Post* the "*end* of revolution," an observation noted with agreement by some Russian journalists, who see in their President the embodiment of Brezhnev: "Putin came to power under the slogan of stability after decades of chaos and disorder."[74] Enter, once again, the famously bushy eyebrows, seen through a most sympathetic lens. To what degree does the decade *redux* of the 1970s mimic the tolerant spirit that we see applied to (and stolen from the drama of) earlier years?

Choosing the 1970s as a time through which to judge the romance of Soviet doctrine today is an increasingly attractive option for directors. This is best shown by the recent docudrama of Brezhnev's final months. The series does much to humanize the politician (played by Sergei Shakurov), to remove him from any specific policy or the consequences thereof. In this tale, staged almost entirely at Brezhnev's dacha, we see him hunting for boar, socializing, watching films, enjoying political jokes about himself, and – most importantly – flirting endlessly with his nurse, played by Mariia Shukshina. Even distant journalists of *Le Monde* noted that the series embodied both nostalgia and a marked human touch, especially in one episode where Brezhnev complains about the quality of kielbasa in rural stores (having chewed it himself).[75] These were even more human qualities than those of "Putin's [own] stagnation."

Another more human and intimate scene was excised in the final cut, in which Shakurov and Shukshina climb into bed together. The importance of this lost episode was well assessed by Brezhnev's granddaughter:

> It was only after six months that I discovered the crowning scene had been cut: Brezhnev comes onto to his nurse and gets her into bed! The viewers were probably supposed to start applauding at that point: "Oh, Brezhnev! Oh, you son of a bitch!" And then in a wave of nostalgia they'd be filled with *pride* for their nation: an old man, but he could still get it done! True, the screenwriters were really flattering Brezhnev by granting him that kind of enormous potency. I'm not sure I can even imagine it ... doing "you-know-what" at the age of 75![76]

The leader's granddaughter was happy that Snezhkin had not made Brezhnev a "walking joke" or, conversely, the embodiment of "spite and anger." It was, she added, the director's emphasis upon familial emotions in a rural setting that made her grandfather come to life. Shakurov, explaining this transformation, said it was done both silently and visually; applying the make-up each morning took so long he would doze off – and then wake up as Brezhnev, unable to rid himself of Leonid Il'ich's shuffling gait or deep, mumbling intonation.[77]

Making emotion credible, however, meant more than greasepaint; it involved contextualizing a number of other personal episodes from earlier in the leader's life, too, so that the private could explain the public. The private itself must be shown *as* public, as in many other "dramatized" histories, such as *The Leningrader* (*Leningradets*, 2005), which tells the fate of the Soviet navy in 1962 through one high-ranking family.

According to this technique in our 1970s docudrama, we see more than one Brezhnev on screen among friends; the younger man, even then a big fan of the opposite sex, is played with similar eyebrows by Artur Vakhi. This actor, too, lost a few scenes on the cutting-room floor. An episode in which Brezhnev awkwardly rediscovers his wife's sensuality after armed service was cut, as were some premonitory funeral scenes.[78] The extremes of sexual release and death are invoked, hinted at, and even filmed, but they do not make it to the television screen. Shakurov, when (re)assessing the years under Brezhnev, likewise saw his hero in terms of a personal, *potential* happiness – rather than its documented realization. This, in turn, shaped his own memories of Brezhnev's eighteen years in office:

> We spent eighteen years under the leadership of that man. We went to political gatherings and sang [political] songs. Maybe 150 thousand people were unhappy, but 150 million were happy with the ways things were. They were completely content. It was an amazing time, one of the best. Brezhnev himself was an interesting guy. He fought on the front-line in WWII, taking part in all kinds of military operations. So those war medals of his weren't bogus. It was only later on that people starting slapping titles on him: "Hero of This and That." There was nobody better back then to run the country. You couldn't say that he was too tough, or that he was very soft, either. He was just perfect.[79]

This nostalgic spirit remained hugely important in 2004–5, when at least ten series appeared both set in and dedicated to parallels with the Soviet experience. Virtually all are discussed in detail in this book. World War Two and the Stagnation appear most often: tales of private social networks under Stalin and Brezhnev:

Moscow Saga (set in the period 1925–1957, Channel One)
72 Meters (late 1980s–early 1990s, Channel One)
Children of the Arbat (1930s–1940s, Channel One)
Beneath the Verona Sky (1980s, NTV)
Twins (1975–2002, Channel One)
Two Fates (1960s–1990s, Channel One)
Bless the Woman (1930s–1950s, Channel One)
Red Square (1980s, Rossiia)
Penal Battalion (World War Two, Rossiia)
Saboteur (World War Two, Channel One)[80]

The balanced, if not frozen binarisms of Cold War détente under Brezhnev ("them and us") allowed for the reinstatement of many Stalinist oppositions at a time when the influx of foreign literature (and influence) was increasingly filtered or curtailed, forcing – once again – a process of national self-definition by negative example. Moneyed, prestigious America, for example, lacked the better, albeit impoverished, workings of Soviet culture. Similar oppositions underwrite today's Russia, such as oligarchs versus the Kremlin, or the Yeltsin "family" versus others, like Putin, from a morally laudable security background (the *siloviki*). Again as in 1970s détente, this configuration is used to criticize, for example, one representative of a group (such as Khodorkovskii) without damaging the overall, desired harmony between the state critic and business *per se*. Individuals are held up as negative examples, whilst the grander groups they come from (business as a whole in this case) are fundamentally left alone, giving an impression of stability that is policed only on occasion – and with commendable reason.

Conclusion: the 1970s enjoy lasting relevance, thanks to managed, moderate binarisms taken in part from literature

> One of the distinguishing characteristics of socialist realist art is its force that unifies people. Bourgeois cinematography affirms and lauds the hero as loner, cynic, individualist and skeptic.
>
> (From a Russian textbook of 1976)[81]

Television is not sidestepping or dismissing the Soviet experience; it is resurrecting it, in large part from literature and post-war cinema. The romance therein, however, is reconsidered and calmly *managed* as a fondly remembered stability of three decades prior. Brezhnev has become the hero or *deus ex machina* of docudramas and several television series because he offers the best of (a riskless) yesterday and thus the hope for a better today. His verbally embodied ubiquity was, it would seem, consoling; likewise, today's TV journalists, often members of that once-consoled generation, admit: "If there are no obvious sensations to cover in the news, we start the broadcast with the President."[82] This happens on almost every single day of the year.

The extreme, ineffable inversions of selfhood documented by Soviet romantics that shunned this risklessness might be easily dismissed as problems of Stalinist maximalism, but they were precisely the metaphors that informed similar, cinematic transitions from Brezhnev's gray stagnation to the very different hopes of perestroika. Two of the biggest hits of 1973, marking Brezhnev's midpoint, turned the materialist (supposedly manageable and effable) goals of Soviet sociology – on any scale – into an elusive, if not desperately desired, target. These are, I stress, but two brief examples of troubled, centrifugal worldviews even during a calm, centripetal decade.

The Stepmother (*Machekha*, dir. O. Bondarev) put a simple family in the middle of heartless Soviet society and recorded it with maximum, almost documentary factualness. The opening shots position the protagonists against the wide background of a sprawling river, to the neo-folk classic song by Liudmila Zykina, "A Mother's Heart" (*Serdtse materinskoe*). As a woman turns on her TV to watch a(n older, yet still relevant) comedy broadcast by Arkadii Raikin, we learn of a mother who is asked to take the orphaned daughter of her husband's previous partner. Discovering the abandoned youngster, standing alone on the road against an enormous backdrop of snowy mountains, the new parents soon see how incredibly withdrawn she is after the death of her own birthmother.

The stepmother perseveres, however, earning her son's hatred and the epithet "idiot" (*dura*) from others. This little girl, Sveta, only comes out of her shell when in the countryside – and bonds with her father only on his combine harvester in the fields. As they grow closer, the father falls briefly ill but "gets a little better right away" when Sveta shows him some bedside care; she even cradles the head of her stepmother, who says, "Things shouldn't be so frightening." But they *are* – and the simple dream of these characters in apparent existence becomes an ideal, one that might slip farther and farther away. It is precisely this film that is used to structure the 2006 TV series *The Gromovs* (dir. Aleksandr Baranov, Channel One). Set in a distant, deeply provincial mining town in 1976, the series includes a discussion of *Machekha* in its opening episode. The movie's emphases and concerns are then used to fashion several moral benchmarks for the remaining eleven installments of *The Gromovs* as a young, broken family endures similar trials and tribulations.

The other big hit of 1973, *Red Snowball-Tree* (*Kalina krasnaia*), is much crueler, making romanticism (which remains unknown and unstated) even more forceful in its response. This tale by "village writer" and director Vasilii Shukshin, the real-life father of Brezhnev's TV nurse, helps us to show the huge overlap between socialist realism's ecoaesthetic and village prose, thus reducing the difference or status of the latter as somehow dissident. It begins with a choir of prisoners singing "Eventide Peal" (*Vechernii zvon*), as one man (our hero) is released at the end of his term, stopping as he leaves to greet both trees and cows. Amid interwoven dramatic scenes and documentary episodes of village life, we see the meeting of the jailbird and a woman – Liubov' – with whom he corresponded while inside. He has a tough time in normal village life, though, is called "prickly" and even queries the *raison d'être* of a man who won eighteen awards as a Stakhanovite.

At a village evening of drunken singing, a local man stops everybody in their tracks with a rendition of "That's Why I Love My Native Russia" (*Vot za chto ia liubliu rodnuiu Rus'*); the male protagonist then wishes that "life could be a little easier, with music, perhaps, so that at long last I wouldn't have to think about anything." The body and heart yearn for a melodic, choral goal that outstrips thought and language, so much so that a stately, more official evening of song rings hollow. The compère says "The country has changed; so have the songs. The people have begun new songs." In the face of such prescriptive claptrap, the ex-con continues to talk to the trees: "Don't worry. It'll soon be warm." They cannot answer and he falls to thoughts of another elusive desire: "What is this? Am I not allowed to be happy?"

Songs he sings to Liubov' cannot remove the pain of social life – of existence in a society that eventually beats him to death in a birch grove, among the trees he adored. He was never able "to be a human being. He was just a rough peasant [*muzhik*]. And there are many like him in Russia." When nearing the ideal boundlessness of everything, the typicality of realism becomes the typicality of embitterment, a lasting struggle with sadness or Epstein's *topos* of the void. It is here that we find ourselves in a stately tradition of national self-awareness and simultaneously distanced from a discernable nation. At this point Latin *telenovelas* step in to help, themselves seen as itinerant, homeless and therefore transferable mélanges of "all things" Spanish and Portuguese. They combine the Spanish bravado of our Russian Don Quixote with the sprawling structure of Golden Age novels. This odd fusion is then colored by a 1970s middlebrow exoticism, by views of foreign climes from the age of Brezhnev.

3 Soaps
The influence of Latin America

[TV series] are a real show of force: uniforms, tanks, shoot-outs, and the Special Forces, too ... I know it's all very exciting, but what does it have to do with Pushkin?[1]

Introduction: making a tradition later to be emulated

Not only are Brezhnev and his era increasingly important in the *raison d'être* of Russian TV drama; that same period was responsible for instituting the genre itself. As a form of storytelling well established in the West decades before, though, how did television series even come to Russia? This remains a tricky issue, since argument continues over how lengthy, serialized "television films" of the past relate to the television series we know today. What is the difference between a long film in four parts and a series in fourteen? Aleksandr Prokhorov has succinctly argued that Soviet television of the 1960s

> articulated its own format of the mini-series, or what critics called at the time the "television film," a narrative developing over the course of several episodes. The rise of the mini-series redefined the meaning of the extra-long motion picture in Soviet culture, [too. Cinema shifted from a] domain of the Stalinist monumental style to ... the domain of the small screen aesthetics.[2]

Grand, cultured cinema and throwaway TV interacted in the 1960s just as literature and TV do today.

If we take the most inclusive view possible, then the granddaddy of all these more serious, longer TV dramas is often said to be *Drawing Fire* (*Vyzyvaem ogon' na sebia*, dir. Sergei Kolosov, 1963–4), recorded at Mosfil'm and commissioned by Gosteleradio. This stirring tale of World War Two spy Ania Morozova and her escapades with Polish resistance fighters was broken into four episodes (96, 76, 77, and 68 minutes). Ironically, as state television then tried to satisfy the public's manifest desire for this type of lengthy "Russian" story, Mosfil'm would gain benefit from real-life Polish and Bulgarian colleagues, too, as budgetary constraints obliged Moscow to borrow Polish TV series to fill primetime schedules (*Four Men, a Tank and a Dog* [*Chetyre tankista i sobaka*, dir. Konrad Natecki, from 1965] and *A Risk Greater Than Life* [*Stavka bol'she, chem zhizn'*, dir. Andrzej Konic, 1967]). Polish series still appear today in Russian TV-translations.³

Issues of sufficient financing in the 1960s were solved with admirable speed. Over 1967 and 1968, for example, 113 TV films were broadcast on the Soviet small screen. Central Television also oversaw the birth of Èkran, an association responsible for many classic serialized films of the 1970s. These included adaptations of the Anatolii Ivanov novels *Shadows Vanish at Noon* (*Teni ischezaiut v polden'*, dir. Valerii Uskov and Vladimir Krasnopol'skii, 1971 [TV]/1974 [cinema]) and *An Eternal Summons* (*Vechnyi zov*, dir. Valerii Uskov and Vladimir Krasnopol'skii, 1973), together with the most famous of all espionage dramas, *The Seventeen Moments of Spring* (*Semnadtsat' mgnovenii vesny*, dir. Tat'iana Lioznova, 1973).⁴

Almost simultaneously, a more modern-sounding detective series had been planned: *Experts Are on the Case* (*Sledstvie vedut znatoki*, multiple directors), which debuted to immediate success in 1971. Ostentatious themes, such as Siberian villages under Soviet power or World War Two anti-Fascist activity, were avoided. The staged scale was small and intense. Popular wisdom tells us that the series' genesis can be traced to the late 1960s, when the writers Aleksandr and Ol'ga Lavrov were asked to help create the drama at Mosfil'm, in part because the studio's director had himself once been a prosecutor. The Lavrovs were already well known for their regular publication of courtroom transcripts in the pages of *The Literary Gazette* (*Literaturnaia gazeta*). This combination of fact and fiction was a hit; the resultant series would spawn twenty-two episodes, the last of which was broadcast as late as 1989.⁵

The parallel and truncated format of "extended television films" (or shorter proto-series) would also blossom in the same period, notably in the very gaudy, melodramatic *Gypsy* (*Tsygan*, dir. Aleksandr Blank, 1979) over four episodes (100, 80, 80, and 85 minutes), together with *The Rendezvous Is Set* (*Mesto vstrechi izmenit' nel'zia*, dir. Stanislav Govorukhin; five episodes) in the same year. Soon to be canonized with equal verve in the 1980s were the Boiarskii-heavy swashbuckling adventures *D'Artagnan and the Three Musketeers* (*D'Artan'ian i tri mushketera*, dir. Georgii Iungval'd-Khil'kevich, 1978; 80, 65, and 75 minutes) and the trilogy spawned by Svetlana Druzhinina's costume adventure *Midshipmen, Onwards!* (*Gardemariny, vpered!*, 1987; 80, 70, 65, and 75 minutes). In today's civic memory, these have walked side by side with the "imperial nostalgia" of a five-film Sherlock Holmes series directed by Igor' Maslennikov between 1979 and 1986, itself fluctuating between feature film and episodic formats.⁶ The 1980s are also punctuated by a neat consistency in the ten 70-minute episodes of *TASS Is Authorized to Report* (*TASS upolnomochen zaiavit'*, dir. Vladimir Fokin,

1984). The emphases sketched here – history, (admired or envied) foreign models, detective work, and an unending struggle with classic literature – would continue to be important.

Many of the early TV films and similar series, however, neither generated exceptional interest nor produced profit. As socialism shuffled inelegantly from the world stage and international awareness grew after the mid- to late 1980s, these Soviet models of television drama began to look woefully old-fashioned. Indeed, within two years of the final Sherlock Holmes film, bold and brash Mexican or Brazilian soaps would appear, purchased *en masse* by Russian channels. We have already heard how influential they would become; they were soon creating serious, if not overwhelming, competition for initial post-Soviet series like *Goriachev and Others* (*Goriachev i drugie*, dir. Iurii Belen'kii, 1992–4) or *The Little Things of Life* (*Melochi zhizni*, dir. Viacheslav Brovkin, Gennadii Pavlov, and Aleksandr Pokrovskii, 1992–5).

In fact it would take several years for Russian studios and TV stations to plan a counterattack against Latin American melodrama. Even in the late 1990s, under pressure from post-default economic restraints, more audacious and parsimonious executives at Channel One decided it was acceptable to slice both *An Eternal Summons* and *Shadows Vanish at Noon* into 52-minute episodes. Each hour could thus accommodate eight minutes of primetime advertising. This ruse allowed Channel One briefly to outpace viewing figures for Timothy Dalton and the American series *Scarlett* (1994), but it was hardly a long-term solution, even if it did show the potential validity of homemade serials amid primetime foreign competition after 7:45 p.m.[7] Any rehashing of old broadcasts was also a long way from what studios really wanted to do: make new, respectable shows and avoid undignified pandering to market pressures. Even today, the head of a hugely influential TV production company in Russia has admitted, "the more television series adapted from novels written by classic writers, the better."[8]

RTR, hoping the canon would make them money, had manufactured two recent and "classic" adaptations of Dumas' *La Reine Margot* (*Koroleva Margo*, dir. Aleksandr Muratov, 1995–6) and *La Dame de Monsoreau* (*Grafinia de Monsoro*, dir. Vladimir Popkov, 1997), ventures that leaned heavily not only on broad French shoulders and the printed page, but also on the admired Soviet Musketeer serials – themselves a jumble of swashbuckling theater, romance, and nationally famous songs. Almost concurrently, an even more staid – yet cheaper – project appeared: *The Secrets of St. Petersburg* (*Peterburgskie tainy*, dir. Vadim Zobin, Mark Orlov, and Leonid Pchelkin, 1994–6), based on Vsevolod Krestovskii's novel *Petersburg Slums*. This attempt at nineteenth-century respectability displayed little of what commentators nowadays call the "nationally specific or homey" features that epitomize so many Russian serials.[9] Hence, complaints continued unabated about pointless television series from the US, while these types of more "literary" narratives buckled under the weight of sun-soaked Latin broadcasts.

Spanish- and Portuguese-language drama came to Russia thanks largely to the equally exotic, Bulgarian-born French distributor Dino Dinev. Unable to convince Russian Central Television that they would adore his 300-kilogram box of Mexican video cassettes, he agreed to let the Russians broadcast the first five episodes of *The Rich Cry, Too* (*Bogatye tozhe plachut* [*Los Ricos Tambièn Lloran*]) for free. Only when studio heads at Ostankino saw sacks of cheery viewer-mail that had literally reached the ceiling did they invest in the soap on a long-term basis.

The Rich Cry, Too debuted the first of its 249 episodes in 1992. Originally scheduled for once-weekly showings on Saturdays, it was soon broadcast five days out of seven. Love came to town. The show's star, Veronica Castro, claimed on a 1992 visit to Russia that her heroine "knows how to fight for her happiness. She is both a woman and a winner." These clichés surrounding feisty, full-bosomed Latin types started to have serious consequences in Slavdom. The 150-episode *Simply Maria* (*Prosto Mariia* [*Simplemente María*]), itself based upon a 1967 Argentinean serial of the same name, enjoyed equal success, growing from a simple premise: the tale of a peasant girl who moves to a big city, where she finds love, money, and adventure – beginning with an accidental pregnancy. Castro herself saw nothing formulaic in this and other plots, though:

> I was attracted to the series because it touches on complex, multifaceted problems, the most important of which is the love of a middle-aged woman for a younger man ... In Mexico, at the start of the twentieth century, that would have looked like a real challenge to society.[10]

At the end of that same century it seemed that only established and yet *innovative* Soviet directors could save Slavic television studios from the challenge of torpor.[11] The strategies regarding any kind of comeback were well documented by the *Independent Newspaper* (*Nezavisimaia gazeta*) in its weekly polling of politicians, public figures, and regular viewers *vis-à-vis* the best, worst, or most memorable TV broadcasts of the previous seven days. We can hear discontent from the very outset: "All those Latin American serials and soap operas are quite simply the stupefaction of society."[12] The kingpins of late Soviet culture were not happy with the alternatives available at home, either: "I can't call the [Russian] serials great works of art. They're pleasant enough, but they've got really primitive screenplays that always hinge on some kind of cruelty – and a requisite criminal component, too" (Georgii Daneliia); "I get irritated by the actors' constant lisping, by all those sentimental women's serials, by the disrespect shown among young people, by their appalling speech and incredible arrogance" (Aleksandr Kushner).[13]

For all this prohibitive grumbling, the Brazilian soap about the abolition of slavery, *Isaura the Slave* (*Escrava Isaura*) – already shown to great acclaim in seventy-nine nations – had scored a massive home run in Russia with its fusion of historical fact, exotic locales, undying love, and moral propreity.[14] The floodgates were open: a deluge of Brazilian serials marked the first few years of post-Soviet life: *Senorita* (*Sen'orita* [*Sinha Moca*], broadcast in 1992); *My Love, My Grief* (*Moia liubov', moia pechal'* [*Meu Bem, Meu Mal*], broadcast in 1993); *The Sweet Spring* (*Sladkii ruchei* [*Riacho Doce*], broadcast in 1993); *Full-Moon of Love* (*Polnolunie liubvi* [*Lua Cheia de Amor*], broadcast in 1994); and *The New Wave* (*Novaia volna* [*Uma Onda no Ar*], broadcast in 1994). Between 1999 and 2001, this influence was still profitable – seventeen Brazilian series were scattered across the networks.[15]

Where could Russia look for long, historical narratives of its own? Logically, to literature (again), maybe even to tales that themselves celebrated the cultural primacy of words. Nabokov's *The Gift*, *The Master and Margarita*, and Pasternak's *Doctor Zhivago* (both as yet unfilmed) were already advocated in 1999 by one journalist at *The Banner* (*Znamia*) as suitable material; by pleasant coincidence Russian serials were starting to enjoy their first serious market share at this time. The same columnist, however, wanted works *by* great writers, not *about* their lives. TV couldn't handle that lofty subject:

> A novel about a novelist is a true staple of twentieth-century Russian culture ... of *high* culture. As the hero of a soap opera or serial, a Russian writer will be dull. You can't hang anything on that kind of figure except outdated ambitions ... New Russia can't garner its identity through the figure of a writer, of literature. It can't repeat or clone some old, nineteenth-century or Soviet notion. It's historically pointless. It's a dead-end. It's a Mobius strip that Russia can never escape from.[16]

One of the biggest problems of cultural escape was the inability of early Russian series in the 1990s to look sophisticated, a predicament caused by little cash, "cheap screenplays, cheap direction, and cheap camerawork, too." Only very recently have things changed: "I find myself rejecting those foreign series. Lately I've been watching our Russian TV series with pleasure."[17] This single and subjective opinion can be easily contextualized with more objective data: in 2002, Russian TV dropped *Santa Barbara* in order to free up space for domestic dramas. Two soon-to-be important production companies – A-Media and Phoenix Films – were simultaneously born. Likewise, if in 1999 Russian series occupied less than 10 percent of primetime line-ups, as noted, by 2001–2 they claimed 46 percent.[18]

The slowly vanquished timeslots of 19:30 (on RTR) and 20:55 (on NTV) allowed homegrown dramas to outperform both *E.R.* and *Walker: Texas Ranger*. NTV even had the audacity to place two domestic serials back to back in the evening slots – and, to the amazement of all concerned, they bumped ORT's national news broadcast (*Vremia*) into second place. Dizzy with the anticipation of sudden profits, RTR crammed six new domestic series into its schedule within three months – and radically increased its market share as a result, from 4 percent to an occasional 25 percent![19] Every channel sat up, dreaming of advertising revenues, which prior to the default had been climbing at annual rates of over 30 percent per annum, reaching $520 million in 1997 – a figure then slashed to $190 million by 1999. These fortunes mirrored the bold Latin dramas that made them.

Giving Moscow a Mexican ethos: *Moscow Saga* (dir. Dmitrii Barshchevskii, 2004), *The KGB in Dinner Jackets* (dir. Oleg Fomin, 2004), and *Penal Battalion* (dir. Nikolai Dostal', 2004)

Audience desire was important even in the darkest years of the USSR; today, market pressures make that same desire still more important. But what if the state takes increasing control and stubbornly subsidizes the tales that *it* wants to see? Happy stories, if shown often enough, might refashion once-sad memories, and as Putin once purportedly said about Russian domestic television: "You could show a horse's ass on TV for three months straight and even *that* would become popular."[20] Those troubled by Putin's black humor think that his media policies indeed boil down to one simple practice: "We'll teach you how to love your nation" and do so in utterly fabricated, trouble-free realms where there was never great interest to start with, such as "patriotic" attempts to win either the Eurovision Song Contest or the equivalent of *American Idol*, known as *Star Factory* (*Fabrika zvezd*), replete with regional champions. In our attempt to divorce studio desire from audience responses to TV-tales of Soviet life today (all over again), web-based discussions and forums should be frequently referenced. They help to blur an apparent, received clarity and create a maximum synonymy between socialist metaphors of kinship (for reasons of politicking or profit) and those of Latin drama.

One of the best examples of how "post-Latin, manqué-literary" series are, for example, remaking the patriotic wartime Soviet experience both universally human and complex has been the twenty-two-episode dramatization of Vasilii Aksenov's three-volume *Moscow Saga*, filmed over two years, due to the size (and busy work schedules) of its star cast: Inna Churikova, Iurii Solomin, Kristina Orbakaite, Aleksandr Baluev, Aleksei Kortnev, Dmitrii Kharat'ian, Igor' Skliar, Marina Iakovleva, and Sergei Bezrukov. The series, set between the 1920s and 1950s, likewise involved so many actors of differing generations that their own family mileposts over time became as important as the subject of the drama. Actors got married and gave birth; directors or producers fell ill, all while canine characters left litters of puppies behind before the final scenes were shot.[21] Sergei Bezrukov lost over 15 kilograms due to the simultaneous requirements of filming his younger, slimmer figure in *A Policeman's Beat* (*Uchastok*); eventually his uniforms had to be sewn anew. Aleksandr Baluev, meanwhile, lost 12 kilograms from working on the saga alone.²² Life outran and shaped the filming of a very soapy timeline.

Unifying today's varied private and celebrity tales, Aksenov's style of the 1960s generation embodied an uncompromising insistence on deciding "whether you're with the Whites or with the Reds." This would hopefully act as a vehicle for ethical issues of Soviet culture and yet still seem attractive to modern viewers, accustomed to the oppositions of simple criminal or police sagas. It would, in the words of Julian Graffy, "support positive Thaw values by looking backwards in order to reclaim and reinterpret Soviet models of plot and character."²³ Straddling three decades from the 1920s onwards, Aksenov's epic of life under Stalin had pretensions towards a latter-day *War and Peace*, full of universal human experience. And still some journalists worried that it might become a "mountain of historical details," interwoven with no less finesse and cunning than Soviet storytelling.²⁴ It is, in fact, the theme of poetry itself that gives the series its most powerful episodes, in terms of either literary debate or the role played by Orbakaite – a doomed restaurant singer, whose rarely voiced, quiet tales of amity would be destroyed by a ruthless, noisy government.

In defense of this tragic work, the author told the *Washington Post* of his intention not to tell viewers anything new about Stalin, but to speak of universal human interaction under pressure: "In any time of terror, we see how people survived, how they lived, how they loved each other, and how they betrayed each other, too." That pressure, said *Children of the Arbat* director Andrei Èshpai (see pp. 94–97), would transform the series' characters. "Some people are crushed, but individuality somehow survives. Humanity survives and love survives, too. We're showing how decisions made at the very top of the Soviet pyramid of power were translated into the lives of ordinary people." The docudrama *Brezhnev* took one man out of dogma in order to reinstate him politically; placed side by side, however, perhaps *Moscow Saga* and *Brezhnev* could *undermine* received hierarchies, too? The issue is very complex, making it hard to define many TV series as either "pro-" or "anti-institutional." One simply goes further than the other.

Despite any admirable aim to undermine, overshoot, or level the erstwhile pecking orders of Soviet life, the human rights group Memorial held that because the state had helped to fund this series it actually reflects Putin's desire to fashion positive impressions of the past, especially because so much archival news footage is spliced with the modern acting. The director of the series, Dmitrii Barshchveskii, spoke clearly to this issue:

> You could argue that now, when there's concern over our nation's direction, the authorities are reminding people that things aren't so bad – compared to what came before. But you could also argue that if the authorities have allowed this film to be broadcast, there's hope that Russia might develop in a civilized manner, too.²⁵

Many people from the generations depicted in the story were asked by newspapers whether or not the spectacle struck them as convincing, passionately engaging documentary material or mere manipulative politicking. Was it *real*? One of the best responses came from Elizaveta Gorbunova, an elderly lifelong resident of Moscow.

> I'm in something of two minds about the film. There are two worlds within *Moscow Saga*, existing simultaneously – and yet unnaturally. The story itself, its heroes and their lively experiences – that's all exciting, and you always wait for the next episode to see what happens next. But as for the backdrop, you just want to telephone the series' producers and explain a thing or two. We grumble about Americans whenever they make films about us, but ... when a Soviet army uniform doesn't conform to historical reality, when characters only drink vodka in tiny sips and their homes are full of unfamiliar objects ... There's a ton of mistakes in each episode.
>
> In 1925 Gradov's wife telephones him by dialing a direct number to his office. But all phone calls back then were made through a "lady operator"! There are concrete slabs all along the tramlines, too. Where did they come from in 1927? Look how the dachas shine with lights in 1941 – during the war. What about the blackout? ... And the [Red Square] Mausoleum looks the same as today; but back then it was covered in cloth, so the Germans couldn't bomb it. How could a general drive along the frontline with his headlights up? Was that so it'd be easier for the Germans to bomb him? Back then there were special slats put on headlights that let only the narrowest strip of light through. Why couldn't the producers invite a consultant who was alive back then and would notice all those historical inaccuracies?[26]

Other people – especially those who lived at that time – had problems with the veracity of the series in terms of what history *looked* like – and yet it was a great success. One journalist proposed that success came from processes of audience recognition, not from any thematic originality. Yet if this reality was not something that could be seen and documented as correct, what was it? What exactly was being remembered? "What's important is the number of recognizable *situations* that these dozens of characters end up in. If you like, what's important is the number of clichés – as many as possible."[27] Social events and networks of redone, recalled empathy made *Moscow Saga* a Stalinist *Santa Barbara*, not just a mountain of ostensible, quantifiable details, which – somewhat ironically – are what make these kinds of broadcasts so pricey.

And on that note, Aksenov himself received Russia's Open Booker Prize at the end of 2004, just after he had seen a shorter, promotional cut of *Moscow Saga*.[28] The author used the occasion to question another paradox or two of recent Russian storytelling today, such as the very prize he was receiving. It was funded by Mikhail Khodorkovskii, a man behind bars for purported abuse of Putin's taxation system. Aksenov had penned a family chronicle both graced by Khodorkovskii's organization *and* blessed by Channel One. Viewers' forums reflected a similar disparity, caught between desires to see ostensible, material veracity and, conversely, enjoy an emotionally engaging event, no matter what it looked like.[29]

Latin dramas and soaps in general, as mentioned, downplay the importance of locale, of recognizable places. They stress spoken interaction instead, but then go further still. The affective load *prior* to (or beyond) speech is what holds audiences' attention; hence the ease with which soapy dialog can be mocked, since its real and complex import lies outside the dictionary. Melodramatic Latin and "daytime" dramas are founded first on speech and then, more importantly, upon the devastating power of what *cannot* (or dare not) be said. Russian drama, at least in the first years of the new millennium, has wavered between these forms of excitement: the ostensible management of visual, often antique display, on the one hand, and the unmanageable revelation of the ineffable, on the other. The latter needs neither cash nor crowds to be impressive.

This difference was also felt on the big screen. Gleb Panfilov's film *The Romanovs* (2000) is based around unseen or little-known aspects of Nikolai II's final hours in forested exile – and yet this modest scale is inverted in the closing, violent frames. A quiet fidelity *despite everything* made a man, his wife, and their children worthy of sainthood; their nothingness in exile is reversed. Simultaneous, awkward tendencies towards both self-aggrandizement and peripherality are equally clear in Aleksandr Sokurov's *Russian Ark* (2002), where the identical, tragic loss of the Romanovs (seen again at a lonely dinner table) is woven into expensive excursions through the Hermitage and, by the end of the film, Russia's entire cultural heritage.

In the same year Aleksandr Rogozhkin's *The Cuckoo* likewise reduced and then dispatched his representatives of nationwide conflict to forests of the Soviet–Finish border. The film involves no more than a couple of soldiers and a local Sami woman, all unable to speak the same language. What first binds them and subsequently transforms them into a grand metaphor for national disaster is something slight, emotionally intense, and endlessly, unavoidably unspoken.

Armed conflict in Aleksei German's bleak, sepia depiction of World War Two (*The Last Train* [2003]) stepped back further still from recognizable space and placed its few, lost protagonists in the middle of No Man's Land, very much in the style of Tarkovskii's *Ivan's Childhood* (1962). His similarly tinted film of 2005, *Garpastum*, trod equivalent ground, comparing the transposable, shifting playing fields of five-a-side football to the wandering, ever-present threat of aimless warfare. All these films downplay both their locale and dialog, yet underscore much grander (or tragically ruined) forms of temporally intense, eventful "locations" as a result.

Over the last few years, cinema's dramatized debates over the whereabouts of national pride continue to constitute tales of small groups bound by trust and/or love; this is often done with television's help and funding. Thus the significance of Russia's military past has been seen in terms of several comrades – trapped in a submarine – under threat from bureaucratic failure (*72 meters*, dir. V. Khotinenko), or two lonely lovers finding dignity amid other failed, bizarre aspects of late Soviet society (*Mars* [A. Melikian], both 2003–4). A quiet, stubborn commitment to friends and sweethearts either betters or redoes the supposed goals of the big society in which that fidelity is tested, as in *A Driver for Vera* (dir. Pavel Chukhrai) or children's films like *Alesha Popovich* (dir. Konstantin Bronzit, both 2004). These are microcosms of a better policy, not just policy *per se*. What matters is *when* (in their lives) these heroes take affective risks, not *where*. Thus the nature of Brazil's or Russia's "national heroes" can dovetail with the apolitical, yet equally patriotic aspects of prior Soviet cinema, as we have see in the 2005 adaptations of Boris Akunin's novels *The Turkish Gambit* and *The State Councilor*, in which *fin-de-siècle* adventure reemploys some of the binarisms of the Great Game.

These same issues of diminutive, often affectionate or "soapy" groups slowly outdoing others' social schemes arose with clarity in the 2004 series *The KGB in Smoking Jackets*. A long series is set long ago – twenty-seven years prior, under Brezhnev:

> The events of the series take place in 1977. Once upon a time Valentina Mal'tseva, journalist at a Komsomol publication, introduced herself [in a misjudged phone call] as "one of Andropov's people." She was immediately visited by all manner of people with those well-known ID cards in red covers. After an unsuccessful trip [for the KGB] to Argentina, she ends up connected to the CIA [Central Intelligence Agency]– and eventually Israel's Mossad takes an interest in this female Soviet journalist, too. One woman drives three of the world's great spies crazy; for KGB agent Mishin, Mal'tesva will be his first love, that of a young man.[30]

Attempting to reconstruct this schoolboy simplicity in ostensible, persuasive reality, director Oleg Fomin had many problems, not least of which was being denied permission to film in Moscow's KGB/FSB headquarters, the Lubianka; the set was moved to a visually similar location in Prague. And yet filming in the Czech Republic, they discovered, would cost up to $2 million if the screenplay was followed literally. Trying to circumvent this expense, the Russian film crew worked on the sly without paying anybody, but since Mishin and Mal'tseva are on occasion supposed to meet in open, public spaces, they could not but attract the attention of others, in particular US tourists. The Americans thought these KGB figures were actually depicting the mafia; the drama looked timeless and a potentially expensive, primarily visual history gave way to another importance.[31] It did not plan this shift, but was so judged by others. Similarly, the crew's efforts in finding Soviet-style kefir or Borzhomi mineral water, Bulgarian cigarettes, and historically accurate cars were not justified, judging by an audience concern for other, less evident emphases.

The nature of these emphases is clear from the outset, in that much of the political wrangling of Mal'tseva's spy work is dictated by her superior, the man whom she once spurned in school (Mishin): childhood experiences dictate movement in the adult and the social worlds. In fact anything resembling a properly "adult" explanation of these events from a political standpoint is often missing, a lacuna highlighted by the frequent repetition of one phrase attributed to the heroine's grandmother: "The less you know, the better you'll sleep." Mal'tseva herself sees so little logic or clarity in the espionage around her that she wonders early in the series if she will ever be able to trust or love another person. An earlier, superior form of social interaction is under threat from cruelty, from men emotionally "abused" in their youth; in fact at one point the KGB's very *modus operandi* is termed mere "provocation" by Mal'tseva, when compared to the better patriotism of those who fought in World War Two.

The fact that this heroine is willing to sleep with the enemy simply because she *likes* an individual is termed "avant-garde"! The harmony she represents is likewise often associated with something equally odd, with song. When stuck in borderland Argentinean forest, skirting the home of soap operas, Mal'tseva sings to herself to stop the loneliness; she chooses the opening song to the 1934 musical *The Happy-Go-Lucky Guys*. Later – with faint irony – she also employs the patriotic Soviet number "Boldly into Battle We'll Go/And Die as One ... " When this fragile jollity is under pressure in moments of danger, Mal'tseva even admits she would rather die in the arms of a pop singer than those of a spy.

Music helps to make her the advocate of a fairer, familial, and often childlike harmony. When asked after a shootout if she is hurt, the heroine says, "Yes; in the head and heart." She is intellectually and emotionally manipulated by Andropov on several occasions, a man who is not shown by TV in a positive light of late. He is juxtaposed with Brezhnev, who is usually absent here from the screen and not linked to any nasty intrigue. The CIA agents refer to Brezhnev as a "mere wind-up doll," but his fair-handed stability is infinitely preferable to Andropov's scheming.

Just as the opposing camps of careerist espionage ("us" versus "them"), so the angry binarism of military conflict sometimes blurs in the hearts of today's TV audience. *Penal Battalion* (*Shtrafbat*, 2004) uncovered a similarly unspoken truth or complexity in Russia's experience of World War Two, one that – paradoxically – would help to *broaden* the definition of patriotism:

> Military historians don't like to talk about the men who served in penal battalions – or about their nameless graves. These were the battalions that "plugged" the most dangerous breaches along the

frontline; they were made to attack the most impregnable German defenses. There was no need to give them ammunition or supplies. Already guilty of something and yet partly innocent, they were mere cannon fodder. They were driven to certain death. Among the conscripts were all kinds of people: the honest and the wicked, ex-prisoners and draft-dodgers, those who fled jail or had stood up against violence. They became nameless heroes who gave their life for the lives of others, for the freedom of their homeland and for peace on Earth.[32]

As in *The Icon Hunters*, *Shtrafbat* has tried, in the words of one of its actors, Iurii Stepanov, to show "there'd been nobody to mourn for these men." A priest on set, again offering documentary consultations, also hoped the drama would bring the soldiers eternal peace after unjust anonymity.[33] *Izvestiia* drew parallels between *Shtrafbat* and documentary cinema; *Radio Liberty* and the newspaper *Moskovskii komsomolets* likewise said it was proof – "at long last" – that "war can be shown as it really was; that TV stations can show reality – if they want to." When *Shtrafbat* debuted, many journalists felt that this documentary patriotism was indeed grander than some forms of Soviet rhetoric.[34] A representative of *Rossiiskaia gazeta* declared *Moscow Saga* and *Penal Battalion* better expressions of social interest than any other shows that season. The public concurred, granting the broadcasts the top ratings slot with a 47.2 percent audience share.

The series makes considerable use of Soviet narratives, perhaps most explicitly in Episode Five, when a nurse is shown reading Ostrovskii's *How the Steel Was Tempered* to a severely burned officer, hospitalized after heroically setting fire to six enemy tanks. Like Ostrovskii's novel, the characters of *Shtrafbat* must live according to the oft-quoted phrase "Going beyond Refusal" (*Cherez "ne mogu"*). Another pivotal phrase, also frequently employed, is the Stalinist slogan that only through dangerous combat can the prisoners "atone for their guilt before the Motherland." And so we move among the troops and their adventures from doctrine to something grander than language, to the realization *à la* Fadeev that "they are not a list of names. These are living people."

Contemporaries of Ostrovskii had also interpreted his understanding of communality as a potential made feasible through inclusive, affective forgiveness. His hero Korchagin smiles: "He smiles like that all the time, and his smile gives off radiant, kind warmth. To smile like that you have to be the kind of person who loves work, loves people, who loves and values life."[35] In a related paraphrase of the novel's *raison d'être*, it was said in scholarship under Khrushchev that Korchagin "went off to fight and bring closer a happy future for both the people *and himself, too*." By turning this novel into a more subjective endeavor, as in *Shtrafbat*, and not a mere embodiment of political prompting, the core venture actually becomes

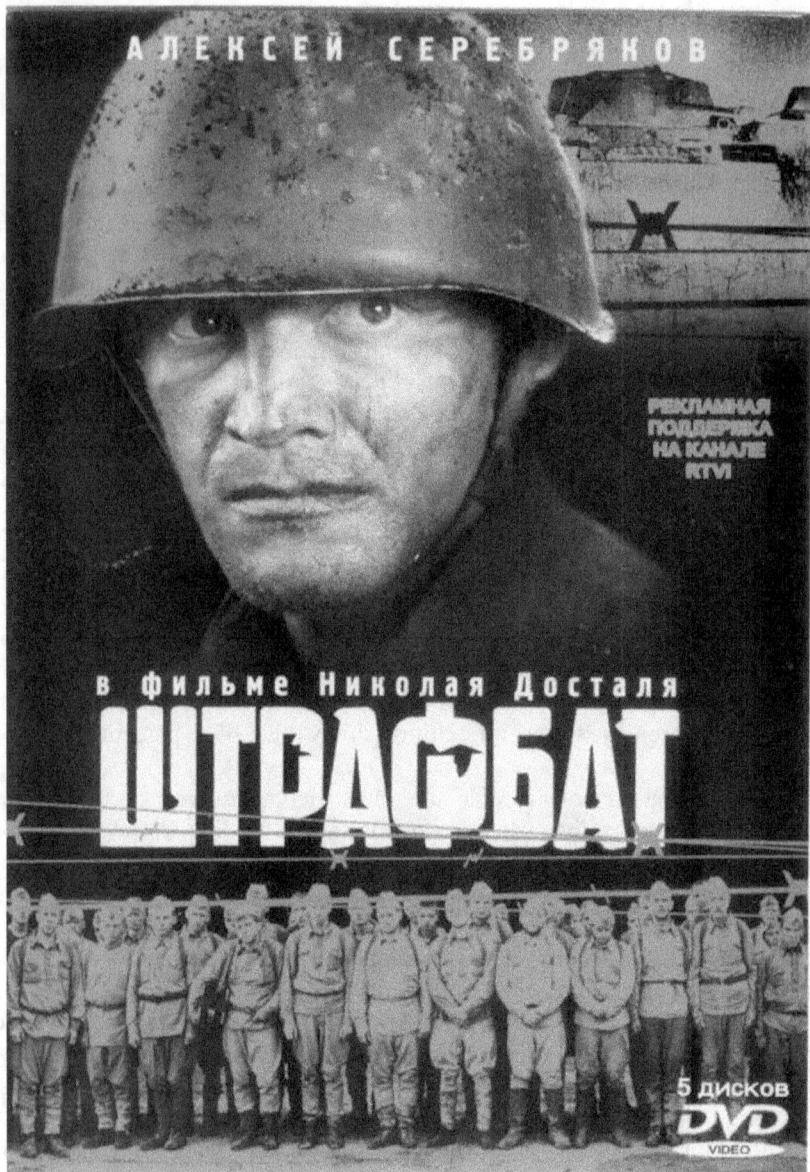

Figure 3.1 Penal Battalion.

bolder. Just as one may turn Korchagin into a man of unending, inclusive gladness, far beyond the sensible, dialectical, or binary limitations of ideology, so his significance snowballs far beyond affairs of state. "The author died, and the legend created about him left also ... The text remained and shows everything: 2 million copies, 5 million, 10 million, 30 million ... "[36]

After all, it is only this affective aspect that would make the book popular with schoolchildren – who couldn't give a hoot about policy. One Soviet schoolteacher in Lithuania suggested that class lectures on the novel should conclude with a reference to the fact that people "in all countries love Pavel Korchagin," and that his story was translated into seventy-nine languages.[37] Despite this ludicrously pompous reference to "all countries," the logic of love remains. In 1935 Ostrovskii wrote to one schoolgirl, "Only now [late in life] do I sense with all my strength the goodness that my book conjured in the minds of young people."[38] In these direct addresses from an author to his young readers (despite their propagation by the state), the intrusion of speechifying is lessened and the differences between happiness and ideological frenzy made clearer. During World War Two, in one telling and similar example from the adult world, a certain Gunner Peshekhonov was killed after shielding a gun port with his body. In his kitbag fellow soldiers found a copy of *How the Steel Was Tempered*, with a childishly naïve and sincere inscription: "Korchagin is a brave, strong person. He will be my favorite hero in life."[39]

In a related fashion, many assumed platitudes of war are turned upside down in *Shtrafbat* over 550 minutes. Fun with a pack of cards can level the difference between Communist and Fascist soldiers; Soviet troops pose as Germans to steal their food and wear the warmer enemy uniforms for extended periods, even if this attracts snipers. Phrases such as "enemy of the people" are applied more often to jealous lovers than anything the state can raise as an object of ideological disdain. Likewise, bellicose aphorisms are applied to familial problems, where they sound even more ominous: "Thrash your own people, so that others will fear you!" The ability of such rhetoric to reflect and accurately mirror the official Soviet enterprise is minimal, for, as one of the characters notes, "the Bolsheviks have always been missing one thing, the *main* thing: love for the people. For them, it was always a means, not an end. The end was limitless power."

The one figure in the series who underscores this love, overtly termed political "abstract humanism," is a priest. Outraged by the destruction of his church, he joins the penal battalion. He, not an officer, teaches the soldiers some of their most patriotic lessons, that – "as hagiography informs us" – even the worst criminal can become a saint. He declares that God sent him to fight in a war that has now become a "holy matter." The priest reads the soldiers the Sermon on the Mount, insisting that the Bible is not "propaganda against the Soviet people." Finally, as we have seen already, music holds characters together under geopolitical duress, but in this case, rather than hymns, the priest leads the battalion in choral renditions of lost and lonely hearts – the gypsy romance "Burn, Burn My Star … " These are the passions that are taken precisely from (or excused by) profitable, passionate Latin dramas, where historical specificity is not the key to persuasion, and they then do double duty in a similar socialist context.

The Cadets (*Kursanty* [dir. Andrei Kavun, 2005]) and *Keys to an Abyss* (*Kliuchi ot bezdny* [dir. Sergei Rusakov, 2004])

The broad embrace of socialist culture on today's television goes further than incorporating people overtly ostracized by the Soviet system or clearly marked as criminals; it discerns variety and complexity among its most conformist members, too. Nothing could be more clear cut than patriotism among *willing* conscripts during World War Two, the young, naïve enthusiasm of cadets, still as far as possible from their first experience of frontline horror. What would melodrama do to their conformist worldview?

> At the basis of this screenplay lie the memoirs of well-known Russian director Petr Todorovskii. The series takes place in the winter of 1942 in an artillery academy at the military rear, where new recruits are being prepared for dispatch to the front. This is the story of boys destined to become cannon fodder; as yet, however, they don't know so. Nonetheless instinct tells them they don't have long to live. We follow the destinies of these young cadets over three months' study, before they're shipped off – young cadets whose remaining time on earth may be those very same three months.

Indeed towards the end of the final episode we are shown the cadets one by one, again in a documentary list reminiscent of *Molodaia gvardiia*. Almost without exception a narrator tells us they will die at the front. Criminal, class, and political divisions are erased, presenting us instead with a universality that, although emotionally persuasive, may not make for good or easy entertainment. The story goes nowhere special.

One viewers' forum dedicated to *Kursanty* said it offered not a happy ending but a "shit ending":

> Life's hard enough as it is – and then TV comes along and spoils your mood even more. Watch any American film about the war and even though the ending may be sad, at least it won't spoil your mood. There'll be hope that life itself or some kind of better existence'll go on, but here ... that's the way it always is in our cinema: a shit ending.

This grimness, however, struck many as being closer to our documentary potential:

> I agree with the person who said it's hard to admit what actually happened. It's one thing if *Kursanty* is good moviemaking, pure and simple, or if there's a good screenplay, but this is all about *life*, too. It's our life, our grandfathers' lives. ... It's sad that things ended that way, but you can't rewrite life, like a movie scenario. As far as I'm concerned, this is

the best possible present to mark the 60th anniversary of the war! A big "Thank You" to those who made the series!⁴⁰

Two of the leading actors here, recently famous from the mafia blockbuster *Brigada*, noted earlier, are Pavel Maikov and Vladimir Vdovichenkov. Both play officers, yet make themselves into most unattractive characters: Maikov morally so and Vdovichenkov physically. Their modern-day glamour is negated. The series demanded a leveling of status; likewise, female star Elena Iakovleva plays a sexually desperate and physically unattractive mother, struggling unsuccessfully with the charms of a cadet perhaps half her age.

The young actor in the central role of *The Cadets*, Ivan Stebunov, took this process even further, discussing the three core elements of his portrayal: "The character, the actor and the human being." Divided as they so often are by the processes of filmmaking and celebrity, Stebunov felt that the subject matter of *Kursanty* had folded them into one. "It seems to me that an actor can't 'play' something that's not within him. It doesn't matter whether I've actually experienced something [i.e. the war] or not. I played something all for the series and so *all* of it's within me now."⁴¹ The show's emotional clout made and molded a life.

It was this spirit of social membership beyond received social categories that informed another popular wartime series, *Keys to the Abyss* (2004). With a cast headed by popular action hero Mikhail Porechenkov, it occasionally made battle a place of social rearrangement, neither the reinforcement of accepted groupings nor politically justified promotions and demotions. That rearrangement hinged on *private* notions of fidelity:

> Springtime 1946. A village not far from Moscow is shaken by a series of rebel attacks and brutal murders. A criminal band headed by Sen'ka Krivoi is creating chaos, a punitive expedition of turncoats and ex-prisoners well-armed with weapons stolen from the enemy. The head of the local police force, Lieutenant Sergei Matveevich Vysik, has been chasing this elusive mob for two months, but all to no avail. Convinced that regular methods won't work any longer, Vysik turns to some frontline friends for help: an old classmate and safebreaker, plus another pal, who is now a card cheat. Both had served under Vysik in a mounted scout division and done their time in a penal battalion. For Vysik, however, these two men are willing to go through hell and high water.

Using the same peripheral soldiers as *Shtrafbat*, this series can shift its emphasis away from the fight for policy or those who make it; instead attention is paid to its purportedly unquestioning recipients. Nonetheless, dogma does stick its nose in from time to time. Little people come to the forefront, the readers and listeners of doctrinaire dictates. What they get,

Figure 3.2 The Cadets.

however, is Vysik, a new version of the stately patrician, "somebody modern, serious, courageous – and to some degree a rather stern patriot."

This phrasing can recall Putin himself. Television presents this same image in tales of presidential planning that seem utopian in their hopeful conflation of disparate entities, like "Honest Bureaucrat," "Responsible Politician," or "Upstanding Journalist." All in all, "a brilliantly rehearsed

Soaps 81

spectacle" made of these stately desires is played out every evening on television. "Viewers nationwide will either applaud or whistle. They could, perhaps, get up and leave, but that's hardly likely. So whoever puts on the best show will be victor" in the competition for public persuasion.[42] With this in mind, Putin held in his 2005 State of the Union address that "we need to create guarantees that will allow state television and radio to operate with maximum objectivity." He also claimed, as so he often does, that the media "operate free from the influence of any groups and thus reflect the entire range of opinions nationwide."[43] This is patently untrue. They must instead show reality in a way that evinces a return to – and respect for – traditions prior to 1991. Quite how this is done, however, and what it means for sentimental, soap-watching viewers are not simple matters. What viewers want (or *expect*), thanks to their experience of Latin drama, and what they're offered are things that do not always coincide.

Conclusion: the Soviet populace helped to construct popular narratives of today redolent of Latin drama

This vital role of audience approval in handling the success or failure of nationwide storytelling is nothing new. Today's audiences are, after all, born of yesterday's, when the Soviet establishment knew perfectly well which books the public *wanted* to read. Even during the 1920s, and then again from the 1960s onwards, major official studies were conducted into readers' tastes and desires.[44] When the authorities, after decades of paper shortages, acquiesced and offered desired volumes in exchange for pulping unwanted texts, the most precious authors – known for ages from the official studies – became evident in select lists: nineteenth-century Russian classics, Shakespeare, Mark Twain, Kipling, Verne, and Hugo. Among factual titles, the public wanted *The ABC of Gardening*, *Advice for Market Gardeners*, and *The Popular Encyclopedia of Medicine*. Adventure, romance, and fruitful domesticity were uppermost:[45]

> In the history of Soviet publishing, the interplay and tension between four sets of interests is a dominating theme. There is, firstly, the [mere] conviction of the Communist Party and Soviet government that the content and circulation of printed matter in the USSR should be controlled by means of ideological guidelines, administrative supervision and the censorship apparatus. Secondly, there are the economic considerations, which favor an efficiently operating industry, the optimum use of limited resources and the minimum recourse to subsidies. Thirdly, there is the strength of professional commitment among many – not all – publishing house staff and authors, and their desire for a reputation among their colleagues and readers which rests on more than officially-inspired commendation. *Finally, there are the variegated and shifting concerns of the huge Soviet reading public, its influence*

> stemming from the freedom, however limited, to read one book rather than another.[46]

Taking into consideration the fact that a smaller number of books would often remain unsold in the USSR than in the US, who was buying them? The state itself was initially unsure, because from 1932 to 1934 the notion of a "'new Soviet reader' was an ideological construct born of frustration with the various unsuccessful attempts [by RAPP and, in song, RAPM] to foster a genuinely proletarian culture."[47] This frustration prompted the massive runs of the 1930s and new attitudes towards librarianship, where professionally trained staff would help to "direct the public's reading" (*rukovodstvo chteniem*). Thus there were lots of new books, a new aesthetic, and a totally new – yet imprecise – view of who a reader was or could become:

> Readers tended to bring the [socialist] novel sharply within their own personal frame of reference. The action of the novel was compared with the readers' own experience of "real life" and assessed on this basis. In an extreme case of the congruence of literature and life, one reader [of Vasilii Azhaev's work] actually recognized events from her own past depicted in the novel [*Far from Moscow*]. The reader was a means of both reinforcing and articulating a range of public values *and* of achieving emotional fulfillment.[48]

This concept of private emotional satisfaction above all (i.e. as underwriting and fueling public values) was evident in how the state went about advocating works for fresh, ideal readers, because the official lists of *rukovodstvo chteniem* were full of exciting but "prescriptive pathos." This emotive distinction of Soviet prose was enormously important in the lists of recommended texts, especially at a time when mass reading took place in public libraries. Emotion would either boost the energy with which state-sponsored novels would try to be "prescriptive" – i.e. sell their worldview – or define the degree to which novels aped the sentimental, engaging pathos of apolitical, aimless, and genuinely popular storytelling, from either non-Soviet times or non-Soviet places. Emotional books were both more convincing and taken out more often. This use of sensibility was vital in fashioning lending tendencies in public places.

From the very start of the USSR, in utterly typical locales like Rostov, say, the need for literature that "isn't boring!" was consistently evident in questionnaires, leading even the Moscow Council of Trade Unions to admit that "entertaining reading" was the prime concern of a youthful socialist audience.[49] Bearing in mind the frequent admissions of wide-ranging official surveys that nobody actually *read* works of literary criticism, an ideally direct, unimpeded relation of typical Soviet readers with the text could perhaps be defined outside critical "guidance," according to a series of principles. These were "understandability"; entertainment value; conservatism of form; the familiarity of characters as a "typological community"; the correspondence of literature and the "everyday consciousness of the consumer"; the "beautifulness" of art; and, finally, a story's "contemporaneousness."[50] Television works along the same lines today.

New readers in a reasonably new society, now or then, have relatively few benchmarks against which to judge a given work of art, torn as they are from the "old world." They therefore judge the success of art by their own, private experience in the ostensible world, becoming co-creators and empirical arbiters of a creative process we assume is simply imposed from above. "The [Soviet] reader," says Dobrenko, "fully recognized the authorial right but all the same was in fact *himself* the author of the story, drawing conclusions from the writer's text that could not be ascribed to the writer (thus the reader agreed with himself)." This approach led readers, just as today, to conclude that events in an unconvincing story "can't be like that in real life!"

The benchmark for persuasive storytelling is not geographic specificity, as the cheap, indoor sets and polyester ball gowns of Latin soaps or *telenovelas* show. Real life cannot be pointed at or confidently named, hence it is easier to say what it "cannot be like." Attempts to say what it *should* be begin, but have trouble gathering speed after the collapse of a socialist ethos. With no long (i.e. still-valued) history or commonly accepted benchmarks for comparative analysis, TV viewers make *themselves* the author of a series' success as they get accustomed to a new culture. The value systems they employ(ed) to do so after the collapse of the USSR have often come from Mexico, Argentina, and Brazil. These systems have entwined so tightly that in the autumn 2006 Russian series *V ritme tango* (*To the Beat of a Tango*) real-life Argentinean celebrity Natalia Oreiro comes to Russia with her soccer-playing husband – so they may find work after Argentina's own "financial catastrophe." Now Latin heroines come to *Russia* to fulfill their dreams. The success and storylines of Slavic TV have bypassed or outpaced the distant continent which they once studied and fondly emulated.

Interweaving with poignant socialist traditions, with that which remained both valid and *unfinished* after doctrine fell silent, Central and South American soaps have helped to (re)introduce affective, interpretational skills. These skills and their resulting expectations are sometimes used to construe the idea of "Putin" himself less as a political individual than as a type of ongoing story. In May 2005 a protest against this type of insistently broadcast narrative led to a meeting outside the Ostankino TV center, home to Channel One. Protestors wore bandanas around their mouths, decorated with a simple statement of audience disapproval when watching any excessively, tediously politicized serial at home on television: "Turn It Off!"[51]

4 Costume drama
"Life as it really is"

> I've served my Motherland all my life. I fought in wars for it; I was even imprisoned for it – and that same country never did me wrong. To you, though, I'm just an old Commie or, as you put it, "pigheaded." Yes I am – and I'm proud of it. I've said it before and I'll say it again: under Stalin, I'd have ... I'd have put you up against the wall.
> (A pensioner's final tirade against the hostile takeover of an equally old helicopter factory by today's oligarchs: *Okhota na iziubria* [*The Siberian Deer Hunt*, 2005])

Introduction: *Bayazet* (dir. Andrei Chernykh and Nikolai Stambula, 2003) and *The Spiral Staircase* (dir. Dmitrii Parmenov, 2004)

If the really important things in "real life" are not tied to a specific name (such as the Party) or place, then what about the importance of a certain time, of history? Some of the very Soviet issues we have outlined so far are just as evident in TV's historical drama. This genre has indeed been permeated by a number of ethical, poignant, and social concerns that run much deeper and longer than any period setting. Take, for example, the nineteenth-century drama directed by Andrei Chernykh and Nikolai Stambula, *Bayazet* (2003). Set amid the Russo-Turkish war of 1877–8, the series depicts the heroic defense of a small Russian garrison "suffering from hunger and thirst, drowning in blood, yet not surrendering the fortress of Bayazet to enemy forces." This rhetoric may remind us of generic Western adventures, especially the 1879 events at Rorke's Drift that inspired the film *Zulu* (dir. C. Endfield, 1964), so important to the early career of Michael Caine. Nonetheless, as the producers of *Bayazet* were keen to tell viewers, their work has a strong domestic and *atemporal* resonance.

> The military and patriotic pathos of the series is softened by a stirring and most dramatic love story. Against the background of common tragedy, amid desperation and death, there lives a pure and yet immoral love: a Russian officer's secret love for the wife of Bayazet's erstwhile

commander. Death alone, almighty death, can destroy the frontier that stands between them.

There could be no clearer example, at least linguistically, of how historical adventure in Russian TV schedules is infused and invigorated with something other than dusty history. Likewise, in the NTV *fin-de-siècle* detective series *The Spiral Staircase* (2004), full of St. Petersburg ghosts and murder victims, Inna Churikova was attracted to a story that relied more upon the quiet, if not timeless, habits of a "Russian Miss Marple" than any crime caused by a given sociopolitical issue.[1] A genre wholly associated, even in the Soviet mind, with Sherlock Holmes, Agatha Christie, or the so-called cozy mysteries is borrowed by *The Spiral Staircase* and then made *endlessly* valid. The historical drama therefore becomes more dramatic than historical (in the factual sense) and relies more upon social history (in the microcosmic sense) than anything doctrinal.

This can warp the distinction between realism and reality further still. In giving the past some (if not more) validity in the present, the distance between the inside and outside of the TV screen lessens, too, such that Russian viewers occasionally see no difference between a "wonderful person" on screen and a wonderful person in daily social interaction.[2] Viewers' experiences, once again, make them authors of this interpretative leap – though we should not forget how disconcertingly close such credulity can be to the story of Victoria Ruffo's deceptive advertisements for MMM.

The difference between these two narratives, between art and (what really looks like) actuality, lies in the seriousness of their dramatic promise. *The Spiral Staircase* is full, if not overloaded with, "theatrical" moments, marked by ladylike screams and unexpected appearances in the dark corners of a large, half-abandoned house. Its entire murder case, however, is conducted tongue in cheek, as if director Dmitrii Parmenov is neither able nor willing to take the expectations of his genre seriously. Both of the plotlines in *Vintovaia lestnitsa*, by way of example, involve an obviously suspicious foreigner.

In the same vein, since most of the action happens wholly within this large house and its garden, many of the episodes are therefore extremely stagy, rarely moving from contiguous chambers. The only open-air scenes in St. Petersburg, for example, are shot on the lawn of the Stock Exchange, a vague indicator of some "life outside." That life, rather worryingly, seems only to promise social disorder that might undermine the show's tidy plot; one of the male characters is loudly upbraided for reading Gor'kii's subversive, dangerous novel *Mother*. Personal history seems happier hiding from a public equivalent so it can keep on having fun.

The nineteenth century: *Poor Nastia* (*Bednaia Nastia*, 2003)

The grandest series in this stagy category, from a purely financial point of view if nothing else, is the nineteenth-century costume drama of 2003 *Poor*

Nastia (dir. Ekaterina Dvigubskaia, Petr Krotenko, Stas Libin [nature scenes], Alla Plotkina, Aleksandr Smirnov, and Petr Shtein). Its producers announced with considerable hubris that after the series' presentation in Los Angeles it would be purchased and displayed in thirty countries, including Greece, Spain, and – ironically or triumphantly – Latin America. The reasons for success on this scale are multiple, but interestingly enough the director of A-Media, which produced *Poor Nastia* (together with *The Brigade* in 2002), said recently that filming the past is always simpler than filming the present.[3] Looking back at history (which already makes sense) is easier than looking around and making sense yourself.

Convinced of this argument, foreign backers quickly appeared to fund the Tolstoian, touristy clichés they expect from Slavdom. A-Media was joined by Columbia Tristar Pictures (who brought *Santa Barbara* to Russia) and Sony. Much money was spent and many tools were borrowed or bought, to the tune of $11.4 million: 42 tons of equipment delivered from overseas; two central sound stages measuring 2,600 square meters, plus fifty-two additional sets; frequent travel to (and use of) more than fifty outdoor locations; 800 costumes; six directors; thirteen screenwriters; and a final screenplay of 9,600 pages, giving voice to the 7,200 people in fourteen cities who passed through casting.[4] The resulting, passionate epic stars some of the prettiest (yet jarringly modern) faces working in television today: Elena Korikova, Daniil Strakhov, Petr Krasilov, and Dmitrii Isaev.[5]

Despite being set further in the past than any other series in this section, *Poor Nastia* claims an emotional relevance in the present:

> 1839: History is moving forward, but human feelings do not change. Love and jealousy, honor and envy, fidelity and disloyalty prevail. Aging Baron Korf has raised Anna as his own daughter. He dreams of watching her on the stage of the Imperial Theater. The beau monde of St. Petersburg undoubtedly sees great talent and a great future in Anna. But very few people know that she is a peasant girl. Prince Mikhail Repnin fell in love with Anna from the moment he set eyes upon her; he, too, is ignorant of her background. Will Repnin be able to preserve this love when Anna's secret is revealed?[6]

These complex social dilemmas and concomitant emotions required 120 episodes to work themselves out. One of the directors (Petr Shtein) drew consciously upon *Gone with the Wind* (Victor Fleming, 1939) to remind him of the "beautiful, powerful blockbuster" he sought for viewers.[7] Similarly, the screenwriters wanted to shape *Poor Nastia* not as an American broadcast (that is, structurally open-ended in case of good ratings and a second series), but as a complete work with "beginning, middle and end," since that – allegedly – is what Slavic audiences want. In structuring the tale, the American members of the team were surprised that their European colleagues expected a screenplay based on "fact," not social gossip or faux mysticism.[8]

"The serial includes a lot of real people and many of the events that made the nineteenth century so rich. To show how carefully the writers related their text to historical truth, we worked with an expert historian and an authority on the history of fashion."[9]

In somehow juxtaposing objective, past reality with the affective power of the narrative, the latter was co-opted into the former: "A fairytale is falsehood, but this falsehood must be counteracted by truth."[10] The producers expressed their intent to prejudice the "objective" aspect of their endeavors. *The Idiot* shied away from ostensible reality, but *Poor Nastia* fosters it. We can sense already another major predicament; even when some of the characters, like Prince Repnin, were the product of screenwriters' fantasy, journalists went to great efforts to prove other individuals had "really" existed with the same name and in some cases were documented by Karamzin: "Repnin is not a real historical personage, but the creators of *Poor Nastia* were no doubt trying to 'connect' him to that well-known family line."[11]

In a similar spirit, some columnists offered their readership endless facts and figures from the series' given period, all in the name of a "truer" context. I have already mentioned the year 1839, when "the Winter Palace was rebuilt after a major fire; monetary reform was begun, resulting in a system based upon silver; the Pulkovskaia Observatory was opened and Lermontov finished the final version of his narrative poem, *The Demon*." Some of those facts may be relevant, but others were not: "At the end of 1839, somewhere between the towns of Vladimir and Moscow, a foreign traveler came across a colossal elephant surrounded by a cavalcade of horses. The elephant was a present from the Persian Shah to Nikolai the First."[12] The documentary evidence was excessive.

Another local problem emerged when the Americans discovered Russian writers were not used to pacing the acts of any given episode so that advertisements would fall into the rhythm of the work, punctuating it with minimum intrusion.[13] Likewise, given the very unusual, unwieldy size of the series, some actors – as noted – worried they would be typecast in this unusually long drama,[14] others that poor ratings would mean being "written out" of the plot by death or accident.[15] A third oddity was the American pace of work. All the technology employed on the set meant that "normal" US production speeds could be met: one day per episode.[16] Perhaps the filming schedule would contradict all possible artistic benefits of a huge budget: "Speed's only a good thing if you're hunting fleas!"[17] Dmitrii Isaev conflated these problems of artistry and speed when he compared the project to a marathon, but the physical labor of each day to filming a one-act play: "Each day's a premiere, an exam."[18] Another of the actors (Daniil Strakhov) admitted that only valerian drops, vodka, TV, and computer games allowed him to "switch off" mentally each evening.[19]

Poor Nastia is indeed a huge, rambling tale on the Tolstoian scale of feature films. In a similarly Tolstoian manner (this time from *Anna Karenina*),

88 *Russian television today*

viewers said that burying a loveable heroine in the middle of so many episodes led to confusion; the series was named after a young woman who often seemed to be absent. What on earth was going on? Just like readers of a serialized romance in the nineteenth century, TV viewers today pondered all possible social relations or combinations in future episodes as hypothetical equations: "Anna + Vladimir Korf = ?"; "Anna + Mikhail Repnin = ?" In attempting to simplify these matters, the most fundamental question of all was posed: "What does Anna want? Love. A real, radiant and all-consuming love."[20] Vanishing in a huge plot and falling in love were supposed to mirror each other: "Do You Like Vanishing into the 19th Century?" asked the promotional materials. Is that movement invisibly affective or theatrical? "Gorgeous costumes and sets. How could they not make you happy? Every little girl dreams of waking up in a place like that."[21]

The 1930s: *Bless the Woman* (*Blagoslovite zhenshchinu*, 2003)

Other big historical dramas of late have been set in the twentieth century, but one in particular is notable for its costumed timescale, like *Poor Nastia*. *Bless the Woman* is the work of Stanislav Govorukhin and has two hypostases, as both a television series and a feature film.

> The heroine's life is shown against the backdrop of actual events in Russia's history, all the way from the 1930s to the 1950s. Together with her husband – a soldier – she travels the nation, trying to find the kind of happiness sought by any woman. All of this takes place during times of repression, war, and social breakdown after the hostilities. Only when she returns to her hometown near the sea many years later does the heroine find, at long last, peace and quiet in her soul.

The movie debuted on August 27, 2003 – designated as Russia's "Cinema Day" – and then opened simultaneously in fifty regions around the nation as part and parcel of celebrations to mark the end of World War Two many years prior. Somebody was keen on making a big fuss with a big story across a big time span. If complex, peripatetic plots might be a marked category of TV's historical melodramas today, then what of the condensed movie version? Can the timescale of a big TV series be abbreviated? The newspaper *Izvestiia* said it had enough plotlines to match the 1,128 episodes of *Santa Barbara*. The television version had a novelistic structure; the feature film, however, could handle neither the scope nor the full extension of any ideas contained in the serial.

In its longer television format, the movie was shown on Channel One. There are reports that Nikita Mikhalkov, too, who has consistently refused to shorten the running time for *The Barber of Siberia* (1999), is planning instead to reinsert the outtakes and edited scenes into the film and run this longer version on TV. The significance of television increases as Channel

One frequently produces films, most notably *Night Watch* and its 2006 sequel, *Day Watch*, the clearest "symbol[s] that television's dictatorship has arrived in Russian cinema."[22] This small-screen authoritarianism pushed *Bless the Woman* all the way to Russia's Oscar nominations. A film existing both on the big screen and TV may seem an odd candidate for Hollywood, but it shows very well the cultural clout enjoyed by television in Russia; it also shows, perhaps, that Govorukhin – who is a deputy in Russia's Duma – can time the production of his patriotic films to help a political career.[23]

As the story maps one woman's life across various key years (1935, 1938, 1941, 1945, and 1958), we are shown periods of Soviet history in a markedly partisan style, hence the rumors concerning the film's political benefit. Govorukhin's cinematic patriotism (re)creates times when "only beautiful girls in gorgeous dresses and expensive shoes traveled on the Moscow subway." The film and its gorgeous, erstwhile Russia were accused of stealing their pathos from all corners of Soviet cinema, an indictment that would reappear after his slavishly "authentic" *Ne khlebom edinym* of 2005. Reliably solid, patriarchal figures seemed plagiarized from *The Officers* (*Ofitsery*, dir. Vladimir Rogovoi, 1971); the depiction of a dramatic female thespian (*à la* Faina Ranevskaia) recalled *The Foundling* (*Podkidysh*, dir. Tat'iana Lukashevich, 1939). In addition, when the heroine of *Bless the Woman* saves herself from the Purges and escapes to an extremely large house in the Crimea, the appearance of yet another dependable man in undependable times reminded some viewers of Aleksei Batalov's role as Gosha in *Moscow Does Not Believe in Tears*.

Using these somewhat grizzled stereotypes to fashion a modern "chick-flick," as it was called more than once, Govorukhin plays into very Soviet notions of what a woman wants – and is. His ideas of romance and loyalty as the benchmarks of a healthy nationalism were occasionally pilloried:

> This ideal woman waits for her intended with a firm bosom and faithful, imploring eyes. She throws herself on his neck even after a three or four-year absence, and doesn't ask where he has been, whom he has slept with, or anything about what he did. She always remembers (as she should) that *he's* the one who decides things for her, everywhere and always.[24]

Worried that the female romantic leads in today's movies look both unhealthy and asexual, Govorukhin chose a young lady from the casting process who reminded him of the Venus de Milo, Aphrodite, and Botticelli's figures – all at the same time: "Of course I wasn't trying to suggest that our ideals of feminine beauty would change after my picture – but I'd certainly like them to."[25] The director explained his decision-making:

> I was guided by intuition. I once read that Fellini said directors very often don't understand what they're filming. A director feels it, but can't define

it with words. And that's how it should be, because to define something with words is to limit it. I've wanted to film "something" for a long time now, but never knew what that "something" was.

It was feminine and it was loved. The film was dedicated "To Our Mothers and Grandmothers." Govorukhin also declared openly in many interviews that he even modeled the heroine on his own mother. Yet this overt referencing of actuality did not stop further criticism of warmed-over Soviet plots and outdated views of how the opposite sex should love. His vagrant heroine, thrown from embrace to embrace, town to town, reminded some viewers of the actresses from *An Eternal Summons*, and his gendered views of trustworthiness continued to raise eyebrows. "Perhaps an ideal woman *should* be like Govorukhin's: fidelity to the grave, and then a new love will come to her as a reward. Perhaps Govorukhin wants to believe that kind of theory. In one interview he said he makes 'anti-cinema' or, if you like, cinema to counter modern cinematography."[26]

Some of the younger women writing in soap forums were less than satisfied with Govorukhin's "anti-cinema" or his ideas of love:

What the hell is kind or humane about this "masterpiece"? You all write about poor women [here in the forum]. The husband almost wipes his feet on his wife, and that's about the extent of his kindness. I've lived with that type of unstable spouse – and I can tell you there's nothing beautiful in it. ... There's no need to "bless this woman" in all her suffering and call it family life. You should *save* women from suffering. Films like this leave the younger generation with the reassurance that, as in the past, a wife is a free domestic laborer, a cook, laundry maid, housemaid, cleaning woman, nanny for the kids, and a passionate lover after the work day. It's all so phony![27]

Poor Nastia and Govorukhin wished to erase the line between fact and fiction with grand, extraordinary storytelling, but did so unnaturally or artificially. The distance between extraordinary and ordinary was a common problem of Soviet storytelling, especially for those such as Aleksei Tolstoi, an author who, as noted by Evgenii Dobrenko, inhabited the gray domain between fiction and fact. "Being a 'figure' in Soviet culture meant being a functionary, since Soviet *culture* [as in Tolstoi] is depoliticized, political power being appropriated elsewhere. The Soviet realist theory of creativity is a sort of 'engendering aesthetic.'"[28] The processes invoked by this kind of engendering, however, can grow so grand that they are no longer political, because they are unmanageable.

If we look at the infamous moment when the Russian government was forced to contemplate a shift from fiction to fact with the Kursk tragedy, the unmanageable and the excessive manifest themselves clearly. When Putin saw the extent of critical coverage and the media's tales of state inefficiency, he personally telephoned the TV stations responsible. What particularly enraged him was the angry testimony of two sailors' wives. "You found two sluts," he screamed, "to drag me down." TV presenter Sergei Dorenko said of the outburst, "These were officers' wives. But Putin was convinced [of his reality] to a degree where neither truth *nor* reality existed."²⁹ The following drama aims to calm down a tad and reclaim the apolitical core of Tolstoi's Sovietness with sympathy, not antagonism. Here we take another step *into* Soviet history in order to bypass it.

World War Two in France: *The Red Choir* (*Krasnaia kapella* [dir. Aleksandr Aravin, 2004])

> You've not understood a thing. You can only think in a straight line, and you don't know what you're worth.
> (Iu. Krymov, *The Tanker "Derbent,"* 1938)

The series *The Red Choir* hoped to address issues of romance, personal and generic fidelity not only by referencing well-known historical events (in this case Soviet espionage work in wartime France), but also by taking much from *The Seventeen Moments of Spring*. Even the mother of the serial's chief actor, Andrei Il'in, said her son plays a better spy than Viacheslav Tikhonov's Stirlitz.³⁰ Viewers' chat forums drew the same parallels between the private and the public, between the micro- and macropolitical, in that the show's love affairs mirrored and yet outdid political allegiances:

> The film is amazing. It's absolutely the right thing to do, showing WWII and secret agents through the prism of human interaction .... We could do with a few more films like that, so young people could see cinema about their own history instead of endless, gory action flicks. I'm so glad that Russian cinema is coming back. Keep it up!

> The episodic historical film *The Red Choir* resurrects the traditions of the Russian spy series. Moreover it's an objective look at the work of secret agents during World War Two. On the other hand, viewers will also see the chief organizers of the Red Choir not just as professional agents, but as vivid characters, too – people who never abandon their wonderful compassion for others. (Promotional text.)

The series centers on the real-world adventures of Leopold Trepper (codename Jean Gilbert), who had been a Soviet agent in Paris – though the producers, as in many Soviet dramas, sometimes use Riga as a mock-up for the streets of France.³¹ The choice of this story is interesting, given that Trepper was Jewish and was rewarded by the Soviets for his priceless espionage work (which perhaps sealed victory at Stalingrad) with ten years in prison.³² *The Red Choir* quickly starts looking like an act of atonement reminiscent of *Bless the Woman*. Its producer, Valerii Todorovskii, first

Figure 4.1 Red Choir.

had the idea of making the film fifteen years prior, yet, just like the team who created *Poor Nastia*, he had no doubts about its contemporaneousness:

> This is a modern story. The series we've made is also modern, and that's really important. Of course there were [past] prototypes and real people behind all of this, but nonetheless it's a flight of fancy. It's a work of art,

not a documentary. The series was made to tell people a powerful story, to excite them.

Some people were excited very quickly. During filming in Paris "proper," an elderly émigré roller-skated up to the crew and was told the film was about Trepper. He skated up to Il'in, peered at his face, and declared: "Yup. Looks like him." He then zipped off.[33] The director addressed these thin lines between fact and fiction, between individual and epoch. In doing so, he slightly contradicted Todorovskii, thus blurring those lines even more:

> Of course there's an element of fantasy. But most of the heroes, together with the basic events in their lives, are strictly documentary. The characters act under their agents' names, not their real ones, so we have the right to at least *some* artistic imagination. Leopold Trepper himself used several names; one of them was Jean Gilbert and that's what he is known as for the entire series. And there's his main protagonist, too, a Gestapo officer – basically the man who broke the Red Choir wide open. He appears under his actual name.[34]

The one surviving member of the Choir, Anatolii Gurevich, was tracked down by the newspaper *Izvestiia* late in 2004. As a real person watching a story that claimed to remake or explicate the actual experience of many people, he likewise found himself stuck between reality and ropey fiction, especially because he hated the negative portrayal of his relatively minor figure in the screenplay:

> I just can't see the series as anything artistic; it's all tied too closely to my life. I can't relate to it as a historical work, either. Not only because Kent (that's my codename) is shown as a traitor. It's simply unbearable to see characters, my colleagues' prototypes, in such primitive and silly stories. I'm sure even the most naïve of viewers – who doesn't know the historical context – will get the impression the Red Choir were a bunch of dilettantes.[35]

Very many viewers said they were reminded of Soviet TV series and were glad *The Red Choir* was "free of all that ideology in Stalinist espionage films... The characters are defined not by class consciousness but by universal humanism."[36] Gurevich, however, remained upset and penned an article, saying *The Red Choir* had more in common with the "style of James Bond" than the day-to-day tedium of spying (a quotidian emphasis nonetheless represented on occasion by antique-laden sets). "What do we get at the end of the series?" asked Gurevich:

> Having taken real events and distorted them beyond recognition, the screenwriters have depicted a different life and different people. The film's creators didn't meet with me (they knew that I'm still alive!). They

took it upon themselves to depict my life as they saw fit; the life of my comrades according to the authors' daydreams.[37]

Gurevich's supporters found time and space to voice the same bitter views on a state intelligence website.[38] In representing history, the filmmakers had ignored the people who constituted it. One overarching, post-Soviet idea appeared to be ignoring the "human facets" it declared to be saving. People were less important than personalities; the idea of camaraderie overshadowed or swamped the actual comrades and the dignified bonds for which they risked their lives.

World War Two in the USSR: *The Children of the Arbat* (*Deti Arbata* [dir. Andrei Èshpai, 2004])

> I'd give every drop of my blood for you! I wouldn't shame you for anything!
>
> (Aleksandr Fadeev, *The Rout*, 1927)

Passions, both directorial and public, seethed around the potentially monumental TV version of Stalinist romance in *The Children of the Arbat*, even though sixteen years had passed since its publication – in essence the same period over which *The Red Choir* had kept its "contemporary relevance." The director said:

> The political aspect of the novel might look a bit naïve today, so it wasn't that important for us. The characters' destinies were much more significant; they haven't aged at all, not even today. We felt it was time to tell the story of one individual's ability to keep things together in an appalling period; the ability to maintain a clarity of vision in freedom's absence – to hold on to sincerity and some degree of self-worth.[39]

The novel was thus tweaked with a "new" relevance. Anatolii Rybakov's novel of absent freedoms had been translated into fifty-two languages after its 1987 publication and the producers matched that scale with modern means: *The Children of the Arbat* cost approximately $300,000. It included location work in Paris, Moscow, Tver', and Nizhnii Novgorod.[40] As in *The Red Choir*, politics were supposedly sidestepped in favor of the personal:

> The series takes place between 1934 and 1943. It is a story that will lead the audience into the Kremlin's offices, through the ambiance of communal apartments, into university lecture halls and prison cells. *The Children of the Arbat* will acquaint viewers with the life and daily routine of a Siberian village, with the towns of Russia's provinces. It ends with tragic events at the start of the Great Patriotic War. The heroes of this tale are down-to-earth boys and girls from Moscow's Arbat,

together with people at the very pinnacle of political power: Stalin and his entourage, Soviet workers, the leaders of academic institutions and of grandiose construction projects. This trilogy tells of all these people and of their spiritual worlds; it outlines their personalities and worldviews in a period that would become hugely significant for Russia's destiny.

Èshpai, despite his experience with the silver screen, was convinced that television could handle this scale by memories of his teacher at VGIK (the Russian State Institute of Cinematography), Tat'iana Lioznova, who had made *Seventeen Moments of Spring*. Musings on David Lynch's *Twin Peaks* (1990) likewise persuaded him that TV could also maintain a sufficiently striking cinematic quality. In an interview with the magazine *TV-Park*, he repeated his disavowal of the political content that once made the narrative so famous:

> Re-reading the novel today, I understood the most interesting thing is the interaction *between* the upper strata of political control and simple human destinies. Just think: so many lives were destroyed by one person's will, by the movement of an eyebrow, an interjection or a throwaway phrase. The theme of internal freedom among people "at the bottom of the pile" is very important here ... . The thing is, though, that freedom is hard to preserve nowadays, too, when individual choice – you'd think – actually has a wider range of options. That's why Rybakov's characters are relevant now, just as they were then.[41]

Something today is as nasty as it was yesterday and it threatens both families and lovers. Èshpai credited the generation of the 1930s and 1940s with a greater willingness to "interact" or socialize candidly than in the present day, when all is deceitful ostentation. TV could show the extent of that emotional openness in the face of malice.

Malice required a convincing portrayal of Stalin. Politics here were replaced by physiology. The hiring of a suitable actor caused great difficulty and involved protracted discussions with well-known figures like Stanislav Govorukhin and Viacheslav Tikhonov. Ultimately, however, the director chose Maksim Sukhanov, probably known best as a kindly, handicapped mobster in *Land of the Deaf* (*Strana glukhikh*, dir. Valerii Todorovskii, 1997). Despite being bald, tall, and only 40 years old, Sukhanov was forced into history and the body of a hirsute, older, and much shorter Stalin. The cameramen worked hard to film him constantly from the highest possible angle, therefore downplaying the issue of physical stature. Sukhanov, in actual fact, was such a difficult hiring that he was ready only when shooting was almost complete and, thus, had to be filmed outside the episodes' "true" or logical order.

Loftiness and chronology aside, Sukhanov also had trouble with the transformation of his face. He does play Stalin in a very disturbing manner, all slouches and accented mumbling; the plastic skin covering his visage mirrors the theatricality of his "Georgian-ness." Though scheduling required that he work quickly towards the end of general production, he (with equal speed) admitted the unpleasantness of wearing a synthetic face overnight and, therefore, returned to more traditional (that is, slower and expensive) techniques: three or four hours each day with the make-up artists.[42] Subsequent critical assessments compared him unfavorably and unfairly to the most famous Stalins of Soviet cinema.

And so a troubled love story was ready to come to television, having waited twenty-one years to be published – and thirty-eight years to be televised. Despite all this attention to historical detail, it had hoped to move away from stressing Stalin *alone*. The series' producer, Andrei Kamorin, again drove home this point, lest we forget: "To say that *Children of the Arbat* is about Stalin is like saying that *War and Peace* is about Napoleon." A desire to preserve the narrative and emotional breadth of the work for love meant that this TV drama should not shrink in the presence of cinema's actual breadth; the small screen needed to establish its own cinematic emphasis on detail (focus) and feeling (an atmospheric or ineffable "air") to claim the literal scale of a big screen synecdochically: "From the very outset we tried to maintain a cinematic language, no matter how hard it'd be. I think we were successful in creating the atmosphere and characters of a movie. I'd never make a serial that didn't have the air of a feature film."[43] Failure, said Kamorin, would come if focus swamped feeling, if history swamped sympathy for the little people who made it – and if the work was wrapped up in some pretension towards "a first-class *Forsyte Saga* with a 'nod' to the BBC."[44]

With Stalin in place, though (as just one man, not an entire dogmatically burdened saga), could the fantasy of little people go to work? With a hopefully convincing sociopolitical counterweight, micropolitical stories could perhaps proffer better versions of its workings. How, then, did viewers react to the depiction of faithful lovers Sasha and Varia (Evgenii Tsyganov and Chulpan Khamatova)? Some contributors to on-line TV forums noted a lyrical fluidity across sixteen episodes that managed to outpace the figure of Stalin altogether. One love story used and then dispensed with the politicking of one leader: "I love relaxing[!] to the series. It's so easy to watch – no effort at all. Things always finish in a way that you want to watch the next episode."[45]

Yet dissatisfaction, on the other hand, occasionally emerged whenever a historically (contextually) accurate mood was totally *absent*. Some emotional states and their depiction were felt to be too modern. Something was being redone, and faultily. Several of the young people playing Komsomol members, for example, were called "hooligans": "It's there in the book, in black and white: 'Open faces, radiant eyes.' But here there's nothing except cynicism or really bad overacting. Where can you find any other kind of face today, though?" The "faces of young people today, in 2004," were no happy alternative, but "there's nothing you can do about it."[46] The ongoing, spirited need of a TV station to emphasize a generation's passion led to overkill with the music, too, because "music [always] dictates a viewer's feelings" and the sound engineers were a bit overbearing. Emotionally, as a result, there might have been problems whenever history was totally suspended, but at least the show looked well funded and had its heart in the right place; at least it was "basically well filmed. And without promoting all that kind of American *chernukha*."[47] It was respectful.

When all was said and done, literary reputation had inspired a series dedicated to the maintenance of that reputation. In addition and consequently, *Children of the Arbat* expressed that respectful desire in a hopeful representation of reality *as* realia (as a physically similar dictator, promised by the producers). The actors do much to struggle against an archaic emphasis, though, and push love to the forefront – in particular Khamatova, who together with Tsyganov enacts in the series' closing episodes one of the most impassioned scenes of love in recent Russian drama. The life-threatening danger of maintaining private (in fact, often illegal) passion in a time of public, objectified fervor is so feral in its expression that the camera can barely keep up. Bodies throw themselves against bare, hollow walls with such disorder that the resulting shots of Tysganov and Khamatova give voice to people more beaten than loved, an image that comes back to haunt us in the very last frames. Their bullet-riddled corpses embrace in the lush, overgrown ruins of a stately edifice. Can the feeling ever escape the physical world, be contemporarily relevant and yet not look false? Some Soviet classics touted by their readers for exemplary accessibility fit the bill well. They show love, care and/or charity in expansive, natural domains that amplify those virtues, the same domains that were supposed venues of clearly expressed, strident Stalinist construction.

Father and son in today's cinema may likewise wander the nation in search of an emotional bond en route to the sea (*Koktebel*, 2003), or reach that same watery expanse to realize the tragic breach between them (*The Return*, 2003). The "active," angry construction of state plans may often lead to a disfigurement of kinships, be it emotional, psychological, or physical (*House of Fools*, 2002; or *My Stepbrother Frankenstein*, 2004). TV storytelling today begins to shape alternatives to this dead-end, where a family narrative can be the key to other, often material successes (which cinema itself has suggested in *A Parcel from Mars* [*Posylka s Marsa*]; *Happy New Year, Papa!* [*S novym godom, papa!*], or *Female Intuition* [*Zhenskaia intuitsiia*]). A family builds things.

Making love work to any one purpose, however, will be tough, since recent movies have made it magical (*Moon Daddy* [*Lunnyi papa*, 2000]; *Fourth Wish* [*Chetvertoe zhelanie*, 2004]; *Dark Night* [*Temnaia noch'*, 2004]), illogical (*Tender Age* [*Nezhnyi vozrast*, 2001]; *Goddess* [*Boginia*, 2004]; *Piter*

FM [2006]), comically dangerous (*It Doesn't Hurt to Dream* [*Mechtat' ne vredno*, 2005]), or, quite literally, directionless (*The Stroll* [*Progulka*, 2003]; *Connection* [*Sviaz'*, 2006]). This aimless, ever-busy process once sat deep in the most clamorous, industrious Soviet stories, like *Cement* (1925, 1932, 1947, or 1950). After all, even in its earliest, most severe edition, the ability of hero Gleb and the collective to manage the most elemental of forces – love, life, and/or (human) nature – is less than assured.

The Thaw and afterwards: *Two Fates* (*Dve sud'by* [dir. Valerii Uskov and Vladimir Krasnopol'skii, 2002])

> She no longer existed: she had drowned in the crowds, disappeared without trace ... There was only a great excited mass of people and thousands of hearts were beating inside him, too.
> (Fedor Gladkov, *Cement*)

Perhaps the best example of a romantically driven familial drama that did not draw upon classic literature or fact but nonetheless aimed for an emotionally absorbing, long-term cinematic sweep across the Soviet experience is *Two Fates*. It takes a step further away from shared or remembered actuality than *Children of the Arbat* in that its love stories are set in Soviet contexts, but employ those contexts only indirectly.

> At the center of the film are two tales of two women [Vera and Lida]. These village girlfriends in the early 1960s have their lives ahead of them; they are both young and beautiful. The Party's regional representative starts courting Vera seriously; Lida is not short of male attention, either. It seems their destinies are thus decided for many years hence. But everything is changed by the arrival of a specialist from Moscow, Stepan. Seeing him for the first time, Vera understands that this is love. Lida decides to use her chance [that is, to manipulate Stepan] and move to Moscow. As so often happens, a friendship between women is ruined because of men. These complex, interwoven predicaments start unwinding in totally unpredictable ways. Masks are removed, revealing the truth – and thus pulling more and more new characters into a whirlpool of events. Our heroines cherish both their dreams and their love through many years. Their private lives develop both dramatically and unexpectedly against the backdrop of the nation's complex destiny.

The closing reference here to things national may make us cringe in anticipation of more politics, but the fates of Vera and Lida (Ekaterina Semenova and Anezhelika Vol'skaia) are very clearly foregrounded. The series dragged some people away from sociopolitical reality with dramatic consequence, especially in a couple of Belarusian villages. Three times in a row, as locals

Figure 4.2 Two Fates.

sat down to watch *Two Fates*, a building somewhere nearby caught fire. The cause of the fires remained a mystery, though some people thought that nouveaux riches were using the empty streets during a very popular TV show to burn down houses – and then buy the land cheaply.[48]

Based upon two popular novels by Semen Malkov, *Ransom* (*Shantazh*) and *Retribution* (*Rasplata*), the broadcasts clearly contained enough successfully chosen elements to keep villagers indoors and produce Moscow investors willing to fund a second series. In blurbs for those future advertisers, we hear about "dramatic intrigue, dynamic action, and romantic conflict":

> All of this excites readers from the very first frames of the series. Semen Malkov, a delicate psychologist and linguistic master, has drawn the world of our contemporaries with unusual focus and brilliance. This all finds voice in the screenplay's details and skillfully crafted dialog.[49]

Investors were no doubt pleased to learn that the screenplay was written by Valerii Uskov and Vladimir Krasnopol'skii, who had brought Russia the airline drama *Beyond Jurisdiction* (*Nepodsuden*, 1969), plus *Shadows Vanish at Noon* and *An Eternal Summons*, mentioned already.[50] Succumbing, however, to the sad, swift "rhythm" of TV work, Uskov and Krasnopol'skii were by now pumping out two complete drama series per season, including the lengthy *Nina* (2001, discussed on p. 128). Some viewers sensed the spirit of a TV Taylorism:

> It looks like a cheap woodcut with all the signs of some weepy Mexican serial transferred to Russian soil ... The characters' experiences are so contrived, all the way from their love affairs to your obligatory historical chronicle that's just stuck in from time to time (Afghanistan, the Putsch, etc.). It's nothing more than "serial feelings" and it moves like a typical serial through the plot lines, too.[51]

Despite this complaint, the show does prove that viewers will happily watch romance dramas according to criteria *other* than historical realia, other than period costumes, plastic faces, or the right furniture. This is absolutely crucial in first recognizing and then bypassing literary, political, and historical specificity.

Conclusion: cash is not synonymous with credibility

If looking real is so important to producers, though, how much money is possibly left to fund quality screenplays and sets, in particular when the best-known thespians can take home much more than $7,000 per day? Ratings (as always) have to be considered, since every percentage ratings point today means more cash from advertisers tomorrow. By way of example, a series with a miserly 1 percent share can easily command more than $2,000 for a 30-second commercial. A show with a 10 percent share over a one-hour episode can bring in $300,000–400,000. An "encore showing" the next morning will conjure more cash still, as of course will later videos and any subsequent sale of the show *in toto* to another channel. What does not manifest itself today is a large amount of scripts, hence another reason for the fuss over Uskov and Krasnopol'skii. Perhaps because television screenwriters often receive little for their work, and so much is being set aside for spectacular verisimilitude, TV stations are repeatedly obliged to screen a large percentage of the material offered them by studios, material that is – as we know – itself produced under time constraints.[52]

Stations need primetime series like *Two Fates*, but even if they order them (that is, if they order precisely what they want) channels habitually cannot fund those dramas to a desired "spectacular" level; TV stations make money from advertising only *after* the serials are shown. This logic suggests that a rough period would be overcome if investment were offered in the short term. Indeed, in 2002 TV advertising brought in $900 million; by 2003 that figure rose to $1.3 billion and in 2004 to $1.78 billion. As money appeared, the production of TV series did not slow down – and the funds needed to "guarantee" a higher quality for future projects started coming in. But it sometimes seems that nobody in the living room cares that much about "quality." The emotional aspect of scenarios needs to be historically accurate, not the costumes, interiors, or make-up.

If so, maybe the success of the cheaper romantic melodramas (the success of thoughts and feeling over objects and locales) suggests there is no need to make classy detective and action serials *all* the time? Some chat-room pundits certainly thought so, but wondered how an emotively driven, often "pure" heroine might relate to the varnished figures of prior prose. In other words, if perfect people are more important than perfect places, does that not start to sound a little reminiscent of prior, varnished decades?

> This tradition [in *Two Fates*] of depicting the hero in social-psychological terms has become daily bread for Russian viewers. Even if it looks a bit schematic, it *is* about those viewers' lives. It helps people to get their bearings in very troubled times. Looking at these heroines, though, I suddenly recalled that I was never very fond of [socialism's] positive heroes. It's so strange to see almost exclusively perfect characters in a twenty-first century serial. It's so peculiar. Do people really have the same spiritual life as these heroines nowadays? Do they have principles? Some might say they're one-sided heroines. In reply I'll say: "So be it, I enjoy their company."[53]

The sentimental, if not loving, contact with characters themselves in love was the series' *raison d'être*, its core tenet. An article in the *Literary Gazette* compared *Two Fates* to the expensive mafia epic *The Brigade* and asked why on earth Russian critics and academics (not viewers) expressed a clear preference for the latter, much flashier serial. The sarcasm here is pronounced: "*The Brigade* is more dynamic, more striking, more shocking. But what about its ideas? Who needs ideas in an age that has none, anyway! We've got freedom!"[54] Despite critics preferring visual qualities to match something Western, the cheaper, emotional clout of *Two Fates* was so strong outside the scholarly community that rumors abounded of high-ranking police officers secretly hooked on the series (and who would on occasion break out in tears!). One acquaintance of lead actress Anzhelika Vol'skaia called her on the telephone with a similarly private response: "Likochka, d'you know what I'm doing now? I'm sobbing my eyes out."[55]

Romantically or sentimentally driven historical serials, by providing connections between then and now, help to stabilize the passage of time. That stability is contingent not upon a well-funded ability to *show* the past, but upon a well-intentioned ability to *empathize* with it. One could side with viewers here and suggest that any steady, heartfelt connections are the workings of an apolitical social network that often makes TV drama, rather than just receiving it. Given, however, the state's ownership of Channel One shares and the less-than-charitable workings of market-driven media, this may be the clever matching and manipulation of viewers' recognizable desires, rather than any homespun process in the hands of TV watchers themselves. Growing skepticism, for example, among Russia's elderly citizens over state altruism during the pension reforms of 2004 undoubtedly hinted that the distance from public endorsement to cynicism may never be that far, even in traditionally autocratic realms.

There have certainly been other historical series of late – such as 2002's *Beyond the Wolves* – which would prompt the public to think hesitantly or cynically about the workings (and our "real" knowledge) of the past. Starring the ever-engaging Valentin Gaft, this series with relative speed (188 minutes) relates a detective's labor during the wet month of March 1946, in a village near Moscow. A solidly built investigator (the ubiquitous Vladislav Galkin), just back from the Front, is sent by his superiors to discover whether some recent and savage murders are, as superstitious locals insist, committed by a werewolf. Suspicion and rumor in the village slowly increase prejudice against one severely retarded resident, cared for by Gaft's character. Charity, love, and attention are the only defense against others' angry ideas and their concomitant social insecurity, which becomes life-threatening: "The series is a mix of mystical horror, a detective series, and the horrors of Stalinism. All the time you're thinking: Is there really a werewolf or is this crime merely the product of cold human reasoning?"[56] The generous, attentive emotions aroused here can, if positive, outline a defense against yesterday's imaginary werewolves or other bad memories. Can they do so, though, against the heartless workings of today's capitalism and the Big City?

5 Melodrama
Little people in the Big City

The Russian backwoods look at us ... A multitude of faces, troubled, joyful and suffering.[1]
(Praise under Brezhnev for A. Malyshkin's *Liudi iz zakholust'ia*, 1937–38)

Moscow is not the countryside: socialist culture and today's notions of nature

In examining the traditions Putinesque television wishes to employ, we have moved from the supposedly geopolitical, imperially bounded concerns of "Soviet" tales to a form of storytelling that – when it's not angry – aims instead for a limitless, truly global and heartfelt notion of social membership. Today's President speaks – as did his predecessors – of unmanageable integration; his narratives require a heritage that cannot be enacted (nor, indeed, was it ever). Political stories and their proposed networks are *desirously* more organic than feasible. Following that assumption, it is necessary to scrutinize the way in which Soviet culture deals with a classic query of Russian literature, of Aksakov and Chekhov, say, when pondering one's relation to the unutterable membership of people within nature: "Could we human beings not learn to live in better harmony with nature, making measured use of her bounty to fill our needs, but without destroying either her beauty or her capacity for self-renewal?"[2] Attitudes to nature (to the romanticism of boundlessness) reveal the spirit of urbanization, of Moscow itself.

Under Lenin's governance, forests, waters, and minerals were swiftly claimed as state property, while huge tracks of uninhabited land were set aside, continuing the Romanovs' regal tradition of *zapovedniki*, i.e. provinces to be free of both development and tourism. These were to be places of ecological study, where man could learn how to live in harmony with nature, rather than falling to the unsophisticated excesses of capitalist rapaciousness. Lenin himself held, in any case, that "replacing the forces of nature with human labor would be impossible." Here the Bolsheviks were furthering a *possible*, well-established Czarist body of ecological thought, working towards the harmonious interaction of man's reason and the environment from the theories of the biologist Vladimir Vernadskii (b. 1863) on the evolution of the planet's biosphere as an open, spectacularly complex system of relations.

Maksim Gor'kii, writing in a pre-Revolutionary context, was among those who spoke up in favor of levelheaded scientific enquiry and conservation before the foundation of the Free Association for the Propagation of Positive Knowledge, headed by ecology activist V.I. Taliev. The *zapovedniki*, held the Association, were the ideal place of such enquiry and should be protected. One of the most valuable national reserves at this time was Askania-Nova in Ukraine; founded modestly in the nineteenth century as a zoo and botanical garden, it still operates today as research center for over fifty species of wildlife: Przewalski horses, zebra, bison, zebu, elks, steppe deer, antelope, and many others. Here the head administrator, Vladimir Stanchinskii, had some surprising, simultaneous theories about man's position in the natural world, allowing a pastoral harmony to inform the goal of harmonious, populated ecosystems.

These theories held that the quantity of living matter in the biosphere is relative to and dependent on the amount of solar energy transformed by photosynthesizing (autotrophic) plants, which Stanchinskii categorized as the "economic base of the living world." He also resorted to the Second Law of Thermodynamics to explicate differing masses between flora and fauna at the biosphere's highest, middle, and lowest levels. The higher a life form, the more energy was lost (as heat), because more effort/energy was needed to find sustenance. The world was therefore organized according to the fluid, imperceptible distribution and application of energy, to the "ubiquitous processes of chemical cycling and energy flow. His work represented an attempt to reduce biological phenomena to a common physical denominator: energy."[3] This early Soviet understanding of ecology as similarly interwoven, invisible forces will be important in later chapters. It is a rarely considered aspect of Soviet realism, though more than evident in today's attempts to label that which luridly flamboyant metropolises *lack*.

Lenin and Lunacharskii, Gor'kii's comrade and colleague, did much to help the creation of wildlife reserves very far from Moscow, and early Soviet conferences helped to prolong the life of a so-called "aesthetic-cultural" view of nature: "Free nature is a great synthetic museum, indispensable for our future enlightenment and mental development, a museum which, in the event of its destruction, cannot be resurrected by the hand of man."[4] In 1924 the Soviet All-Russian Society for Conservation (VOOP) was founded, and at its opening celebrations a congratulatory speech was read by Lunacharskii, a man able to see the relevance of his politicized words for open-armed, big-hearted social acceptance in both pastoral and ecological contexts.

Once Lenin had passed away, Stanchinskii's generous and *laissez-faire* attitude towards the forces of nature came under ever-increasing pressure, especially since the notion of "pure" science was slowly but surely being viewed as fundamentally bourgeois. By 1927 parks were viewed as more research-oriented than anything wholly aesthetic. Forests, rivers, and huge tracts of the steppe were manipulated in the name of socialist advancement. Stalin was interested in a more profitable, pragmatic attitude towards nature as a source: even the Academy of Sciences' magazine *Nature* was accused of *overly*-social, non-ideological comprehensiveness, being "the only journal where you can turn one thousand pages and never encounter the terms *socialism, communism, dictatorship of the proletariat*, etc."[5]

The Russian countryside remained a faultless, fondly remembered byword for social interaction, yet its quintessence stays *beyond* the socialist lexicon. It is a plenitude prior to language, as are the emotions and nostalgic, if not "childish" sentiments thereof. All three states (organic, nostalgic [or "folded"], and affective) are closer to Freud's "oceanic feeling" of membership. This feeling is useless for policy; it is excessive.

In Russian TV's neo- or proto-socialist tales that address these issues, Putin complains, for example, about children's television and its lack of suitable role models, for it is the grand, open expanse of an affectively driven worldview (ironically that *of* the children) that politics needs. It is the viewpoint that "elected" officials must aspire to – yet they can neither name nor equal.[6] Given the overriding importance documented thus far of "lack" or lacunae as a major theme for Russian TV drama, tales of a life *without* nature are ubiquitous. They, by reverse example, are founded upon a deep distrust for moneyed, urban "reality." The difference between towns and trees was extremely well documented in the roller-coaster experiences of Alena Babenko's heroine, Nina, for the rather mannered, if not histrionic 2005 series *Vaniukhin's Children* (*Deti Vaniukhina*, dir. Iurii Moroz): "Alena follows her loved ones from a village to Moscow. She finds out that she's pregnant, almost goes crazy, has a stroke and loses the ability to speak."[7] This chapter focuses on other metropolitan illnesses, on human nature *without* nature; after all, it took a bittersweet 2006 *comedy* series called *Nine Months* (*Deviat' mesiatsev*) for Russians to talk "seriously" about poor women having babies in affluent Moscow.

Life Lines (*Linii sud'by*, 2003) and *Hope Leaves Last* (*Nadezhda ukhodit poslednei*, 2004)

Russia's President often invokes the speechless, murky workings of capital as primary antagonist in his struggle for freedom and rectitude. The prototype of so many TV series in this rubric, *Moscow Does Not Believe in Tears*, is actually not associated today with acquisitiveness, neither thematically nor in terms of its director's future wealth. Vladimir Men'shov says he made no profit from the Oscar-winning Moscow family drama: "Not a penny." This is despite the fact it was seen by 85 million people, played in 20 Moscow movie theaters simultaneously, was purchased by 100 nations, and took $2.5 million at the US box office (after savvy American distributors bought it for a mere $50,000).[8] Today's tales of Moscow, set in similarly familial contexts, are gloomier because these patterns of career, profit, loss, and gain are no longer hidden.

The ensuing opposites of "individual and city," "small and large," or "inside and out" constitute the dominant structures in this rubric. The tale of a provincial figure (literal or metaphorical) who makes his/her way into the capital (or any other center of desire) from the kinder countryside is, in fact, so widespread that it requires subcategories, perhaps by degrees of success – in other words, where the hero or heroine finds him/herself on the road to accomplishment. We will therefore briefly sketch three such subgroups: TV series set at the bottom of urban society, tales of scrappy ascent, and, finally, narratives of vertiginous fame and fortune.

One of the most impressive stories of love-hungry bottom-feeders is *Life Lines*, produced by Valerii Todorovskii and directed by Dmitrii Meskhiev. Todorovskii has explained his own understanding of Russia's centripetal social movement:

> We live in a country that moves in forceful, often bloody ways. It doesn't always comprehend its own direction – neither the price to be paid nor the number of its victims. Nonetheless it *does* move and, when all is said and done, that movement has to result in something.[9]

In dramatizing patterns of social mobility, Todorovskii hoped to avoid the principled triteness of stories designed, as he put it, to clarify "Ten Ways to Improve Your Life." Aiming, therefore for some kind of verisimilitude without the narrow focus of a principled pamphlet, he called *Life Lines* "a huge modern novel":

> The main heroine here is, of course, Fate, that inimitable scoundrel and magician. Early one morning our provincial heroes step onto Moscow soil, both scared and full of bright hope. Yet they cannot imagine what awaits each of them within a month. The renowned movie director Dmitrii Meskhiev describes this brand new project as "a film about provincials and Muscovites. About people who've arrived in Moscow and try to establish a life in this beautiful and terrifying city. For some of them, things come together easily and simply; for others all hopes are dashed. The destinies of newcomers and Muscovites crisscross. For some this will be a fleeting encounter; for others it means a life-long relationship."

Viewers were impressed by this intricate crisscrossing of plotlines, but wondered if so much attention had been paid to artistry that veracity, in the most mundane sense, had fallen through the cracks. One example offered was the odd speed with which a married wounded officer – played by Sergei

Garmash – is granted an apartment (and the speed with which that same, barren apartment is then decorated for the couple).[10] Considering that the series touches upon all forms of love (familial, paternal, sibling, and even extra-marital), the types of desire that drive such connections were swamped by an unfeasible art, by slightly forced contrivances. That skill was not even exclusively optimistic, for the drama does much to outline radical compromises that dreamers make in Moscow, such as the on-stage career of Konstantin Khabenskii's singing hero. Nonetheless, documentary values were occasionally replaced by the arcane elegance of "fated" interaction.

Validating a narrative technique over sometimes displeasing reality is a stance that obviously runs the risk of undermining emotive veracity. This loss of likelihood is equally evident in a more recent, lighter STS series that debuted in the winter of 2004, *Hope Leaves Last* (dir. Evgenii Sokolov):

> Has your husband dumped you? Have you been fired? Have tricksters and scoundrels grabbed your apartment – while you've ended up in prison? Never give up! You can always find a way out of the most difficult situations. The main thing is never to lose spirit, your sense of humor, or your sense of self-worth.[11]

A bighearted, bold humor runs through the series' romantic stories, underwritten primarily by the wide-eyed pantomiming of Nonna Grishaeva, but any such offhanded jollity may, paradoxically, be the gift of those urbanites who have nothing to hope for. The loveless can crack a joke or two, since there's nothing else to do. People facing the risk of choice, however, cannot afford always to look on the bright side of life, hence the greater misery of both romantic and kindly subplots in *Life Lines*.

Metropolitan progression and aimlessness, chronology and nomadism, urban "somebodies" and rural nobodies are inseparable in Soviet society and beyond. Alain Badiou, considering these oppositions, holds that Soviet society embodied a dovetailing of plenitude and absence, something and nothing twice over. These bonds are discernible if we approach socialist culture through "Sartre's conception of radical subjective freedom as *being* nothing, as an objective nothingness, or *néant* – that is, a freedom that determines its existence at each moment, as an ongoing 'creation ex nihilo' – and Marx's conception of the proletariat as *having* nothing, 'nothing to lose but their chains.'"[12] Today this role of absence (and all-consuming, paradoxically enticing presence) is played not only by the ineffable promise of nature that cannot be spoken. It is also mirrored by the center of an absent empire towards which rural or provincial people (*with* nothing) still strive and where they often *find* nothing of worth, either materially or ethically.

Cinema has made this clearer still. Among Russian movies with international budgets, the two performances by Vladimir Mashkov in *The Quickie* (2001) and *Oligarch* (2002) do so with the wealthiest, crudest lucidity; their sinister tales of ruinous cash take place in L.A. and Moscow. Money and the absence of stable, time-honored hierarchies reflect one another; they lead to the type of frenzied or predatory behavior in films such as *In Motion* (2002), where Moscow's get-rich world of tabloid journalism and scandal leads to an accelerated, if not frenzied editorial style. Calm, social cohesion is absent.

An Ideal Couple (Ideal'naia para, 2001) and *Request Stop (Ostanovka po trebovaniiu*, 2000)

This capital strain (in several senses) within today's emotionally driven films and series leans somewhat heavily on the 2001 drama *An Ideal Couple*, directed by Alla Surikova and starring Aleksandr Baluev with Alla Kliuka, who is recognized now more for TV work on Dar'ia Dontsova's detective series than anything from her late-Soviet filmography. The drama tells of two foreign tricksters far from Moscow who come to Russia, finding both love and financial intrigue as they do so. It enjoys such a following even today that the moderators of several chat rooms sometimes need to calm people down:

> Please don't post things like "Super!" "Best of all," "Don't like it," "Get off!" and so forth. We'll delete those posts and leave only what's genuinely interesting. Anything offensive or rude will be removed at once! And don't put much faith in short messages sent from one and the same computer, either; trust a range of messages from a range of people.[13]

In 2001 several actors – like Baluev – started popping up with increasing frequency and success. Work was available and dramas picked up speed. As the public's attention turned from cinema screens to television sets, journalists wondered if TV might even become "the salvation of Russian cinema," having recovered from the recent stock market crash so quickly.[14] Cultural deliverance lay, in this case, in the hands of two love-struck criminals, who – opposed to any prior, honorable heroes – "care nothing for eternal life. They'd prefer to get everything they can here, in *this* life." Surikova was keen to point out in interviews, however, that these were principled thieves, "the grandchildren of Robin Hood!"[15] Criminality existed willy-nilly, so love could purportedly teach one urban crook to steal from another (worse) felon, thus putting immoral gains to moral ends. At approximately the same time, *Request Stop* debuted on Channel One in an attempt to conjure a latter-day dreamer with reasonable odds of victory. The promotional rhetoric used a few years later when the series was sold to REN-TV makes this more than clear. Here is Aleksei Slapovskii's perfect skeleton for the perfect post-Soviet drama, even playing with a phrase or two from Mexican serials as it ponders the role of love amid socio-economic turmoil in the Big City:

> We've not yet come to our senses, but life has already dragged us off in all kinds of directions. Nothing but princes and paupers, queens and

Melodrama 109

Figure 5.1 Request Stop.

Cinderellas, the rich (who "also cry") and the poor (who also laugh). Without even going anywhere, we've suddenly ended up in different worlds. And people from different worlds don't usually cross paths. Yet sometimes those paths *do* cross in chance and strange ways, leading to the most unpredictable consequences. At a certain request stop on the outskirts of a typical Russian town, that is, at a place where the bus

110 *Russian television today*

driver will only stop if you *really* ask him to, a mild-mannered man stands in the rain. His name is Smirnov. He has decided to go to his mother's place after a minor spat with his wife Natasha. A beautiful woman, Irina, drives past in her dazzling car from her dazzling life. She's business-like, liberated, and independent. (There was a husband, but he got sick of it all.) She drives her car through a puddle (accidentally) and soaks poor Smirnov from head to toe. She'd only have to laugh and drive on ... yet either from some whim or a sudden act of genuine kindness she picks up Smirnov, takes him home, dries him off, and warms him up. Then she releases him back into the world. She wasn't attracted to him – after all, he does have a few odd quirks. He gets totally drunk after a single glass of wine and faints if anybody shouts at him.[17]

This odd couple grows closer and closer to love, for he brings her a charming, sometimes dangerous naïvety from the grassy provinces into a world where benevolence and charity are rarely a good (or profitable) idea. When we take these disarming innocents and transfer them into society, Smirnov (Dmitrii Pevtsov) and Irina (Ol'ga Drozdova) are habitually defined through gendered expectations or sweeping generalizations, as noted earlier: kind women help and improve rough men through romance. Conversely, kind men like Smirnov might fix strong women. They could fix the post-perestroika, haggish, and hardhearted female bosses of the song "Working Woman" (*Delovaia zhenshchina*) by Laima Vaikule and Valerii Leont'ev way back in 1986. She says: "You! You there! Why are you sleeping at work?" He replies: "I was visiting my friends yesterday. Dancing, too. I'm very sorry!" Cities can do something unnatural to those in love.

Another Life (Drugaia zhizn', 2003), A Bomb for the Bride (Bomba dlia nevesty, 2004), and I Love You (Ia tebia liubliu, 2004)

I saw a play about a young schoolgirl educating some old, silver-haired professor. *Everybody* was in tears, audience and manager; even the box-office girl downstairs was wiping away her tears with three-ruble notes ... Honestly, Soviet sappiness is dreadful!
(Leonid Leonov, *Skutarevskii*, 1932)

A good example of this modern, iron lady of the Big City is offered by *Another Life*, a tale of Moscow-bound provincials starring Channel One morning TV host Ekaterina Strizhenova – as a TV host. Juxtaposed with the capital (by a four-hour drive) is a tiny village, where a woman with child and motorcycle-collecting husband suddenly feels very disappointed by her fate. She decides to look for better love and a better address, and thus instigates a story evoking sympathy for those stuck in the lifeless provinces, while criticizing their occasional recourse to desperation. The director and

Figure 5.2 Another Life.

screenwriter, Elena Raiskaia, hoped that *Another Life* would survive in the sea of dramatic serials for three reasons: first, because "Life can actually be interesting without gunfights and criminals"; second, because "Viewers will never tire of the relationships between a man and a woman"; and, finally, because "We've found a new narrative form here. Our series is one big talk show, where the heroines each tell their story." The series uses a celebrity to play a celebrity and as a result the romance remains far from most people's normality. The same is true of *A Bomb for the Bride* (dir. Aleksandr Pavlovskii), which employs Vladimir Vishnevskii as a game-show host and moderately gifted singer Iuliia Nachalova as a singer. Their show is supposed to help couples win cash and prizes they will need to improve their new, shared bank accounts.

A similar focus upon the individual within Moscow's upward socialization comes in the series *I Love You* (dir. Viacheslav Krishtofovich, 2004), a rather banal title that sadly resulted from dropping the original name of Ekaterina Vil'mont's novel, *I Want a Babe on Rollerskates!* (*Khochu babu na rolikakh!*):

> For many years, the heroine of this series was only ... a wife. Caring, faithful, and dedicated. She [Aleksandra] loved her husband, a well-known actor, without reservation and assumed he felt the same way. It turned out, however, that things weren't quite so sunny; in an instant her secure world falls apart. How hard it is to start all over again! But she gets through all the hardships, showing exceptional character as she becomes happy, famous, and wealthy ... And, most importantly, love – the main thing in life – will warm her heart once again.

Starring the statuesque Mariia Shukshina from *Brezhnev*, this story starts with marital pressures caused when her actor-husband suddenly becomes an overnight success in an Italian production – and is thus surrounded by hordes of young female fans. Fortune visits the husband, leaving the wife with only tough choices. The popular magazine *TV-Seven* (*Telesem'*) was willing even mid-series to put its faith in her *fate*, rather than worry about the *choice* of infidelity made by her husband (Iaroslav Boiko). Destiny and doubt are all mixed up. "Will Sasha be successful? Yes, of course! ... A new life, new love, and a wonderful future."[18] The underlying idea that fate decides all and happiness is synonymous with fame (requiring no more than patience) led to significant audience sympathy: "The serial really kept my interest. It seems I experience all the blows in Aleksandra's fate together with her." Those blows, however, are often countered by Aleksandr Abdulov's character, offering sage advice, fidelity, and loads of money or love from the sidelines. Likelihood here looks unlikely.

Side by Side with Love (*Parallel'no liubvi*, 2004), *Society Pages* (*Svetskie khroniki*, 2002), and *Polka-Dot Heaven* (*Nebo v goroshek*, 2003)

> Love, life, and his whole heart – he knew he could trust them to her; she'd never spoil or harm them. Everything in him was open to her; nothing was left except Dasha herself. And she *knew* so.
> (Galina Nikolaeva, *Bitva v puti*, 1957)

I Love You, incidentally, is far from the only romantic serial in which Abdulov plays a fairy godfather. This role is a troubling one in the romantic melodrama, for it suggests that the grandest love needs the biggest bank account, and here we slip into some of the beachfront banalities of the *telenovela*. In *Side by Side with Love*, mentioned earlier, money, Muscovite (criminal) acumen, and political clout are all terribly sexy. The serial is remarkable in that its hero, played by Igor' Lifanov, offers without contest the most browbeaten protagonist of any romantic drama. Though now very successful, as a child he was dragged into a world of child slavery, pedophilia, and snuff movies. Lifanov himself, the star of many action series on television, here moves in his own romantic biography from less than nothing to everything – yet we see none of this happening. People just happen to be rich and just happen to save the occasional heroine. It was all just supposed to happen, given time; he moves to the countryside to learn how.

The same is true of the rather tedious *Society Pages* (dir. Valerii Zelenskii and Andrei Kuznetsov), which, although involving the adventures of a magazine staff "behind the scenes of bohemia," revolves around the growing love between a famous photographer (Galkin) and a TV host. Before their friendship even starts looking like a romance, we have what the promotional materials aptly call a "beautiful couple." Things are the way they are. Another series that ends in equally well-financed happiness whilst incorporating the provincial thematic is *Polka-Dot Heaven* (dir. Vladimir Balkashinov). It both plays upon the type of centripetal tales outlined so far and acquires a second "provincial" aspect in that it was filmed and funded by the Ukrainian TV industry. Here the Moscow heroine moves far away from the capital and finds both financial and familial success. Perhaps this was why the series would hopefully mark the "renaissance of Ukrainian cinema."[19] Not only was filming south of the border cheaper, but the crew did not even wait for seasons specified in the screenplay; autumnal scenes were shot in fur coats – when in actuality the outdoor temperature was over 30° Celsius.[20]

Sweating all the way, the actors and actresses plowed through an eight-episode series in two months, producing the dramatic tale of an innocent's education in the world of greed and greenbacks:

> It all begins with a train accident. The main heroine (Klavdiia) finds a baby girl (Zhenia) by the riverside. Somehow this youngster has survived the catastrophe. Klavdiia takes Zhenia to a hospital in the nearest small town. Not long afterwards she adopts the girl and establishes the town's first casino.[21]

Promotional materials fleshed out this mysterious brevity:

> A young and enterprising woman from Moscow, Klavdiia, having amassed a decent sum of money, leaves the capital once and for all. She sets off for the deep provinces in order to bring them civilization. She starts by opening a casino in a small town. The rural residents meet this Moscow guest somewhat coldly, with distrust and caution, and then the people who lose their income to Klavdiia's casino enter into direct conflict with

her. A woman will always find the strength of endurance within her, though, despite all the scheming of her enemies and any failures in her private life. Klavdiia manages to re-establish the club after it is burnt down – and at the same time raise a little girl she found as a toddler on the side of the road. Similarly, she also manages to discover, at long last, her "other half" and starts living happily.

If this is starting to sound a bit silly or far from feasibility, TV audiences thought so, too. Given the fatalism (or mysterious destinies) outlined thus far that viewers often seem to accept, any wild manipulation of another social realm can seem rather unconvincing:

> There's one crowd scene in the casino bar, where everybody's smiling and happily dancing along to some criminal song that does nothing more than underline the crisis in this TV genre. Where can you find a casino were the public smiles so much – *and* applauds the artiste?[22]

Dear Masha Berezina (*Dorogaia Masha Berezina*, 2004)

Moneyed, deterministic and Moscow-centric dramas have been most spectacularly represented by the condescension of *Dear Masha Berezina* (dir. Ekaterina Dvigubskaia, Petr Krotenko, Stanislav Libin, and Aleksandr Smirnov), a series also blessed with the most ostentatious of websites. Worryingly fond of its own affectedness, the site – among other bells and whistles – intended to bless a few viewers with a rare chance to enter its world, either virtually (real-time chat with the actors) or temporarily (a small walk-on part in the series). The opportunity to be blessed by that which cannot be freely *chosen* leaves the prizes' recipients shell-shocked, especially one young man:

> I *want* to be famous. I know people like turning *women* into celebrities, but that's so unfair! How are men any worse? I'm such a great fan of movies, too. I watch all the new releases ... Starring in a TV series, it seems to me, will be a great way to start showing myself "on stage." I must say, though, that I'm not an actor – and never will be – but it'll be interesting to try myself in this role, to see myself on the screen and in the company of stars. It'll be a new experience, so why not?[23]

The chat-room passions were occasionally just as fervent in their defense of gloss: "WHY D'YOU KEEP COMPLAINING ABOUT AN'KA FOR? SHE'S A SUPER HEROINE AND IF YOU DON'T LIKE HER, THAT'S YOUR OWN OPINION – SO KEEP IT TO YOURSELF ... !" Yet the comeback lacked no verve: "IT'S CRAP: I just don't like this serial. It's too much like films from Hollywood. 'Romance à la Hollywood.' Basically it's utter shit."[24] The centripetal, but very un-provincial tale of model Masha returning to Moscow after the catwalks of Paris, Milan, and London was – like *Poor Nastia* – shot using American technology and cost about $100,000 per episode. Parallels between the two series can be further justified because many of the budgetary and teamwork figures coincide. Jumping each and every time to meet these new, expensive benchmarks, Parisian scenes would be shot exclusively in Paris (not Riga) and only the finest hotels, banks, bars, and shops would be employed for Moscow episodes.[25]

What is interesting, however, is how the series' rigid thematic stereotypes, offered to viewers from afar (culturally speaking), were contradicted by its structure. The producers stayed barely ahead of each broadcast date, altering storylines according to audience reactions. This approach, though stressful, allowed episodes to reference recent events directly, such as Mariia Sharapova's Wimbledon victory in the summer of 2004. Viewers did not want anything except happy material, no matter its unattainability in a lofty class. As the main actress, Anna Azarova, noted in an interview for the magazine *Your Leisure Time* (*Vash dosug*):

> We're filming a fairy tale about a beautiful life. Beautiful people, cars, clothes, homes, and love. We're all already tired of the negativity in our own reality. When I myself go home tired after work and push a button on the TV remote, I feel I need a fairy tale, too.[26]

It was hoped that the needs of beauty-starved viewers would increase both audience share and creative activity at STS (founded in 1996). In 2004 the channel ran 27 series in its schedules, as opposed to 87 on Rossiia.[27]

Keen to start its salvation with a bang, STS planned the debut of this A-Media/Sony Pictures epic right after the final whistle of 2004's European Football Championship. The opening credits might therefore reach the 100 million viewers who could not reach for the remote fast enough.[28] Given the tedium of that final match, STS's audience was no doubt keen on excitement, in fact $6 million worth – "a budget to make *Isaura the Slave* or *Kamenskaia* jealous!"[29] An unreal financial plan, piggy-backing on Europe's greatest sporting event; an unreal plot and fairytale resources: *Dear Masha Berezina* soon overshadowed any kind of contact with the outside world on a human scale. STS even placed a clock in the corner of the television screen, counting down to the 21:00 start of the series. The clock looked remarkably similar to the same logo used by other channels to remind viewers of impending daily news broadcasts.[30] *Masha Berezina* would tell you all you need to know about the world.

In this light, consider the recent success of STS that – in the eyes of some – has forced even NTV to follow suit and abandon political critique. Since undergoing a change of management in May 2002, its core audience of 18–45-year-olds has risen by 54 percent. It has overtaken NTV and become the third-largest purchaser of series, after Channel One and Rossiia. It shows no news, replacing bulletins with comedy and feature films; Russian broadcasts constitute 40 percent of the line-up and the rest are foreign.[31] No station is growing faster. Director Aleksandr Rodnianskii, commenting upon this editorial framework, has noted:

> STS has positioned itself in the market not just as an entertainment channel for young people. It creates a domain of positive emotions, a world of beautiful and strong men, a world of beautiful women. It's a window onto another world, instead of being a window onto the courtyard of your apartment building.[32]

We will return to the equally positive and beautiful comedies of STS in Chapter 6.

The flipside of this approach can be just as successful, too. Attracting public interest by manipulating a large number of darkly funny, *negative* examples is the most famous example of social discord, Dmitrii Nagiev's show *Windows* (*Okna*). It uses actors to play out their angry, urban disputes in the style of *The Jerry Springer Show*. Very often these disputes have been performed with sufficient understatement that millions of viewers take them as reality, despite the impractical reasons for which the participants supposedly reach a social impasse. They typically concern generational or marital disagreement over some form of loss – money, housing, employment, prestige, or a once-faithful spouse – caused by the greed of another. Such is the assumed nature of typical lives and really typical people in Moscow.

Typicality or verisimilitude vs. Moscow's reality TV

If Moscow's allure causes so many *unnatural* social problems, maybe verity (human nature) could be best observed in an isolated bubble, in a social laboratory with no address – a place that is nowhere in particular and therefore potentially *anywhere*. According to this logic, reality TV could help us to see how human interaction, divorced from the faceless socializing of gigantic cities, operates today. Maybe the "harmonious networks" of beloved Russian storytelling would then come to light? In bringing a potentially universal actuality to television, the first, most famous step was ventured by the 2001 reality series *Za steklom* (*Through the Window*), a version from TV6 of the popular Western *Big Brother* broadcasts.

Six contestants were locked in a tailor-made apartment, itself housed inside Moscow's *Rossiia* hotel, though the city itself was out of bounds. The players were left to go about their lonely business, leaving some to suggest that the idea of a "game" *per se* was unlikely to foster parity. Indeed the participants' presence in this ongoing competition was decided by public vote, by exclusion, leading to the gradual choice of a winner who would receive an apartment (worth approximately $30,000 at the time). Over the initially planned broadcast period of thirty-four days, interested parties could follow the three men and women either during regular TV broadcasts (commented upon by psychologists) or via a live, 24/7 web feed.³³ At the same time as this voyeurism, an equally piquant, formless (and thus "real") chat show was also enjoying great success: *Dirty Laundry* (*Bol'shaia stirka*). Everything was being hung out – for all to see.³⁴

Politicians were soon complaining that this *unfiltered, unmanaged* reality was straying at times in the direction of "pornography," and indeed one male contestant left *Za steklom* with relative speed after his fiancée declared that his behavior, seen nationwide, was starting to dishonor her family.³⁵ Nonetheless, the show's website logged over 13 million hits in the first three weeks; pirated highlight videos also appeared in the capital's marketplaces after sex between two contestants was recorded on film.³⁶

This purportedly Russian chaos had a foreign precedent. The Dutch company Endemol, responsible for the very first closed-door reality show, was outraged at *Through the Window*'s abuse of a copyrighted format and immediately declared it would prosecute TV6.³⁷ Nineteen stations around the world were already making similar broadcasts and paying a license fee; the Russians had refused to cough up. Business practices outside Moscow's *Rossiia* hotel were spoiling (if not manipulating) those inside with unreasonable promises of self-promotion.

These calculating broadcasts had begun to appear when Boris Berezovskii was the major shareholder of TV6; he, perhaps as a result, decided simultaneously to use that channel for a strangely dual purpose. He began maximizing the station's political critique (which was financially risky) whilst pandering to the lowest, most profitable common denominators in his entertainment listings. His aesthetic standards would bankroll the risk of passing judgment on the Kremlin. After all, the TV advertising market had grown 74 percent between 2000 and 2001, to a record high of $400 million; over the same period US TV advertising revenues had fallen by 11 percent. Things were looking up, thanks in part to cheap, scheming, and socially perverse reality shows.

Moscow's profit margins would continue to alter the nature of actuality; the longer the show, the happier the advertisers. Most successful in this regard has been the related reality broadcast of *House 2* (*Dom 2*), still ongoing (each and every day) two years after the arrival of its initial contestants. The format has since been purchased by Sony, despite discussion of its "immorality" in the Duma. Based on a similar elimination process to *Za steklom*, this show involves a group of young people building a house together just outside Moscow; as the construction work progresses, romance between the players either blossoms or founders. Long-term couples are afforded better accommodation, while unloved players face a greater chance of exclusion. Eliminated contestants now easily outnumber the remaining six "core" couples. Their fame has reached the point where their real lives, filmed around the clock, have engendered other forms of lucrative fantasy: these include recording music, performing in massed holiday concerts, starring in films, and hosting their own talk shows.

The young "builders" range from 18 to 30 years in age, and come from all across Russia; provincial participants outnumber those from big cities. Together we watch them lead their lives over a time span that puts several long-lived dramas to shame:

> This project has lasted a very, very long time. Over this [two-year] period we've seen song and dance, romantic dates and break-ups, jealousy, intrigue, love-triangles, and fisticuffs. We've even seen a couple of weddings! True, nobody has had any babies yet, but perhaps that's just a matter of time?

Overseeing the private performances are the two young female presenters, Kseniia Borodina and Kseniia Sobchak, daughter of St. Petersburg's first post-communist mayor. Both these adjudicators of others' fates are the darlings of Moscow's nightlife. Sobchak advertises a number of perfumes and fashion houses. She also plans to enter politics.

Other shows have used measured eliminations or exclusion to observe behavioral changes in claustrophobic actuality. The best example here would be the NY-based *Hunger* (*Golod*), the format of which amazed some Western observers:

> The pitch for the show? Thirteen Russian twenty-somethings who don't speak a word of English are brought to a house in Queens. In order to eat they either complete a task given by the producers or they go out into the city and try to get it themselves (like Kristina Kalinina, who made $112 by going up to men and screaming, "Give me money and I'll take off my clothes and dance!"). Once a week a pair of contestants goes out into the city and competes to see who can get more money or food. The pair is then flown back to Russia where the audience decides who should stay and who should go. The winner of the show gets a $2,000 monthly pension for life ... So, how long till [the US channel] FOX picks up *Hunger* and sends some Americans to Moscow?[38]

The Russian promotional materials, however, drew a much more dignified parallel with an event from Soviet history that had once become the subject of many songs. In 1960 four Soviet soldiers had been cast adrift in a boat off the coast of Sakhalin for forty-nine days and nights, by which time they had eaten their boots, belts, and even an accordion. They were saved, well on their way to Hawaii, after a chance discovery by American sailors. "The whole world," said *Golod*, "admired the courage and endurance of these Soviet soldiers, who resorted neither to madness, nor to cannibalism. The Russians held this feat of their own military men in the highest possible regard."

After 106 days, *Hunger* was won by a certain Katia Nemova. In her victory interview for the host station, TNT, she first insisted that everything had been filmed as part of real-time actuality. No screenwriters, said Nemova, had been involved in any artificial, predetermined adventures. The experience had taught her what she was capable of, that she could "achieve something" in life.

One media analyst, drawing a parallel between these reality shows and Russia's TV dramas or post-Mexican soaps, pondered the common issue of "reality" therein. She concluded that their tactics of claustrophobia made events *unreal*, since a third of reality shows worldwide produce a nervous breakdown in one or more contestants. The resulting, voyeuristic *Schadenfreude* of *Dom 2*, *Golod*, and other series was, held the analyst, a consequence of massive emotional suppression under the Soviets. Affective expansiveness was "inherent" in the Russian people, but it had been unable to express itself until now – hence the slightly warped, if not hysterical, nature of these broadcasts. They were turning an urgently desired, long-constrained affect into desperately sought, "almost narcotic" drives for frankness. That honesty, however, was unable to shake off the conditions placed upon it by audience expectation (for sex, profanity, and so forth).[39]

Other instances of this format have also been taken wholesale from the West, even more directly than *Za steklom*. Two good examples are REN-TV's *Temptation Island* (*Ostrov iskushenii*) and Channel One's *Survivor* (*Poslednii geroi*, literally *The Final Hero*). Of the latter we hear that

> four single couples set off to a distant exotic island, where they'll put their relationships to the test. Upon arrival the couples are broken up and sent far from each other, to different hotels. These divided pairs [between 21 and 31 years of age] won't be able to communicate directly. Besides exotic nature and ocean beaches, our contestants will also find "tempters or temptresses" of the opposite sex. These are young, single and active people. Our fun-loving travelers will be happy to start a relationship on this island, and maybe even find their destiny ... The divided couples will go on lots of dates with their tempters; maybe that'll lead to new couples and new relationships, too.

Properly licensed this time (via FOX), with no complaints from Hollywood, *Ostrov iskushenii* offered little in the way of originality, since by the time it ran in Russia versions had already aired over the last four years in Britain, Australia, France, Germany, Spain, Greece, Hungary, Belgium, and all across Scandinavia. It was hosted by Vladislav Galkin, thus bringing the ideas of serialized (make-believe) stories and biographies even closer. Interestingly enough, just before the series began, Galkin said anybody who puts their lives through a process such as *Temptation Island* is not within the framework of objective actuality; they are, he believed, willingly submitting their reality to manufactured changes that constitute something else entirely, a "parallel potential." Irina Varlamova, producer of the series, clarified this difference succinctly when she said that this latent, analogous form of authenticity had one significant downside: *cruelty*. It would make the Russian version of *Temptation Island* different and "more entertaining." No single term, it seems, better defines the failure of reality TV to attain or even reflect a historically validated, endlessly desired *habitus* from literary Russian storytelling.

Various seasons of *Poslednii geroi* tried similar uses of an "exclusive" cruelty, set in progressively more exotic locales, each time in the name of a 3 million ruble purse. The shows moved between Panama (for the debut season of 2001), Malaysia, and Haiti, at which point the contestants were no longer badly behaved plebs but *bona fide* TV stars – or at least those who could do with a little extra publicity: Ekaterina Semenova, Iuliia Nachalova, and Zhanna Friske, for example, all starred in the 2003 series.

The most consequential of all these overlaps has been the musical talent series *Fabrika zvezd* (*Star Factory*), in the spirit of *American Idol*. It has currently offered the nation five separate competitions on Channel One. This potentially endless series "offers young talent a unique opportunity to present itself [in the Moscow arena], to find its place on today's musical Olympus and enhance today's music business. Come on and join in the production of our Factory's stars! Take part in the voting! For the very first time you'll see how new stars are born on the Russian stage."

Among the show's more famous judges is chanteuse Alla Pugacheva. Her reasons for taking part speak once more to a *possible*, "parallel" amelioration of reality in the middle of Moscow. Her own website tells us as much. Pugacheva stands against urban, unfair providence – all in the name of little nobodies. The relation of the following quote to *Fabrika*'s evenhandedness or actuality is, however, open to considerable debate; recent editions of the show have included young contestants who are already of some renown. The most egregious example of this was St. Petersburg vocalist Zara in 2006:

> Pugacheva's unique quality is a finely-honed sense of equality. Bad people who fall into her "bio-field" either become *good* people, or they vanish completely. She can be a saint or a sinner; she can be awful, too – just like any other woman. People love, fear, respect, and worship her. Pugacheva's songs help people to survive, to believe in themselves. There's never been any aggression in her songs. She's been called a "secret weapon" because she has always helped people dream of something better.[40]

Equally consequential and magnanimous judges in this production of starry-eyed expectancy have been musical producers Igor' Matvienko and Maks Fadeev, together with well-known composers Igor' Krutoi and Igor' Nikolaev. They help to "guide typical groups" of approximately twenty young boys and girls through twelve weeks of grueling competition. Occupying Channel One's busy "Star House" in Moscow, they may call friends and relatives only once every two days. Approximately 400 letters a day arrived at Channel One during the 2004 shows in the hope of reaching the participants, yet none, says the station, made their way through the

800 staffers working on the show. This, once again, is improbable, given that the rules regarding phone-based texting were considerably weaker. Each of the contestants, it was rumored, got about 100 messages per day. Texting was then overshadowed by the high degree of web-based traffic (including forums), constituting a total of 3.6 million hits on the show's site.

All this activity has a goal: exhibition. It is social only because it is directed towards strangers; the claustrophobic confinement of passionate, frequently peeved youngsters is eventually transported to the grandest of all Moscow stages for collective, far-reaching concerts. The finale of the 2003 series gathered 17,000 people in Moscow's Olympic stadium. At the end of the 2004 season, one of the contestant winners, Nastia Stotskaia, likewise took part in a five-hour musical concert at the Kremlin, broadcast from coast to coast. It was hosted by the singer Valeriia (the "voice of Russia") and the nation's most famous impressionist, Maksim Galkin. These are not isolated examples of well-funded pomp; the nationwide interest in *Fabrika zvezd* now leads on a regular basis to many musical extravaganzas in which well-established stars (such as Pugacheva's daughter) and neophyte contestants sing together to mutual benefit or profit.

The degree of cynicism regarding Moscow's reality and talent shows has grown in recent years. Producers' rhetoric habitually stresses evenhandedness, but in doing so it merely hints at a supernatural triumph for those people who would never normally dream of such things. If the wealthiest, most influential (or adept) bribers would keep winning reality shows, the public could at least take heart in a comforting fatalism. Everybody, however, is offered everything in longwinded pledges, but nobody gets anything. Thus is Muscovite reality presented; no wonder TV's heroes and heroines keep escaping to the countryside, as we will see on many occasions.

What remains is a *managed*, restricted, or proscribed version of expansiveness, the product of a 1970s Brezhnevian tradition. The best example thereof is the messy, "speakeasy" format of Channel One's 2006 talk show *No Hang-Ups* (*Bez kompleksov*). Supposedly an adlibbed interaction with stars and audience, where the host Lolita Miliavskaia "hides nothing and judges nobody," the broadcasts stay firmly within the twee, tidy limits of a profitable daytime format. Miliavskaia herself, born in 1963, is a perfect product of this managed generation, which, as mentioned earlier, constitutes 70 percent or more of today's TV staff.

Conclusion: wary of "unnatural" excess, today's TV borrows a middle ground from Brezhnevian traditions (and their loss)

> All I can see inside myself is a throng of intersecting lines; one of them flies upwards, beyond the limits of my paintings.
>
> (Leonid Leonov, *Skutarevskii*, 1932)

Russia's impoverished public and wealthy performers, the men and women like Miliavskaia who once took solace from the songs of Pugacheva, do so now from the films of that long-gone era. They turn to the movies of Brezhnev's office, which pepper TV line-ups every single New Year's Day and Christmas, in fact whenever families come together. As noted in this book's Introduction, the most widely accepted stories told during Russia's biggest celebrations come from the 1970s. Brezhnevian films, in other words, are the most popular and profitable during holiday primetime. They tell us a great deal about the desired and desiring worldview of those who grew up with them.

These movies show a slow loss of respectful peace and quiet as cities became greedier prior to perestroika. By the late 1970s, for example, the social ideals of cinema had turned often to the highly successful genre of musicals (Pugacheva's *Zhenshchina, kotoraia poet* or Sofiia Rotaru's *Dusha*) and gentle comedy (like *Ironiia sud'by* or *Sluzhebnyi roman*), all of which I have examined in detail elsewhere. The slightly later box-office success of the early 1980s took elements of this musical or social harmony into more adventurous (and more frightening) territory. They chart much of what today's audiences *lament* at Christmas and New Year. The effort to vivify absent social bonds in late Brezhnevian cinema (and somewhat beyond) is the same effort under threat from Moscow's influence today. These parallels are made by the journalists who grew up with the former narratives – and today publish critical articles about the latter.

One very indicative feature here is *Mechanic Gavrilov's Favorite Woman* (dir. P. Todorovskii), a simple and touching tale of yearning in 1981. A middle-aged lady – Rita (Liudmila Gurchenko) – waits for her groom on her wedding day, but he does not turn up: "You can have a husband and still be very lonely," she says. Strangers offer her some solace on the city street (wine and a sandwich), while Rita herself helps a much younger couple decide their marriage plans during an outdoors tiff. She even lends the fiancée her own dress: this sad act embodies the universally social existence eluding Rita herself. Ashamed to face acquaintances at her own failed reception, she gets *another* stranger to pretend to be Gavrilov, introduced as the hero of Rita's whirlwind romance. Suddenly Gavrilov does indeed turn up: he had defended a woman's honor at the flower shop, got into a punch-up and was delayed at the police station. Only luck, it seems, can make an ideal come true, where "you can't *imagine* what happiness this is," a subjective, unpredictable, unspoken aim, one unobtainable through specific or practical effort.

One of the most impressive hit films in its determination to save a happy social existence in a worsening society came in 1985's *Flight 222* (dir. S. Mikaèlian). Here we already feel the grim pressures of perestroika on the calm, modest desires of the 1970s. The movie concerns a sportsman on tour in New York with his wife, a dancer. The husband suddenly, even to the amazement of his spouse, runs off to the bright lights of the Big Apple and asks for political asylum. As the two nations involved sort out the matter of the wife's desires (or try to interpret those familiar desires for political gain), the troupe's airplane is delayed on the tarmac, unable to leave for Moscow. Pugacheva's song "Starry Summer" (*Zvezdnoe leto*) plays in order to calm people in the cabin, as the US or Soviet authorities try to force the woman's hand. She, however, starts to sense a better, quieter "social being" amid the passengers than she does with her selfish husband. "I understand everything," she says. "It's extremely simple. He has stayed behind."

The worse the relationship and the pushier the politicians, the jollier and more successful the relations between passengers; they realize a happy state of cohabitation in their metal, successfully social bubble on the runway. The passengers escape the nastiness of New York (and Moscow politics) because they are nowhere in particular. They sing "Happy Birthday" to one another, plus famous songs from Soviet children's cartoons. The passengers know what they want and need among each other, whereas the politicians have no idea what the wife wants; she says almost nothing during the entire film. Finally, inspired by her fellow passengers, she announces that she wants to go home. "Home" does not imply a motherland but "my mother and my friends at work." Her husband begs her to stay, but she flies off to continue the messy, multiple searches for selfhood among many little people, rather than the false, quotidian attempt with one poor spouse.

By 1986, a time we associate with a break in the Soviet aesthetic or the emergence of anger and political critique, our social, choral ideals *continue* to be sought in a way that has little to do with glasnost. This is the sentimental, wantonly minorized vein that runs through to today's TV stories. In the film *Forgive Me* (*Prosti*, dir. È. Iasan), we begin with an atmosphere of tense friendships and sometimes cruel mockery in a group of female lab assistants: "You're in a collective, not the jungle!" Marriage reflects the same malaise: "All women realize their husband's infidelity sooner or later" – and indeed this is what the main character discovers. Since "we live to work and not vice versa" in the USSR, a solution to this mishap will not come easily. In a tale as cruel as *Kalina krasnaia*, the heroine flees to the house only to be mugged – and apparently raped. Only now is there some vague reconciliation between the central couple. Surely, if documenting reality means this much wretchedness, is there not some hope for an all-encompassing, accommodating, and affective aesthetic *somewhere else*? Hope comes, as ever, in two ways: a reduction in the scale of social projects and recourse to the unspoken, geographically indeterminate workings of compassion that socialist art often invokes with reference to an unpeopled wilderness or music.

In Karen Shakhnazarov's hugely popular comedy of 1986, *The Courier*, laughter also helps, via irony, to reduce the likelihood of big drama or clumsy problem-solving. A boy's parents get divorced; hence we begin with a socially orphaned Soviet citizen. The scale could be no smaller as social groups hold out against the cruelty of perestroika. Russia does nothing for this young man, Ivan; he and his friends are happier break-dancing to Herbie Hancock, a type of music that means more than the civic pride of

Lev Leshchenko's civically responsible hit song "Parental Home" (*Roditel'skii dom*) that we hear playing in the background during one screaming match. He says he will burn down the apartment and hates his own mother. Thankfully employment offers a possible alternative to this wretchedness.

A job as a courier takes him to the house of a professor and her attractive daughter, but the father is initially disgusted by Ivan's "nihilism and rudeness," by his one "principle of social existence: a good wage and as little work as possible." Out of lazy interest Ivan asks his friend if *he* has any principle of social existence. The friend stutters, stumbles and finally relies upon utterly unconvincing rhetorical cliché, merely repeating something he would have learned in a late-Soviet classroom: "The principle of humanism."

Ivan slowly gets to know the professor's daughter and shows her, amid his dreams of Africa's wilderness and Masai warriors, some nearby wasteland where he believes a leopard lives in secret, having once escaped captivity. The professor slowly warms to this sluggish bravado or truthfulness that reminds us of *L'Étranger*, but the daughter, conversely, starts to find it somewhat tiring. This unsuccessful construction and dismantling of fickle social relationships only resolves itself at the very end of the movie. Ivan asks his friend once more what his dream in life is; the friend says he wants a winter coat. Ivan gives him his own new coat in silence. One tiny moment of an ideal (inspired by the virtues of a distant wilderness) survives amid angry parents, a failed romance, a sad apartment, and divorce. Over and over again, this dreamy, rarely seen ideal will be connected with a breakdown of the subject–object divide and the open, non-urban spaces of the world's biggest country. This chapter has focused on negative examples.

The use of love among villagers to advocate (or make) *better* cohesion was adopted more explicitly by Channel One in its 2004 mini-series that drew, once more, on the Shukshin family – *Shukshin's Stories* (dir. Arkadii Sirenko). Compared to the jingoism of US primetime, this patriotic retrospection of Brezhnevian backwaters (already redone in the present by *Okhotniki za ikonami*) is quieter, empathetic, and, as a result, harder to express. Its use of modesty, mercilessly self-deprecating humor, and unexpected love to socialize lonely figures is sometimes complicated, especially when their multitude approaches a synonymy of everybody and nobody.

Realizing an ideal "non-Moscow" is not easy. In looking to connect people beyond the received boundaries or limiting sets of mapmaking and history, many TV series have had difficulty balancing ahistorical love and passion with the related, busy environments of period costumes, antiques, or other specific references. Argument continues over the importance of sociohistorical context and ways in which viewers might need or want it. Is it more important to show and retell (that is, correct) the past or, conversely, stress themes that survived *despite* the reality captured in received histories? These two goals overlap but remain distinct.

This confusion underscores a delightful comedy series of 2006, *The Enchanted Village* (*Zakoldovannyi uchastok*). Written by Aleksei Slapovskii, it tells of a Moscow hypnotist who tries to bewitch a series of dachas, the residents of which are troubled by a range of social woes: infidelity, alcoholism, and various failed "business" ventures. Can a lost, rustic peace be reclaimed, at least by the "magic" of hypnotism? This wonderful, sleepy state might bring a fleeting happiness, but "what'll happen when everybody wakes up?" In a Tolstoian spirit, the hypnotist tells the villagers during one session: "You're all a part of the universe, an inseparable part." This insight is not easily gained. One local resident stops drinking and garners a similar sense of "oceanic" wonderment by staring endlessly at plants, fields, and thunderstorms. This behavior, though, strikes his wife as *so* abnormal she begs him to start drinking again; his consolation comes from singing old Soviet songs by Mark Bernes, wistfully, with a close friend across a twilight pasture.

For any new story of love or social linkages to survive or improve upon old Soviet narratives, there are degrees of feasibility viewers will accept. The same is true of stories set in the present, where today's urban and market-driven values are overwhelmingly oppressive. Hence the amazing frequency with which fate and destiny in Moscow are mentioned. Yet these forces are never really explained; dramas like *Life Lines* or *Two Fates* include love's victory, yet do so in ways that leave the *workings* of fate unexplained. Nobody really cares, however. In a land where love was so often trampled by urban dictate (*Deti Arbata* being a perfect example) viewers simply have to believe in a better, hidden force. And they do, because so many believe that society's urban ills are just as predestined – as are the lives of heroines, the classic victims of melodrama, either in crowded, heartless Moscow or in distant meadows.

6 Heroines
Airports, planes, and wedding trains

> We are not always able to combine patriotic responsibility for Russia's destiny with what Stolypin once called "Civil Liberties."
>
> (Putin, 2000)

Beloved (*Zhelannaia*, 2003) and *Nina* (2001)

The most typical heroines on today's TV who struggle with an urban destiny, social objectification, or marital convention can perhaps be divided into three groups: those of the past, those of the present, and those thrown back and forth – either metaphorically (that is, by financial machinations) or physically (by railway systems and airlines, for example). Destabilization is one step closer to nothingness. The 2003 series *Beloved* (dir. Iurii Kuz'menko) outlined the first of these groups very politely, as an initially confusing soon-to-be unruly desire from someone's history:

> The present day. On her sixtieth birthday Mariia Grigor'eva receives an envelope from a stranger. Inside she finds a ring and an open letter signed with the pseudonym "Your Sweet Little Hedgehog." Mariia recalls that she used the nickname for all her numerous lovers. She is mentally transported to the past in order to understand who could have sent her such a touching letter.

Based, once again, on a novel with a more interesting title (Iurii Perov's *The Full-Figured Beauty* [*Prekrasnaia tolstushka*]), the series juxtaposes personal passions with the room for movement afforded by social convention. Kuz'menko maintains, therefore, that *Beloved* could never have been screened during the Soviet period, if for no other reason than it shows a woman passing through a great number of sexual relationships, one of which involves a political figure (clearly based on Beriia) exercising his fantasy in tights and a tutu.[1] These oddities, hidden from the public eye, are combined with equal, ever-present attempts to capture forgotten, once-evident details from daily life, in particular in terms of domestic furnishings. The problem

Figure 6.1 Beloved.

of a reality felt or remembered versus "stuff" comes back from shows such as *The Idiot*. The artistic director of *Zhelannaia*, Valentin Gidulianov, also worked on *The Rendezvous Is Set* and – just as before – spent endless hours scouring antique shops. Likewise, in the first few episodes Mariia (Ol'ga Vechkileva) is only fifteen years old; in order to resurrect her private and public age, costume designers took her dress patterns directly and scrupulously from magazine cut-outs of the 1950s.[2]

This objectification of Mariia's dizzying affairs amid archived magazines, paper cut-outs, and bric-a-brac also occurs as textual reductionism. The number of her (already numerous) relationships with men in the series is less than in the novel; additional lesbian adventures were also cut from the TV version. Her early attempts to instigate a miscarriage and avoid marriage are much less dramatic on screen, reduced to jumping down from chairs and cupboards, time after time.[3] Even the psychological horror of Beriia (Viktor Sukhorukov) is made ridiculous rather than criminal. This desire to *show* desire yet keep it free from excess or excessive political intrigue is evident in quite a few television shows. Heroines are scattered amid objects and others' objectionable behavior, but they often remain separate from the extremes of what, ironically, is real life. Much is hinted at (by analogy or banality); almost nothing troublingly explicit is named.

The 2001 romance *Nina* is another good example. It tells – not unlike *I Love You* – of a woman's rise and fall (and rise again) in the worlds of business and love, yet the latter barely manages with great effort to elude the shadow of the former in the plot:

> Famous model Nina adores her profession; she is a loving mother and a faithful wife. Her life, however, changes radically after the disappearance of her husband Sasha. A happy life and career are lost forever. A meeting with Mikhail resurrects her hope for happiness and love. All is going well, but Aleksandr suddenly appears from nowhere. The weight of the past changes her life yet again.

Promoters felt (no doubt correctly) that an avoidance of excess would make the series maximally palatable:

> The basic dramatic intrigue here will keep both guys *and* gals happy ... There's the favorite combination of your typical, sexually repressed Lara Croft fan: spirited action with some bandit punch-ups and a sensual heroine – who every now and then needs to extricate herself from some "spicy" situation or other.

Almost magically, the heroine always manages to "preserve a sense of virginal honor" and find romance, too. By using a little of everything but nothing much in particular, the "punch-ups won't get dull and there won't be too much weeping going on."[4] Specificity did not seem profitable; the plot outline used for domestic sales similarly condenses both generic sampling and vague social groups to the point of childishness or, to be honest, illogicality and incomprehensibility. The confusion leads to stories of movement and social passage, underscored by placing them within the world of transportation. The resulting narratives reexamine – yet again – some cherished Soviet motifs of interaction.

The Station (*Vokzal*, 2003), *A Passenger without Baggage* (*Passazhir bez bagazha*, 2003), and *Heaven and Earth* (*Nebo i zemlia*, 2003–4)

> [In the future] it will be hot, noisy and happy. Just like Baku on a holiday ... Trains will travel from Kazan' station, painted with the words *Moscow-Kara-Bugaz, via Tashkent-Krasnovodsk*. A health resort will be opened in the gulf, where there's the best air in the USSR. How about that, eh?
>
> (K. Paustovskii, *Kara Bugaz*, 1932)

This quote is extremely optimistic; of course, no such singular network was ever completed to match Paustovskii's daydreaming. Even nowadays Putin says in his televised town-hall meetings that Russia lacks any "universal resource" or one means for economic progress and must thus work in "various directions."[5] Multiplicity is lauded, here as fiscal deterritorialization, yet its closely supervised "variety" is invoked with such insistence, especially against the background of increasing social cynicism, that it simply becomes a lament for singularity. This repetitious lament has, as noted, been deemed "the Kremlin's own TV series."

Hopes for nationwide machinic (i.e. quixotically kind and aimless) interaction, actually made possible *by* machines, have therefore remained disappointing, unfinished biographies, shifting back and forth without discernible progress. People, places, and genders never slipped their shackles and so we arrive at the simple, building-block plots of today, pushing passive lovers from unit to unit. This is regularly expressed in a directly physical manner – on trains, for example. Precisely this type of interaction is multiplied many times over in the railway series *The Station* (dir. Andrei Kavun), full of helpless lovers, jobless adults, and reasonless terrorists.

Filmed primarily in a Minsk terminal, the show was – despite the strength of these passions – criticized by the actual employees of the station for being emotionally engaging yet "virtually criminal" in its ignorance of actuality, such as the screenplay's incorrect use of shunting-yard regulations, which dictate the movement of rolling stock on screen. A local newspaper published a very long article to show that small, specific actuality (ignored by the series but everywhere in the actual station) was no less interesting, all the way from trouble with the homeless to helping an abandoned baby – or a recent adventure with $8,500 left anonymously in a luggage locker:

> Here the paths of regular local people and successful businessmen all crisscross; nimble thieves and wayward girls, the lives of tramps and eternally nomadic gypsies, thrown in the gutter. Any station is made of endless meetings and departures; constant expectations and endless highways. A station isn't made of buildings and trains, but of passengers and employees. A station is everyday life, flowing before our eyes yet simultaneously hidden from us all.[6]

The central romance here involves the station manager (Valentin Smirnitskii) and our heroine, a young, emotionally troubled junior employee (Svetlana Antonova). Both have been through tough times (divorce and poverty). This leads to a most unconventional romance – Smirnitskii is no matinee idol. The stakes are raised considerably as rumors of a terrorist attack on the station grow from episode to episode, and in the end Oksana (Antonova's character) saves the manager when an attack does indeed take place and a bomb is detonated on board one of the station's trains. These lovers are dragged great distances through diverse biographies, only to be torn from one another permanently by the dangerous political principles of others.

In *A Passenger without Baggage* (REN-TV), a young woman is horrified to discover than her husband has hanged himself on the night train between St. Petersburg and Moscow. Here we make the uncomplicated step from the *end* of a romance into the detective story. Love – barely hinted at in early references – drives the subsequent criminal investigation. The heroine cares because she once *cared*:

> It all begins with the suicide of a completely level-headed man. Why did a photographer from a modest studio decide to end his life on the St. Petersburg to Moscow train? He was found in the carriage toilet, hanging from a camera strap. Right away his wife Iana must explain the conditions surrounding this bizarre fatality. In the course of her subsequent amateur investigation, some secret negatives pop up – of course – together with an equally secret woman and a large amount of money. It turns out that the husband had amassed terrible debts and was even forced to sell his parents' dacha. Then death starts claiming the innocent employees of the husband's studio – with both precision and brutality. Iana's investigation reveals that some unknown criminals want to frame her. Evidence left at crime scenes points to her indubitable guilt. Now she absolutely has to figure out the circumstances surrounding her husband's death, to remove all suspicion from herself, if nothing else.

This story (the first of three based on an Anna Malysheva novel) consists of four episodes. Each series was shot by a different director, leaving Malysheva's brokenhearted heroines floating between varied executive desires and genres: psychological drama, detective tales, and a thriller.[7]

Among these tales of "transported" individuals, the sixteen-series *Heaven and Earth* is especially impressive, employing two stars from *The Brigade* – Ekaterina Guseva and Vladimir Vdovichenkov. It was again directed in Minsk, this time by Viktor Sergeev, who has a reputation for making "women's dramas" even though he oversaw the third series of *Gangland Petersburg* (*Banditskii Peterburg*, 2001): "I like films centered around a female character and in this series the women are undoubtedly stronger than the men." Ekaterina Guseva agreed, saying that her childhood impressions of a stewardess' life proved to be wrong, since it soon became clear that airline careers are "hellishly difficult."[8] The fact that she was performing simultaneously in the Moscow musical *Nord-Ost* did little to lessen the difficult workload; she would travel back and forth between the two cities on night trains:[9]

> The action takes place in the imaginary town of Surdiansk. Relations are strained between our heroine (a stewardess called Marina) and her husband, airline captain Viktor Shvedov. Viktor, despite problems both at home and with his health, refuses to grant Marina a divorce. [On a routine flight,] the airline *Aviakom* receives a threatening note: "The steel bird will also fall." Several passengers receive the same note. Panic sets in on board and the air stewards try to calm the passengers. After the incident Marina promises her husband that from now on they will always fly together.

The show was deliberately shot in winter, so the major actors would (hopefully) be free for a lengthy commitment. Nonetheless, either budgets or timetables proved to be problematic, as Guseva's experience already shows: the biggest male star – Aleksandr Baluev – was sidelined early in the plot by a heart attack, throwing her into the limelight very quickly. Baluev assessed the romantic problems caused by his absence as follows:

> Pilots are special people. Without love, so to speak, they just can't fly. Without love a pilot is not a pilot ... It's not clear what's most important for my character. His sweetheart or the skies. That was probably the most important moment in the role that I tried to make use of.[10]

The male aspect of the romance is again presented as an existential issue, one that can proffer a superior alternative to other, more grossly social choices.

The emotional conundrums surrounding Guseva's character were occasionally overshadowed by petulant nitpickers from the aviation profession, as was the case with *The Station*. Their criticism ranged from uniforms that were the wrong color to airplanes that do not crash "properly."[11] Separating the emotional choices from the material ones (in terms of career, cash, and production values) was not going to be easy. Perhaps in deliberate and admirable avoidance of material(istic) fussiness, Guseva tried hard later in the series to vivify some dreadful problems of paralysis with no more than her eyes. She remained in that immobile state for several episodes.[12] This degree of affective intensity led ultimately to parallels with Arthur Haley's *Airport* (dir. George Seaton, 1970). The series was thus colored "through and through with both love and respect for stewardesses, those 'swallows of the sky.'" It was, with this powerful romantic undercurrent, also the first series starring Vdovichenkov devoid of shooting and fighting (as, for example, in *The Brigade, Bimmer* [*Bumer*, dir. Petr Buslov, 2003] or its sequel two years later).

The connections of Vdovichenkov and Guseva to *The Brigade* and *Nord-Ost* are very important, since both productions were lauded and lambasted as deeply Russian tales of the here and now. Both juxtapose love with other forms of desire, be they political or purely avaricious. Based on a Soviet adventure story of Arctic aviation, *Nord-Ost* is:

> an explanation of the Soviet past in personal, not political, terms. Moreover, it projects the past onto the present, seeking continuity. [It is] a symbol of Russia – not of the new Russia, but of a country with tradition, rather than one where traditions were severed.[13]

Mark Lipovetsky, in a related observation, extends that same historical project to various stable characteristics in the reworking of a private Soviet past. In other words, private experience might be used to bridge the gap caused by politics in 1991. The lyrical experiences in post-Soviet dramas, says Lipovetsky, often constitute a simple opposition of good and bad characters; a frequent reliance upon military conflict to drive the plot; an already "psychologically shaped" protagonist drawn from heroic archetypes; the insignificance of romance, plus recognizable references to Soviet works and to well-known Western genres.[14] I would certainly not go this far, and take big issue with the removal of romance, but the idea of calm, private continuation is very much at work.

The ability of anybody actually to get *anything* done is moot, though, as we see. I would be inclined at this stage to side instead with arguments made in Anthony Olcott's study of popular fiction in Russia and the morality therein. The principles that underlie romance on Russian TV are often the same ethically underwritten and wisely chosen options that structure detective shows. They are not overtly political and are made within a restricted, romantically social space:

> The code of morality lies not in individual acts, but rather in the purpose for which an act was undertaken, or the intent that lies behind it. If the purpose of an act is to serve private ends or advance individual interests, then the *detektiv* [detective series or story] will view it with suspicion and probably condemn it outright, no matter how apparently benign the act may be. Conversely, as long as the purpose of an act is to serve "the people" or the disembodied State, the genre accepts it as good – even if property is stolen or people killed.[15]

Private actions, therefore, echo and effect public states. Such ideas, as Olcott notes, go back further than post-Soviet concerns. They predate Marx, bearing instead the mark of a religious orthodoxy that maintains the inherent sinfulness of humans (especially in any division of selfhood from the community); and yet, according to the same outlook, all people bear the potential likeness of God. These pious views of behavior in detective stories can move further still from policy, in fact from history altogether, when they touch upon the nature of power in all social structures (and, therefore, in both law and order):

> Paradoxical as the argument may seem, the genre of the *detektiv* could be said to be elaborating a view of good and evil that in fact makes crime fiction impossible, or at least unnecessary. If there is no substantial barrier between good and bad, [that is,] if [human] law by definition contravenes [truly universal, socially unprejudiced] justice, and if crime and law enforcement are going to battle one another to a draw for all eternity, then the conventions of crime fiction – at least as defined by the Western countries that gave birth to them – have no place in Russia. The genre refuses to show that crime may be stopped, that good may triumph, or that humans may grow less evil.[16]

If the room for altering the legal status quo is so small, then, not surprisingly, a somewhat fatalistic Manicheanism can result for the heart, too. Love becomes a harbor from the eternal vacillation between happiness and harm, yet – in theory – it *makes* happiness also. Heroines move back and forth across a philosophical playing field that never alters and still, for all that, remains a mystery worthy of Sherlock Holmes.

Dasha Vasil'eva, liubitel'nitsa chastnogo syska (*Dasha Vasil'eva, Amateur Private Detective*, from 2003), *Samara-Gorodok* (*The Sweet Town of Samara*, 2004), *Vsegda govori vsegda* (*Always Say Always*, 2003), and *Bliznetsy* (*The Twins*, 2005)

> The world opens up like a rebus. I see a host of figures: people, horses, carts, cables, machines, steam, letters, clouds, mountains, cars, water ... I don't understand how they relate to one another. But I know that they do. There's some kind of mighty interaction. I know it for sure ... and believe it. But I just don't *see* it. It's so infuriating – to believe and yet not see!
> (V. Kataev, *Time, Forward!*, 1932)

The Dasha Vasil'eva series, based upon a very successful run of detective novels by Dar'ia Dontsova, begins with a rather silly premise. Giving voice to Russia's eternal Francophilia, our eponymous heroine is placed in the elegant suburbs of Paris through the unconvincing workings of fate; we also see her working actively, though modestly, as a private detective. The ability of a female lead to adopt the role of, say, Helen Mirren's high-ranking detective Jane Tennyson in *Prime Suspect* (1991–2006) is so unexpected and unfounded in the Russian TV tradition that it is handed over to irony or jocularity:

> This is an unusual Cinderella story ... Dasha Vasil'eva, the modest teacher of a Moscow institute, receives an enormous inheritance. She

moves with her children and cats to a luxurious mansion in the suburbs of Paris. Peace and quiet, however, don't suit a Russian woman who has been burned in her struggles with destiny. This new lady-millionaire finds new meaning in her life working as a private detective. Having solved one case, she does not then rest on her laurels; she gets enormous pleasure from her hobby, whereas the Russian and French police get nothing more than a big headache.

This Cinderella reference is important in that is both employed on a regular basis for promotional materials and applied to heroines who struggle against circumstance only to be saved not by effort or intellect, but by other, better circumstances. Take, for example, the 2003 series *Always Say Always*, which bears a strong resemblance to the plot of *Nina*. The heroines are even physically similar, but what is interesting in this case is that Mariia Poroshina's character is accompanied most of the time by a clowning sidekick, the bubbly redhead Tat'iana Abramova. Whatever drama or destiny is faced by Poroshina brings her slowly to a philosophy of resignation. Any feisty assertions to the contrary, that success is possible with effort, are handed over to Abramova and thus to humor. Willful self-definition is most often possible thanks only to other people and good fortune, neither of which is expected or predictable:

> *Always Say Always* is a story of transformation, but it's more complicated than a banal Cinderella story. It tells of a woman in the grip of circumstances that she must learn to handle. Nonetheless, the heroine's success is balanced by all the experiences she'll have to endure. Without these misfortunes the heroine wouldn't have the energy, ideas, or people to help her build a new, interesting, bright and different destiny. Life is not as it seems – and sadness, no matter how terrible, can perhaps be the only way to summon the strength for change.

A 2004 provincial drama, *The Sweet Town of Samara*, works along similar lines; it helps to dovetail this and the previous chapters by showing how Moscow can be "escaped" with metaphors of transience or travel – away from Moscow. The activity of its heroine is increasingly dispersed through (or made manifest *by*) a wandering social network, through the kind of caring ties that are found in rural societies, not big cities. Dmitrii Diuzhev again undermines his gangster-like persona by playing a Moscow hockey star tongue in cheek; eternal heartthrob Dmitrii Kharat'ian also makes admirable fun of his cultural status. Nonetheless, the latter character, affiliated with a small mental hospital in the very rural-sounding backwater of Zaprud'e ("Beyond the Pond"), gives voice to increasingly serious observations as time goes on.

The heroine of the drama, Varvara, is a well-known and successful figure in the Moscow fashion scene; she is engaged to marry Diuzhev's character, Nikita. Unbeknown to all, Varvara is still legally married, however, and needs to return to Zaprud'e for an official divorce from husband Lenia (Kharat'ian). Initially she gets little sympathy from Lenia and, to make matters worse, Varvara was a most unpleasant and manipulative local beauty in her youth. People in the village are not happy to see her again and nobody is terribly keen on bending the rules to get her divorce filed quickly. The judge will not take a bribe and her old teacher will not forge a graduation certificate.

Meanwhile the Moscow subplot involves a Latin pop diva, Natalie Ortega, who inspires a young rural girl to enter a competition that will win her a dinner with the singer. Much is said about the prearranged and unfair nature of such "contests" and, in addition, the rural youngster is duped by a Russian woman pretending to be the singing star. She is robbed of all her money, a denouement that sets the tone for another plot twist. Nikita falls in love with the spoiled Ortega; the screenplay makes it clear that they deserve each other.

In distant Zaprud'e, however, Varvara admits her partial guilt in this situation; once upon a time she had dumped Lenia at their wedding reception. It soon becomes clear that she had done so only because a malicious admirer of Lenia had spread false rumors of his infidelity, hoping to ruin their happiness. When this is understood, the marriage of Lenia and Varvara can be reestablished and their life made anew among many friends in the sunny countryside.

If *The Sweet Town of Samara* posits the improving fate of a heroine among an increasingly open landscape, *The Twins* (*Bliznetsy*) pushes that spatial logic even further. This 2005 series, starring Èl'vira Bolgova and Andrei Sokolov, spent approximately $3 million in order to record "love and genuine human emotions" amid criminal intrigue spread over two decades in Moscow, Tashkent, Samarkand, Samara, Novgorod, St. Petersburg, and London.

After an ill-advised love affair with the daughter of a Soviet official in 1986, Detective Erozhin (Sokolov) accepts a transfer to Uzbekistan in order to avoid any professional fallout. There he makes contact with a fellow police officer, a friend from his student years, Vakhid. Erozhin learns that Vakhid's daughter Fatima had always been a major headache for the family and has now left home, committing a series of crimes across several Asian republics. Bolgova, playing the role of Fatima, in fact had to play three different sisters, and so our theme of self-realization is physically dispersed, too, not just across space, but across the forms of different (and yet closely related) people. The film crew handled flashback scenes of the threesome by swapping a couple of newborn babies every so often and, subsequently, in teenage scenes, a couple of 14-year-old twins. In adult episodes, it falls to Bolgova to show a more complex experience through more roles, whilst simultaneously adopting the "unifying" gait and speech patterns of Russian-speaking Uzbek women.[17]

Using doubles or split-screen techniques, Bolgova's movement across the TV screen was often quite literally drawn on the floor, so that any subsequent movements of another sister could be pasted into scenes without the technical problems caused by overlapping bodies. Stuntwomen and naked screen doubles (shot from behind) were likewise employed, multiplying Bolgova's presence on screen further still.[18] And yet, for all its complexity, the plot of *The Twins* seemed so familiar and natural to Russian viewers that one journalist even suggested that it had been taken from several Bollywood movies and their folkloric origins, loved for decades by Slavs.[19]

Bliznetsy was actually taken in part from the real world, since Erozhin and Vakhid are both based upon actual policemen from Moscow and Samarkand. The relationship between them, among subplots of bribery or infidelity in the Uzbek police force, was therefore too real for the Uzbek government; although much of the series was filmed in Samarkand and flatteringly showcases a great deal of local architecture, Uzbek state television banned *Bliznetsy* from the airwaves, declaring its subject matter contrary to the "national spirit."[20] It had dragged its heroine too far from home, making her subject to the shuttling patterns of the international drug trade. If a storyline becomes too long, the same problem can emerge; a hero or heroine will be pushed and pulled in so many directions that the unity of a "story" vanishes altogether. Perhaps by simply lengthening a narrative, TV shows could approximate a post-Soviet realism more successfully than reality TV – one that would speak both to an enduring "unity" *and* to its troubling dissipation in "life as it is."

Drugs, bombs, and endlessly mobile heroines: *The Airport* (*Aèroport*, 2005–6)

The most important change in TV series since 2005 has indeed been that of length. The dimensions once possible with foreign funding (in *Poor Nastia*, for example) are now being investigated by domestic sponsors. Needless to say, this grand gesture is made easier by cutting back on expenses. Long stories today are, therefore, frequently filmed in enclosed, contemporary spaces, producing an aesthetic akin to sitcoms or American daytime drama. One of the most indicative and lengthiest examples of late has been the NTV series *Airport*, directed by Egor Grammatikov and Aleksandr Gur'ianov:

> An airport is a tiny country with its management, workers and servants, its police and medical center; the difference is that there are many more newcomers than natives. Dozens of airplanes fly in and out every day, while thousands of passengers pass through the buildings. Sometimes one or two of them will stay, falling in love with this strange life between Heaven and Earth. *Airport* is a television series with elements of comedy, melodrama and detective fiction. The main thing, however, is the people: the employees of various airport services and the passengers of all ages, creeds and colors. They all have their problems, their joys and sorrows.

Figure 6.2 The Airport.

Each and every one of them has a unique destiny; sometimes it's comic, sometimes dramatic, but it's always interesting. After all, the workers of any airport are one big, rock-solid family. And as in any family, passions can boil over, too: conflicts, drama, jealousy, plus – of course – heavenly love, because airports are the "Gateway to the Skies"![21]

The series deliberately chose a large group of unknown actors, allegedly not from financial considerations, but from the desire for increased realism; approximately 250 actors were squeezed into a terminal at Moscow's Vnukovo airport. By removing any "stars," by removing the *sine qua non* of a classic or literary adaptation, *Airport* could thus move closer to an actual, "living organism."[22] Due to the problems of piracy experienced by *Doctor Zhivago*, by way of illustration, this cheaper and organic serial (which had no pretensions to "the level of Spielberg") would in fact go head to head with Pasternak's classic on Belarusian TV – and do very well indeed.[23]

The series begins with some students on a guided tour of an already busy and brand-new airport; added to this social multitude are the cleaning staff, air crews, shop assistants, security guards, and many other characters bound by their workplace – though separated by promotion, professional status, prejudice, and secret yearnings. Early on we are shown a young female journalist posing as a cleaner in order to unveil what she believes is a major scandal, but she is quickly upstaged by the first real drama of the series. A Russian man arrives with his girlfriend from Dushanbe; he is using her as an innocent courier for a shoulder bag of drugs. When they are stalled in customs, he panics and flees, leaving her with the bag. She cannot believe her future fiancé has vanished, especially since he has all the money from the recent sale of her apartment in Tajikistan.

Meanwhile, a senior pilot has suddenly to "placate" a drunken passenger. He does so with a well-placed fist, only to learn that the passenger is a local bigwig – and the pilot is soon out of work. Cash, provincial origins, and status in the Big City are, once again, swiftly outlined as major reasons for conflict. Any possibility for harmony is embodied by one of the upper-level officials and his wife (a stewardess); unable to have children of their own, they ponder adoption, a choice that is seriously, slowly considered over many episodes before it is undertaken.

In a similar spirit, as the lure of abandoned drugs leads to the arrest of a few social undesirables, the girl used as a courier is saved from both homelessness and poverty by employment in the airport bar. In this manner she, too, slowly socializes herself as an orphan into a busier, public world. As the undercover journalist says of this increasingly hectic space: "D'you know what passions there are in this place?! Real comedies and melodramas." The distance between them, between laughter and heartbreak, is sometimes very small indeed.

Happiness and sadness are often kept uncomfortably close, as when the banned pilot celebrates a small success over the arrogant man he punched; he is offered work by a new airline, only to suffer a heart attack immediately afterwards. Self-determination is often difficult in this environment, where – in the words of a property developer who plans to extend the construction of future terminals over local dachas – "There's no time for compassion here." The *need* for compassion, however, is always nearby.

One example: pitied by an airport policeman, the girl from Dushanbe is given a dress to wear for a business function, and turns into an absolute princess. The policeman thus falls in love with the same woman he recently arrested and imprisoned. This kind of small, unexpectedly granted haven is vital when one is surrounded by temptation (a boy tries marijuana), avarice (scam artists rob the jewelry store), and the pressures of big-city business (a bureaucrat's young wife mistakenly poses for a Moscow "men's magazine"). The major characters try very hard to realize their modest futures and not to be bitter, because "cynics are nothing more than disillusioned romantics."

The forces that control these little transitory lives within the airport are recurrently anonymous. By way of illustration, the businesswoman who hired the banned pilot then inexplicably fires him because she was told to do so "from above." Meanwhile the mysterious operations of Russia's Tax Inspectorate, used so violently in real life, are blamed for ruining the finances of the barmaid's husband. (During Episode Twenty-Two, in fact, their malicious workings are referred to over and over.) The same barmaid is then approached by an old friend, now an army officer; he declares his undying love for her, but he has soon absconded to Rostov with a bag of cash; we never know quite why. Many references are made in the series to the "heavenly" nature of flying as an escape from these strange, spiteful systems of the world below: "What's that beneath us?" "Clouds." "So we're already in heaven!" Faith alone does not help; by the middle of the series we have been exposed to faux nuns (who solicit cash for non-existent convents) and icon thieves, preying on the personal debts of baggage handlers in order to get some export "assistance."

Love and marriage are the only serious alternatives to volatility. The manager whose (uncomfortably youthful) wife poses for a magazine yearns increasingly for the stability of his first marriage, especially because the latter woman is always close by, herself a senior stewardess. The show's most eligible bachelor (the in-house doctor) and most attractive single woman (another stewardess) are involved in a large number of amorous adventures with various people, but older and wiser figures, including a card-playing conman, tell them both individually and regularly that marriage alone will bring them tranquility in a fickle world.

Love, however, is not risk-free; it can bring considerable damage in its wake whenever it goes wrong. During an episode that involves a bomb threat, the "terrorist" who compiles an explosive device in the Vnukovo toilet is shown merely to have been unlucky in love. It transpires that he was only trying to protect his father from prosecution, a criminal being transported through Vnukovo under police supervision. That risk, despite its public failure, brings father and son *closer*. Their love runs to illegal extremes, both binding and tearing them apart.

Later, in a related episode, two wheelchair-bound couples are offered the chance to enter a dance competition in Paris, thanks to the "charity" of a local politician. His fake friendship and paternal affection are outdone by the invalids; miraculously, one of the handicapped men stands up briefly in order to save a girl from falling down an escalator. He then places the new joy or faith in his family over and above the competition, its once-in-a-lifetime trip, and any political benefit. He stays home and does not travel.

In a very similar fashion, another family later on weighs the benefits of emigrating to Canada versus love and responsibility for their father, even if he is an alcoholic. The family wins. This ethic is extended to foreigners, too; an American businessman abandons his high-flying career for a penniless female artist in Russia. Love is bigger than (and prior to) politics: "If you don't fight for your girl, you won't fight for your country." There has to be a private, excessive source of signification for public systems to draw upon. Heroines embody that source in a time-honored fashion.

This fight for "what's yours" often involves a grim insistence upon compassion when logic suggests otherwise. In one late episode we see a young writer who is asked to fly to India; he is asked to pen an article and thus impress a travel agent sufficiently that the agent will then bless the writer's marriage to his daughter. This young man, however, suffers from a terrible fear of flying, so he does his "research" on India in the airport bookshop. His fiancée discovers this long series of deceitful charades, trip after trip, but she plays along with an additional "flight" to Israel (thanks to some appropriate, foreign-looking souvenirs purchased in Vnukovo), so that the marriage can go ahead.

She *pities* his weakness, worries, and social failings; together the two of them will build something better, a stronger, shared unit. It is the risk of doing so, however, that takes our unmarried doctor and stewardess almost thirty episodes to even begin "opening up their true feelings." Similarly (and equally late!), when the girl from Dushanbe finally feels at home in her new world, her boyfriend suddenly reappears. He is virtually insane after various financial failures. He kidnaps his old girlfriend ... but is shot dead by the girl's suitor from the police station as the boyfriend readies his pistol. This extremely precarious drama comes not long before the closing scenes, when – just as in the beginning – another group of students is taken on another tour of the airport. Thus end the first thirty episodes and another ninety begin as multiple female protagonists are moved around, forwards and backwards in search of Heaven.

An old-world bravado to inspire today's heroines, stuck in the Big City

> Man trembles; he is a leaf on a huge and beautiful tree. His is the sky and his is the earth, and *he is* the sky and the earth. It's so good to believe everything, to know and to love everything.
>
> (V. Ivanov, *Armored Train 14:69*, 1922)

In clarifying the dispersive, endlessly displaced and yet national spirit of our modern Russian stories, we find there is, as suggested, much in common between their desired (i.e. never attained) typicality and the "oceanic desire" of romanticism. The insistence of socialist theory that realism capture a given epoch in all its dialectical significance can, likewise, be reinterpreted as the insistent shuttling of a romantic back and forth between people and places, moving slowly toward (i.e. desperately hoping for) an affecting/affected union with oceanic "life as it is." Our homeless heroines occupy a similarly quivering state on the edge of actuality, on the edge of a vacant wilderness.

This tentative, drifting form of selfhood, divorced from urban and doctrinal singularity, is not new. It is a product of socialist storytelling. Konstantin Fedin used his memories of Vsevolod Ivanov to highlight it – the desire to affect an interpenetration of nature, man, and a variegated, itinerant concord *beyond* language. "Vsevolod's favorite words are joy, eternity and wind."[24] These three nouns alone have been fine antidotes to the stabilizing, stagnating tendency of Soviet *habitus* both when Ivanov wrote his stories and (even more so) when they were republished during the Stalinist purges. They show the kind of supra-national expansionism that, for instance, troubles today's neo-Stalinist autocracy in Uzbekistan, especially when its sense of safe containment is destabilized by desire(s), by TV tales of endlessly mobile women as in *The Twins*.

Ivanov's three nouns underscore cinema of the time as well and have given contemporary television some time-tested ways to do them justice (visually) and allow for an escape from dogma (emotionally, as in *Deti Arbata* or *Moskovskaia saga*). Visual tales from the time of Paustovskii's and Kataev's achievements help us to understand even better why Stalinist and Brezhnevian cultures invoke the greatest nostalgia. Today's schoolchildren, as shown in Chapter 7, are told to watch precisely these hit films of the 1930s to put the true emphases of modern storytelling back in a *better, wider* context. Here we sense echoes again of Putin's famous opinion that only the heartless do not regret the collapse of the USSR, but only the brainless would try to reinstate it. It remains a never-achieved and tragically mismanaged project, ushering in metaphors of destiny that leave heroines high and dry.

Iskateli schast'ia (*The Seekers of Happiness*, 1936), directed by V. Korsh-Sablin, sketches the early outlines of this heartless tragedy and does so in empty, address-less nature – in the overpoweringly social, yet unpeopled realm *almost* promised by our shuttling, homeless actresses. This film spoke of Jews dispatched on trains to inaccessible Birobidzhan, the newly founded "autonomous republic." These displaced people all make their ramshackle home within new and common farm labor, within an empty, endless wasteland; all except one man (Pini), who is obsessed with discovering gold. As he pans, his avaricious glee comes in stealing *from* the landscape, not from working within it. Against a backdrop of never-ending, misty lakes, Pini almost kills a fellow farmer in the battle for some gold dust. He tries to flee across a river to China, but is caught and shown that his "gold" is in fact worthless iron pyrite. Amid this drama's closing speeches it requires a grandmother to celebrate the return of family, the land, and the state's "generosity." Dogma quickly pretends to be domestic and matriarchal.

Heroines, however, do indeed inspire better bonds. The same year consigned some Komsomol members, both male and female, to a desolate northern shore in the adventure *Semero smelykh* (*The Valiant Seven*, dir. S. Gerasimov). Just as *Iskateli schast'ia* is awash with Jewish folksongs, so this second movie of friendship is often punctuated by the Soviet classic number *Leisia, pesnia* ("Roll Onward, Song..."). In "good" Arctic weather of sunshine and minus 15° Celsius, these brave, crooning pioneers head out to help a sickly Inuit; charity is mapped out in the middle of nowhere. Again, as in *The Seekers of Happiness*, a similarly shared enjoyment of meager provisions is offered as cause for (modest) solace during tough Arctic effort; private acts crown the public project. This theme of diffident, yet stubborn social units is highlighted elsewhere when characters sense great pain on seeing their absent colleagues' empty bunks – or framed pictures of cherished, absent parents.

Their diffidence amid Arctic blankness is established by numerous shots of tiny, dark, fur-clad figures against an overbearing, white nothingness. Occasionally these dots seek or hug one another. They dream of a more welcoming environment, of sun-drenched Poltava, "where the apples and cherries are blossoming." Similarly, although *Leisia, pesnia* is a swaggering shanty about "storming the seas" by decree, *Semero smelykh* ends with a handful of lovers deciding to stay on at the freezing outpost, an earnest decision made to the strains of the same melody. Even the team's young cook is inspired to stay longer by the love of a woman for one of his friends (without which the project would have fallen apart – and everybody would have gone home).

Music often helps a heroine to inspire and then manage these projects, as in the 1936 score by Dunaevskii and Lebedev-Kumach for the comedy *Devushka speshit na svidanie* (*She's Off on a Date*, dir. M. Verner); two Muscovites travel southwards, far away from the big city, in order to enjoy a holiday amid apples, cherries, and palms. The comedy comes from ways in which urban bureaucratic meddling continues to haunt them, as in Dunaevskii's and Lebedev-Kumach's project for the following year, too: *The Well-To-Do Fiancée* (*Bogataia nevesta*, dir. I. Pyr'ev). Here a Ukrainian *kolkhoz* is introduced to viewers through the charm of farm workers singing as they traverse golden harvest fields. Government administration in the form of an unattractive state accountant spoils the possible romance of two workers, Pavlo and Marinka, purely out of jealousy and spite. In a village where courting couples are literally flushed from the bushes at bedtime, the state tries to upset the type of harmony between Marinka's love and nature that is musically cultivated in dolly shots moving *with* (not ahead of) the farmers and their threshing machines.

Against undulating, continuous crops, the accountant sings satirical songs and lewd gypsy romances to discredit Pavlo, but eventually is urged by love to admit his awful behavior, making a confession which the festive farmhands immediately accept, giving him a bicycle as a present! Cinema of this most awful – and yet fondly remembered – period both visually and melodically stresses organic nature (sunshine, wheat fields, holiday resorts, and/

or whirlwinds) over politics as a desired form or locus of social cohesion. Can a similar philadelphia or poetic montage survive today, especially in a world that judges detective or mafia tales to be the best, most representative, and most profitable? The Dasha Vasil'eva series and *Always Say Always* handed over women's self-determination to humor and, in doing so, left little room for seriousness amid the criminal social forces that both shape modern Russia and negate any ecological or organic potential. Before examining the criminal or detective series *per se*, therefore, the squeamish workings of heroines amid wholehearted, unadulterated humor deserve a closer look. Humor incorporates objects of desire yet tries to laugh off their absence; it tries, ironically, to make nothing out of something (i.e. out of *nothing's* very promise).

Sitcoms: someone else's happy story versus homespun blogs

Absolutely vital in the development of comic heroines has been the Moscow production company A-Media noted earlier and formed in 2002, which today creates a line-up of funny shows that fill the primetime schedule of STS to great effect. Its combined output of soaps and TV series in 2005 was 800 hours.[25] One of the most commercially successful has been *Ne rodis' krasivoi* (*If You Weren't Born Pretty* ...), an ugly-duckling tale than began on Colombian television. It enjoyed success in Germany, Israel, and India before being bought by A-Media from Sony International.[26] The German version, interestingly, had made its main female actress especially unappealing by placing her childhood in unfashionable East Germany. Socialism, it would seem, can nowadays kill your chances of getting a date.

During the peak seasons of *Ne rodis' krasivoi*, five episodes a week were shot at the Moscow studios. The leading actress, Nelli Uvarova, was not allowed to be seen looking attractive in public until the final show aired – and her heroine's dreams realized. The promotional materials explained this growing tension and audience expectation:

> This is the story of Katia. She works as a secretary in a company called Zimaletto. Although nature has blessed her with great intellect, a wonderful character and a pure spirit, no man – alas – has ever cast an interested glance in her direction. But ... despite her unremarkable appearance, Katia still dreams about love and happiness.

We must wait with her. The sometimes music-hall humor of this series is emphasized by the endless, unnatural arrangements of small, wisecracking groups at work. Two, three, or four people chip in with suggestions of how to help Katia ... but her problems endure.

Another heroine in the same line-up has it no easier, specifically in A-Media's version of the ABC serial *Grace under Fire* (1993–8). Brett Butler's Russified heroine, once upon a time called Grace Kelly, is here played by the ever-excellent

Tat'iana Dogileva and now known as Liubov' Orlova. She lives in a forgettable, sleepy rural community within striking distance of Moscow called Babkinsk. Here Liubov' (i.e. "Love") suffers from the same problems documented in the US version, such as a bad factory job and an even worse ex-husband. Much of the original's prickly wittiness has survived in the Russian remake (thanks, once again, to Nonna Grishaeva) – and the show's sets (Orlova's living room and kitchen) have a marked similarity to the original ABC stage. Sony, after all, maintains the right to final edits of any scripts and related visual material.

Maybe these copycat shows aren't even "Russian" any more? In the summer of 2005, British research was published into the formula of a universally "perfect" sitcom. This formula has been referenced by the Russian press in the light of STS and its comic line-up, together with a few worries about the impending arrival of even more remakes:[27]

> The scientists found that the comedic value of a sitcom was determined by multiplying the recognizable qualities of the main character by their delusions of grandeur. This is added to the verbal wit of the script and the total is multiplied by the amount someone falls over. The total is divided by the success of any scheme during the show and the difference in social status between the highest and lowest ranking characters is then added.[28]

These categories, strict as they are, may indeed prove a guide to future evening schedules, especially where a heroine's unsteady social status (or her husband's posturing) is so often threatened by Moscow.

Russia has struggled with the sitcom format for years, and these copycat shows mark the first real breakthrough since *Strawberry Café* (*Kafe Klubnichka*) in the late 1990s – which nobody remembers. The interior and exterior of the café's forecourt looked cheap to the point of cynicism and Channel One's daytime broadcast schedule did little to help the show judge itself against serious competition. The most telling attempt thus far to stay domestic has been the TNT show *Sasha Plus Masha* that uses two- or three-minute, often unrelated (but genuinely droll) sketches about a typical young woman and her partner. Here is how the "non-Sony," truly Russian couple is promoted:

> She's no supermodel; he's no Di Caprio, either. They don't live in Paris. They're just the same as you and me. They love one another, but that doesn't stop them arguing. They lead a typical life and they've got hundreds of stories about how to live together. Masha loves her mother, Sasha, sex and sad movies; she doesn't like stupid jokes, horror films or football. There are two things she can make from nothing: a salad and a mountain out of a molehill. She'd love to give up smoking ... and get married. Sasha loves football, motorbikes and computers. He doesn't like

taking ages to get dressed, his mother-in-law or conversations about babies. Life for him is a complete funfair – where Masha's the main attraction!

For all this admirable effort, the most popular *bona fide* sitcoms still come from once-foreign material. The best and funniest example of an STS, peripherally shunted heroine is another Sony collaboration entitled *Moia prekrasnaia niania* (*My Fair Nanny*). The basic structure, as can be seen from the plot synopsis below, is taken directly from the CBS New York sitcom *The Nanny* (1993–9); here a Queens accent is swapped for a Ukrainian equivalent and Broadway becomes the theatrical world of Moscow:

> The show takes place in Moscow, where thirty-year-old Vika Prutkovskaia lives. Until she was fifteen, Vika lived in [laughably provincial] Mariupol'; now she's on the outskirts of the capital, working in a small boutique that belongs to her fiancé Anton. Vika wants to get married, but it turns out that Anton isn't ready yet. Moreover, he has another woman in his life; he fires Vika so that his new fiancée can take her place. Vika starts selling cosmetics door-to-door. She'd have gone on living this simple life, the kind that millions of our viewers know so well ... if she hadn't one day knocked on the door of the Shatalin family, who were looking for a nanny. This only happens in the movies, but suddenly Vika finds herself in the stylish apartment of theater producer Maksim Shatalin! That's the kind of thing most of us can only dream about!

This series exploded with such success over 2005 that box sets were on sale by New Year 2006, offering 104 episodes on ten DVDs, together with additional recordings of the show's "200 best jokes." By February of the same year the lead actress was already winning newspaper polls as the nation's favorite heroine.[29] These accomplishments have taken the host channel by surprise, but STS has quickly learned to milk the situation. Episodes can now run up to three times a day (morning, primetime, and midnight), constantly pulling in a market share of up to 38 percent.[30] The work involved here is intense, all in the name of what general director Aleksandr Rodnianskii has often called the desire of STS to proffer a reality that doesn't exist, but *ought* to.[31] Rodnianskii's plans thus do not differ in any way from the identical phrasing used to promote Nikita Mikhalkov's nostalgic and patriotic epic of 1999, *The Barber of Siberia*.

Each episode in this popular version of what life ought to be costs about $50,000 to shoot – at the rate of one show per day until twenty-five storylines have been committed to video. The American version of the show had 130 episodes when it finally went to syndication; when STS was planning the Slavic equivalent, twenty of these were deemed unsuitable for Russification, since the humor was too culturally specific.[32] The six editions needed to make 110 from 104 were saved for festive timeslots in the 2005–6 New

Year's line-up. STS had no qualms about running against major feature films on opposing networks.

So what of our provincial heroine's fairytale in the Big City? The likelihood of marriage between nanny and employer (Anastasiia Zavorotniuk and Sergei Zhigunov) always looks greater than it did between Fran Drescher and Charles Shaughnessy in the original version. The possibility of our heroine "coming home" and reaching her goal is *almost* offered, over and over, to the point where some viewers start to tire of the suspended tension: "Will Shatalin and Vika get married this season? Of course not."[33] In order keep more patient and forgiving viewers interested, the series employs a large number of guest stars and singers, which does not stretch credulity, given Shatalin's work as a theater producer. Fedor Bondarchuk even took time out from filming his *Company Nine* epic to play a small role. Bondarchuk's post-Soviet patriotism fits neatly with the show's intentions, despite any apparent discrepancy between frightening wars and funny marriages. In one interview, by way of illustration, the pivotal character of the butler (Boris Smolkin) was asked to play a game of word association. To the word "song" he answered "Dunaevskii"; to the word "victory" he replied, "Second World War." Even the funniest shows are carrying some serious, socialist baggage from Stalinist cinema of the 1940s. They do so both happily and earnestly.

Rumors are told of child-minding agencies around Russia that now get phone calls from people who insist on "a nanny *just like that*."[34] Building a bridge between fantasy and reality is helped somewhat by the fact that Zavorotniuk's own life shares some parallels with her well-traveled heroine. She struggled for a few years in Los Angeles as an actress, but returned to Russia in order to stay close to friends, family, and the language she realized would be inherent in any future, potential success.[35] She had to make way for destiny and/or chance. She had failed the casting call for *Poor Nastia* and was only invited to try for *Moia prekrasnaia niania* after 1,500 other actresses had been interviewed. The invitation came totally unexpectedly – by phone when she was on holiday in Anapa.[36] Zavorotniuk (a mother of two) also maintains that she shares with Vika the traits of "a loving, faithful individual who would never do anything to hurt the kids."[37]

The ability of our peripheral Ukrainian nanny or other "dispensable" heroines to fashion their own biographies often seems very much in doubt. So much so, in fact, that the theatricality of the show's kitschy appearance and frequently physical humor recalls many facets of *I Love Lucy*, a parallel that was often drawn in the 1990s with Drescher's own humor.

It is, perhaps because of this increasingly frantic comedy from an often desperate society that people have begun to use new media in order to write their own lifelines *beyond* TV, in the aimless spirit of gonzo journalism. In the summer of 2004, *Nezavisimaia gazeta* expressed its hope that Russian newspapers and television might become kinder, more humane and fairer (i.e. more realistic) in their reflection of actuality. As an example of how to write your *own* story and do so in a way that was gently, admirably shapeless or open to chance intrusion, the newspaper went in search of video bloggers who draw directly upon Hunter Thompson for their inspiration.[38] People have started plotting their own entertaining lifelines as funny or fascinating yarns. Debates over who owns the rights to storytelling have become an enormously important part of Russia's cultural landscape, especially in the form of piracy. The private stories open to legal dispute here can be short three-minute songs or three-hour films.

As early as 2000, the Russian media started showing interest in the fate of American website mp3.com, not only because of the legal aspects, but because digital formats might allow people to establish their own personal archives and private soundtracks, irrespective of geography and bank accounts. Russian arguments over the legal aspects of up- and downloading biographies began to sound loud and clear:

- What if an individual *wants* his story to be heard and downloaded?
- How do I know if the individual *didn't* want me to download it?
- What if I download a song and it turns out to be something entirely different?
- Hyperlinks often take me where I don't want to go. Is that my fault?
- Am I to blame if some spammer sends me a file I don't want?
- Other people can find and abuse my passwords to media-rich sites with no great effort.[39]

The massive *means* used to fight private storytelling in America were compared by the Russian press to their "laughable" results; Russia aside, illegally downloaded narratives worldwide (of both songs and film) were outnumbering legal purchases three to one. The horrible failure of Sony's XCP anti-piracy software late in 2005 did little to placate individuals; in fact news of the previous year that America's recording industry had 2,454 copyright cases running simultaneously – most of which were failing – brought some Slavic observers considerable joy. This in turn irked Western media moguls, of course, especially since the US government has recently claimed that $6 billion of fair trade is *not* taking place due to pirate production in Slavdom.[40] Even when Russian mp3 sites do operate legally, they charge for an entire album or film what an American consumer would pay for a single song – and so the US industry loses even more.

The first six months of 2004 in St. Petersburg alone witnessed twenty-six copyright-abuse cases, since 80 percent (if not more) of audio-video material on sale around the city was assumed to be pirated. Whatever the eventual outcome of these cases, however, the often unfunny, deterministic storytelling of Moscow's state-run media has meant that some viewers and listeners in the nation's backwaters have already turned their technical savvy to other ends, in particular to videocasting. Here, perhaps, at long last are mobile forms of self-definition, safe from the damage done by one's (unfashionable, underfunded) address.

Information about podcasting started coming seriously to Russia in 2004 from a number of sources: word of mouth, search engine rubrics, news stories, and links to overseas, English-language web pages. Slowly the nation started bypassing Moscow television by investigating a form of "Do-It-*Yourself* Reality Shows," the term given to Russian podcasts by our gonzo youngsters. The most famous exponent of this medium has been ex-MTV Russia presenter Vasilii Strel'nikov; he used it to come in from the rural cold:

> For twelve years I talked with the entire world; I presented musical programs, read the news and was the happiest guy on Earth. After all, people heard my voice in the furthest corners of the planet! There are no words to explain that kind of feeling! ... Nowadays everything's a lot simpler. In order to broadcast to the whole world you don't require powerful transmitters or special studios. You can do it from your bedroom via the internet! It's called podcasting, from the words "I-Pod" and "Broadcasting." All you need is a PC or a MAC, a soundcard and a microphone! Download the free Audacity MP3 recorder for Windows, Mac or Linux. That allows you record and edit sound files ... Record your show – about 10 or twenty minutes. It could be a story about your life, your friends, family, work or study. It's a kind of "live magazine." The whole planet will hear you![41]

Quite frequently this activity has been defined by the Russian press as "personal media." You show the world what you would like it know: the long, intermittent and awfully provincial stories that would otherwise go unnoticed. Coherence is thus given to peripheral, oft-"transported" members of society. Some of podcasting's ardent, anarchic members even hope that it will "kill" radio altogether.[42] Bloggers and podcasters are riding a wave that observers believe will constitute a worldwide audience of 75 million listeners by 2010. The minority will soon constitute a majority ... or so believe the rural romantics.

Any possibility for change and social agency in the narration of new stories, however, has a very long way to travel. Strel'nikov, in a witty aside, has recently recalled the text of what he holds to be Russia's first podcast, placed upon his personal site. Having been away from Moscow's TV stations for several years, he decided to return from the uninhabited edges of the map: "Hello, kids. I'm Vasilii Strel'nikov. Thanks for visiting our site. I'm alive and well. I'm on my pension and living in the forest!"[43] No wonder these tiny private chronicles of self-made agency are again handed over to humor and self-irony. Ukrainian nannies from Mariupol' only seem believable when filtered through irony, and forty-something VJs spend as much time mocking their own, ongoing (yet increasingly famous) diaries as they do composing them. Hence the ironic TV series.

7 Comedy
Nervous giggling and its serious object

Putin's rhetoric is an amazing, really strange mishmash of ideas. They come from modern, liberal political jargon ("The Market," "Reforms," "New Technology'), the lingo of some Stalinist empire ("Traitors," "The Dictatorship of Law"), the political terminology of Pobedonostsev's era ("Russia's Enemies") and a hotchpotch of army or prison slang like his famous "We'll kill 'em in the shithouse" – all of which has opened the path to millions of simple Russian souls.[1]

Post-Soviet classrooms and the dismissal of chronology

This cutting assessment of how Putin tells a nation's story comes courtesy of late St. Petersburg poet Viktor Krivulin. He maintains the president's stylistic searching is born of an awkward awareness that Russia's erstwhile power structures are now completely absent. This discomfort is then exacerbated by a secondary, repressed uneasiness regarding his ambiguous status as the nation's "chosen" leader. Thus he zips back and forth between styles, hoping to persuade the various factions of a huge society – including himself. Other commentators today propose that Putin's manufactured demeanor and humorless gravitas may in fact be dictated more by pandering, consciously or otherwise, to the big, important members of the G8, as seen in *Lichnyi nomer*.[2]

Nobody at home is sure which style to take seriously, because the lines between self-assured pomp and heavily subsidized self-delusion are sometimes very thin. This same stylistic slippage feeds into the importance of ironic television series – and, consequently, into the fate of the Soviet tradition as a whole, a timeless issue well underlined by the Channel One mystical thriller *Khiromant* (*The Palmist*) of 2005. A young man sees "the sign of Stalin or Hitler" printed on the palms of today's future tyrants, because "times may have changed, but people are still the same."

Part of this quandary has been audible in Russian schoolrooms for some while. As the Soviet Union vanished in the 1990s, it presented itself to the schoolchildren who would grow up to become today's television target audience. Their teachers wondered what could possibly be salvaged from the literary canon. Many schoolbooks of the 1990s begin with an open admission of revisionism and related problems. When talk turned to the classics like *How the Steel Was Tempered*, for example, children were offered the following caveat:

> In conditions where social mores are being reevaluated, our attitude also changes towards works which even in the recent past were at our bedsides. These were books whose heroes were models for our lives and destinies ... [The problem is that] we today simply can't comprehend or believe the happiness of a generation that sacrificed its life so "there'd be no dark stain on the Revolution's scarlet banner." An individual who fights loyally for a grand idea will always be attractive to readers' hearts. Today we need those lessons of history.[3]

Soviet storytelling was reassessed *en bloc*. It was suggested, even in schools of distant Cheboksary, that Soviet socialist realism should in retrospect be defined as "critical-affirmative realism," as it neither lost the critical tendencies of nineteenth century practice nor reached the difficult, forgiving goal of an art form that was entirely affirmative and therefore open to all kinds of change, intrusion, or influence.[4] In view of the fact that Gor'kii was now rarely referred to in schools without "a mocking shade of irony," did other aspects of his spoiled "grand idea" still warrant the attention of young people and their educators?[5]

One important classroom anthology of 1994 interpreted that literary "grandness" not as specifically Soviet but as "an eternal dream of mankind," the magic inherent in any secular text that takes upon itself an "Evangelical" function. On the road to a salvationary "grandeur ... we achieved nothing. Or, more accurately, we achieved a great deal, but at a cost we never foresaw. More often than not, we simply didn't get what we reckoned on. But the dream remains, all the same. Is it even achievable?"[6]

In general, reassessment of "the dream" led to kinder questions like this: "Are Gor'kii's works relevant now, when the role and significance of the Revolution in the life of our country [are] being examined? In all probability: Yes."[7] One reason given to school kids to support this view was that Russian culture cannot be positioned either inside or outside of the Soviet Union. It is the property neither of the émigré intelligentsia, nor of the internal, "underground" writers who worked with such difficulty under dictatorial constraints. It is *all* of the above, inside and out, approved and disapproved, spiritual and atheist, home and away: "In a wonderful manner all of these multihued extensions gradually interweave in a complex, but unified, polyphonic sound. Russian culture did not self-destruct. Once again, it triumphed."[8]

Exam questions in Moscow in 2001 also asked children why the 1930s may perhaps not be a hopeless "dark tunnel" in Soviet history. What if, they continued, we include the happiness of popular movies and musicals of the time?[9]

This same textbook explained its step away from political oversimplification in a useful introduction, casting a simultaneous glance back to the generation raised under Brezhnev that now makes television programs about the period:

> Your older brothers and sisters (not to mention your parents) read in their textbooks that the main (or only) tradition of Russian literature was founded in revolutionary and liberating ideals. Today that view is being reconsidered. After all, the revolutionary tradition was only one part of Russian literature's rich and expansive nature. It had many moral orientations, a profound spirituality and humanism. It was the source of both the [secular] State *and* a religious or philosophical understanding of the world.[10]

A Russian-language Latvian textbook examining literature of the entire twentieth century, also published in 2001, summarizes much of what we are documenting in terms of a hopeful passage from words to silence, logic to love, city to nature, and from things exclusive to those accepting. It records the fact that in March of 1988 at a late Congress of the Soviet Writers' Union, a Latvian writer defined the three major themes facing literature as "ecology, language and history." A fellow countryman took the stand and repeated this concern for the "ecological environment." This came at the same time as Valentin Rasputin's interview with the magazine *Smena* after he had been able to avert disastrous governmental plans to redirect several Siberian rivers: "I'd like more than anything to be busy with literature right now. But things don't work out that way."[11] Literature and ecology, say today's teachers, were both interrelated and equally pressing at a recent time when the Soviet Union was evanescing once and for all, when rhetoric meant less and less.

There is little agreement even today over which stories should be saved in the public memory. In February 2003, 100-volume sets of classic Russian literature (all the way from medieval annals to the present) were sent to every Russian school. Production costs ran to 170 million rubles for the first edition alone. These books were hardbound, published by the Drofa house and financed by the state (i.e. at taxpayers' expense). Standard school holdings, said the education minister Vladimir Filippov, were "downright outdated."[12] The choice of writers from the late twentieth century caused much argument, because authors sympathetic to Putin's policies found much more space on the printed page; critical darlings, genuinely popular, and scandalous writers were all simply absent.

The selection of authors for the Soviet period was, however, both more interesting and less contentious. Writers of those decades known well to Western readers were often blessed with individual, even multiple volumes to their name: Sholokhov, Pasternak, Bulgakov, Zamiatin, Solzhenitsyn, or Platonov, by way of example. Gor'kii is one of the few writers with three volumes, giving voice to the Soviet tradition in its early, less strident form. He is joined by various contemporaries who, as proposed, are perhaps "more"

Soviet: A. Tolstoi, Fedin, Ivanov, Kataev, Leonov, and Paustovskii. These authors have been drawn upon in the course of this study, since they dovetail with television yarns today; they combine both majesty and modesty. Irony and humor on the small screen help gingerly to map out a similar style at the end of a grand, canonical tradition. Humor helps when nobody knows quite what to say – or how to say it.

The UPS Agency (*Agentstvo NLS,* from 2001), *Sisters* (*Sestry,* 2004), and *Women in a Lawless Game* (*Zhenshchiny v igre bez pravil,* 2004)

A genre popular in Russian storytelling today is the "ironic detective tale," looking with a wry smile at our yarns of masterful criminals or sage, perspicacious detectives. A good place to start would be the wonderful series *The UPS Agency* (dir. Dmitrii Parmenov). While there are certainly romantic tendencies in the TV adaptations of Dar'ia Dontsova's books mentioned earlier, they usually take the form of middle-aged modesty and are consigned to the level of subplot. *The UPS Agency*, however, is driven wholly by affairs of the heart. First of all, the agency's very name includes an abbreviation for "Unusual Private Situations." Cases cracked by the agency's three young (and amateurish) detectives always involve somebody's amorous or familial mishap. Second, the three young people find, given their age (early twenties), that sexual tensions buzz between them from time to time. These two issues make for a muddle of romance and other emotional schemes:

> The agency's youthful colleagues have handled ... all the tricky intricacy of other people's confidential affairs. They've broken through webs of intrigue and tracked down brides who vanished on the eve of their wedding ... Each of the films in this series is unique, separate, and unconnected to the others. That's why it's hard to define this serial's genre.[13]

The magazine *TV-Park* distinguished this series from other works by its "kindness and irony," since it treats off-hand love stories as high drama. The host station, TNT, explained further how kindness forms a work ethic:

> The UPS Agency takes on any case that a normal detective would happily turn down. In order to see each case to the end, various disguises are needed; the threesome needs to adopt all kinds of strange personae and enter the world of their adversaries. But in any situation, even the trickiest, the trustiest weapon of all will save our heroes: humor.[14]

Affirmative, inclusive kindness and humor counteract the cruelty of typical melodramas – they offset Muscovite emphases. Not only is the series set and shot in St. Petersburg, but the show's promoters make much of the provincial origins of its actors (from Vologda and Poltava). Smaller characters from smaller towns will be loved by more and more people. The small reflects and makes the big:

> I [Igor' Botvin] lived in Moscow when I was in the army; I was in the Spetsnaz. Then I went home to Vologda. I slobbed around for a bit and then made a break for it – to Petersburg where my sister lives. Lived there for a while, went out and about … I liked the place. So I went home, grabbed my stuff and moved to Petersburg for good.[15]

As a result, the "lad from Vologda has become the idol of Russia's women right before our eyes." When he finally traveled back to his village after a ten-year absence, "he went to visit all the friends and acquaintances that used to laugh at him. Some had become alcoholics, some had got married …. Now they looked at Igor' with respect and asked him all about working in TV."[16] He had worked his way into the hearts of young girls amid St. Petersburg's classical beauty with bodybuilding and an enduring admiration for Arnold Schwarzenegger.[17]

The parallel systems of love and provincial inclusiveness are furthered by the fact that the series' crew prides itself on wanting to shoot outdoors without drawing any attention. In one instance

> there was a sign hanging at the entrance to a gas station: "Dear Drivers! Don't be concerned. We're just filming." The crew occupied a motel, set up their apparatus and lighting. And the drivers who came by to grab a bite, or the long-haul truckers setting things up for a stopover, paid no real attention to what was going on. They all quickly went away, each on his own business.[18]

The quiet, ironic, and iconoclastic treatment of detective stories with friendship and flirting adopts a grander scale in *Sisters* (dir. Anton Sivers), produced in 2004 by Dmitrii Meskhiev and Valerii Todorovskii for Rossiia. The satirical linkages between romance and wrongdoing are extended in *Sisters* as domestic spats and broken hearts turn into *bona fide* criminal activity:

> Each of the three charming sisters has her own destiny, her own profession, and her own men. Nina is married to a successful surgeon but prefers to earn her living by driving cars [into Russia] from abroad. She is forced to take on this dangerous work after her husband starts having problems on his job. The middle sister, Alla, is a beautiful red-haired business lady, while Masha, the youngest, works at a TV station and dreams of becoming a famous journalist. Life in this big family is far from simple – every one of the sisters has a strong character and will stand up for what she believes in.

Figure 7.1 Sisters.

Dragged into and out of various (male) schemes, the sisters' proximity to a normal relationship grows in an inverse relationship to the adventure. The more chaos, the less romance; the more romance, the greater peace, quiet, and chances of a pleasing denouement. The greatest juxtaposition between male destruction and female emotional construction comes late in the twelve-episode series when Masha (Liubov' Tikhomirova) is drugged in a café by a

Comedy 155

deranged photographer. Already cursed with a boyfriend who is often drunk and always indecisive, she now awakes from the pills and cognac to discover she is bound, gagged, and trapped within a locked mansion somewhere at a mystery location. Male conceptions of love are more than proprietary.

The confusion, car chases, and shoot-outs that mark the lives led by such strong-headed characters are aptly captured in the title of the 2004 Rossiia series *Women in a Lawless Game*, made by Iurii Moroz, the director of the detective series *Kamenskaia*. Here, too, the love of women is potentially a driving force. As Moroz himself has said, the series is:

> a real melodrama of love and that's what it shares with *Kamenskaia*. There are five central heroines; initially I undertook this project to try and look at love's various stages. There's the first sentiment of a very young girl, the fortuitous love of a mother, and the late, but extremely feisty romance of a grandmother who's still in the prime of life.[19]

> The wheel of fortune interweaves peoples' destinies in magical ways. It gives rise to new connections and changes the world around us all. At the center of the story are three women: Mariia Petrovna, Elena, and Alka. Three generations of women in one family – each of them is fated to meet her true love. The grandmother will find her final love; the mother's love will be unexpected and brief. The daughter's love will be her first. No matter how each of their fates comes together, no matter what difficulties fall to their lot, these women are sure of one thing. Only love can overcome misfortune. (Promotional text.)

The various plots are entwined not so much by shared knowledge among characters as by a tongue-in-cheek narrative amplified by quirky comments upon frozen frames, on-screen text, and other games played with the acceleration/deceleration of events passing before us. Much of this is very reminiscent of *Amélie* (dir. Jean-Pierre Jeunet, 2001). The workings of destiny are so complex they can only be described in a childlike or mocking, disjointed fashion which does little to aid comprehension. One connection between such social conjecture and real life (that is, between fairytales and feasibility) is made by the casting of musician Garik Sukachev, who plays himself as a singer admired by one of the sisters from afar. What brings all the characters together, such as the husband of a car accident victim and a divorcée looking for a fresh start, is devotion – either among adults or for a young woman in difficulty after an unexpected pregnancy.

That Balzac Age, or All Men Are Basta . . . (Bal'zakovskii vozrast, ili Vse muzhiki svo . . . , 2004–5)

If the success of these series and their aspirations to realism are dependent upon the *reflection* of something (very often fated) rather than the creation of something bold and socially subversive *ex nihilo*, then a problem hovering forever in the background is whether these series also "re-present" somebody else's (already presented and accepted) reality, perhaps that of American studios. Of late, the loudest and most publicly discussed example of cultural fawning outside of sitcoms has been the relationship between NTV's romantic series "for middle-aged women" *That Balzac Age, or All Men Are Basta...* (dir. Dmitrii Fiks) and HBO's *Sex and the City* (1998–2002).

The difference (which could either complicate or negate accusations of plagiarism) between the two serials is defined as follows:

> We've got people here [in Russia] who can talk about love, too; they can talk about sex without prudishness and vulgarity. They can do it with *humor*. That's what makes our version no less interesting – sometimes more so, actually. Nonetheless the main heroine in this serial remains Love, even if She isn't mentioned in the credits. This is Love in all Her manifestations and misfortunes, Love through tears and laughter. On their way through life these four girlfriends will encounter wealthy admirers and youthful lovers, charming rabbis and gorgeous (albeit suspicious-looking) guys. Each of the heroines will have to answer the question: "Are all men really basta ... ?" Is it worth giving up and surrendering to life's unfairness? Or, despite it all, *not* give up hope and keep on believing there's a prince out there somewhere waiting for each of them on a white horse? A prince who's briefly lost in the labyrinths of the Big City?[20]

Even if this is a convincing definition of difference, it leans terribly heavily (and carefully) on the model it claims to disown. This was hardly a series composed in a carefree, slapdash manner, either: 250 actresses were tried for each of the four female roles:[21]

> Singing the tune of this American serial to a Russian melody, the [Slavic] screenwriters ignored some key circumstances, such as differences between cultural traditions ... [The authors forgot] that talking about "you-know-what" in public in Russian or English are two totally different things. When four female New Yorkers, all wealthy and successful, emancipated women, give forth on the nuances of an orgasm or the correct relationship between penis length and vagina width, it seems neither tasteless nor vulgar. The linguistic peculiarities of the great and mighty Russian language are such that even if we ignore the comedic element of the serial, it all looks helpless and unconvincing.[22]

The women's magazine *Kleo* went as far as tabulating the similarities between the two shows and even matching the characters one to one: Sarah Jessica Parker and Iuliia Men'shova; Cynthia Nixon and Lada Dens; Kim Cattrall and Zhanna Èpple; Kristin Davis and Alika Smekhova. In addition,

Figure 7.2 That Balzac Age.

the male partners seemed to repeat various New York characters, just as the roles of the cities themselves (New York and Moscow) overlap. The differences, somewhat harshly, were here defined as dramatic ability, the number of awards won, and the number of episodes (99 versus 12): "Twelve doesn't seem like a lot but, on the other hand, there's no need for any more. Please, no more!"[23]

For all that, the debut in June 2004 was a hit, allowing NTV to outstrip Channel One in primetime – a very rare event of late. Even more surprising, a large part of the show's audience was stolen from the classic detective series running simultaneously on Channel One and discussed below, *Streets of Broken Lights* (*Ulitsy razbitykh fornarei*). Doubts had persisted right until the debut, since a late spring or early summer release never bodes well for a healthy market share – especially in a cold country like Russia, where good weather means bad TV statistics. But many people were happy to stay home and follow the romantic adventures of four women questioning traditional notions of age and gender. As Iuliia Men'shova put it:

> If you live with the feeling that you're 30, that you've got a child and have been dumped, then of course your personal life is going to come to a standstill. What matters here is not the man, not the child, but how you see yourself and your age ... Some ladies sit at home and suffer: "I'm 30, I've got no husband. Poor me, what am I to do? 40 isn't far off!" They've just got divorced, the pain hasn't passed yet, but she's already driving herself on so she can jump into another marriage as soon as possible. Get a grip! Look after your kids first of all! A husband will turn up sooner or later.[24]

Fate and self-definition walk hand in hand. The latter is an American import.

The Literary Gazette was unimpressed. It judged the series from the standpoint that "generic, narrative and intonational unpredictability" are always the key to good storytelling, whereas NTV was offering "graphomania" and a "clearly unprofessional," if not "helpless," screenplay. Any attempt to match *Sex and the City* in a land that never had its own sexual revolution was bound to look sad and silly.[25] The problem was not new: the Soviet women's magazine *Female Worker* (*Rabotnitsa*) had never looked anything like *Cosmopolitan* and the Russian show's dialog remained stubbornly on the level of "mentally retarded seventh-graders," which didn't help matters.[26]

Yet that purported retardation or unshakeable Slavic air could perhaps help to foster the show's success, as the journal *Ogonek* thought. The American HBO series had not garnered especially high ratings when it ran in Russia; a local version with a local reality surely stood a better chance?[27] It could even help people by offering them emotional support grounded in identifiable domestic experience:

> There are so many women like that in [our] life. They could learn from others' [dramatized] mistakes. It's not a perfect game to play, of course. Nor, come to that, are the show's plots perfect, either ... But what *is* ideal in our life? The main thing is that it's nice to watch. It may not be for everybody, but lots of people *will* like it. It's not "Cinema for Everyone," but it's certainly for a lot of people.[28]

Comedy 159

Soldiers (*Soldaty*, since 2004), *The Bachelors* (*Kholostiaki*, 2004), and *Next* (since 2001)

Here we see irony applied to three other, less girly topics: military service, the "drama" of bachelor life, and crime. *Soldiers*, dedicated to the first of these rubrics, has enjoyed great success. It had already run to an eleventh series by the spring of 2007 and remains a good example of how funniness and insecure patriotism frequently inform each other:

> Two friends, having lost contact with on another in civilian life, unexpectedly meet in the Military Enlistment Office [when drafted for national service]. A big-city playboy and a village lad will now trudge their way through service together. As usual, doing one's civic duty always involves lots of things that go wrong. The biggest disaster of all is their "comrade" commander, played by Boris Shcherbakov. He's a textbook officer; the kind that wouldn't climb the Alps for anything – and so ends up in a ton of jokes instead. His new recruits encounter everything, all the way from hazing to going AWOL [absent without leave]. And every so often, in a non-regulation sort of way, romance blossoms in the troops, too – between a nurse, a major and a foot soldier. That's the kind of love triangle that even Shakespeare would envy.

The series has turned out to be the most successful project of its kind for the host station, REN-TV. This is due not so much to the enduring popularity of Shcherbakov or to the more modish reputation of costar Pavel Maikov, but the fact that army service is a virtually universal experience. Each of the actors has appeared in newspapers, turning the severity of two years in the military into nationally fond memories, jokes, or even recipes for very simple pleasures enjoyed by recruits "back then" with virtually no ingredients, such as potato pancakes.[29] *Soldiers* in fact benefits from a special popularity with émigré audiences, too, perhaps as a vicarious, cathartic experience of genuine danger (in Afghanistan or Chechnya) avoided by those whose forefathers left the USSR.

In a similarly broad gesture across the social canvas, the series entitled *The Bachelors* debuted in October 2004. The Moscow setting immediately invited parallels between the show and its female forerunner, *That Balzac Age*. In fact some viewers even complained that the (irritatingly persistent) theme music and title sequences had been swiped from *Sex and the City*. This Muscovite male edition was dedicated to "four bosom buddies, tied by an undying love for pretty young women." The men in question are Oleg (Oleg Fomin), owner of a lingerie store; car salesman Anatolii (Evgenii Stychkin); heart surgeon Dima (Dmitrii Pevtsov); and ladies' man Gosha (Marat Basharov). Although all four actors are married in actuality, the producers were not concerned about their commitment to verisimilitude,

160 *Russian television today*

since bachelor life – like military service – "is something we've all been through at some point."[30] These are four guys for whom women are a "measure of ambition, self-justification – and faith in oneself":

> We meet these four inseparable friends at the very moment when one of them, Dima, is being dumped by his wife. The second bachelor, Oleg, is suffering fits of jealousy from his partner; the third is being introduced by his mother to yet another "girl from a good family." The ex-wives of the fourth bachelor, Tolia, keep coming back to him. In other words, there's no room for boredom in the lives of these four handsome buddies.

The demands placed upon the actors in their depiction of "absolute" normality were considerable. It takes twenty-four episodes for them to overcome their typical if not "ridiculous phobias and complexes." Pevtsov said that humor and emotion in the series were central to any convincing portrait of ordinariness. Typical experience was therefore tied closely to self-doubt, silliness, and a drawn-out, gentle complexity. Irony, by making pomp difficult and decision-making less arrogant, came closer to something beyond self-assured platitudes. "Playing this particular bachelor," he said, was "more difficult than bringing a murderer, woman or some nervous wreck to the screen." Stychkin concurred, stating that humor and self-deprecation would be crucial in capturing a fleeting "golden mean" between crude caricature and mere vulgarity.[31]

Yet despite any aspirations towards universality, this would still somehow be a very "Russian" project, in opposition to what Basharov has termed the "conveyor" style of screenplay production in the United States.[32] Important here is the degree to which improvisation was permitted on screen; normal, adlibbed, and spontaneous behavior would hopefully save the show from anything formulaic. In fact Oleg Fomin went as far as saying that "almost every" scene would end with some off-the-cuff inventiveness.[33] Using these techniques, Basharov was pleased that *Bachelors*, along with more and more of Russia's TV series, was able to avoid accusations of "shabbiness."[34] This was certainly true enough to attract the interest of several stars from other art forms, playing in secondary guest roles, such as leggy Anna Semenovich from the ensemble *Blestiashchie*:

> What could be more enjoyable for a young (or not so young) secretary, editor, translator, teacher, office manager or even her ambitious assistant than a long tale of pure, happy – or unhappy – love? A love unburdened by material worries, by relatives or any other grim obligations? A story about men; not the smartest, not the brightest, not the best bred ... but nonetheless indispensable *men*? The kind who're around for just one day, for a night, for a year – for life, even? What, too, could be more pleasant for our own overgrown, flighty "playboys" than a story of wish-fulfillment – about successfully conquering a woman? A story unburdened

by all the consequences of that love – which makes the story no less cheerful ... ?³⁵

The jokes come fast and furious in the series, which involves so many failed relationships with so many women that at times it seems completely unstructured. Refusing to take itself too seriously, it has numerous in-jokes, too, for example about the endless, wandering plot of *Poor Nastia*, patriotism ("one's wife, like one's homeland, is never chosen"), or Soviet rhetoric (the turning of one life, not society as a whole, from "fairytale into reality"). The loss of a girlfriend is directly paralleled with a Soviet officer's loss of life, while the desire to flee a difficult relationship is justified by Gor'kii's departure for Capri in times gone by.

As this flippancy may suggest, the series makes fun of its own unwillingness to shoulder grand themes. Troubled females suffer from what the four men call the "Anna Karenina" syndrome, and any talk of virtues learned from Dostoevskii is dealt with on purely sentimental, not intellectual terms. The antics of these four adults (and their companions) are better handled by quotes from Soviet cartoon characters (Karlson) or pop-lyrics, either Soviet (*Stoiat devchonki*) or modern (*Aleshka* by *Ruki vverkh*). The heroes even undermine their own story by remarking, for example, that today's untalented actresses work on TV (not in live theater or film); likewise they adopt the ironic addressing of the camera begun by US series such as the mid-1980s *Moonlighting* (ABC). This silliness extends to the outright plundering of scenes from recent and renowned romantic comedies, like the massed stampede of brides usurping Renée Zellweger in 1989's *The Bachelor* (dir. G. Sinyor).

The same happy irony hangs over *Next* (rarely referred to by its Russian title *Sleduiushchii*), starring Aleksandr Abdulov as crime kingpin, Lavr. Based around the relationship between Lavr and an unexpectedly discovered son, the series in each of its three hypostases has placed a clear moral dilemma before its hero: crime or fatherhood, crime or peaceful retirement, and crime or married life. Each of the options, between what might become Stychkin's caricatures or simplified vulgarity, is defined by the promotional staff at REN-TV as an "uncompromising struggle," yet the show always treats that dramatic duality with a light sense of humor.³⁶ It's so serious it has to be funny; if the characters didn't laugh, they'd cry.

Various institutional stereotypes are politely ridiculed. Parenthood is often referred to as nothing more than funding a child's education with well-timed bribes; Lavr's bodyguards satisfy their desire for a macho outlet by shooting empty bottles, even though his newly found son shows them that football does the job just as well. Questions over Lavr's sexuality, given that he is of "solid" age and still not married, are dismissed as nonsense, since he is "a Bolshevik" – synonymous here with warm-blooded heterosexuality, to borrow a phrase from Ian Fleming.

The series' screenwriters were aware of their silliness, but still built the narrative on a serious, well-intentioned, and sentimental foundation. The story is emotionally credible. When Lavr reveals to his lost son that he is indeed the boy's father, the youngster asks: "You're my father? This is some kind of Mexican serial!" Lavr replies: "I don't care if it's a Brazilian one! A fact remains a fact" – and it has emotional, civil validity as a result.

What exactly is post-Socialist irony hiding from?

    Russia's national resources are its greatest wealth.

(Putin, 2001)

As already noted, Putin's official stance on the social role of television has for years made much of its relationship to freedom, for "without truly free media, Russian democracy will not survive, and we will not succeed in building a civil society."[37] And yet for all the related governmental grumbling over ethical standards on some channels, it is universally accepted by the public that money decides almost everything on the small screen. The promise of (fundable) airtime and/or the removal of government support is what makes broadcasting legally and fiscally possible.[38] Freedom, therefore, remains nothing more than an abstract entity; hence the jokes.

    This continuing state of (constrained) affairs is lambasted by independent domestic journalists as extremely damaging for the development of either long-term, competitive market forces or a truly democratic dissemination of public information.[39] Bemoaning the same situation, today's Communist Party also notes a widespread loss of faith in the media, together with any shared dream or ideal that might be represented visually on television – especially if today's viewers are spoiled by obsessions with easy money in Moscow. They seem happiest of all with the Russian version of *Who Wants to Be a Millionaire* (false hopes of wealth), Dmitrii Nagiev's scandal-show *Windows* (false stories of family discord, played by actors who appear real), or Leonid Parfenov's revisionist history of the late Soviet period on NTV, *Namedni* (cancelled by the Kremlin as false).[40] No wonder, once more, that irony is so pervasive.

    All this joking around invites us for the remainder of this book to examine some serious solutions; they will be ways to move from humor to hope, from squeamishness to something socially expansive. Irony, after all, has its limits, as shown by the second (2005) season of *Bal'zakovskii vozrast*. What was tongue in cheek for the first series, discussed above, became noticeably darker in the second, when our four heroines (still in need of a job, spouse, or both) bump up against issues of abortion, prostitution, and other unfunny hindrances on their way to what they desperately hope will involve a glass slipper. Jokes about social inclusion are no longer funny when the object of desire vanishes altogether. What seemed possible in the past for a quartet of adult women has vanished in the present; it would appear they wanted too much. Something, when excessively sought, becomes nothing. As we know, however, the import of diminution or nothingness in the city is very different *outside* of metropolitan contexts. Singular, urban desires – because of their unfunny, thanatic failure – validate by negative example a different form of minorized singularity in a different place.

These processes of negation (or the positive elimination of a greedy, "splendid isolation") are *known*. Muscovite greed actively, consciously avoids its challenges, as established by the prior generation – hence the touching, yet ironic use of Soviet narrative in today's tales of love. Socialist story arcs promised so much, yet were decimated by prior politicking; all the same, they still evoke an eternally "salvationary," vertiginous risk to move beyond their doctrinaire, collective aspects. A desire for *non-communitarian* existence, for alternative (and apolitical) groupings, often resides *within* the socialist canon, within the extremes and excess that today's heroes and heroines pretend to find funny.

Given our emphasis upon Dobrenko's definition of Soviet culture's organic idealism and TV's demonizing of Moscow, one socialist story gives especially telling expression to the idea that Putinesque narratives (as primetime *or* policy) must reference, yet dare not/cannot enact. Leonid Leonov's *Russian Forest*, first published in 1953, gives wonderful voice to dreams of macrobiotic inclusiveness that, although *born* of Muscovite pragmatism, overshoot common sense altogether in a series of Spinozistic metaphors for perfect, aimless socialization. Being nowhere in particular becomes a better, if not perfect, form of almost anti-humanist presence. In our ironic TV series, a superior social or amorous existence is often expressed through provincial or rural states, through "non-cities." Leonov's novel shows us how goal-driven processes of inclusion can begin a similar *epoché* of non-verbal and non-linear states beyond the dehumanizing "labyrinth of the Big City." It shows what lies beyond the last and saddest joke of all, beyond the self-deprecation of Russia's little losers, raised under Khrushchev and Brezhnev.

The book focuses upon the long, slow intellectual competition between two forestry researchers: Ivan Vikhrov, who represents Leonov's attitudes towards social existence; and Aleksandr Gratsianskii, the embodiment of a more predatory, Stalinist eco-view. *Russkii les* begins just before the outbreak of World War Two. Vikhrov's daughter has been convinced by Gratsianskii of her father's scientific and ideological "errors"; it takes considerable time (and effort during the war) for her to realize the tragedy of her misjudgment.

It transpires that Gratsianskii, a one-time revolutionary, had in decades gone by actually been involved with the Czarist secret police as a turncoat, something he somehow manages to keep hush-hush. This dark secret is mirrored by his plans to plunder Russia's wilderness, with scant regard for subsequent environmental damage. As his schemes fall apart, he is even revealed to be a spy for the Australian secret service (since the storyline has now reached the time of the Korean War). Gratsianskii eventually commits suicide. His dramatic denouement, however, brings little calm because "the death of Stalin was no guarantee of the end of the Gratsianskii type."[41]

Leonov's novel marks the epitome of the Soviet ecological/realist novel. It marks the early steps towards Brezhnev's fondly remembered 1970s, when the grandest social designation of all, "Planet Earth," would come to mean "natural and harmonious connections formed between people and nature"; it would be made synonymous in academic literature with "home, mother or family."[42] The novel merges the micro- and macropolitical by stressing the former and shifting it *away* from urban, machinic production.

This is a "patriotic book, born of the love that a nation's son has for his native people." It is the consequence of "massive generalizations," i.e. the realist practice of "generalizing details," pushed to the point where they leave Soviet society or people altogether and head out into the empty taiga. They overcome the linear, shuttling pathways of our transported heroines, back and forth. Linearity becomes an eventful "interfusing of the epoch's quintessential forces."[43] This is not a stable political tract but a happening in the Badiouian sense, so vast in its philosophical purview beyond the bracketing processes of nationalism that it has usually been discussed in religious terms since 1991.

These strands of an apophatically defined, materialist "deliverance" merge in a long forestry lecture given by Professor Vikhrov. Here, as opposed to Gratsianskii, he advocates a socialist existence both in and *as* nature. The ideas informing his speech underwrite the most philosophically important story under investigation in our entire study, perhaps in all of Soviet literature. The lecture, strange though it may seem, was lauded even at the time of its first appearance as irreproachable propaganda, as "a lofty sermon of love for one's homeland."[44] It lies at the core of a long novel that nonetheless appeared even in the 1950s to be less stridently progressive than an "exchange of calls or motifs [*pereklichki*] between the past and present."[45] This shuttling procedure occurs sensitively and spends as much time looking backward or sideways as it does forward: "Nature actively participates in the destinies of the older and younger generations, from their first spark of self-awareness to the awful torments of World War Two – a time when nature herself sheltered her children. She did so as a mother."[46]

These affective, microcosmic, and familial metaphors have underwritten almost all of our TV series. *The Russian Forest*, by using those images for something other than unidirectional policy, becomes a "labyrinth of opinions, events and conflicts," as schoolbooks note today.[47] It goes nowhere special, yet resides *everywhere*; it was repeatedly drawn upon in schools during perestroika to educate today's adults with alternative forms of communality. Here are some nationwide homework questions from 1986:

- Which of Leonov's books do *you* value most highly?
- How do you feel about Leonov's fight for the preservation of nature?
- What makes Leonov's work valuable for work in schools?
- What is it about Leonov's works that makes them difficult to study?[48]

The active, yet "difficult," participation and subjectively "valuable" interdependence of people *as* nature starts to constitute endlessly social, Deleuzian machines. Their mutually beneficial interactions are industrious, not industrial. "The field and the forest," says Vikhrov, "are the most powerful of machines, which convert the sun's energy and the soil's fertility into the essential products of our existence ... Of all the machines that are working for us, the forest is one of the most durable, but also one of the hardest to repair when it breaks down." Self-deprecation, the inverse of urban chutzpah, is the key to this machinery's ongoing success and it is often instigated best of all by humor. The interaction of comedy, doubt, and social drama in cinema from the time of *Russian Forest*'s publication shows the role of humor in fashioning narrative forms to outlast the rigors of Stalinism, full of hope for something better – for Brezhnev's calm. These are the movies to show ironic TV the ropes; they show what comes *after* the irony.

Conclusion: ironic TV needs a little help from the past to get serious

> Tolstoi said that a man's like a fraction in which the numerator is reality and the denominator's what he *thinks* he is. The bigger the denominator, the smaller the fraction; if the denominator is infinity, then the fraction equals naught. Good that, isn't it?
>
> (Vasilii Azhaev, *Far from Moscow*, 1948)

A very quick glance at the cinema of the same period hints at how a massively popular, "less linguistic" art form might help to illuminate prose. Cinema used comedy to investigate the post-Stalinist modesty that would become so seriously important for storytelling. It was founded on provincial, outlying, or peripheral plots – on little lives, structured affectively. Both socially and geographically, a wilderness and distance from the Soviet center could lead to something very special beyond irony.

The major comedy synonymous with Leonov's novel was also the first feature film of the Soviet Union's finest comic, Arkadii Raikin: *We Met Somewhere ...* (*My s Vami gde-to vstrechalis'*, dir. N. Dostal') of 1954. The entire motion picture is aesthetically estranged from po-faced norms, for Raikin introduces the plot as if within a variety performance (i.e. as skits of events recalled) and is himself playing the role of a comic on holiday. Only after mocking a few grand centralized forms of Soviet art does the story begin: one figure pilloried, for example, is a member of the Soviet Composers' Union, whose bathetic, symphonic style quickly "descends" into the jazz of Leonid Utesov's *Masha*, a song about raunchy flirtation over steaming cups of tea.

It is worth noting in brief that Utesov's timeless value – as a funny force that can be used or abused by politics – was just as clear in the 2006 biopic *Utesov: A Lifelong Song* (*Pesnia dlinoiu v zhizn'*). The series, replete with badly dubbed ditties, is also loaded up with ham-fisted Jewish "revisionism" and shot on cheap video, the trebly qualities of which don't help scenes of misty nostalgia. Utesov changes shape too often, too; the thin and wiry actors who vivify his youthful years somehow become shorter and fatter as time passes. Yet, for all these faults, the endless importance of witty, throwaway one-liners is well stressed, be they spoken or sung. As Utesov's father says with regard to the Revolution: "Workers of the world unite, anywhere you like; just don't do it in my kitchen." Hence Raikin's invocation of a funny tradition in order to reconsider something revolutionary; humor creates a different viewpoint with a series of roles or disguises.

In a similar vein and in the same year as *We Met Somewhere*, the hit comedy *Dragonfly* (*Strekoza*, dir. S. Dolidze) took an isolated figure, a little nobody, and watched her work through the various tiny guises of romance. The title is the heroine's nickname: she is definitely flighty and must be the worst librarian in the USSR, dealing poorly with readers' requests for both Gor'kii's *Mother* and Sholokhov's *Quiet Flows the Don*. She tries hard to catch the attention of a handsome young architect and, due to a bureaucratic muddle over surnames, finds her (ordinary) self elevated wrongly to the status of Hero of Socialist Labor.

It is decided that only work will save Strekoza from this and other mix-ups. Worried at first, she applies her favorite songs to the workday and things soon go swimmingly. Her new social success is celebrated in a national magazine and color photo-spread, an event that coincides with the success of her courtship. The love story is resolved and the final scenes show the couple walking away from the camera, gathering poppies in a faraway, blossoming, and sunny Georgian mountain valley.

If we move to other funny blockbusters later in the same decade, the grandeur of the open countryside is likewise replaced by the big, equally grand emotions of endearment. In the comedy classic of 1957, *Up High* (*Vysota*, dir. A. Zarkhi), the lofty pinnacles of Soviet construction and their scaffolding workers become a metaphor for the dizzying challenges of romance. The woman in this improbable love affair (played by Inna Makarova) is a gutsy, assertive tomboy who smokes and drinks with the best of them, though we discover that her own, marginal state as an atypical female is a consequence of being orphaned during the war. This leads us to hypothesize that her dramatic behavior is massive overcompensation for some troubling lack. When she gets dressed for a date, in fact, her potential boyfriend describes her garish garb as "a South American traffic light." Something unfunny is missing.

It is only when the man involved – Kolia (i.e. Nikolai Rybnikov) – is in danger after a fall that she reveals her true feelings, especially because it transpires that he, too, has no relatives and so she comes to visit him in hospital. In a serious admission she makes only to a doctor, we discover: "I love him." It is only after *and because of* this silly love affair that she then enters public existence, becoming a member of the Komsomol; her father was a forest worker and she declares her wish to continue some public traditions. The Soviet subplot works and survives only because of the ironically "industrious" love story; the love story, likewise, works only because it is elevated high above the intrusively social streets of the Big City. Four years later, these same two lovers would in fact be transported outwards, not upwards – all the way to Leonov's snowy Siberian forests for a similar yet *brighter* love story: *Devchata* (dir. I. Chuliukin).

If there were no minor tale, from two orphans on the edge of society, the major plot of the forester's daughter and her commitment(s) would founder. Given the enormous distances between two people and everybody, between heady romance and social propriety, are there any guidelines at all? Here the role of law and order is extremely important in today's socially responsible drama. A rule or two might lessen the nervous laughter. Here the extremism that underlies the chapters thus far becomes something more modest: the need to discern a worldview approaching clarity whenever crime makes the machinic, caring goals of *Russkii les* impossible. After all, whenever burgeoning social production has trouble, it must still, willy-nilly, defend itself against illegal, lawless destruction. Lovers and jokers are rarely left alone to experiment in peace.

8 Law and order
Making sense of *something*

> Just because you don't know about IT, that doesn't mean IT is unreal.
> (Tagline for NTV's sci-fi mystery *The Bureau* [*Kontora*, dir. Dmitrii Parmenov, 2006], borrowing heavily from FOX TV's *The X-Files* [1993–2002])

Early adventure series under Putin: getting a grip on humorless disappointments and social failures

In looking at the themes of law and order, it seems reasonable to contextualize mystery series and/or thrillers according to the years before Putin's inauguration in March 2000, his first term (until the landslide of December 2003), and then the second, current term in office (since the spring of 2004). The earliest shows in this chain were often the simplest, too, displaying a marked structural naïvety. In the mid-1990s, for example, viewers were offered Vadim Derbenev's *On the Corner of Patriarch's Ponds* (*Na uglu u Patriarshikh*), wherein a policeman, investigating a ring of international antique smugglers, "very unexpectedly finds his true love, too. She is called Natasha. She's intelligent, slender, and mysterious – a complex individual." The connection between the two plots was less than natural. There was an awareness amongst studios prior to the Default that these types of TV series needed to be both exciting and emotionally engaging, but the relationship between the two intentions looked either contrived or simply non-existent.

A more persuasive interface of public and private plots would be developed in future years via increased thematic intricacy, as shown by the subsequent evolution of *Patriarch's Ponds*. The second season of 2001 involved the same central character of Sergei Nikol'skii (played by Igor' Livanov), but criminality had now blossomed beyond cops and robbers. It consisted of burglary, robbery, blackmail, drug trafficking, prostitution, *and* corrupt politics, i.e. the forces still battled weakly by love in today's feature films like *The Point* (*Tochka*), *It Doesn't Hurt* (*Mne ne bol'no*), and *Junk* (*Zhest'* [all 2006]). All were quickly included in the early episodes of *Patriarch's Ponds*, blurring any clear-cut definition of modern society and its negative operations. As promotional texts of the time told us, with such frenzied activity at work, "Nikol'skii's private life isn't at all easy."

In fact the third season in 2003 pushed the hero out of this discordant workplace altogether, into private investigations. Nikol'skii was detached from the reassuring support of a state institution; his individual presence was minimized, whilst that of surrounding society was amplified and complicated. The former was placed within the latter – and self-assured agency became harder and harder. In a male parallel to our love-hungry, ironic heroines, therefore, the simplicity of police work amid binary oppositions of "Good vs. Bad" was likewise no longer convincing.

Heroes, just like heroines, sought healthier social bonds. Crime was everywhere, making the development of a normal family life tougher. This led honest upholders of the law to *leave* agencies which supposedly embodied the legal codex. The nature of law and order outside those agencies was (and remains) the core social quandary of the criminal drama.

Similar tendencies were evident elsewhere within the same timeframe, analogous problems that (as with romance) could lead to a trivializing, self-defeating wittiness. It was easier to laugh things off. The late 1990s also produced criminal tales, like Igor' Maslennikov's *What Did the Deceased Say?* (*Chto skazal pokoinik?*), that admitted most of their "unbelievable plot twists" were better handed over to satire. According to this logic, the show's producers cast several nationally renowned tragicomic actors of old, such as Oleg Tabakov and Oleg Basilashvili. Not only does this story pit one isolated lady, privy to a secret code, against an entire bevy of baddies out to kidnap her, but the "unbelievably complex" plot reverses any typical primacy of good over bad. It then lets crime chase its target further still, from country to country: Denmark, France, Greece, Brazil, and Poland. The story never goes anywhere.

In *The Dossier of Detective Dubrovskii* (dir. Aleksandr Muratov, 1999), starring the popular Soviet actor Nikolai Karachentsov, this growing intricacy was expressed neatly in blurbs designed for the national press:

> The time has passed when our nation enthused over the adventures of incorruptible policemen and fearless KGB agents. Nowadays the hero of a detective story is more likely to be a private detective than just an honest policeman. Detective Roman Dubrovskii, who used to serve in the Moscow Criminal Investigator's Office, finds himself dragged into an enormous political intrigue that touches upon the interests of Russia's most influential people. The Federal Security Services suspect Dubrovskii of committing a murder. He is pursued by an outraged gang of forgers; virtually alone Dubrovskii must oppose a powerful criminal organization that aims to reach the height of political power. He plays cat-and-mouse with these criminals, cracking safes and saving charming women as he does so. His life is full of chases, shoot-outs and terrifying

mystery. But he sees his case through to the end, afraid of no risk, keeping to his principles and maintaining a sense of humor.

The implicit need for at least some moral constancy in a terrifyingly mysterious world was best embodied by the figure of Lekha Nikolaev, played by Mikhail Porechenkov in the series *National Security Agent* (*Agent natsional'noi bezopasnosti*, 1998–9). The directors (Vitalii Aksenov and Dmitrii Svetozarov), the production team of *Russkoe video*, and TNT were all keen to remind viewers that Nikolaev did not drive an Aston Martin, nor did he drink martinis (either shaken or stirred) – "but he's still way cooler than his British colleague." The affluent assuredness of James Bond was totally out of place in Russia's shady social developments; instead the producers equated him with the fighting spirit of a bulldog, struggling against seemingly insurmountable odds. His bravery was dictated neither by rulebooks nor ideology, for "being an agent is not a job. It's a matter of heart and soul." His membership in the world here is felt, not spelled out in codices.

The series enjoys great popularity even today, perhaps because the hero adopts so many roles and guises for each adventure that variety (or credulity) can be stretched liberally. Talks were held in the spring of 2005 about the possibility of a sixth series, but according to industry rumors Porechenkov was unhappy with both his salary and the show's production standards.[1] This, after all, was a role that had spawned "Russia's cult actor and number one sex-symbol." Even after he scaled these dizzy heights of public adoration, Porechenkov was not keen on jettisoning the bulldog stereotype, irrespective of actual wealth or renown. It was easily (if not identically) transferred to his 2005 ORT drama, *Officers*, with its explosions, romantic intrigue, hackneyed talk of military "fidelity," and lumbering soundtrack full of whining guitar solos. This no-nonsense approach to macho characterization often shone through in interviews, where, for example, he said a good shot of vodka was his preferred form of relaxation after a long day, rather than any swanky nightclub.[2]

Lekha Nikolaev was not the kind of hero to bother with matters of family life, however. Some characters of this period find domesticity difficult; others spurn it altogether, and here we see an important difference from many of today's popular shows. Life outdoors circa 2000 is simply too time-consuming: "People like my hero never get married. They go through life alone."[3]

Analogous loners appeared in other simultaneous series. *Bourgeois' Birthday* (*Den' rozhdeniia Burzhuia* [dir. Anatolii Mateshko, 2000]) used an orphan, strangely nicknamed in his youth, as the male hero of a rags-to-riches tale. Here the eponymous outsider, played by Valerii Nikolaev, makes his way "into" normalcy – but his hard-won stability is soon undermined; in the second NTV season of 2001 a spectacular fire claims the lives of his wife, son, and grandmother, thus clearing the floor for another ascent from nothing whatsoever to something very impressive. He begins the search for his family's killer, hiding the fact that he survived the fire.

Confident manipulation of society seems only possible if that same society presumes your absence. Nobody can hurt you if they can't see you. This is the premise that underlies subsequent broadcasts like Dmitrii Svetozarov's *Baron by Name* (*Po imeni Baron*, 2002), following the career of an unwanted Jewish boy, born during evacuation in World War Two, who has even managed to forget his own name. Crime and a suitable moniker make him what normal society could not.

One might argue that this theme is also part and parcel of series such as *Brigada* or *Gangland Petersburg*. They all follow a generational line, documenting the social maturation of shunned Soviet youngsters raised amid the manners and morals of a totally different environment. The latter series, which forged the career of Dmitrii Pevtsov, involved at one point in 2000 a plot in which two university friends find very different fates in post-Soviet Russia. One becomes an investigator, the other a criminal after life-changing experiences in Afghanistan, yet even the more upstanding and institutionalized of the two is obliged to look "beyond the law" for social clarity and fairness, for the people who murdered his parents. Thus "both heroes have to experience a great deal: fidelity and betrayal, love and hatred, desperation and compassion – in other words the cruel struggle for survival."

This generational theme, roiled by social entanglements, would become very common in the near future, since even older, wiser figures could not cope with contemporaneity. *The Detectives* (*Syshchiki*) starred Boris Shcherbakov in 2001 as a wise social elder, who understands that "experience, quick wits, intuition and a sense of humor are a detective's truest friends, even in the most unusual of situations." A Soviet training, said directors Uskov and Krasnopol'skii, counted for little after 1991.

Similar in its quiet, anxious design was the series *Mr. Boss* (*Grazhdanin nachal'nik*, dir. N. Dostal') and the dramatized life of Senior Detective Pafnut'ev, played by Iurii Stepanov. Although a high-ranking official and thus hopefully privy to the philosophical certitude of Shcherbakov, Stepanov's character must frequently employ "unusual methods" in order to deal with criminal processes. He is unable to speak with certainty of the very social networks he is protecting – or those to which he answers. He is far from his object of social desire. What was needed at this point was the kind of work that could produce a mélange of all of these extreme tendencies or stylistic shifts. It should bridge (or deconstruct) past, outdated binaries, and, by paradoxically *returning* to that past, claim to document "life as it is."

Absorbing senselessness in order to clarify matters

Another Nikolai Dostal' drama, *Stiletto Knife* (*Stilet*, 2003), proclaimed itself a successful attempt to "interweave various plots from diverse genres in a single network: tragedy, melodrama, action, and thriller. Its heroes are striking representatives of modern life in which, as we know, there's room for success and envy, betrayal and murder – but there's also love, friendship, decency and honor." The simultaneous drama *Fifth Angel* (*Piatyi angel*, dir. Vladimir Fokin) likewise trumpeted a movement towards something multigeneric. It hoped to link drama and a detective series whilst leaning heavily on the comic talents of those such as Liia Akhedzhakova to "make sense of life in our country today." Only a mess would make sense, be it ecological or chaotic and urban. Laying down simple rules for society did not appear feasible. The 2004 series *Against the Flow* (*Protiv techeniia*, dir. Anatolii Mateshko) also tried a similarly untidy line of inquiry, casting Mikhail Porechenkov in an unexpected, more romantically inclined role.[4]

This was a good idea. Since the start of the twenty-first century, Russian television has established an entirely new generation of these stars, known only to the small screen. Many of them are a complete mystery to large numbers of émigré audiences, living overseas and raised on the big-screen actors of Soviet cinema. People like Porechenkov can bring with them a large amount of generic baggage, even after a few years of fame. Sometimes this may be of detriment to an actor's career (as typecasting), but it can – if inverted – also have a very positive effect too, in the slow movement towards the multigeneric TV series.

Take, for example, Èrnest Iasan's *The Mole* (*Krot*), which began on Rossiia in 2001 and follows a similar interest in multiple roles. One of its stars, Dmitrii Nagiev, was already extremely well known for his work as witty DJ and comic parodist (on the show *Ostorozhno: modern!*) and would soon become nationally notorious for the faux reality/talk show mentioned previously, *Okna* (see p. 116). He brought artistic deceit to a tale of its social equivalent, and as a result viewers recognized their own environment (even in a story that offers some of the stagiest, unnatural dialog of any post-Soviet drama – the opening episode alone is a fine catalog of rhetorical and technical clichés, soon to become unfashionable). The show was summarized as follows for viewers:

> Those who work in the Special Services use the term "mole" to refer to somebody burrowing their way into the criminal world. In order to become that kind of agent, a mole must give up everything: his friends, home and even his family. His operations must avoid any kind of false move or hasty action. The criminal world has never shown pity for anyone – nor will it. Criminal Investigator Sergei Kuz'michev sets off to Moscow with the aim of infiltrating a criminal group. He pretends to be a kid from the countryside who has arrived in town to make some cash. Sergei thus manages to gain the trust of bandits – and starts collaborating with them. This mission can have fatal consequences. Sergei struggles against an enemy that is smart, sly and has a great deal of influence. The mole needs not only to get his job done; he has to save his own life, too.

As Putin's second term began, another – more successful – attempt at generic complexity came in the form of *The Midday Demon* (*Demon poldnia*). It is set with almost Chekhovian simplicity on a misty lakeside and with a minimal number of actors, headed by Nikolai Dobrynin, Sergei Chonishvili, and Anzhelika Nevolina, plus a star turn by singer Maksim Leonidov. The demon of the title refers to the difficulties of encroaching middle age at forty, to a muddle of new and contradictory worldviews encountered for the first time. Just as the characters in the series deal with the legal, emotional, and physical difficulties of aging, with a major crime, jealousy, and infidelity, so the house in which these events unfold was once a meteorological station that monitored nature's changes with confidence – but is now obsolete. In the words of director Aleksei Kozlov, the building is "both a symbol and barometer, measuring the onset of inclement weather."[5] One of the most successful dramas of crime in recent Russian television thus, ironically, removes almost all the guns, explosions, bullets, and Moscow gloss. It sticks a tiny group of people in the middle of foggy nothingness and hands crime over to the small, unpredictable tensions caused by the success or failure of love.

A comparable structure was evident in REN-TV's *Hallucination* (*Navazhdenie*, dir. Anna Legchilova) of 2004, in which a girl – played in her adult life by Tat'iana Arntgol'ts – witnesses a murder. She is obliged to flee her home and abandon her parents. On returning in future times to these places and people, an intriguing family drama is folded neatly and consequentially into the criminal plot. The minor issues of small-scale interaction, shown as erratically, realistically complex, underwrite the major ones. This serious process mirrors the role of self-deprecation in ironic TV; Arntgol'ts also starred in a 2004 parody of criminal movies with Pavel Maikov, *New Year's Day Is Cancelled*, a knockabout physical farce based on the bungled burglary of a supermarket. Genres were overlapping with increasing speed.

The 2004 series *Count Krestovskii* (*Graf Krestovskii*) played a similar, albeit slightly less amusing game, using motifs from Dumas' *The Count of Monte Cristo*. In this case, Aleksandr Baluev's character (Èl'brus Tamaev) is raised by his father and blessed with a happy Soviet schooling, during which he finds both companionship and affection. Urban post-socialist culture, however, brings other, destabilizing experiences: "The betrayal of friends, the loss of a loved one, and the loss of freedom." Affection and liberty try to reinstate themselves in "a tale about self-worth and revenge, about moral choices that everybody faces – sooner or later. This is a story of love, freedom and *universal* forgiveness." The private is public; it is consciously and emotionally so away from the metropolis.

It takes us a while to realize as much, however, since the expensive services of Baluev are not offered on screen until the fifth episode. From this point on we see an individual struggle with social temptations that began just before perestroika, "under Chernenko. These were drugs, foreign culture, one-armed bandits, and mini-bikinis." Calling himself a man "of a previous epoch," Baluev is taught the skills to survive in today's world by his fellow prisoner (orchestrated to the strangest of jazz interludes). When, in times to come, he reestablishes himself in urban society, he invests substantial sums in children's homes and returns to Russia icons that had been wrongly (i.e. profitably) "exported."

Interviews with the stars and crew of the series revealed that a work of classic literature had embodied some classic, overarching values to make this kind of generic mixing possible.[6] Something affective underwrote a classic work of the French language, once upon a time endorsed by Soviet schoolrooms, and that influence in turn blessed a story of loss or entrapment among a few isolated, modern characters with maximum relevance. The director, Ramiz Fataliev, maintained that these values were not to be used for any moralizing, but simply in the hope of evoking a sense of collective empathy: "If a viewer's heart responds to our romantic, slightly naïve story, then our work is done."[7]

Baluev, however, was not completely in agreement with Fataliev. The actor remarked that even now he misses the structural simplicity of, say, German children's detective shows like *Commissar Rex*, where "everything's the way it should be ... First there's a murder, then somebody leaves some traces behind, and [finally] people turn up. They ponder things and figure it all out."[8] Simplicity was fondly remembered, especially when it came to notions of justice.

Indeed, there is still airtime for generically straightforward series on today's television, such as the well-armed criminal drama *The Warrior* (*Boets*) or Vadim Shmelev's *A Game of Survival* (*Igra na vybyvanie*, both 2004–5); the latter, once again, stars Pavel Maikov. Both contain amorous elements, in these cases women who need saving. Of the two shows, *A Game of Survival* has the more interesting structure, designed to heighten the tension of that gender-specific salvation. The residents of a luxurious Moscow apartment building all receive anonymous threats, with $5,000 demanded from each flat. Each day the sum is not met one resident of one apartment will be killed – and the total ransom (of $1 million) will increase by $100,000. Maikov was attracted to the project not only because of its potential as a vehicle for a positive hero, but also because the significance of dramatic tension was zealously guarded by the producers. Not even the actors knew the final denouement as they filmed each episode.[9] Veracity and verisimilitude needed to be *unstructured*, even if people like Baluev wanted to see the simplicity of children's television in real life.

The four big stars of *Brigada* (Maikov, Bezrukov, Vdovichenkov, and Diuzhev) have all moved towards more positive roles since their rise to fame. This shift towards an ethical stance that may be employed by policy and yet *escape* it is increasingly important today. The criminal known as "The Gambler" who hunts down the apartment's victims in *A Game of Survival* uses Shakespeare, Dovlatov, and Bulgakov as texts with which to encode secret messages. He steals the social significance of art to aid his skewered notions of "propriety" and pays an extremely high price for doing so. Once more television draws upon classic literature, in this case upon the cost of spoiling its social use and/or relevance.

Also in 2005, the series *Firefighters* (*Ognebortsy*, dir. Isaak Fridberg) struck an excellent balance between the adventure film and other, willfully complex (i.e. "truer") subplots. It blended adventure and other elements in the tale of a homeless man saved from an inferno at the expense of a fireman's life. Inspired to adopt the career of his deceased savior, this tramp (Denis Ragozin) works hard to earn both the respect and forgiveness of his adopted workmates. Ragozin, in addition, has already lost his wife to a wealthier man from Central Asia.

He learns how to make himself anew not only through guilt over the fireman's demise, but also because a retired and invalid colleague (Dmitrii Kharat'ian) instills in him the sense of civic duty he once felt when defending Moscow's White House. Kharat'ian's character is the grandson of a high-ranking firefighter and therefore heir to what he neatly calls the "Hero of His *Own* Union" (*Geroi sobstvennogo soiuza*). He even wears his father's suits, because a modern firefighter cannot afford normal clothes.

These social bonds need to be fixed, especially when some of the other characters show how badly they can be spoiled. Classic Soviet actor Lev Durov plays an ex-fireman who has become a mafia player, a man who once saved lives but now aspires to the role of a criminal authority. Ragozin struggles against similar lapses in his own life. Eventually he gets to know the widow and daughter of his savior. When he manages to find sufficient money to refurbish their emotionally empty home, the daughter wonders if he is "a millionaire, just like the Count of Monte Cristo," a literary reference made not only in Baluev's series, but in *The Spiral Staircase*, too. Eventually the world is put back in its place by a storybook model and Ragozin becomes something similar, but better. He becomes a model member of a model team, a social unit so much in harmony with the world that when it loses a fire truck in a forest fire, Ragozin and the firefighters feel as much pity for the scorched trees as they do for their ruined equipment. Nature mirrors the most successful and least structured of all desirable social linkages.

Harmony and decency are a rare (and therefore often-validated) grouping. One's vocation and a private life still remain very hard to combine, to the point where we encounter the tellingly titled *Men Don't Cry* (*Muzhchiny ne plachut*, dir. Sergei Bobrov), based on the detective work of a very mild-mannered investigator, Sergei Ivanov. When the first few episodes debuted on Rossiia in 2005, the press remarked that the main barrier in combining life, "law, and order" nowadays is honesty. Dishonest people find it easier to get things done; decency is a quality more likely to complicate than resolve matters in today's culture.[10] This problem has become so widespread that a show such as Iurii Kuz'menko's *The Truckers* (*Dal'noboishchiki,* from 2001) has taken its freight-hauling, decent heroes all across the lush, unmapped

Russian landscape on their deliveries, but, no matter where they go, all manner of unsought adventures caused by greed and pettiness are always close by.

Well-muscled rectitude and mother nature: *The Sarmatian* (*Sarmat*, 2004) and *Taiga: Survival Course* (dir. Aleksandr Aravin, 2002)

Honest decency is empathetic towards complexity (i.e. accepting of others). The real litmus test for this worldview would, with time, be expressed generically, as different subplots or narrative styles experienced by small ensembles. It would also be subjected to unpredictable, dangerous society *per se*. The two most radical examples thereof are in this subsection; they use the violent disorientation caused by war and mechanical disaster to remake decent actuality in the middle of boundless, inhospitable wildernesses. The values of lone, broad-shouldered heroes are remade in the middle of nowhere by redefining their selfhood as part of (or wholly in the networks *of*) profoundly social, "un-lonely" nature, where – ironically – nobody lives.

Putin's first term in office created a welcoming environment for noisy action series that demanded scant mental effort from the viewers. On the heels of presidential posturing *vis-à-vis* Chechnya, dramas appeared in the style of 2003's *The Nation Expects* (*Rodina zhdet*, dir. Oleg Pogodin) that revolved around the new threats of terrorism and the old treasure of oil reserves. Advertising materials showed the cast, headed by Valerii Nikolaev, Iurii Solomin, Dmitrii Diuzhev, and Mariia Kivva, standing legs apart, all in camouflage and very heavily armed. This masculine spirit, arms akimbo, would continue to find an audience, as with *The Sarmatian* (*Sarmat*) in 2004, again tied tightly to newspaper headlines:

> Special Forces commander Sarmatov has been on missions in almost all the world's danger zones. He's the hero of several wars where Soviet forces took part in "limited operations." And now Sarmatov, the "Sarmatian," has an especially important mission: to steal American super-agent Matlaw from a neighboring eastern nation. Matlaw is always surrounded by professional security, but Sarmatov's division is made entirely of experienced veterans. The mission is successful, albeit at a high price. All of Sarmatov's troops perish and he, heavily wounded, falls together with the kidnapped Matlaw into the hands of opposition forces. Sarmatov is considered dead.

One of the men lost in this mission of 1989 floats off down a mountain river and Sarmatov notes that he looks like a crucified figure. The Christological theme of military demise that underwrote Soviet classics like *Chapaev* or *How the Steel Was Tempered* continues here, relative to the characters' isolation from bureaucratic society or a hierarchical HQ.

Law and order 177

Figure 8.1 The Sarmatian.

Sarmatov's men do not understand why their own nation does not rescue them; in the same vein the hero divorces himself from ideology in order to aspire to something grander. "I don't serve the Communists," he says. "I serve my motherland. Russia has a past and a future." Something, therefore, is being impeded by bluster; something closer to a truer patriotism. The spoiling of Russian social development in the 1990s under Yeltsin is forecast for Sarmatov by a tribe of people who live in the mountains and worship fire; the political future is told from an isolated valley, by a man who lives alone among nature:

> After the Great Northern Land falls apart, there will be much blood and many tears. The lust for gold will spoil its leaders. Even greedier people will then come to power, sharing among themselves that which belongs to everybody. There will be little hope for the children and elderly people will be dishonored, too ... You [Sarmatov] may serve Duty, but Love will be your salvation.

That may sound a tad hackneyed, but it attracted Lev Durov, if for no other reason than television now offers better employment than cinema. Some of Durov's fans were unimpressed:

> I check all the TV stations in the evening and start feeling like crap. It's like we're all living in prison camps. I'm so sick of these *Cops on Broken Streetlights*, *Agents of National BMWs* and the other stuff that just copies them! Blood, shootouts and punch-ups ... You get the feeling that Russia's completely made up of cops or criminals ... They're identical, too. How much more can we take? I've almost stopped watching TV altogether! And what about the quality of these serials, eh? They all look so worn out.[11]

One of the problems here was time constraints, the degree to which money or minutes sufficed in any broadcast to exercise a sense of novelty without jeopardizing potential profit margins. Serials may be long, went the argument, but to what degree can they capture the "documentary" drama of life itself? One viewer of *The Sarmatian* made the rather scathing comment that even in some extraordinarily long series such as *Moscow Saga*, life-changing events such as an abortion could be forgotten in five minutes, because the plot must always run off to other characters or other plot twists – all of which are punctuated by advertisements, too. The same viewer said it would be better to take a similar episode from Sholokhov's *Quiet Flows the Don* "and that's something you'd remember for the rest of your life."[12] Television drama, so keen to match literature's cultural prestige, had trouble avoiding cliché when it came to tales of law and order.

All the same, *Sarmat* tried hard to invoke spaces and time spans beyond its ostensible limits. Using direct references to both World War Two Soviet spy drama and the troubled hero of *Crime and Punishment*, this show also includes several clear examples of a bigger, better ecological life. We hear the reminiscences of Russian POWs who see an encroaching hailstorm while in enemy confinement. They suddenly get undressed and perform some "incredible dance of unity with one another" under the thunder and hail. The enemy guards, suddenly inspired, do the same; together they all – allies *and* enemies – reach a stage of "collective catharsis."

Sarmatov himself, with his vision magically restored by love for his wife and family, makes the equally unpredictable decision to join those he loves, to leave political or military service. This is contextualized by hints of a miraculous Easter resurrection:

> That's just the nature of Russian people ... and nature is nature. For the same reason you can't ask yourself why the grass is green or snow white. It's just the way that the world is; the best thing we can do is try to improve that world – just a little.

Dramas became increasingly keen on leaving their adventurous protagonists in the middle of nowhere in the hope of a similar epiphany, where – as we hear from *Sarmat* amid the bombs and bullets – "Russians can dissolve in nature; they can become an inseparable part of it." Nonetheless, cash tried very hard to oust the importance of anything natural. The drama *Taiga* of 2002 used the premise of a Russian criminal who has stolen cash from the Chinese mafia; a small aircraft carrying the key protagonists is subsequently forced to land amid Siberian forests, thus producing the elementary plotline of a fight for survival amid human greed and nature's indifference.

The twelve episodes are set almost entirely in the wilderness, where the victims make their lives anew, both simpler and better: "We can live more simply and accept things are as they are on Earth." Several references are made by these people to their adventures as soap-like and to the TV series they are missing at home. One of these missed dramas is fifty episodes in length, "but the main thing is it'll all be about love." A younger heroine dismisses all such broadcasts as "cheap old Soviet stuff" (*sovok*), but the TV watcher stands her ground; these and other shows are "about our life ... when things were happy and interesting." Continuing her argument she asks: "What didn't you like about communism? Don't you think we lived well?"

Fighting each other, wolves, and bears, these initially antagonistic characters slowly grow closer – and eventually escape *en masse* along the river, under a makeshift Russian tricolor. Patriotism is made in the backwoods, a space now lost to urban sprawl, the laws and order of a decent, empathetic nationhood are also made in the fondly remembered networks of childhood, an existence lost to adulthood (a state shaped *by* urban sprawl).

The rules of childhood, forgotten over time: *The Maker of More Misery* (*Umnozhaiushchii pechal'*, 2005)

Oleg Fesenko's financial drama of 2005 uses money in the same way that *Sarmat* uses martial politics. *The Maker of More Misery* begins with an honest, open friendship between three boys, a linkage that social pressures will

Figure 8.2 The Maker of More Misery.

subsequently ruin. Money, careers, and crime will slowly come between these men and the one woman they all love; in this respect the series has an almost identical structure to 2004's *The Three Colors of Love* (*Tri tsveta liubvi*, dir. Dmitrii Svetozarov). One of the boys in *The Maker* becomes a business magnate, another a police officer, and the third an Olympic athlete. Tensions over the years reach the point where one-time friends cause each other's imprisonment and even plan each other's murder – a long way from the boyhood nicknames they once had for one another: Faithful Steed, Sly Dog, and Wily Cat. Viewers said that these childhood subplots "went somehow deeper than your typical shows about friendship and killers." They were more "real."

One of the three actors, Anatolii Belyi, who plays the series' financial magnate, drew another parallel between real life and the greater "profundity" of this show by referencing in interviews his own poverty prior to the drama's success: he had once sold vacuum cleaners door to door.[13] Though many analogies were made between the figure of Mikhail Khodorkovskii and Belyi's character (Serebrovskii), the actor held that he was depicting real and universal stages of psychological development, rather than making a specific political point or limiting his portrayal to caricature.[14] This refusal to endorse simplicity was summarized more successfully by one of the female leads, Dasha Moroz: "It's a melodrama and a detective story, half and half ... with action, too."[15]

And so this drama employs several genres to show a multitude of ever-changing states. In response to this modern mess, however, it does eventually offer something of a simple (though elusive) solution, that of camaraderie and emotional parity which might be regained. Herein lies the great importance of this show. It draws upon the established significance of childhood and family as an ideal, yet in between the lost idyll and its almost impossible return, we see some of the closest parallels to modern actuality in any TV drama: the obvious references to Khodorkovskii, despite Belyi's claims. These extend even to the point of physical and sartorial likeness, to the same silver hair and the same spectacles.

This show, therefore, makes a very Putinesque point in its redoing of financial, perhaps illegal, chaos, yet it proffers a solution that lies *beyond* political control: childhood memories. It promises not the arrival of something as yet unknown, but the possible return of that which was possessed long ago. Once again, therefore, dogma may employ these metaphors of affective cohesion, but their realization lies beyond pragmatism. They reach the unmanageable scale that we see, for example, in *KGB v smokinge*, where Comrade Mal'tseva is told by a Catholic priest that "divine assistance" can be better understood as "us, as people, goodness, and children." She maintains that fear alone moves the world, but the priest counters her cynicism: "No, love does. You already know so."

This materialization reminds us of Gor'kii's *Mat'*, where a revolutionary, fluid, and familial ardor can lessen the conceit of selfhood so radically that it challenges the boundaries of materialism: "'She is speaking God's words!' a man shouted hoarsely and excitedly. 'God's words, good people! Listen to her!'" In a book where "the House of God is the whole earth," we start to see once again the common ground with *Cement*, even, which overtly references the link between Spinoza and socialism. It makes the one materialist narrative of socialism multiple – and begs the individual to be stubbornly cheerful. Since these are skills and scenarios valid under any form of oppression, the incipient literature of socialism is teaching its readers how to go beyond its tenets and, paradoxically, survive its own messy heritage thirty-five years later.

In the related early stories of the USSR, a body enters (i.e. is constituted by) everything and therefore the *destruction* of any one body in armed or unfair conflict – hopefully – would alter nothing. This supra- or anti-humanist jeopardy in Gor'kii's novel was called the challenge of a "genuine artist, one who creates a new world *together with nature and society*, opening the hidden potentials of the real world."[16] This intersection of nature and society is done affectively. Emotions, as nature's kindred spirit, are forever and always en route elsewhere. Their goalless passage is an embodiment of latency, an ever-present anticipation and awareness of yet another, unexpected connection or "genre" of an(other) affect or machinic thrust. The edges of a departing past (childhood, for example) or already-minorized events and phenomena thus come back to rejoin the center when remembered, pitied, or promoted. Hence, perhaps, Gor'kii's desire to "turn [even] the backwaters of Siberia into the flourishing corners of culture."[17] Invisible powers would alter ostensible geography by *copying* it, yet this would remain a rarely enacted ideal.

The Maker of More Misery begins a long way from the invisible. It starts in the world of Mal'tseva's fear, where oligarch Serebrovskii is willing to pay his old friend $120,000 per annum to handle his security, which – apparently – will be "much cooler" than anything the president has. Likewise, in the same wealthy spirit, the series is peppered with product placements, in particular for well-known brands of beer, vodka, and for Mastercard. (The irony of pandering to business in order to lambaste cupidity was seemingly lost on the series' producers.) We are told that Serebrovskii's mother had raised him to be a member of the intelligentsia, but today, when money decides everything, he thinks he will succeed only if others "fear and hate" him. This ungrateful son then dismisses the cultural importance of lengthy kitchen conversations under the Soviets as nothing more than the guarantor of "schizophrenia and piles."

We later learn that his father had been the chief engineer for the famous Soviet explorer and pilot Chkalov, but was arrested as a result of Stalinist paranoia. The son is now taking his revenge on a past society that ruined his own familial equivalent. One of Serebrovskii's victims later guesses as much, and asks him if his modern cruelty is perhaps the result of poor relations with a father. These Freudian conclusions are extended to relations between the three friends, too. The one woman who has connected them since schooldays through her friendship, love, and/or marriage says these men are actually identical. God, she assumes, had made one perfect man, but then split him into three personalities; each third was afforded its individual destiny.

When this fractured unity is put under greater stress after financial markets collapse beneath Serebrovskii, he considers killing the friend (Ordyntsev) who had become a policeman. Ordyntsev turned the tables on his wealthy acquaintance when he saw that fiscal values were ruining a shared past. As Ordyntsev indeed says to the third friend: "I'm afraid he's going to shoot me in order to forget about our past ... but it's terrifying to live without a history." The adult, forward-looking world cannot totally extricate itself from a pre-verbal, pre-adult past without considerable violence.

This bewilderment could only be greater if there were absolutely no distinction between adult life and adult fictions, as we saw in *The New Don Quixote* of *Rostov-Papa* much earlier (see pp. 8–13) – and this is indeed what happens when the 2005 series *Circumstantial Evidence* (*Kosvennye uliki*, dir. Viacheslav Krishtofovich) offers us a writer of detective stories, Igor' Feonov, whose own life becomes the object of police investigation. A crime is committed according to the plot of his latest – unpublished – story, a trick also used in *The Spiral Staircase*. It becomes totally unclear whether life is being penned by an absent "divine" author or merely repeating the banal plots of an amateur novelist. If life has any statutes, their origin is indistinct.

Perhaps thanks to the rare gifts of Sergei Makovetskii in the main role, *Circumstantial Evidence* produces – at the very least – "a detective story against the backdrop of family drama" that investigates some fundamental questions of collective existence, of private and literary histories: "What kind of man does a woman need? What kind of man does a young woman need – and what kind of man does an elderly woman need?" These snowballing, self-complicating meta-tales reminded some people of the 1970s' quietly complex, metaphorical cartoons by Iurii Norshtein held in such regard by cinema juries and academia today. And yet, if actuality is as messy as these mixed tales would have us believe, other viewers want to *escape* reality; they yearn for the simple stuff:

> This isn't a serial, it's a nightmare. I've watched three episodes already: THREE. And not a single person has been killed. What the hell's going on? It's a Russian TV series, a detective series to boot, and in three episodes they haven't killed anybody. How people can watch it, I've no idea. I still have hope, some small and fleeting hope, that they'll beat somebody up or bump them off.[18]

Some concluding rules for embracing a big-screen ecology

> Above all, we should acknowledge that the collapse of the Soviet Union was the major geopolitical disaster of the century.
>
> (Putin, 2005)

In essence, all of the TV series which ponder (and then proffer) some social law and order do so by advocating a *risk*. Instead of suggesting the violent elimination of otherness, they promote a risky, almost impossible entry into organic, decentered selfhood. In the series *Nebo i zemlia*, discussed above (see pp. 130–2), which also involves long-term considerations of how to "bump somebody off," a soon-to-be-murderous air hostess played by Mariia Golubkina shoulders a major grudge against her airline employers. In one particularly tense moment she draws a parallel between excessive work or effort and the philosophy of Soviet literary hero Meres'ev, himself from the 1946 *Tale of a Real Man (Povest' o nastoiashchem cheloveke)*.

Although made with slight bitterness, Golubkina's parallel begs brief consideration; it shows the role of affective membership in a bigger and better family than politics can offer, especially if one is trying to avoid penning a tragic or illegal autobiography. Once more tales of World War Two find great application in today's peacetime. They show how the risky rules of a dispersed selfhood can so often be confused with (or halted by) the laws of armed conflict.

Povest' o nastoiashchem cheloveke was so important, it would be republished in 180 editions and 49 languages; a total run of almost 10 million copies. It was penned over nineteen days at the end of the war, after author Polevoi had met the real-life counterpart of his hero, Meres'ev, who had been shot down in his plane in April 1942, shattering both his legs. He had dragged his body for sixteen days and nights through enemy territory to a reach a partisan unit. He was then flown to Moscow, where both legs were amputated. This is the incredible, perilous effort in the name of some shared ideal that Golubkina evokes with the bitter knowledge that it is *absent*.

Meres'ev must believe in his future with greater vigor than the massed, militarized, or logical world of others. In the following depiction of a dogfight the antagonism of two worldviews is as tense as humanly possible; the price to pay for failure is death. Meres'ev triumphs – not in the name of the bellicose state, but in the name of the woman he loves:

> He prepared for instant death. Suddenly, when it seemed to him that he was within arm's length of the German machine, the German pilot lost his nerve and leapt upward; the blue sunlit underside of the German machine flashed like lightning in front of him. In that instant Aleksei pressed all his triggers, stitched the German with three fiery threads and forthwith looped the loop; and as the ground swung over his head he saw an airplane fluttering helplessly against its background.
>
> *Ol'ga!* he yelled in frenzied triumph, and forgetting everything he spiraled down in narrow circles, accompanying the German machine on its last journey, right down to the red, weed-covered ground, until it struck the earth and sent up a column of black smoke. Only then did his nervous tension and tightened muscles relax, leaving him with a sense of intense weariness. He glanced at the fuel gauge. The pointer was trembling almost at zero.

This is the jeopardy of a social realism in a well-armed social sphere, the documentary aesthetic pushed to its own, unnatural limits such that it reveals its opposite; the repetitiously private sentiments of a lover increase such that he dissolves in frantic attempts to accept the entire world, all its details and members. He will do *anything* for his girlfriend as a man with "a keen mind, a good memory and a big heart." Policy hijacks this enthusiasm – and does very little with it.

The role of recollection here remains important, given series like Niiole Adomenaite's *The Hunt for Cinderella* (from 1999), in which the *loss* of memory makes criminal activity a great deal easier; the series' heroine is manipulated in order to assassinate others. Conversely, in *The Diary of a Murderer* (dir. Kirill Serebrennikov, 2002) the work of a young librarian helps to find possible links in local archives between a series of modern crimes and equal violence in the same region many decades earlier. In 1919 a young man had lost consciousness prior to his execution, when he was offered a last minute plea bargain: to shoot the other prisoners or die with them. When he awoke among their bodies, he assumed that he had indeed shot them. His amnesia becomes a loss of sanity and social attachment.

Meres'ev embodies a hazardous defense against this loss. After all of Polevoi's equally dangerous adventures, supposedly enacted in the name of Soviet law and order, he can "add a happy [molecular] ending to the story. After the war he married the girl he loved and they now had a son, Viktor. Meres'ev's old mother came from Kamyshin and is now living with them, rejoicing in the happiness of her children and nursing little Meres'ev." The 1948 film version by Aleksander Stolper amplifies these issues of choral affect and embodies more of the lost categories or laws that often make TV dramas of this section so sad; it also underlines how the themes of (emotional) presence and fast, fleeting (physical) absence can be intermingled so successfully in very "Russian" tales of wartime pilots even now, like Aleksandr Rogozhkin's *Transit* (*Peregon*, 2006).

One of the earliest scenes after Meres'ev's plane crash is shot from above, showing a bent propeller and two indistinguishable forms on the snow: a pilot – and a bear. When he is eventually in hospital after this ordeal, the hero is cast in chiaroscuro, long shadows, and the emptiness or silence of the wards; together these emphasize the need for at least two people to battle the soul-destroying isolation. The hospital scenes lack music or even non-diegetic noise from the neighboring wards and corridors. In fact the film as a whole is remarkably quiet – nurses react in great silent sympathy with patients facing amputation, for example. Empathy outdoes talk or professional rhetoric concerning wartime civic duty in the face of private suffering.

The first break in this serenity and the first key unit of any future, complex choral principle comes when the pilot's physiotherapy (involving a prosthetic limb) takes the romantic – if not desperate – form of dance lessons across an empty, institutional dance floor. In fact as Meres'ev gets better and needs to reprove his worthiness as a Soviet pilot, he does so by dancing, by showing the bold, risky, and bodily expression he learned from correlations of love, attention, and affection.

These melodramatic extremes of martial conflict, however, need – as ever – a calmer, unarmed counterpart. Another simultaneous hit film helps us to see some symmetry with the ineffable role of family or love. *Together* they embody the aesthetic drawn upon by Putinesque storytelling. In the second drama, *The Village Schoolteacher* (*Sel'skaia uchitel'nitsa*, dir. M. Donskoi), also known by its subtitle as *The Cultivation of Feeling*, a young girl (Varia) prior to World War One in a St. Petersburg academy both sings of "how it seems I'm in love" and realizes she is the only graduating student with a desire to go and work deep in the countryside. When she arrives, her dreams are immediately spoiled by scenes of domestic abuse and the crudity of an alcoholic singing a darker, yet related song of prisoners, deceased parents, and family duty beyond the far eastern shores of Lake Baikal (*Po dikim stepiam Zabaikal'ia*). Trying to put things right, Varia says that she will teach the kids "how day becomes night, why the wind blows and whither rivers flow." She conducts ecology classes outdoors in order to explain bird flight, harvests, and rainbows, as a result of which the drunk's son is inspired to sit the acceptance exams at a major school – but he runs up against pre-Revolutionary snobbism. The teacher, too, had lost her fiancé to the equally cruel Czarist police a little earlier; she sympathizes with him.

The Revolution comes – an event heard about in song before news reports or journalistic rhetoric – and the teacher defends her school against local violence. Her perilous role as multiple, massed mother to the "blind kittens" she has raised and educated has produced a "love that cannot be killed." These same students then serve to defend the larger, metaphorical motherland against the background of the famous propaganda poster, "The Motherland Is Calling You" (*Rodina-Mat' Zovet*). In the closing moments her love for the students becomes *their love*, both for her and among themselves. Varia vanishes into an adoring crowd or emotional ocean of her own making. She has done as much as possible; her risk (first within and then beyond dogma) paid off – and in these crowded frames she becomes as small as possible.

The hazardous self-affirmation (*away* from atomistic selfhood) shown by Varia and Meres'ev underscores today's TV narratives, both dramatically and politically. Their visual drama is affective, whereas politics puts more faith in the lexicon. A long-lived hope for their amalgamation leads today's academics to write to Putin, making sure that Gor'kii is well represented with public memorials, albeit as "a living man, not as a mummy."[19] Several Russian psychologists in 2005 even hazarded the generalization that Putin and Gor'kii are men of the same "social type," wavering between the need to control events and a greater, more ethically laudable alternative that would paradoxically mean *sacrificing* control in a moment of risk.[20] Gor'kii's biography and the aesthetic he spawned show this tragic disparity between an excessively, hazardously striking narrative and managed, real-world pragmatics; the most popular criminal series of all give cause for a little optimism by balancing law, order, and hazard.

9 Criminal series
Soviet traditions come home

> "You can't defeat the world all on your own. Have the courage to admit and accept that."
> (One detective to another in *Philip's Bay* [*Bukhta Filippa*], dir. A. Tsabadze, 2005)

The bad guys: *Zona* (*Prison Colony*, dir. Petr Shtein, 2006)

As the book reaches its final chapter, the synonymy of length and persuasiveness on TV needs once more to be addressed after *Aèroport*. How long can TV series continue in their considerations of ostensible reality and be convincingly real? Is there a maximum limit? One joke concerning the detective series *Kamenskaia*, examined in this chapter, certainly suggested as much; the actor Sergei Garmash, having learned that *Kamenskaia* would "enjoy" a fifth series, begged to be shot dead in the fourth. Elena Iakovleva, who plays the eponymous heroine, was scared of being left with minor actors if Garmash left, and so she threw herself in front of the bullet.[1]

Without doubt the best example on Russian television of a domestically produced serial that attempts to avoid this semi-serious problem is 2006's *Prison Colony* (*Zona*), which, although initially limited to a run of fifty episodes, neither numbers nor names those episodes on screen. What results is the chronotope of an atypically small space (a single prison) and considerably more time, all in the attempt to capture a better, less edited view of hazardous actuality.

The following quotation is used for promoting the series: "The colony is not a territory, but a test. A man can either withstand this test, or be broken by it. His ability to withstand it depends on his sense of self-worth and an ability to distinguish between importance and transience." The stories used to bring Andrei Tarkovskii's phrase here to life (from his 1979 film *Stalker*) were taken *from* life, from the memories of real prisoners. The series includes a reasonable amount of actual prison slang, too, although the entire drama was filmed in an abandoned factory not far from Moscow, lined with convincing furniture and fittings, some donated by prisoners themselves. Other details and habits also help to define daily life "inside": the prisoners, as per internal lore, never play cards at the table, for example. They are not allowed by the authorities to have money or knives, either – and so they cut their bread with taut threads. These and other oddities are all documented.

Zona begins with the suspicious suicide of a prison officer, an occurrence that takes on increasingly criminal overtones with each and every installment. As is already evident, the lines between law and order are fuzzy; this is without doubt the one series in this book that would trouble the Russian state more than any other, for the authorities are shown as malicious, scheming, and frequently lacking the honor of thieves. The role of one of the main officers was even played by a real-life ex-convict. Law and order sit side by side, because – in the words of director Petr Shtein – "Prison is a parallel world that nobody wants to acknowledge, but it *does* exist; the line between our world and that of the prison is so fine, anyone could transgress it in a split second."[2]

The screenwriters gathered *Zona*'s storylines in prisons, labor camps, and transfer stations all around Russia. Travel issues aside, another major complication presented itself, for the writers had to sneak their texts past the internal censorship of the prison system.[3] Their success in preserving these anecdotes intact led the show's producers to declare *Zona* the first TV series in Russia based on documentary evidence, or at least so close to actuality that the line between drama and "some kind of reality show" was invisible.[4] This was unexpected for a Russian audience, the startling "combination of both police and prisoners' stories" in one small and very social sphere.[5]

Equally odd was the appearance of Shtein himself on set, producing a contemporary prison drama after his famous involvement with *Poor Nastia*. He jumped from costume drama to cellblock intrigue, consciously bypassing the phenomenon of action series altogether. Shtein discerned themes of self-determination and social constraint that could link a well-moneyed past to an impoverished, incarcerated present – yet to some viewers they seemed strange enough to be humorous. Several cruel individuals drew parallels with the American *Police Academy* franchise.[6] In some interviews, perhaps as a result, Shtein almost seemed to denounce the former romantic project, claiming that the American sponsors had "loathed him for struggling against the idiocy of their foreign subject-matter."[7]

There was little to laugh about in the work schedule for *Zona*; filming ran only slightly ahead of broadcast dates. Ideally, once again in avoidance of openly admitted financial issues, the studio claimed that this double progression allowed them to alter both the series' "accents" and its actors according to audience reaction. All in all, a marriage of viewers and thespians would allow increased sympathy for the inmates:

> Compassion and the ability to forgive have always been inherent to Russians. There's a good reason why people used to bring presents to the prison gates on holidays, including those who had nothing to do with the inmates. We're not trying to whitewash our prisoners, to romanticize

their portrayal on screen. We just want to let people know what still goes on behind those walls; we want to show them peoples' lives, the laws and concepts of honor and fairness according to which prisoners live. Yes, they've committed crimes and get punished according to the law. That's the price they pay. But in prison they run up against other kinds of cruelty and injustice too, often from the very people who're supposed to *uphold* the law.[8]

The series, as suggested here by its producers, was forced to define and justify itself very quickly. NTV was "asked" to broadcast the show later at night (11:30 p.m.), but it fought its way back to primetime. One or two newspapers said the time shift was enacted at the personal request of Putin, as – perhaps – was NTV's decision to cut the total number of episodes from 100 to 50. Many people were upset by this apparent censorship, since *Zona* was enjoying a 20 percent audience share, pulling in more viewers than the President's press conferences.[9] Some provisional prisoners even threatened to slash their wrists if they were not allowed to view the show, since "lights out" was always scheduled for 10 p.m. Conversely, prison officers wrote to the national press, angrily declaring that *Zona* "crudely distorts reality." It calls into question the "honor and dignity of hundreds of thousands of people who work with prisoners. These people fulfill one of the most difficult state functions: the correction of those who have *transgressed* the law."[10]

The newspaper *Trud* even maintained that Shtein had actively summoned hatred for the forces of law and order, a subversive gesture for which *he* should be incarcerated:

> We ask ourselves – what was the point of making this series? To scare us, to provoke or spread chaos, to further divide this derelict society of ours? Or is to popularize some kind of criminal idea, that all policemen are bastards and then ... "Arise Mighty Nation"?! We've been through all that several times before, so why pour oil on the fire? Maybe that kind of thing will make somebody feel a bit better. Who, exactly, we can only guess.[11]

This rhetorical question was answered by the newspaper *Komsomol'skaia Pravda*; bearing in mind that adults know prison life "isn't exactly a rest home," only adolescents would watch *Zona* with any devotion, learning as a result how to use prison slang – and many other forms of nastiness.[12] Aiming to calm these increasingly angry voices, Shtein responded elsewhere that a degree of self-censorship was applied by the crew, since (for example) we do not see the prisoners using the cell's toilet, nor do we hear *that* much swearing. The director was simply trying to reveal a massive, hidden cross-section of Russian society. A million people are imprisoned each year nationwide; an additional 300,000 are hired by the state to watch over them.[13]

In essence, the most telling and typical responses came from two groups: ex-prisoners praising the accuracy of the series, and other viewers who felt sorry for the heroes of *Zona*, especially when they had heard that only 10–15 percent of people incarcerated in Russia are of actual danger to the outside world. This snowballing sympathy led to a great deal of viewer mail, in fact "tons of it," because despite any enduring, "criminal romanticism" (*blatnaia romantika*) the general public remains in complete ignorance of real prison life.[14] A lengthy interview on *Radio Svoboda* addressed this issue; it came to the conclusion that there is a big difference between "entertaining people with nastiness, fear and aggression" and talking of their *causes*. The latter activity would be much more alarming for the government.[15]

The establishing shot of each episode moves in from open countryside to this enclosed, dangerous multiplicity. This documentary air is enhanced by the fact that episodes are, as mentioned, neither named nor numbered, as if an ongoing flow overshadows any episodic compartmentalization. Likewise there is no ADR work; the entire dialog is recorded live. This realism is immediately underscored by the cruelty of prison officers in the opening scenes, beating recently transported inmates in order to establish their insignificance: "I am Lord God – and you are shit!" One of these officers is quickly so drunk (after being abandoned by his wife) that he must be tied to a radiator: "Welcome to Hell!" Only the care and attention given to an abandoned kitten make him forget a world so vindictive; even the woman who handles inmates' packages from relatives (the sole bearer of happiness) has herself to drink heavily. These people have good reason to hate the world: the drunk officer is subsequently told to drown his kitten.

The fundamental event that brings narrative progression into this unending misery is the suspicious suicide of an officer. Tensions surrounding the crime dictate shifting relations among the prison staff. With regard to the prisoners' interaction, a constant (albeit slow) movement of new inmates back and forth through the space of one cell shapes the drama therein. Status in the outside world is of occasional importance "inside," especially if a character was once a major criminal figure, but in essence the most intelligent of detainees eventually finds common ground with the most physically dangerous. This harmony is a necessity, for – in the words of one character to a novice – "If I were in your position, I wouldn't go around looking for enemies."

In this unnaturally peopled environment, it is almost impossible to hold on to private belongings (watches, jackets, and wedding rings all go missing), but since so much is stolen so often, ownership *per se* is undermined and this, paradoxically, leads to another leveling force. These genuine bonds of friendship and consolation can rarely be expressed out loud, however; the series often cuts to an overhead shot, as seen on CCTV. Somebody is always watching and waiting to ruin any camaraderie – though we are not told who. Once again the actual source of power (and violence) is unnamed.

These two forces, official and unofficial, visible and hidden, battle one another for fifty episodes, often according to an awkward pun invoked by one inmate: the struggle between "Law and Justice." The former is in uniform, and, given that "Fate" is, not surprisingly, mentioned so often by detainees, *The Prison Colony* leaves an overriding impression that retribution will come, sooner or later. Hence the worries noted above among both viewers and commentators that *Zona* is deliberately, dangerously seditious.

Its rebellious atmosphere is fueled by several outrageous scenes of injustice, the first of which involves a prisoner refusing to sing at an officers' function. He undergoes a forced rehearsal of the World War Two classic about a soldier's fidelity (*Temnaia noch'*), but the staff requests soon lapse into the famous criminal ditty "Thieves' Love" (*Vorovskaia liubov'*). The officers assume they can bribe the singing inmate with a better cell, microwave, and fridge, but it all goes horribly wrong. The singer is punished for his pigheaded nature by being thrown into an unfamiliar cell, where he is raped. He barely maintains his sanity, whereas the wife of one upper-level official has already lost her mind. Her husband is left pondering the tragic irony that she may herself need to be "incarcerated."

Against the background of these grim events there develops perhaps the most important plotline. An American in his early twenties (Dennis) is thrown into prison and himself charged with rape; he is stripped naked, hosed down with freezing water, and stuck in a one-man cell so narrow (the so-called *kishka*) that he can only stand. Close to despair, he still sings "America, the Beautiful" as loud as hazardous pluck will allow. Once released into a common cell, he maintains a naïve faith in the court system, but occasionally breaks into fits of incredible profanity (that are not translated into Russian). He is quickly accepted by the prisoners, who try to educate him regarding his real "legal" status: "There's none of your American law here in Russia. And there never was, either." By this stage, the claustrophobic sets and consistently low lighting have already persuaded us of the general hopelessness. It is so divorced from anything natural that when, in one rare instance, a prisoner is released for good, he stares at the boundlessness of the sky and then joyfully buries his face in unpolluted, "pure snow."

The American is told by his antagonistic lawyer that an unnaturally long sentence can be avoided if $200,000 is wired to a Russian account from a wealthy uncle in Detroit. Not only, however, has this relative been estranged from Dennis' family for twenty years; it later transpires in the series that there is *no* pending case against him (and that the uncle has long since died, anyway). Dennis is denied any chance to read the Russian legal codex in his cell; the copies in the prison library are deliberately torn and soiled, making the text illegible: "This isn't justice; it's a farce!"

The bonds he forms with cellmates henceforth get stronger. He is given the nickname "Raven" as a sign of courteous empathy and is sung the time-honored dirge "Black Raven." This is an important gesture of acceptance. It leads another prisoner to sulk when he gets an unwanted nickname; he is called "Dope" (or "ram"; *baran*) instead of "Baron." Dennis and another man in the same cell (framed for a commercially driven murder) are afforded a special status in that their innocence and honesty is assumed by other inmates. The elders help to educate, raise, and protect Dennis, who subsequently admits to being a virgin. The senior inmates arrange for him to be visited by two prostitutes, as "nobody ever gets out of the *zona*, believe me." Even if physical release is possible, mental and emotional escape is often not, because (in a related aphorism) "if you ever deal with the cops, you'll never break free."

One of the nastiest figures embodying this stalemate is a female prosecutor, who in later episodes is promoted to chief officer. She is more than happy to manipulate friendships, conjugal visits, and even drug addictions in order to get the results she desires. She is the quintessence of the death and destruction that pervade her ranks; this thanatic association is so strong that when another officer is (with difficulty) persuaded to give a blood transfusion to an elderly, hardcore criminal, the latter undergoes a religious conversion! He calls the officer's kindness "amazing, unbelievable," or even "cruel punishment" that goes beyond anything resembling a comprehensible norm (*bespredel*). Any risky removal of an established binarism in the world is painfully incomprehensible to him – and, indeed, when he reads biblical passages to his cellmates they only want to hear about "an eye for an eye."

The officers would be equally groundless without the existence of their assigned, assumed "enemy." One of them, making reference to a classic Soviet cartoon (again by Norshtein), says that outside of the prison he would be "lost, just like that hedgehog in the fog." Later another of his colleagues admits with self-deprecating humor that whenever he leaves the prison complex he suffers from immediate agoraphobia.

A major character who appears "from the fog" in later episodes to challenge these heartbreaking oppositions is a priest, Father Mikhail. He was once a soldier and saw active service in Afghanistan. Although a human, finite representative of a ubiquitous, eternal God, he is amazed that the female prosecutor knows so much about what happens in the prison – the realm where she acts as a bitter, omniscient deity. Many of those in uniform are called "petty demons." Yet another official, giving voice to this demonic trait, tells the priest that he, too, "speaks about goodness, but he does so with 'different words.'" Life in the prison, he adds, is like a "war zone," but Father Mikhail insists it is "too early" for the officer to give up on himself. With this and other statements, the priest becomes a sorely needed representative of some ineffable, chancy excess beyond the limits of a dual structure.

This risk is given voice only by the mentally ill spouse mentioned above; she tells her husband that all the prisoners should be freed, for then "we'll *all* be free," inmates and staff alike. She runs to one cell in order to inform the prisoners. Even though they know of her husband's lofty rank, they dismiss her idea as hazardous. It could not possibly be true: "There aren't any fools here." The newly Christian prisoner says that spiritually "we're all free already"; his clever idea is handed over to irony because it is potentially, dangerously *true*.

It is, eventually, the American Dennis who takes this leap of faith; he asks Father Mikhail to christen him. Dennis now acts as something of a litmus test for the other prisoners. He must endure the greatest degree of transformation, because he arrived from as far from the *zona* as possible. He does so and finds a solution to the claustrophobia, a way to both build upon and outshoot the friendship of his cellmates. Verbalizing this step for us, he says that his adventure was supposed to happen for a reason, so that he could escape living to "a strict plan." This inflexible plan was made of commonly acknowledged, "progressive" stages: college, a good job, and the unavoidable need to define further success in monetary terms alone: "Only here do I understand what it means to be free."

As Dennis manages a degree of freedom, the noose tightens around several of the officers when investigation of the opening "suicide" intensifies. At a party to celebrate the lead investigator's promotion, a congratulatory package explodes, killing a female colleague; earlier a friend of his had died after a glass of poisoned cognac. Simultaneously, the prison's female doctor is under great pressure from her violent husband (also a guard) to stop both talking about the investigation and "flirting" with her criminal patients. His violence, in fact, forces her to look for solace and she falls desperately in love with one of the prisoners. The contact between them is formed at a moment of maximum jeopardy – and as a result pays the greatest rewards. The inmate came from a family of circus performers, which is a world maximally distant from the prison, as the doctor herself points out during one of their clandestine meetings. The circus is made of "laughter, applause and bright lights. The only things here are misery and fear."

The fact that these two people come together is even more astonishing when we consider how they met; the doctor's husband in an earlier fit of unjustified jealousy stripped his wife half-naked and threw her into the prisoners' cell. It was the circus performer who showed her the greatest kindness, shielding her from the possibility of rape with care, compassion, cups of tea, and candy. A man who has nothing and is kept permanently *away* from society offers, ironically, a solution applicable to one and all. This is because, as we're told in one of the very last episodes in a comparison of prisons and the outside world: "There's more truth in here than there is outside."

The good guys: *Streets of Broken Lights* (*Ulitsy razbitykh fonarei*, from 1997) and *Kamenskaia* (from 1999)

> Success [in battle] never has and never will depend on position, or equipment, or even on numbers – least of all on position. It depends on the feeling that's in *me* ... and in *him* ... and in every soldier.
>
> (Lev Tolstoi, *War and Peace*)

Zona comes on the heels of several nationally popular detective series, often based themselves upon populist paperbacks written "for one and all." This lighter genre has its detractors, a strain of discontent that led to the severity of *The Prison Colony*. A couple of years ago, *Art of Cinema* (*Iskusstvo kino*) outlined its own dissatisfaction with the quintessential post-Soviet detective TV story *Streets of Broken Lights*. The article's author, Aleksandr Rogozhkin, blamed Russia's lack of experience in "long" series. In this particular series he discerned a lack of continuity twice over: both stylistically (that is, between episodes) and in the behavior of the main characters. The absence of discernible plotlines on many occasions was replaced by nothing more than "an excessive plenitude of everyday elements and details." Able to muster a few positive thoughts, Rogozhkin said the broadcasts at least expressed some simple "Russian" notions of fairness and justice. Yet these resulting opposites (narrative/visual convolution and ethical ease) contradict each other, he admitted; so much so, in fact, that the mental effort required in following the plot makes it hard for viewers to engage key events emotionally. The head is so busy the heart cannot catch up.[16]

Rogozhkin may be wrong in some respects. After all, the show both was and remains popular! The charm of this wandering, cheap format is such that when compared to the dreamscapes of *Dear Masha Berezina* it starts to look extremely convincing. Confusion on the set between actors and real policemen is reported by newspapers, reminding us of the inexpensive and provincial *The UPS Agency*.[17] The show has not only slipped back and forth modestly between fact and fiction; it has also moved unsurely between TV stations because of its popularity. Originally released on TNT, it ended up on ORT in 1998 after Kirienko's Default, which wiped out the advertising world and led to much head scratching among cash-strapped TV producers. But the next, second series of *Streets* moved suddenly to NTV, which had noted the show's éclat on TNT and ORT and thus outbid them both.

Because the controller of ORT, Konstantin Èrnst, had now missed a chance to continue the broadcasts, he announced his intention to make an identical mirror-show, a decision the head of TNT maligned as a "dearth of good ideas."[18] ORT nonetheless began its copycat serial, the naturalistic, morally muddled tale of "real" policemen *Lethal Force* (*Uboinaia sila* [multiple directors, from 2000]), starring the same cops plus Konstantin Khabenskii. It was only after protracted legal discussions that ORT was forced to return the staple characters of *Streets* to the show on NTV.[19]

In essence, though, this story constitutes what Russians refer to as a "man's serial" and, for all the domestic scenes or marital problems that we see in *Streets*, it was *Kamenskaia* that made married life a major part of how real life "outdoors" is understood. *Streets of Broken Lights* uses scenes of romance under stress to add a quotidian yet secondary element; *Kamenskaia* puts love and married life on a par with police work. Both series have on occasion been criticized for excessive violence, yet love and respect at home attain their full social weight in the latter, which is based on novels by Aleksandra Marinina usually grouped under the term "women's detective fiction" (*zhenskii detektiv*).[20]

The series stars the nationally renowned actress Elena Iakovleva as the eponymous heroine, but even she was hired only after long debates concerning possible alternates: Polina Kutepova, Mariia Aronova, Elena Tsyplakova, Vera Glagoleva, and Ol'ga Drozdova. The ultimate choice was obviously successful, since a recent television survey to find the "Nation's Number One Hero" put Anastasiia Kamenskaia in fourth place, after Putin, Sakharov, and Solzhenitsyn![21] Whenever she is asked about similarities between herself and that female hero, Iakovleva almost always limits matters to the smaller, domestic facets of her alter ego:

> Like my heroine, I like to drink coffee. I drink martinis, too, but I prefer *demi sec*. Like Kamenskaia, I'm not crazy about computers. I don't wear prescription glasses. I dress very much like her – jeans, a cap, jacket, skirt or a short sheepskin coat. That's almost exactly like Nastia. But she [eventually] went off at some point to the registry office in an elegant gown, whereas my husband and I popped in to register ourselves in between rehearsals and an evening performance – literally in our jeans and sweaters![22]

> On one and the same day in different Moscow wedding registries, two brides are shot point-blank. Red on white: the color combination to entice an unidentified maniac. Perhaps that's how a spurned woman takes revenge? As fate and circumstance would have it, Anastasiia Kamenskaia is getting married in the same registry office as the murder victim. Maybe some photos, taken by a photographer moonlighting at the ceremonies will help the investigation? (Promotional blurb.)

Iakovleva is well aware that these parallels between life and drama can be consequential. She was told by young girls after the ominous 1989 hit *Intergirl* (*Interdevochka*, dir. Petr Todorovskii) that they wanted to become prostitutes, whereas today police cadets write on their exam papers that they wish to emulate Kamenskaia.[23] The series' producer, Valerii Todorovskii, believes people need these parallels, since (as suggested above) they both replicate and construct fundamental social connections. He draws a nice parallel between a comforting TV series and being at summer camp, where in each room there's always some twelve-year-old boy who is asked to tell an ongoing story each night before bed: "Come on, tell us that story! Where did it get to last night?" He maintains that the same happens in hospital wards and, allegedly, in prison colonies, too. The key element to all these narratives, be they verbal or visual, is that they must overlap with a commonly felt, shared certainty. This quality distinguishes them from soap operas. Todorovskii holds that because soap operas operate "above" reality (unnatural money, atypical beauty, etc.), they cannot function in Russia; if quotidian (actual) experience were at any point compared to the imaginary tale on screen, the fictional edifice would crumble.[24]

The avoidance of deception in *Kamenskaia* has been successful – and not just for the lead actress. Even a secondary figure, Sergei Garmash (who plays Kamenskaia's colleague Iurii Korotkov), has enjoyed sufficient popularity in his own romantic yet down-to-earth subplots to warrant parallels with the fame of Stirlitz. This odd comparison between a love-struck policeman and a Nazi officer is possible because Garmash played Richard Heydrich in *The Red Choir*. Garmash has, in fact, acted in several of the series under review here and is very much a TV staple after appearances in *Life Lines*, *Beyond the Wolves*, and *The Brigade*. In one recent interview he defined the attractiveness of serials for the "Russian mentality" via three key emphases: "Crime, a family chronicle, and a long, drawn out love story."[25] They are inseparable, hence our discussion of doe-eyed romance among hard-nosed cops.

If figures of the hearth or heart (no matter what they do for a living) embody better philosophies of social being, perhaps they qualify as heirs to the long-lost label of "intelligentsia"? If so, these are not the lonesome, library-bound thinkers of prior decades. The prestigious *New Literary Review* (*Novoe literaturnoe obozrenie*) has pointed out that today's characters of learning and intellect (such as detectives) must – according to the "demands of mass culture" – be shown knee-deep in "real problems of daily life." In one episode, for example, Kamenskaia ponders whether to buy some expensive orange juice:

> "It'd be pleasure incarnate, of course, but it's so expensive ... That kind of packet would last for four days if I only drank it in the morning, and even then it'd come to almost 2,000 rubles a month." Kamenskaia had taken time off in May but hadn't gone anywhere. Instead she'd taken on a little hackwork – translating a detective novel from the French – then blown all that money on some lavish pleasures. She'd bought 30 packets of juice, a few jars of coffee, and three boxes of good cigarettes.[26]

Thus, argues the *New Literary Review*, the heroine is an admirable figure because she uses her mind and intellect in the real world – hopefully to solve problems – and as a detective that means she works to the public good. Any individual prone to detachment among his/her musings should wise up, be good, and get social ASAP.

Turetskii's March (*Marsh Turetskogo*, from 2000)

> Heroism, the love of freedom, fortitude, a proximity to the Russian people, a synthesis [*sliianie*] with the massed soldiers, an emotional temperament, passion, and a gift for music.[27]
>
> (A schoolbook's celebration of Chapaev's qualities in 1984)

These conclusions about *Kamenskaia* can be transferred to another Rossiia show with which it is often advertised – as a kindred spirit in aesthetics and airtime: *Turetskii's March* (dir. Mikhail Tumanishvili) stars Aleksandr Domogarov, an actor already very prominent in historical TV drama. The bravado of courtly heartthrobs is shifted to the police force: "The show's hero is Special Investigator for the State Procurator's Office, Turetskii. He's unbelievably smart, independent, and honest. The main thing, though, is that he struggles successfully against corruption, against criminals and 'businessmen' who don't keep their hands clean."[28] Given Domogarov's status as an established TV star and sex symbol, those "admirable" social qualities often dovetail with his ability to conquer hearts as well as criminals.[29] His affairs come at the expense of his marriage; the actress playing his wife (Marina Mogilevskaia) is the embodiment of marital martyrdom. Here the "female" emphases of *Kamenskaia* become another "men's serial," for there is *much* drinking, smoking, winking, and fishing going on:

> A wave of murders involving major bankers has rolled across Russia. What is it: a war between financial factions that's risen to the surface? Maybe fighting between bandits? "Big shot" Aleksandr Borisovich Turetskii is brought into the case. His version of events – the final version – turns out to be the only correct one.

If, on the other hand, romantic characteristics (oriented towards male or female viewers) *connect* several serials – made by the same TV channel and advertised on the same posters at the same bus stops – does this not hint at an impending homogeneity, gendered categories aside? For some people today, it certainly does; once again *Zona* felt a need to break out from these limits. The routine of many shows can sometimes overlap with the routine of characters' professional activities, leaving a gray sameness redolent of socialist tedium, of "warmed-over, Soviet officialdom":

> [In the case of Turetskii,] you might have a beautiful girl who's trying to explain with broken, indistinct phrases that she's in mortal danger. But Turetskii coldly insists on the facts of the matter – and until those facts come to light he's ready to walk away, pure and simple, leaving the girl to destiny's whim. So it's no big surprise that during an intense shoot-out with some murderers who've turned up, Turetskii takes quite a while to realize they've already shot her ... It looks like this hero's in no position to save anybody from death, because he no longer has the inner strength to worry about another person's existence. Whenever Domogarov has to show his reaction at a friend's death, it all looks extremely cold and mannered.[30]

Here, too, the emphasis on details such as shared drinks between the "lads" in the Procurator's Office reaches the point of a "profoundly modern [and irritating] naturalism." Hence, perhaps, the reaction of some viewers today: "I really don't like Domogarov. He plays his role badly and it's all too affected. The series is a big disappointment for me." It would appear that when the social membership of actors around Turetskii (in particular Vladimir Il'in and Boris Nevzorov) is both institutionalized (in the form of the state procurator) and then directed back *upon* forms of society in somewhat forceful, if not sexually patriarchal ways, it unnerves some people. Policemen are supposed to aid, that is, *be* the social within a largely predestined, Manichean scheme (the Channel One series *Khiromant* makes this clearest of all). Self-assured ladies' men who use the institution of their employers smack on occasion of Soviet cockiness or *chvanstvo*. Already a star from swashbuckling historical dramas, Domogarov had brought that troubling baggage with him to the police series. Kamenskaia *doubts*; Turetskii *does* –; yet at times with unfeasible self-reliance. He occasionally becomes a social and sexual fantasy.

The Brigade (*Brigada*, 2002) and *Borderlands* (*Granitsa*, 2000)

> There are times we still don't appreciate our freedom; even less often do we handle it well. A creative application of energy, resourcefulness, a sense of measure and the will to win cannot be introduced by governmental decree.
> (Putin, 2004)

Pushy heroes caused problems in Russia's most famous mafia tale of lifelong fidelity and philadelphia: *The Brigade*. It had few qualms advertising itself explicitly in the spirit of *One Upon a Time in America* (dir. Sergio Leone, 1984) or *The Godfather* (dir. Francis Ford Coppola, 1972). Some journalists even detailed specific episodes taken directly from the second and third parts of the *Godfather* trilogy (1974 and 1990), yet were also willing to say that *The Brigade* follows "the standard path [of a Russian mafia film] – from a happy-go-lucky hooligan to big-time racketeer. Then we see participation in all kinds of economic 'schemes' and finally your patriotic Mafioso – who can't bring himself to sell arms to Chechen warriors."[31] Nonetheless, everything depends on trust and amity:

> This is the story of four childhood friends. They're typical Moscow guys: Sasha Belyi, Kosmos, Pchela, and Fil. They grew up together around the same courtyard. Together these four buddies decide to make a little extra cash, but an inadvertent murder ruins all their plans in a second. Their lives suddenly become a gamble; a risk that's too great for them ... but there's nowhere to retreat. And so the four friends map out a path for themselves in the criminal world. By destiny's will they become one of Moscow's most organized and prominent criminal gangs.

The series went on to make the actors household names; so much so, in fact, that – as with *Kamenskaia* – several articles appeared, sympathizing with current stars of TV and cinema who had missed out. Sergei Bezrukov's

Figure 9.1 The Brigade.

central role as the bandit Sasha Belyi was discussed in the same breath as Konstantin Khabenskii and even Vladimir Mashkov. Ekaterina Guseva's role as Belyi's wife had almost fallen to Inga Oboldina and Mariia Golubkina.[32] Not long after the debut, frantic questions already sounded as to the possibility of a sequel. One of the four central actors, Pavel Maikov, quipped: "Have you watched this [first] series to the end yet?! [Maybe] we all get killed, so what kind of sequel could there be? Do you want 'Return of *The Brigade* Zombies'?"[33]

Winning both the casting call and the hearts of impatient millions, Bezrukov's position at the head of the series has now made him one of TV's cultural arbiters; he is constantly asked, as with *Esenin* or *Master and Margarita*, about the current state of television drama, about its leanings towards positive or negative heroes. It is here that *The Brigade* differs from *Turetskii's March* in its potential *vis-à-vis* social models. Bezrukov has said, for example, that the adaptation of Dostoevskii's *Idiot* will incline kids towards good books (and away from computer screens), a positive attitude extended by the contention that all his on-screen characters, including Sasha Belyi and Vronskii (in the adaptation of *Anna Karenina*), are likewise positive.[34] Since when did mafia figures give advice on socializing children with love and respect?

The possibility of squeezing constructive meanings into a criminal drama series came in part from a relative lack of blood and guts (compared with analogous films). The director and screenwriter Aleksei Sidorov wanted "lots of psychological, quotidian episodes instead. And *love* scenes, in the good sense of the word – without vulgarity ... The Russian public adores Belyi for the way he loved [not for his criminal guile] ... Young people today have lost the ability to love, they've lost the idea of fidelity."[35] Here is where friends and lovers overlap, where *Turetskii* falls behind in a cloud of dust. Masculine camaraderie requires two things as the foundation of a credible series: a deeply loved heroine (acting as ethical yardstick for the outside word) and an *equal*, oppositional force in that same outside world against which the hero is judged. *Turetskii*'s characters, though hugely admired, sometimes lean so heavily on assurances (on themselves, on their rock-solid friendship) and the institution they represent that they start to seem Soviet (in the sense of being monolithic), as opposed to Sasha Belyi *et al.*, who salvage the romanticism of much earlier Soviet narratives. *The Brigade* is romantic in terms of both love and twentieth-century literary chronology. Both those categories embody forms of desire. State institutions desire nothing; they already embody everything.

"Everything" can be avoided with "some-thing(s)" in particular. The quotidian elements so closely tied to *The Brigade*, together with a vital love theme, underwrite the scale of this project and prompt the analogies with *Once Upon a Time in America*. *The Brigade* was shot on 350 locations and includes 110 speaking roles of consequence; it made use of 900 costumes and for one shoot-out alone needed 500 holes in the wall to reflect all the shots supposedly fired.[36] There is a limit, however (as one might expect), where this enterprise becomes excessive and again looks naturalistic; that is, it sidelines the human element and/or "institutionalizes" itself in TV line-ups through the unassailable size of its machinations. Maybe *The Brigade* is popular purely because it has the funds to show itself more often than other, similar broadcasts?

If so, we reach another Soviet dilemma: are viewers and readers simple, passive recipients of Moscow's centralized culture or do they guide TV listings with their decision to watch (or not to watch) a given broadcast? The former, sadder possibility is sometimes encountered:

> The thing is that viewers are like children. They adore reading what they've read 100 times before and watching what they've already watched. If TV stations show us [the elderly comics] Petrosian, Stepanenko, and [the variety show] *Anshlag* every day, then we'll start loving Petrosian, Stepanenko, and *Anshlag*.[37]

This observation, by *Art of Cinema* editor Daniil Dondurei, was seconded by TV presenter Aleksandr Liubimov, who claimed that TV stories engage viewers' emotions, "not their head. They sort of rehash a viewer's impressions from life ... while distorting them a bit." *The Brigade*'s producer, Aleksandr Inshakov, objected to this sorry viewpoint at a television roundtable; he maintained there was no such influence of TV on life, that is, no such thing as a film whose events then came to life *in* life. This seems moot, however, even in the context of *The Brigade*, given that several instances have been recorded in Russia of young boys killing their contemporaries on the explicit model of this series.

One of the show's other producers, Anatolii Sivushov, holds that the broadcast's influence on life has been positive, and here we come full circle – to the earlier contention that Sasha Belyi actually teaches viewers to love. Sivushov said that the adventures of Belyi and his friends could justifiably be cataloged under a subheading of "The Russian Mafia through the Eyes of Mothers and Wives."[38] This constant interlocking during most episodes between crime and romance or (subsequent) familial ties has even conjured parallels – yet again – with both the maudlin tradition and episodic structure of *Moscow Does Not Believe in Tears*.[39] Paradoxically, it was said that *The Brigade*, in order to reach the high moral ground held by Men'shov's film, had to show wrongdoing by its heroes because any tale of great wealth accrued after perestroika among *honest* characters would convince nobody. It had to involve criminals, said one journalist, since nobody would believe a tale of honest policemen and their love lives. *The Brigade*, walking this contrary path, "tells of good things ... The heroes are continually obliged to decide what's more important for them – real friendship or huge amounts of money. They resolve these issues with complete dignity "[40]

Since *Moscow Does Not Believe in Tears* and *The Brigade* both take place over very long periods of time, being tales of change and chance, it is interesting to see how children perceive these processes of dignified maturation. Given the importance of love, what girls have to say is of particular significance, especially in response to a hackneyed boyish remark:

> They're great guys. Great friends, too. It's too bad that they got into arms dealing, though. I liked the figure of Fil best of all, because he's an athlete. He's reliable and always cool (Artem, 11 years old).

> What do mean, they're "great"? Look how many bad things they did to other people ... Sure, there was a strong friendship between the men, but that's not enough to make me respect bandits. It's a good thing *I* don't have friends like that (Lena, 16 years old).
>
> I'd like to be Belyi's girlfriend. I like a life with adventure. But it wasn't worth killing the people who killed his friends. That could go on forever! ... It's better to have less money and live quietly. I felt sorry for Belyi's family. His wife and son will be shaking with fear for the rest of their lives. The film is a warning to all girls and guys who still don't understand what big money leads to – or what happens when you're greedy for power (Ania, 11 years old).[41]

In an interview with a major Moscow newspaper, Bezrukov said the series is "about *life*. The fate of both the nation and mankind. It's about the fact there's real friendship and real love. I hope young people, despite all of my hero's charm, won't take him as an example to follow, because you'll pay three times over for that kind of life." His co-stars agreed and said the series centers upon "friends who are trying to build a life for themselves – all on their own" (Vladimir Vdovichenkov); Pavel Maikov was even more straightforward in his definition. *The Brigade* is, quite simply, "about love and friendship."[42]

If violence, justice, and friendship can be commingled, though, are we really escaping the kind of dilemma in which *Turetskii's March* found itself? The problem does not go away in the Russian press today. One correspondent has suggested that these combined qualities of the central characters amount to the standard Soviet depiction of military officers, not bandits or criminals:

> There's strict adherence to one's word, plus heroic acts in the name of both friendship and love ... And how beautiful and faithful their girlfriends all are! The true ideal of a Russian officer's wife! They don't ask their husbands about work ... They understand that it's the fate of all men to go off into the fog and then call home, overcoming the agony from a shot to the shoulder: "I'm with a friend at his dacha. Everything's just fine."[43]

This inclination towards a reliable past – rather than the risk of something new or very foreign (in the sense of uniqueness) – was likened on one web forum to the difference between a solid, unrefined, and plagiarized *Snickers* bar and infinitely superior Swiss *Lindt* chocolate: "It's a cinema-clone, a 'Dolly the sheep' in comparison to normal, healthy animals."[44]

The retro-series (consciously or otherwise) of dignified social "officers" within the male adventure rubric has become increasingly popular, and was foreshadowed by dramas like *Borderlands: A Romance of the Taiga* (*Granitsa: Taezhnyi roman* [dir. Aleksandr Mitta, 2000]), made in eight episodes for TV as well as being whittled down to two hours for the cinema:

The action takes place in the 1970s. Our heroes are the officers and wives of the Far Eastern Border Garrison. Although the [social] world of these characters is a small one, that same small space is home to an entire range of human relations: love and betrayal, friendship and bitterness, mutual assistance – and jealousy to the point of madness.

Director and screenwriter Aleksandr Mitta "obviously wanted to make the kind of TV program that nobody has made for ages [that is, since the 1970s themselves]. First of all, it would plainly be a TV novella centered not on one destiny, but on lots of them, all entwined. The characters would develop as they go along, too."[45] Using the geographic, social, and historical sweep here, not only does the romantically driven TV series expand beyond its usual limits, but kindred dramas draw both increasingly and positively upon Soviet experience under Brezhnev. This historical insistence, given Putin's stance towards the media, again may be cause for concern. Nostalgia has a downside, too.

In December 2004 the independent monitoring group Freedom House used its global survey "Freedom in the World" to downgrade Russia from "Partly Free" to the lowly status of "Not Free": "Russia's status fell because of the flawed nature of the country's parliamentary elections in December 2003 and the presidential elections in 2004, the further consolidation of state control of the media and the imposition of official curbs on opposition political parties and groups."[46] One story in particular has addressed some unhappy issues of legality amid *happy*, rural networks with particular success and popularity.

Village life to a nostalgic theme tune: *A Policeman's Beat* (*Uchastok*, 2003)

We want all our law-abiding citizens to be proud of our law enforcement agencies – and not cross the street whenever they see someone in uniform. There can be no place in law enforcement for people whose primary aim is to fill their own pockets.

(Putin, 2005)

A Policeman's Beat (dir. Aleksandr Baranov) is the very quiet television series in which Bezrukov starred after *The Brigade* had come to an end. Here, after *Borderlands*, is the workshop of the new positive hero, the place where he will grow:

Forest, forest all around. Fields. Villages. Little houses. Basically nothing special, if you don't count the fact that Sergei Bezrukov is walking around the village. There's a strikingly handsome bloodhound beside him. Bezrukov is silent. For a while. The bloodhound talks to him. Sometimes. Together this odd couple is investigating the matter of

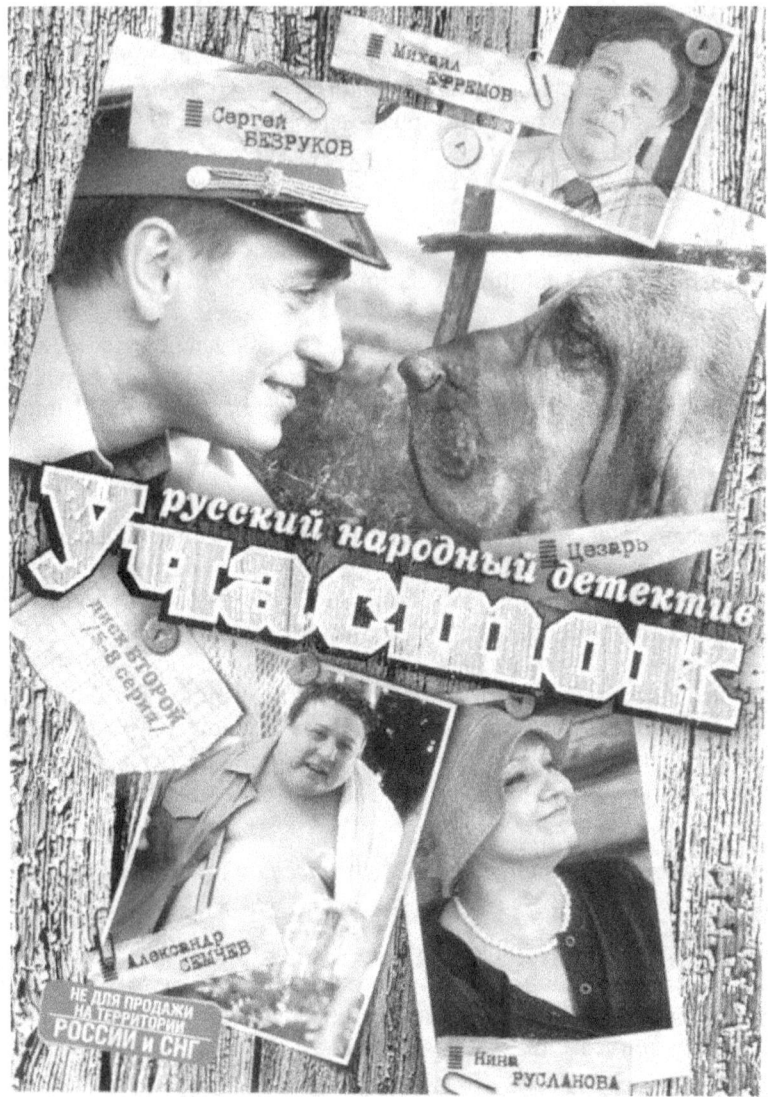

Figure 9.2 *A Policeman's Beat.*

a stolen goat. A nice little scene ... that took about a million dollars to make.[47]

The broadcasts, running at the same time as *Two Fates*, took a massive 49 percent share of national primetime; *Two Fates* took 42 percent in its timeslot. *The Brigade*, by comparison, hit its peak at 40.2 percent. Nostalgia and countryside romance, on the edge of (but not wholly *in*) an institution, were back in a big way:[48]

Policeman Pavel Kravtsov is a rather strange person. If he has to handcuff somebody he apologizes and asks if the cuffs pinch. He's ambitious but honest; he's young but pensive. You won't make much of yourself in a city police force with that kind of "investment" in your career. And so Lieutenant Kravtsov, a city boy through and through, ends up in the backwater village of Anisovka as a regular policeman. It's a bit like exile or an unwelcome business trip. And then there's the argument he had with his wife – over a complete misunderstanding. It was about Kravtsov being married to his job, when that same job (in the form of his boss) isn't exactly holding onto him ... Having left everything behind and taking only his beloved dog Caesar, Kravtsov heads off for Anisovka where he starts getting used to the place.

The future implications of this stencil, whereby institutional figures are viewed through personal, romantic relationships (in this case with Mariia Poroshina) can be seen already. The publishing house and broadcasting network Palmyra (*Pal'mira*) has created an annual competition called "Russian Theme" (*Rossiiskii siuzhet*) in order to rally good, positive heroes with the following phrases:

The world we live in tomorrow depends on the world we're shown today! Look to the future positively. The competition's priority is the search for works that show a positive side of contemporary life, works that form the image of a positive hero. Works that affirm human virtue. We're in favor of depicting heroes who can, in today's complicated circumstances, make a career for themselves by honest means. A career, success, and material self-sufficiency *are* attainable in Russia without recourse to corruption, crime, and treachery.

The magazine *Ogonek* offered these same ideas to a panel of industry experts as a context in which to discuss *A Policeman's Beat*.[49] The author of the screenplay, Aleksei Slapovskii, likened his hero (with scant modesty) to Dostoevskii's Alesha Karamazov and Prince Myshkin. He claimed that writers will never find positive heroes in the real police force, since "it's 99% corrupt – from the top down." Hence his desire to create a fictional – if not salvationary – representative from the long-lost 1 percent, a "positive hero [just like Sasha Belyi] who's not made for political posters. He's the kind of person who makes a life for himself, by himself. He doesn't lie around on the stove" like the lazy men of Slavic folklore. He is saved from the Big City by rural existence.

The show was lauded for sounding the death knell of ten years of "hellish" TV and news centered both on violence and the enduring misery of *chernukha*. In this series "everything ends well because we have Officer Kravtsov – a knight beyond both fear and reproach. Not only does he believe sincerely in the triumph of justice and the law, but he defends them, too. By doing so he affirms similar beliefs in the viewer. And who, upon seeing all that, wouldn't jump for joy?"[50] Indeed, this may be cause for delight, but the same writer remarks that at some point (or limit) it all starts smelling like the well-polished past in the spirit of the retro-concerts *Old Songs about What Matters* (*Starye pesni o glavnom*) or Alla Pugacheva's dreamy classic of 1979 also mentioned earlier, "Starry Summer" (*Zvezdnoe leto*).

Bezrukov jumps into the proceedings and once again insists that *all* his heroes are "positive," that *A Policeman's Beat* does not "rehabilitate" an old and obsolete prototype.[51] Boris Grachevskii, director of the ageless children's series *Mishmash* (*Eralash*), has concurred. He insisted the show is busy solving issues of human interaction rather than dramatizing an obsessive, greedy interest in hard cash.[52] Pushing that parallel a little further one could take issue with Bezrukov, though, because *Uchastok* could undoubtedly be likened to the Brezhnevian "village" detective stories of Officer Aniskin (*The Provincial Detective* [*Derevenskii detektiv*, dir. Ivan Lukinskii, 1968]; *Aniskin and Phantomas* [*Aniskin i Fantomas*, dir. Mikhail Zharov and Vladimir Rapoport, 1974]; and *Once Again Aniskin* [*I snova Aniksin*, dir. Mikhail Zharov and Vitalii Ivanov, 1978]). Likewise, "it's not exactly *Cossacks of the Kuban* [*Kubanskie kazaki*, dir. Ivan Pyr'ev, 1949], but all the same this project does has a positive aura."[53] The debate continued:

> There's a lot here that's just made up – and there are way too many "coincidences." What we're shown as happening over one year in the village wouldn't happen over 100 years in a real village. But all things considered I like it. It's not dull.
>
> Where would you see an officer like Bezrukov? He only knows about village life from books.
>
> It's a good-natured film – and that makes for a very strange combination. But is that so bad? The situations in the series are lively enough – things happen a little too often [in the village], as other people have pointed out. But what d'you want? You'd never watch real village life on a day-to-day basis! They [the producers] show well the Russian tendency to screw things up; they show our passion for boozing and for anything that's offered us free of charge, etc., etc. I vote FOR this kind of series with both my thumbs – and all my toes.[54]

The parallel with the legendary musical *Cossacks of the Kuban* is helpful, since it also makes much use of the landscape to build optimistic metaphors. Maybe this is also the format of the future? Pyr'ev's opening scenes in 1949 are of peopleless wheat fields; the smoothly rolling blades of a combine harvester come into shot, and an opening song of love and plenitude rings out across the countryside. Soviet songs, still loved today, bolster the narrative ("As once you were, so still you are ... " ["*Kakim ty byl, takim ty i ostalsia* ... "]); numerous people adopt melodies sung at first by one person. This leads quickly to the workplace harmony of multitudes and the harmony of farm workers' music. In fact, when these mellifluous groups take the form of an amateur variety concert, we see a reverse process as the affect of the sung lyrics inspires the audience to love, to note the "warning signs" of their fluttering hearts.

Harmonic rustic emphases are a basis of Cossack society. When a young woman at a ball spurns an official, she declares the evening "un-Soviet!" Romance, not rhetoric, will fix the problem and make the evening Soviet. Farms at this time compete over a new piano that is for sale; they dream of the jazz, Chopin, and Soviet variety numbers they could play upon it and prove their *kolkhoz* "isn't an old village." When love and music do indeed come together in a resolved romantic plot, the lead couple moves off towards the horizon as the credits get ready to roll – and the lovers are followed by the plows of massed agriculture across the screen, not vice versa. Big plans follow in the successful, exemplary footsteps of little harmonies.

The *Aniskin* analogy is just as helpful. (Surely the name of the village in *A Policeman's Beat* – that is, Anisovka – is not a coincidence?) It results in plots with "little blood, lots of humor and life-affirming motives."[55] Millions of viewers agree, even if some question the intentions of this "neo-eco-realism" used to frame the tale of a divorced policeman painfully preoccupied with a villager's wife as he solves myriad crimes, none of which displace the yearning of his lonely heart. Love is always there, working hard, in this case to the quiet theme tune sung by Bezrukov himself, placing modern police work in the context of nature and the nation: "Why do the birch trees rustle in Russia? How do they know everything? They stand by the roads, white trunks leaning in the wind, and sadly let their leaves fall."

Bezrukov sings this with Nikolai Rastorguev, lead singer of *Liubè*; the band is famous for wearing military uniforms on stage whilst encouraging great respect for the army and police. Their videos are awash with Soviet nostalgia – and as a result Rastorguev counts many statesmen among his fans. His most famous song, *Kombat*, was dedicated to the fiftieth anniversary of World War Two and so three-minute texts about birch trees in police series recall stories about loud patriotism, but what exactly is being taken or remembered from the greatest conflict in the nation's history? What are Rastorguev and Bezrukov invoking in the countryside?

An interesting and instructive parallel here might be the film *The Hearts of Four* (*Serdtsa chetyrekh*, dir. K. Iudin), which was made for release in 1941, deemed ready for great success, but due to the hostilities was shelved until 1944. At that time it indeed met with loud public approval, garnering almost 20 million viewers across the USSR. Popular notions of good, convincing entertainment were unhampered or unaltered by war. They underwrite a sense of continuity that can be drawn upon by Rastorguev, employing both policy and a grander (quieter) force of social cohesion through emotional or musical harmony.

This particular musical vaudeville concerns a misunderstanding between lovers, in particular between the male suitors of two sisters, of one young and flighty girl and her older or somewhat severe sibling. The elder woman is a fledgling mathematician and gives lectures at a summer camp to soldiers; one of them quickly admits to an officer that he is in love, prompting the officer to say: "Everything's in order, then!" The odd, sometimes dizzy dictates of love surpass those of the parade ground. The officer even offers help to the subordinate soldier in writing a successful love letter.

The military world often coincides with the amorous, but even so the new Soviet sensitivity – of these two "women who always prefer feeling to reason" – struggles to align "modern" ardor with what the sisters read about love in their "bourgeois" novels of the nineteenth century. (The term, in fact, is employed throughout the film with great irony.) The mathematician, thankfully, comes to recognize a different sense of order in the world, one more cordial than anything formulaic. She hears a wise old professor quote Pushkin and the poet's thoughts on repetition or willed, unpredictable desire: "The heart burns and loves once more, for it cannot but love."

Gradually this pattern overrules everything arithmetical, as love triumphs; the mathematician (Galina) gets a kiss – and the camera spins round and round! Both girls find boyfriends and decide to stay in the countryside, not the city. As they wave at the train going back to Moscow in the final frames, we see them waving at us. We are the ones going back to the city. The challenge to find love is now ours – and people like *Liubè* sing of that challenge today; it stands before us as we enter the metropolis, where our unity will be under considerable threat.

The experiences of the maturing heart kept on going, whether there was war or not. They also bolstered the greatest motion pictures at the other end of the hostilities. A duty to one's sweetheart was given the most contemporary relevance in *The Number One Gloves* (*Pervaia perchatka*, dir. A. Frolov) of 1946, telling of a promising new boxer and skills so graceful they are termed a "symphony" by his trainer on several occasions. As a man from the Siberian taiga, out of place in the Big City, the boxer puts his sweetheart above Muscovite competitions and dreams of being with her around a silent, distant forest campfire one day. A misunderstanding between them spoils things, though, and he heads home in a terrible huff. After a week(!) traveling by train eastwards, he has a change of heart in the middle of the Siberian wilderness. He brings this newfound organic wisdom back to his girlfriend – and with her devotion alone finds the inner strength he needs to wear "the number one gloves of the USSR."

This movie underlines the codex of popular, truly significant entertainment, of hopes and dreams in a dictatorial society after World War Two; a longing for victorious amity (stronger than the ailing body or heart it fuels) to inspire Russian society through tough years of deprivation and reconstruction – even now. It comes to Moscow from the middle of nowhere, one or two people at a time, because it's *supposed* to belong to nobodies – to the workers told by dogma itself that they "have nothing to lose."

10 Conclusion
Fighting the good fight

> The state cannot demand faith, prayer, love, goodness or conviction from its citizens. It cannot regulate scientific, religious and artistic creation ... It should not intervene in moral, family and daily private life. Let us not forget this.
>
> (Putin, 2005)

A bighearted leap away from humanism

It would seem that a need to accept love's destiny (that is, "because I can do so little myself") is also what drives the need for the battling heroes of detective series like *Kamenskaia* to be socially *active* ("I hope those heroes can at least do *something*, because I cannot"). Love and barely self-sufficient detectives are both embodiments of social amelioration. Detectives, as we have seen, also *need* that love in their own private lives – in domestic emphases that must be palpable, lest we fall to the complaints suffered by confident, institutionally sustained Turetskii. Even detectives must be romantic and it is their small, often unworkable dream (not dogma) of social betterment that allows for some aspects of Soviet storytelling to be redone, as in *The Brigade* or *A Policeman's Beat*. Storytelling is redone with romance. Without the roles of Guseva and Poroshina, these two series would be completely different (that is, considerably uglier).

It takes little to turn lovelorn tales like *A Policeman's Beat* into politics and at this point we can only trust that Channel One stays on the right side of the line. Nonetheless, we should already be grateful that most of the TV series outlined here express a Slavic social yearning without recourse to the cultural kowtowing of *That Balzac Age*. One very bad example of self-demeaning citizenship, though, was 2004's *Sister Swap* (*Rodstvennyi obmen*, dir. V. Kott). Despite an expensive roster (Kristina Orbakaite, Dmitrii Pevtsov, Marat Basharov, and music by Igor' Krutoi), its love story is a sad spectacle.

With awful irony, this very Muscovite romance includes much that made Russian TV so provincial until recent times, including that enduring curse of the Slavic screen, post-sync dialog. Whenever live speech does remain in the final cut, it is from the noisiest locales (inside cars, on sidewalks) and once-audible words are completely swamped. Other old-time sins include female voices used for children; the crew's equipment or limbs straying into frames; outrageously hackneyed attempts to pass off Russian actors as wealthy, stylish English-speaking executives – and the endless, strained ignorance of a returning émigrée (Orbakaite herself) that obliges most Russian characters to explain various loveable clichés of Moscow life (drink, laziness, bad diet, smoking, etc.). Love of another land promises nothing good. Love of the girl next door is both fine and poignant. It also makes for better television and a better philosophy. It may even make for a better society; all we can hope is that politicians don't start telling us so.

Thus we come to the end of our study with a few concluding thoughts to synthesize many objects of attention. Although the theoretical observations peppered throughout this monograph have made neither frequent nor lasting reference to the speculative practices of ecocriticism, additional parallels are always possible – correspondences to give our examination a single overarching purpose. Nature, the environment, and their combined philosophical significances for socialist-inspired culture before or after 1991 have certainly been important from the outset. We have seen, for example, the recurrent use of socialist tales as a call to forms of deeply social selfhood beyond urban existence and the bounds of the human body. Through a desired (and ever-desirous) membership in choral forms of nature, much socialist storytelling advocates a risky "leap away from the rhetoric of humanism."[1]

That leap away from one self and/or one singular goal has reemerged in TV storytelling of recent years. Visual media can potentially outdo the compartmentalizing, segmenting, and metonymically structured narratives of goal-driven oratory. Kinetic, visual media can embody the affective, directionless *intentions* of language. Just as Gor'kii's *Mother* becomes in 2001 a novel based wholly upon the "ability and need to love, inherent in *every* woman or mother,"[2] so the increasingly personal, poignant, and quieter reconsideration of the Soviet tradition in a "natural," visual framework *prior to (or aside from)* the pathos of ideology's wordy infringement makes things gradually more complex for viewers and their processes of socialization. Teachers in Moscow ask children today why the 1930s may not be a low point in Soviet culture. What, they ask, if we include kinder, more mobile phenomena – such as the lyrical, popular movies and musicals of the time? We have done precisely that, and as a result our impressions of logocentric, dogmatic, and obsolete Soviet culture hopefully change; they become increasingly multifaceted. Television series continue to investigate that complexity, even with an archival interest such as *Kazaroza* (2006), which dramatizes the tragically bigoted, murderous passions surrounding Esperanto's potential in early Soviet society.

In Dmitrii Fiks' related police series *The Lawyer* (*Advokat*, 2004), a compromised journalist tells his junior colleague that he needs some simple, "patriotic" language to discredit a busybody investigator who has arrived from Moscow. The newcomer spells trouble for the local administration. "Do you know what patriotism is?" asks the editor, checking that the colleague is aware of what's required. The investigator (Zimin) is played by Andrei Sokolov, who among other duties handles a case of prejudice against a young Armenian man, made a scapegoat for a murder. Local people are happy to lean on their simple, jingoistic axioms and condemn the Armenian. When justice is brought to court, Zimin informs those present that not only do "we get the power structures we deserve," but each of us bears responsibility for both the good and evil and society.

"Nobody knew the Union would fall apart," says another character in defense of this ubiquitous, outspoken malice, but politics are neither prior to nor the cause of private values. Quite the opposite. When asked how honest he is in his own social dreaming, Zimin asks in turn whether this interlocutor wants "the honest word of a Pioneer, or the honest word of a lawyer." The former was once a wonderful benchmark, but was eventually spoiled. Zimin hopes to start again, to offer a similar honesty and do it better – the way it should have been in the first place.

One of the most interesting developments today has been an extension of these detective series' fatalism to the point where even willful figures of the *early* Revolution are forced to stop and ponder their presumed degrees of agency in shaping themselves or their nation. In 2005 Channel One funded Vladimir Khotinenko's lavish, ten-series drama *Death of an Empire* (*Gibel' imperii*) starring absolutely everybody: Sergei Makovetskii, Chulpan Khamatova, Aleksandr Baluev, Mariia Mironova, Andrei Krasko (now tragically deceased), Marat Basharov, Dmitrii Pevtsov, Vladislav Galkin, Fedor Bondarchuk, Konstantin Khabenskii, Iurii Kutsenko, Mariia Poroshina, and many others. It aimed to create a "psychological portrait [of the Revolution]... and not a concrete passage of events." It investigated the clash of two worlds, one conservative and frail, the other revolutionary and reckless. Here, in the adventures of imperial investigators on the trail of political, dangerous subversion, we see some of the values endorsed by our Soviet-inspired series; they are, however, virtues and failings that now have application or origin *before* anything Soviet. They often come from art more than policy, from the past more than the present, perhaps because – as James von Geldern has said of Soviet popular culture – sentimental love and patriotism "thrive best when men and women accept their traditional roles ... [or when] citizens accept traditional national identities."[3] These traditions are very old and bring us full circle to literature's role.

Lermontov's narrative poem *The Demon* is used here as a key text for deciphering secret messages; Dostoevskii's novel *The Devils* and Blok's play *The Puppet Show* (*Balaganchik*) are discussed in terms of their social relevance. The canon is perhaps telling a story that *never* changes; both Pevtsov and Makovetskii say on different occasions that their characters "do what they must," although "what will be will be." These heroes, carried in death as a Christ upon the bayonets of others, show a modern relevance amid networks of ineffable, unchangeable events that is enormous. "The Revolution," says another character "has no dignity or principles or tradition." It does, but it would never truly recognize or enact them. Towards the series' close, Makovetskii notes that after the Revolution "there will be nothing." Therein lies the problem; there *never* was nothing in the Badiouian sense.

Perhaps no series says this more clearly and quietly than 2004's *The Savior beneath the Birch Trees* (*Spas pod berezami*, dir. Leonid Ėidlin). On Moscow's outskirts, where birches once stood, a small church, previously made a prison, goes back to what it always did: helping people. Today it houses a self-confessed "neorealist" writer penning the events experienced by those who work or pray there. Finances and/or fiancées come and go "at God's will" throughout the episodes. Numerous references are made to the sentimental, social goals of Soviet culture, though the charm of Liubov' Orlova and her musicals of the 1930s are here enjoyed by a rather "simple," childlike man, perhaps unfit for modern interaction. Simple ideals do not come easily to our adult world; even the final frames leave the narrator yearning "for some kind of [shared] happy ending" in a direct address to the audience. It takes bravery to operate a normal existence today. In one scene where an Oscar-blessed star of Brezhnev's cinema, Irina Murav'eva, is upset about her life that seems "like a Mexican series" and about prayers said in the church for soap stars, the priest (Iurii Beliaev) sends her off to a better story of very similar desires. He tells her to stop watching the Mexican stuff, to "go home and watch *Chapaev*."

If viewers like Murav'eva's worried heroine rely on state-funded melodrama for resting places or ontological security, they will get even more security from looking (or yearning) further still into the past. Brezhnevian drama sought for conservatism, for a managed multiplicity as "cozy" detective or Holmesian tales, but recent series like *Gibel' imperii* or *Spas pod berezami* suggest that any *juste milieu* might be outrun by a desire for even greater retrospection, for even older, clearer oppositions. These are found in times and places further and further from anything resembling socialist or Soviet experience.

Often important in this slippage – once again – is the role of non-urban existence, for example in 2004's *Esenin*, also discussed earlier (see pp. 57–9). This eleven-episode drama depicts Esenin – *the* Soviet poet of the countryside – as accepting of the Revolution only because he once upon a time believed its talk of a "peasants' heaven." On seeing the execution of some farm workers from a train window, however, he comes to define socialism as nothing more than an "emotion for slaves." Despite being funded by Channel One, this series first embraces, but then outpaces, any practical ideas we hear from today's Duma. It is excessive to the point where it invokes its opposite – in this case a critique of socialism – yet it does so in ways taken *from* the musical, naturally and/or biologically harmonious metaphors of Soviet literature.

Conclusion 213

The first thing Esenin looks for after imprisonment is his "dear, native" accordion; when he is attacked by his soon-to-be murderers, he uses the same tool of concord to physically beat back the secret police. In a related spirit, when stuck in Berlin with Isadora Duncan, he meets Gor'kii in a restaurant – and is inspired to try a wild, unbridled folk dance. Later still in exile he says: "I love my homeland, you see? There's no way I can live without her. I love her grey skies and landscape. It is the *landscape* that gave us Pushkin, Lermontov, Tolstoi, and Dostoevskii. Anyone who stays in emigration is betraying that land." He goes back to his home village of Konstantinovo and is immediately asked by an elder: "Are you a communist?" "No," replies Esenin; "Thank God." By the end of this first day back in the fields he stands alone on a hilltop, surveys the interminable countryside that "gave birth" to literature, and says, in our time-honored Spinozistic mode, "Forgive us, Lord."

The investigative work done to discover the "truth" about Esenin's death takes place in 1985, in other words under Gorbachev. These cruel, post-Brezhnevian times are shot in pallid tones; the more brightly colored footage is saved for Esenin's life. The detective heading this revisionist case is referred to directly as a latter-day Stirlitz, a kinder spirit from the calmer 1970s. And indeed this kindness is needed. At the poet's funeral we are given yet another list of friends and family members who will be destroyed by the Soviet system, one after the other, as in *Molodaia gvardiia* or *Kursanty*.

Upon its commercial release on DVD, the series' credits employed four diverse stanzas from Esenin's passionate poem of 1914, *Rus'* ("Ancient Russia"). As the director frequently makes clear, this is a work for which the poet was awarded a gold watch in June 1916 after reciting it to the Empress and her daughters. The poem places its author in the middle of inexhaustible blueness, a realm that *also* gives voice to impending, nameless disaster as the clamor of ugly crows. Tiny domestic spaces or refuges amid this emptiness are palpable, too. A poet lauded *by* the Soviets is placed in a fuller, fairer context by a purportedly neo-socialist TV network, yet Orthodox and imperial realms of the countryside are treated with much greater affection. There is nothing positive whatsoever in the depiction of government during the poet's lifetime (or, come to that, in the 1980s, either). Storytelling, which we often see beginning with the gray, "non-politics" of Brezhnev's hushed 1970s, is taken further from the present day by many TV dramas, further from concrete times, and placed in networks closer to either (an even older) faith or some Spinozistic, ecologically driven filigree.

It is very difficult, therefore, to conflate political rhetoric and today's television in Russia, even though such assumptions are the norm in Western journalism. Truer, perhaps, is the enduring relevance of a key quandary outlined in our Introduction, offered by Mikhail Epstein, himself drawing upon the awful finale of Nikolai Gogol's *Dead Souls*. Russia's vastness, it was claimed, inspires both a sense of nothingness (of a place too big to see) plus some insistent awareness of a great heroism required to do that magnitude justice. Talking practically of such matters, as Esenin learns, is impossible.

Pavel Lungin's eight-episode fantasy upon Gogol's stories for NTV, *The Case of the Dead Souls* (2005), uses precisely the same passage quoted by Epstein. It asks us whether there can possibly be any "Russians who don't love to gallop" into the boundlessness of their country(side), even though they're *always* unaware of what lies ahead? These well-liked, requoted cultural designations may be Slavic clichés, but they have enormous cultural relevance for those people who constitute (i.e. speak of) that same culture. The same banalities not only drive stories of self-definition, but frequently fall foul of their own expansiveness, of an intellectual, inhuman scale inspired by the world's greatest *natural* expanse.

In Lungin's TV series, a government envoy travels to unknown villages in the middle of nowhere in order to bring law, order, and other loudly spoken dictates to the criminal case of some missing peasants, these "dead souls." Filled, however, with his own pomp and circumstance whenever surrounded by little nobodies in nameless villages, he soon begins to overshoot his own rhetorically defined grandeur. After excessive eating and imbibing, he saddles a makeshift wagon and declares his intention to grace this backwater with St. Petersburg's policies. Horribly drunk, he gets ready to whip the horse into action and chase his chosen criminal across the landscape, for "what Russian does not love to gallop?" Within ten seconds, the horse has slowed to a lazy trot and its political rider is already sound asleep. The horse, however, keeps going. Spurred into initial action by its big-talking rider, the animal strolls inexorably off into unmapped, quickly darkening forests. There, say two locals, beyond the end of those maps, both ravenous wolves and dreadful roads await him, "for such is the law of nature."

Esenin and *The Case of the Dead Souls* are just two more examples of how television series in Russian today have overshot anything resembling a standard, effable patriotism or socialist retrospection. The empty object of (ne'er-realized) socialist dreaming that has driven many of Putin's narratives may be swallowing itself. The problem is, as we have seen, that this object of desire offers no resting place as it "gallops" further like Gogol's drunken and self-assured dignitary. This desire produces narratives that shift into wider and riskier realms; taken to extremes, they invoke their opposites. They search for an ontological security further and further into the past, long before the Revolution, and therefore start designating *socialism* as the negative by which they can define anything "positive." Such is the dilemma of televised storytelling today, state-run or otherwise, in the world's biggest country, where endless forests, Esenin's soothsaying crows, and Gogol's starving wolves define the true, natural laws of the land.

Filmography

Television series and related shows

Advokat (*The Laywer*). Dir. Dmitrii Fiks. 2004.
Aèroport (*The Airport*). Dir. Egor Grammatikov and Aleksandr Gur'ianov. 2005–6.
Agent natsional'noi bezopasnosti (*National Security Agent*). Dir. Vitalii Aksenov and Dmitrii Svetozarov. From 1998.
Agentstvo NLS (*The UPS Agency*). Dir. Dmitrii Parmenov. From 2001.
American Idol (FOX reality show). USA. From 2002.
Aniskin i Fantomas (*Aniskin and Phantomas*). Dir. Mikhail Zharov and Vladimir Rapoport. 1974.
Anna Karenina. Dir. Sergei Solov'ev. (In production, 2005–2007.)
Anshlag (*Full House*, RTR/Rossiia variety show). From 1993.
Baiazet (*Bayazet*). Dir. Andrei Chernykh and Nikolai Stambula. 2003.
Bal'zakovskii vozrast, ili Vse muzhiki svo ... (*That Balzac Age, or All Men Are Basta ...*). Dir. Dmitrii Fiks. 2004–5.
Banditskii Peterburg (*Gangland Petersburg*). Dir. Vladimir Bortko, Viktor Sergeev, Vlad Furman, and Andrei Benkendorf. 2000–3.
Bednaia Nastia (*Poor Nastia*). Dir. Ekaterina Dvigubskaia, Petr Krotenko, Stas Libin, Alla Plotkina, Aleksandr Smirnov, and Petr Shtein. 2003.
Bez kompleksov (*No Hang-Ups*, Channel One chat show). 2006.
Blagoslovite zhenshchinu (*Bless the Woman*). Dir. Stanislav Govorukhin. 2003.
Bliznetsy (*The Twins*). Dir. Zinovii Roizman. 2005.
Boets (*The Warrior*). Dir. Dmitrii Lesnevskii. 2004.
Bogatye tozhe plachut (*Los Ricos También Lloran* [*The Rich Cry, Too*]). Mexico. Dir. Fernando Chacón. 1979.
Bol'shaia stirka (*Dirty Laundry*, Channel One chat show). From 2001.
Bomba dlia nevesty (*A Bomb for the Bride*). Dir. Aleksandr Pavlovskii. 2004.
Brat'ia Karamazovy (*The Brothers Karamazov*). Dir. Iurii Moroz. In production 2006.
Brezhnev. Dir. Sergei Snezhkin. 2005.
Brigada (*The Brigade*). Dir. Aleksei Sidorov. 2002.
Bukhta Filippa (*Philip's Bay*). Dir. Aleko Tsabadze. 2005.

Chetyre tankista i sobaka (*Four Men, a Tank and a Dog*). Poland. Dir. Konrad Nalecki. 1965–9.
Chto skazal pokoinik? (*What Did the Deceased Say?*). Dir. Igor' Maslennikov. 1998.
D'Artan'ian i tri mushketera (*D'Artagnan and the Three Musketeers*). Dir. Georgii Iungval'd-Khil'kevich. 1978.
Dal'noboishchiki (*The Truckers*). Dir. Iurii Kuz'menko. 2000–4.
Dallas (CBS soap). USA. 1978–91.
Dasha Vasil'eva, liubitel'nitsa chastnogo syska (*Dasha Vasil'eva, Amateur Private Detective*). Dir. Anatolii Mateshko, Oleg Fesenko, and Andrei Marmontov. From 2003.
Delo o mertvykh dushakh (*The Case of the Dead Souls*). Dir. Pavel Lungin. 2005.
Demon poldnia (*The Midday Demon*). Dir. Aleksei Kozlov. 2004–5.
Den' rozhdeniia Burzhuia (*Bourgeois' Birthday*). Dir. Anatolii Mateshko. 2000–1.
Derevenskii detektiv (*The Provincial Detective*). Dir. Ivan Lukinskii. 1968.
Deti Arbata (*The Children of the Arbat*). Dir. Andrei Èshpai. 2004.
Deti Vaniukhina (*Vaniukhin's Children*). Dir. Iurii Moroz. 2005.
Deviat' mesiatsev (*Nine Months*) Dir. R. Gigineishvili. 2006.
Dnevnik ubiitsy (*Diary of a Murderer*). Dir. Kirill Serebrennikov. 2002.
Doktor Zhivago (*Doctor Zhivago*). Dir. Aleksandr Proshkin. 2006.
Dom 2 (*House 2*, TNT reality show). From 2004.
Dorogaia Masha Berezina (*Dear Masha Berezina*). Dir. Ekaterina Dvigubskaia, Petr Krotenko, Stanislav Libin, and Aleksandr Smirnov. 2004.
Dos'e detektiva Dubrovskogo (*The Dossier of Detective Dubrovskii*). Dir. Aleksandr Muratov. 1999.
Drugaia zhizn' (*Another Life*). Dir. Elena Raiskaia. 2003.
Druzhnaia semeika (*A Happy Family*). Dir. Iurii Stytskovskii. 2002–3.
Dve sud'by (*Two Fates*). Dir. Valerii Uskov and Vladimir Krasnopol'skii. 2002.
Dynasty (ABC soap). USA. 1981–9.
Ego zhena (*His Wife*). Dir. Oleg Massarygin. 2006.
E.R. (NBC drama). USA. From 1994.
Eralash (*Mishmash*, ORT/Channel One comedy). From 1975.
Esenin. Dir. Igor' Zaitsev. 2004.
Fabrika zvezd (*Star Factory*, Channel One reality show). From 2002.
Forsyte Saga (NET [for US] drama). UK. Multiple directors. 1969–70.
Gardemariny, vpered! (*Midshipmen, Onwards!*). Dir. Svetlana Druzhinina. 1987.
Geroi nashego vremeni (*A Hero of Our Time*). Dir. Aleksandr Kott. 2005.
Gibel' Imperii (*Death of an Empire*). Dir. Vladimir Khotinenko. 2005.
Golod (*Hunger*, TNT reality show). 2005.
Goriachev i drugie (*Goriachev and Others*). Dir. Iurii Belen'kii. 1992–4.
Gorodok (*Small Town*, RTR/Rossiia comedy). From 1993.

Grace Under Fire (ABC sitcom). USA. 1993–8.
Graf Krestovskii (*Count Krestovskii*). Dir. Ramiz Fataliev. 2004.
Grafinia de Monsoro (*La Dame de Monsoreau*). Dir. Vladimir Popkov. 1997.
Granitsa: Taezhnyi roman (*Borderlands: A Romance of the Taiga*). Dir. Aleksandr Mitta. 2000.
Grazhdanin nachal'nik (*Mr. Boss*). Dir. Nikolai Dostal'. 2001.
Gromovy (*The Gromov Family*). Dir. Aleksandr Baranov. 2006.
Hill Street Blues (NBC drama). USA. 1981–7.
I Love Lucy (CBS comedy). USA. 1951–7.
I snova Aniskin (*Once Again Aniskin*). Dir. Mikhail Zharov and Vitalii Ivanov. 1978.
Ia tebia liubliu (*I Love You*). Dir. Viacheslav Krishtofovich. 2004.
Ideal'naia para (*An Ideal Couple*). Dir. Alla Surikova. 2001.
Idiot (*The Idiot*). Dir. Vladimir Bortko. 2003.
Igra na vybyvanie (*A Game of Survival*). Dir. Vadim Shmelev. 2004.
Instruktor (*The Instructor*). Dir. Evgenii Serov. 2003.
Jeffersons (CBS comedy). USA. 1975–85.
Jerry Springer Show (NBC chat show). USA. From 1991.
Kafe Klubnichka (*Strawberry Café*). Dir. Iurii Belen'kii. 1996–7.
Kamenskaia. Dir. Iurii Moroz. From 1999.
Kazaroza. Dir. Alena Dem'ianenko. 2005.
Kazus Kukotskogo (*Kukotskii's Case*). Dir. Iurii Grymov. 2005.
KBG v smokinge (*The KGB in Dinner Jackets*). Dir. Oleg Fomin. 2004.
Khiromant (*The Palmist*). Dir. Andrei Bormatov. 2005.
Kholostiaki (*The Bachelors*). Dir. Pavel Bardin. 2004.
Kliuchi ot bezdny (*Keys to an Abyss*). Dir. Sergei Rusakov. 2004.
Klounov ne ubivaiut (*They Don't Kill Clowns*). Dir. Sergei Borchukov. 2005.
Kommissar Rex (*Commissar Rex*). Dir. P. Ariel and W. Dickmann. Germany. 1994–2004.
Kontora (*The Bureau*) Dir. Dmitrii Parmenov. 2006.
Koroleva Margo (*La Reine Margot*). Dir. Aleksandr Muratov. 1995–6.
Kosvennye uliki (*Circumstantial Evidence*). Dir. Viacheslav Krishtofovich. 2005.
Krasnaia kapella (*The Red Choir*). Dir. Aleksandr Aravin. 2004.
Krot (*The Mole*). Dir. Èrnest Iasan. 2001.
Kto khochet stat' millionerom? (*Who Wants to be a Millionaire?*, Channel One game show). From 2001.
Kursanty (*The Cadets*). Dir. Andrei Kavun. 2005.
Lednikovyi period (*Ice Age*). Dir. Aleksandr Buravskii. 2002.
Leningradets (*The Leningrader*). Dir. Konstantin Khudiakov. 2005.
Linii sud'by (*Life Lines*). Dir. Dmitrii Meskhiev. 2003.
Liuba, deti i zavod (*Liuba, the Kids and the Factory*) Dir. Leonid Mazor. 2005.
Liubov' kak liubov' (*A Love Like Any Other*). Dir. Aleksandr Nazarov. 2006.

Marsh Turetskogo (*Turetskii's March*). Dir. Mikhail Tumanishvili. From 2000.
Master i Margarita (*The Master and Margarita*). Dir. Vladimir Bortko. 2005.
Melochi zhizni (*The Little Things of Life*). Dir. Viacheslav Brovkin, Gennadii Pavlov, and Aleksandr Pokrovskii. 1992–5.
Mesto vstrechi izmenit' nel'zia (*The Rendezvous Is Set*). Dir. Stanislav Govorukhin. 1979.
Moia liubov', moia pechal' (*Meu Bem, Meu Mal* [*My Love, My Grief*]). Brazil. Dir. Reynaldo Boury, Paulo Ubiratan, and Ricardo Waddington. 1990.
Moia prekrasnaia niania (*My Fair Nanny*). Dir. Aleksei Kiriushchenko. 2004–5.
Molodaia gvardiia (*The Young Guard*). Dir. Sergei Lialin. 2006.
Moonlighting (ABC comedy). USA. 1985–9.
Moskovskaia saga (*Moscow Saga*). Dir. Dmitrii Barshchevskii. 2004.
Muzhchiny ne plachut (*Men Don't Cry*). Dir. Sergei Bobrov. 2005.
Na bezymiannoi vysote (*At an Unknown Height*). Dir. Viacheslav Nikiforov. 2003–4.
Na uglu u Patriarshikh (*On the Corner of Patriarch's Ponds*). Dir. Vadim Derbenev. 1995–2002.
Nadezhda ukhodit poslednei (*Hope Leaves Last*). Dir. Evgenii Sokolov. 2004.
Namedni (*The Other Day*, NTV documentary). 2003.
Nanny, The (CBS sitcom). USA. 1993–9.
Navazhdenie (*Hallucination*). Dir. Anna Legchilova. 2004.
Ne rodis' krasivoi (*If You Weren't Born Pretty . . .*) Dir. Aleksandr Nazarov. 2005.
Nebo i zemlia (*Heaven and Earth*). Dir. Viktor Sergeev. 2003–4.
Nebo v goroshek (*Polka-Dot Heaven*). Dir. Vladimir Balkashinov. 2003.
Next (*Sleduiushchii*). Dir. Oleg Fomin. From 2001.
Nina. Dir. Valerii Uskov and Vladimir Krasnopol'skii. 2001.
Novaia volna (*Uma Onda no Ar* [*The New Wave*]). Brazil. Dir. Lucas Bueno, José Carlos Pieri, and Cecil Thiré. 1994.
Ofitsery (*The Officers*). Dir. Murad Aliev. 2005.
Ognebortsy (*Firefighters*). Dir. Isaak Fridberg. 2005.
Okhota na iziubria (*The Hunt for Siberian Deer*). Dir. Abai Karpykov. 2005.
Okhota na Zolushku (*The Hunt for Cinderella*). Dir. Niiole Adomenaite. 1999–2000.
Okna (*Windows*, TNT talk show). 2002–4.
Okhotniki za ikonami (*The Icon Hunters*). Dir. Sergei Popov. 2005.
Ostanovka po trebovaniiu (*Request Stop*). Dir. Dzhanik Faiziev. 2000, 2001.
Ostorozhno, modern! (*Look Out, It's Modern!*, STS comedy). 2000–4.
Ostrov iskushenii (*Temptation Island*, REN TV reality show). From 2001.
Parallel'no liubvi (*Side by Side with Love*). Dir. Dmitrii Mednov. 2004.

Passazhir bez bagazha (*A Passenger without Baggage*). Dir. Khuat Akhmetov. 2003.
Peterburgskie tainy (*The Secrets of St. Petersburg*). Dir. Vadim Zobin, Mark Orlov, and Leonid Pchelkin. 1994–6.
Peyton Place (ABC soap). USA. 1964–9.
Piatyi angel (*The Fifth Angel*). Dir. Vladimir Fokin. 2004.
Po imeni Baron (*Baron by Name*). Dir. Dmitrii Svetozarov. 2002.
Po tu storonu volkov (*Beyond the Wolves*). Dir. Vladimir Khotinenko. 2002.
Pod nebom Verony (*Beneath a Verona Sky*). Dir. Vladimir Krasnpol'skii and Valerii Uskov. 2005.
Polnolunie liubvi (*Lua Cheia de Amor* [*Full-Moon of Love*]). Brazil. Dir. Marió Márcio Bandarra, Flávio Colatrello Jr., José Carlos Pieri, and Roberto Talma. 1990.
Port Charles (ABC soap). USA. 1997–2003.
Poslednii geroi (*The Final Hero*, Channel One reality show). From 2001.
Prime Suspect (Granada TV drama). UK. From 1991.
Prosto Mariia (*Simplemente María* [*Simply María*]). Argentina, Brazil, Mexico, and Peru. Dir. Carlos Barrios Porras, Walter Avancini, Benjamin Cattan, Enzo Bellomo, Arturo Ripstein, and Beatriz Sheridan. 1969–89.
Protiv techeniia (*Against the Flow*). Dir. Anatolii Mateshko. 2004.
Riabynia Izaura (*Escrava Isaura* [*Isaura the Slave*]). Brazil. Dir. Milton Gonçalves and Herval Rossano. 1976.
Rodina zhdet (*The Nation Expects*). Dir. Oleg Pogodin. 2003.
Rodstvennyi obmen (*Sister Swap*). Dir. Vladimir Kott. 2004.
Rostov-Papa. Dir. Kirill Serebrennikov. 2001.
Samara-gorodok (*The Sweet Town of Samara*). Dir. Pavel Snisarenko. 2004.
Santa Barbara (NBC soap). USA. 1984–93.
Sarmat (*The Sarmatian*). Dir. Igor' Talpa. 2004.
Sasha + Masha (*Sasha plus Masha*) Dir. Dmitrii Fedorov. 2004–5.
Scarlett (CBS drama). USA. Dir. John Erman. 1994.
Semnadtsat' mgnovenii vesny (*The Seventeen Moments of Spring*). Dir. Tat'iana Lioznova. 1973.
Sen'orita (*Sinhá Moça* [*Senorita*]). Brazil. Dir. Reynaldo Boury and Jayme Monjardim. 1986.
Sestry (*Sisters*). Dir. Anton Sivers. 2004.
Sex and the City (HBO drama). Multiple directors. 1998–2002.
Shtrafbat (*Penal Batallion*). Dir. Nikolai Dostal'. 2004.
Shukshinskie rasskazy (*Shukshin's Stories*). Dir. Anatolii Sirenko. 2004.
Sladkii ruchei (*Riacho Doce* [*The Sweet Spring*]). Brazil. Dir. Reynaldo Boury, Luiz Fernando Carvalho, and Paulo Ubiratan. 1990.
Sledstvie vedut znatoki (*Experts Are on the Case*). Dir. Viacheslav Brovkin, Iurii Krotenko, Viktor Turbin, Vasilii Davidchuk, and Gennadii Pavlov. 1971–89.
Soldaty (*Soldiers*). Dir. Sergei Arlanov. From 2004.

Spas pod berezami (*The Savior beneath the Birch Trees*). Dir. Leonid Èidlin. 2004.
Starye pesni o glavnom (*Old Songs about What Matters*, Channel One variety show). From 2000.
Stavka bol'she chem zhizn' (*A Risk Greater Than Life*). Poland. Dir. Andrzej Konic. 1967.
Stilet (*The Stiletto Knife*). Dir. Nikolai Dostal'. 2003.
Svetskie khroniki (*Society Pages*). Dir. Valerii Zelenskii and Andrei Kuznetsov. 2002.
Syshchiki (*The Detectives*). Dir. Valerii Uskov and Vladimir Krasnopol'skii. 2001.
Taiga. Dir. Aleksandr Aravin. 2002.
TASS upolnomochen zaiavit' (*TASS Is Authorized to Report*). Dir. Vladimir Fokin. 1984.
Teni ischezaiut v polden' (*Shadows Vanish at Noon*). Dir. Valerii Uskov and Vladimir Krasnopol'skii. 1971.
Tri tsveta liubvi (*The Three Colors of Love*). Dir. Dmitrii Svetozarov. 2004.
Tsygan (*Gypsy*). Dir. Aleksandr Blank. 1979.
Twin Peaks (ABC drama). USA. 1990–1.
Uboinaia sila (*Lethal Force*). Multiple directors. From 2000.
Uchastok (*A Policeman's Beat*). Dir. Aleksandr Baranov. 2003.
Ulitsy razbitykh fonarei (*Streets of Broken Lights*). Multiple directors. From 1997.
Umnozhaiushchii pechal' (*The Maker of More Misery*). Dir. Oleg Fesenko. 2005.
Utesov: Pesnia dlinoiu v zhizn' (*Utesov: A Lifelong Song*). Dir. Georgii Nikolaenko. 2006.
V kruge pervom (*The First Circle*). Dir. Gleb Panfilov. 2006.
V ritme tango (*To the Beat of a Tango*). Dir. Aleksandr Pavlovskii. 2006.
Vechnyi zov (*An Eternal Summons*). Dir. Valerii Uskov and Vladimir Krasnopol'skii. 1973–83.
Vintovaia lestnitsa (*The Sprial Staircase*). Dir. Dmitrii Parmenov. 2004.
Vokzal (*The Station*). Dir. Andrei Kavun. 2003.
Voskresen'e v zhenskoi bane (*Sunday in the Ladies' Bathhouse*). Dir. Dmitrii Astrakhan. 2005.
Vsegda govori vsegda (*Always Say Always*). Dir. Aleksei Kozlov. 2003.
Vyzyvaem ogon' na sebia (*Drawing Fire*). Dir. Sergei Kolosov. 1963–4.
Walker: Texas Ranger (CBS drama). USA. 1993–2001.
X-Files (FOX drama). USA. 1993–2002.
Za steklom (*Through the Window*, TV6 reality show). 2001.
Zakoldovannyi Uchastok (*The Enchanted Village*). Dir. Aleksandr Baranov. 2006.
Zhelannaia (*Beloved*). Dir. Iurii Kuz'menko. 2003.
Zhenshchiny v igre bez pravil (*Women in a Lawless Game*). Dir. Iurii Moroz. 2004.

Zolotoi telenok (*The Golden Calf*). Dir. Ul'iana Shilkina. 2006.
Zona (*Prison Colony*). Dir Petr Shtein. 2006.

Feature films

Among the Soviet films of greater consequence to our study, the numbers in parentheses after older entries refer to viewing figures in millions.

9 rota (2005) F. Bondarchuk.
32-oe dekabria (2004) A. Muratov.
72 metra (2003) V. Khotinenko.
Airport (1970) G. Seaton.
Alesha Popovich (2004) K. Bronzit.
Amélie (2001) J.-P. Jeunet.
Anna na shee (1954) I. Annenskii (31.9).
Antikiller (2002) E. Mikhalkov-Konchalovskii.
Azazel' (2003) A. Adabash'ian.
Bachelor, The (1999) G. Sinyor.
Ballada o soldate (1959) G. Chukhrai (30.1).
Beloe solntse pustyni (1969) V. Motyl' (34.5).
Beregis' avtomobilia (1966) È. Riazanov (29).
Bespokoinoe khoziaistvo (1946) M. Zharov (17.79).
Bitva v puti (1961) V. Basov (38.3).
Bogataia nevesta (1937) I. Pyr'ev.
Boginia (2004) R. Litvinova.
Bol'shaia zhizn' (1939/1946) L. Lukov (18.6).
Bourne Supremacy, The (2004) P. Greengrass.
Brat (1997) A. Balabanov.
Brat 2 (2000) A. Balabanov.
Brilliantovaia ruka (1968) L. Gaidai (76.7).
Bumer (2003) P. Buslov.
Bumer 2 (2005) P. Buslov.
Chapaev (1934) Vasil'ev brothers.
Chelovek s bul'vara Kaputsinov (1987) A. Surikova (39.8).
Chetvertoe zhelanie (2004) O. Perunovskaia.
Chetyre (2005) I. Khrzhanovskii.
Daite zhalobnuiu knigu (1964) È. Riazanov (19.9).
Delo bylo v Pen'kove (1957) S. Rostotskii (30.5).
Delo No. 306 (1956) A. Rybakov (33.5).
Delo Rumiantseva (1956) I. Kheifits (31.76).
Den' polnoluniia (1998) K. Shakhnazarov.
Devchata (1961) Iu. Chuliukin (34.8).
Devushka bez adresa (1957) È. Riazanov (36.5).
Devushka speshit na svidanie (1936) M. Verner.
Die Hard (1988) J. McTiernan.

Dnevnoi dozor (2006) T. Bekmambetov.
Dom durakov (2002) A. Konchalovskii.
Dom, v kotorom ia zhivu (1957) L. Kulidzhanov (28.9).
Dusha (1981) A. Stefanovich (33.3).
Dva boitsa (1943) L. Lukov.
Dvenadtsat' stul'ev (2005) M. Papernik.
Eger' (2004) A. Tsatsuev.
Ezhik v tumane (1975) Iu. Norshtein.
Few Good Men, A (1992) R. Reiner.
Garpastum (2005) A. German.
Godfather, The (1972) F. Ford Coppola.
Gone with the Wind (1939) V. Fleming.
Gusarskaia ballada (1962) È. Riazanov (48.64).
Happenstance (2000) L. Firode.
Idi i smotri (1985) È. Klimov (28.9).
Interdevochka (1989) P. Todorovskii (41.3).
Ironiia sud'by (1976) È. Riazanov.
Iskateli schast'ia (1936) V. Korsh-Sablin.
Ispytanie vernosti (1954) I. Pyr'ev (31.9).
Istrebiteli (1939) È. Pentslin (27.1).
Ital'ianets (2005) A. Kravchuk.
Ivan Vasil'evich meniaet professiiu (1973) L. Gaidai (60.7).
Ivanovo detstvo (1962) A. Tarkovskii.
Izobrazhaia zhertvu (2006) K. Serebrennikov.
Jurassic Park (1993) S. Spielberg.
Kalina krasnaia (1973) V. Shukshin (62.5).
Kamennyi tsvetok (1946) A. Ptushko (23.17).
Karlik nos (2003) I. Maksimov.
Karlson vernulsia (1970) B. Stepantsev.
Karnaval'naia noch' (1956) È. Riazanov (48.64).
Kavkazskaia plennitsa (1966) L. Gaidai (76.54).
Kliuch ot spal'ni (2004) È. Riazanov.
Koktebel' (2003) A. Popogrebskii, B. Khlebnikov.
Kramer versus Kramer (1979) R. Benton.
Kubanskie kazaki (1949) I. Pyr'ev (40.6).
Kukushka (2002) A. Rogozhkin.
Kur'er (1986) K. Shakhnazarov (31.9).
Kutuzov (1943) V. Petrov (17.73).
Letiat zhuravli (1957) M. Kalatozov (28.3).
Lichnyi nomer (2004) E. Lavrent'ev.
Liubimaia zhenshchina mekhanika Gavrilova (1981) P. Todorovskii.
Liubov' i golubi (1984) V. Men'shov (105).
Lost in La Mancha (2002) T. Gilliam.
Love Actually (2003) R. Curtis.
Lunnyi papa (2000) B. Khudoinazarov.

Machekha (1973) O. Bondarev (59.4).
Maksimka (1952) V. Braun (32.9).
Malenkaia Vera (1988) V. Pichul (54.9).
Malysh i Karlson (1968) B. Stepantsev.
Mars (2004) A. Melikian.
Mechtat' ne vredno (2005) E. Lavrent'ev.
Mne ne bol'no (2006) A. Balabanov.
Moi svodnyi brat Frankenshtein (2004) V. Todorovskii.
Moia liubov' (1940) V. Korsh-Sablin (19.2).
Molodaia gvardiia (1948) S. Gerasimov (42.4).
Moskva slezam ne verit (1979) V. Men'shov (84.4).
My s Vami gde-to vstrechalis' (1954) N. Dostal' (31.5).
Ne khlebom edinym (2005) S. Govorukhin.
Ne khodite, devki, zamuzh (1985) E. Gerasimov (29.4).
Nebesnyi tikhokhod (1945) S. Timoshenko (21.37).
Nepodsuden (1969) V. Krasnopol'skii (43.3).
Neulovimye mstiteli (1966) È. Keosaian (54.5).
Neveroiatnye prikliucheniia ital'iantsev v Rossii (1973) È. Riazanov (49.2).
Nezhnyi vozrast (2001) S. Solov'ev.
Nochnoi dozor (2004) T. Bekmambetov.
Nochnoi patrul' (1957) V. Sukhobokov (36.42).
Novyi god otmeniaetsia! (2004) V. Shmelev.
Odinokim predostavliaetsia obshchezhitie (1983) S. Samsonov (23.2).
Ofitsery (1971) V. Rogovoi.
Okhota na piran'iu (2006) A. Kavun.
Oligarkh (2002) P. Lugin.
Once Upon a Time in America (1984) S. Leone.
Ottsy i deti (1983) V. Nikiforov.
Peregon (2006) A. Rogozhkin.
Pervaia perchatka (1946) A. Frolov (18.57).
Petr pervyi (1937–8) V. Petrov.
Pirates of the Caribbean (2003) G. Verbinski.
Piter FM (2006) O. Bychkova.
Podkidysh (1939) T. Lukashevich.
Podniataia tselina (1959–61) A. Ivanov (30.2).
Poezd idet na vostok (1948) Iu. Raizman (16.1).
Police Academy (1984) H. Wilson.
Poslednii poezd (2003) A. German.
Posylka s Marsa (2004) I. Kozhevnikov, V. Donskov.
Povest' o nastoiashchem cheloveke (1948) A. Stolper (34.4).
Prishla i govoriu (1985) N. Ardashnikov (25.7).
Progulka (2003) A. Uchitel'.
Prosti (1986) È. Iasan (37.6).
Pyl' (2005) S. Loban.
Quickie, The (2002) S. Bodrov.

Raznye sud'by (1956) L. Lukov (30.69).
Reis 222 (1985) S. Mikaèlian (35.3).
Romanovy (2000) G. Panfilov.
Romans o vliublennykh (1974) A. Mikhalkov-Konchalovskii (36.5).
Rozygrysh (1976) V. Men'shov (96).
Russkii kovcheg (2002) A. Sokurov.
S novym godom, papa! (2004) O. Perunovskaia.
Sadko (1952) A. Ptushko (27.3).
Saving Private Ryan (1998) S. Spielberg.
Sel'skaia uchitel'nitsa (1947) M. Donskoi (18.11).
Semero smelykh (1936) S. Gerasimov.
Serdtsa chetyrekh (1941) K. Iudin (19.44).
Sestry (2001) S. Bodrov.
Shirli-Myrli (1995) V. Men'shov (135).
Shiza (2004) G. Omarova.
Shkola muzhestva (1954) V. Basov (27.2).
Sibirskii tsiriul'nik (1999) N. Mikhalkov.
Sluzhebnyi roman (1977) È. Riazanov (58.4).
Sobach'e serdtse (1988) V. Bortko.
Soldat Ivan Brovkin (1955) I. Lukinskii (40.37).
Speed (1994) J. de Bont.
Stalker (1979) A. Tarkovskii.
Stariki razboiniki (1971) È. Riazanov (31.5).
Statskii sovetnik (2005) F. Iankovskii.
Strana glukhikh (1997) V. Todorovskii.
Strekoza (1954) S. Dolidze (29.62).
Sud'ba Mariny (1953) I. Shmaruk (37.9).
Sud'ba rezidenta (1970) V. Dorman (28.7).
Svad'ba s pridanym (1953) T. Lukashevich (45.4).
Sviaz' (2006) A. Smirnova.
Svolochi (2006) A. Atanesian.
Tanker Derbent (1940) A. Faintsimmer.
Temnaia noch' (2004) D. Astrakhan.
Tikhii Don (1957–8) S. Gerasimov (47).
Tishina (1963) V. Basov (30.32).
Tochka (2006) Iu. Moroz.
Traktoristy (1939) I. Pyr'ev.
Tsirk (1936) G. Aleksandrov.
Turetskii gambit (2005) Dzh. Faiziev.
Utomlennye solntsem (1995) N. Mikhalkov.
V dvizhenii (2002) F. Iankovskii.
V shest' chasov vechera posle voiny (1944) I. Pyr'ev (26.1).
Vernye druz'ia (1954) M. Kalatozov (30.9).
Veselye rebiata (1934) G. Aleksandrov.
Vesna (1947) G. Aleksandrov (16.2).

Vesna na Zarechnoi ulitse (1956) M. Khutsiev and F. Mironer (30.12).
Voditel' dlia Very (2004) P. Chukhrai.
Voina (2002) A. Balabanov.
Voina i mir (1965–7) S. Bondarchuk (58).
Vokzal dlia dvoikh (1982) È. Riazanov (35.8).
Volga-Volga (1938) G. Aleksandrov.
Vozvrashchenie (2003) A. Zviagintsev.
Vsadnik po imeni Smert' (2004) K. Shakhnazarov.
Vstrecha na Èlbe (1949) G. Aleksandrov (24.2).
Vysota (1957) A. Zarkhi.
West Side Story (1961) J. Robbins and R. Wise.
Zavist' bogov (2000) V. Men'shov.
Zemlia Sannikova (1972) A. Mkrtchian (41.1).
Zhenshchina, kotoraia poet (1978) A. Orlov (54.9).
Zhenskaia intuitsiia (2005) O. Bairak.
Zhest' (2006) D. Neimand.
Zhestokii romans (1984) È. Riazanov (22).
Zhivoi trup (1968) V. Vengerov.
Zimniaia vishnia (1985) I. Maslennikov.
Zulu (1964) C. Endfield.
Zvezda (2002) N. Lebedev.

Notes

Introduction

1 Pesmen, D. *Russia and Soul: An Exploration*, Ithaca: Cornell University Press (2000), 4.
2 Ibid., 16.
3 Epstein, M. "Russo-Soviet Topoi," in Dobrenko, E. and Naiman, E. *The Landscape of Stalinism*, Seattle: University of Washington Press (2003), 280.
4 Clark, C. "Socialist Realism and the Sacralizing of Space," in Dobrenko and Naiman, 9.
5 Lahusen, T. *How Life Writes the Book: Real Socialism and Socialist Realism in Stalin's Russia*, Ithaca: Cornell University Press (1997), 26.
6 "Postmodernism, Communism, and Sots-Art," in Balina, M., Condee, N., and Dobrenko, E. *Endquote: Sots-Art and Soviet Grand Style*, Evanston: Northwestern University Press (2000), 17.
7 Ibid., 25.
8 Dobrenko, E. "The Disaster of Middlebrow Taste," in Lahusen, T. and Dobrenko, E. (eds.) *Socialist Realism without Shores*, Durham: Duke University Press (1997), 158.
9 Dobrenko, E. *Aesthetics of Alienation*, Evanston: Northwestern University Press (2005), 124.
10 See, for example, *TV in the Russian Federation*, European Audiovisual Observatory (March 2006), 7–8.
11 Boym, S. "Paradoxes of Unified Culture," in Lahusen and Dobrenko, 124.
12 Epstein, M. "Postmodernism, Communism, and Sots-Art," in Balina, Condee, and Dobrenko, 19.
13 See pre-release notes in "Reportazh so s"emochnoi ploshchadki," *Ruskino*: http://www.ruskino.ru/motor/motor.php?folder = egozhena, or "Reds in the Bed: Stalin's Sex Drive Exposed," *Scotland on Sunday*, 3 September (2006).
14 Beumers, B. *Pop Culture Russia! Media Arts and Lifestyle*, Santa Barbara: Clio (2005), 72.
15 Introduction to Hutchings, S. and Vernitskaia, A. (eds.) *Screening the Word: Russian and Soviet Film Adaptations of Literature*, London: Routledge-Curzon (2004), 19–20.
16 On this issue, see Larsson, D. "Every Picture Tells a Story: Agency and Narration in Film" (2000), www.english.mnsu.edu/larsson/nargent.html.

1 Action heroes

1 Timofeev, L. *Russkaia sovetskaia literatura*, Moscow: Prosveshchenie (1972), 331.
2 "Ritorika Putina: Tri istochnika i tri sostavnye chasti," *Russkii zhurnal*, 5 June (2003).
3 Beumers, B. "To Moscow! To Moscow? The Russian Hero and the Loss of the Centre," *Russia on Reels: The Russian Idea in Post-Soviet Cinema*, London: Tauris (1999), 76–91.
4 "Sud'ba otechestvennogo kino – Putin posetil Mosfil'm," *Reklama-Online*, 3 November (2003).
5 "V prokat vyshel novyi otechestvennyi blokbaster," *News.ru*, 15 December (2004); and "Marshevyi perelom," *Rossiiskaia gazeta*, 3 December (2004).
6 "Zvezda/The Star," *Variety*, 22 July (2002) and Kazakevich, E. (1963) "Zvezda" *Sochineniia v dvukh tomakh*, Moscow: Khudozhestvennaia literatura (1963 [vol. 1]).
7 "Kino i gosudarstvo: Kto kogo imeet," *Nezavisimaia gazeta*, 24 December (2004).
8 "Il-76 do Rima ne doletit," *Rossiiskaia gazeta*, 9 December (2004).
9 "Vash 'lichnyi nomer,'" *Rolan* #44, November (2004).
10 "Lichnyi nomer – novyi russkii blokba$ter," *Utro*, 9 December (2004).
11 Koropeckyj, R. and Romanchuk, R. "Ukraine in Blackface: Performance and Representation in Gogol's Dikan'ka Tales, Book 1," *Slavic Review* 62 (2003): 525–48.
12 Prokhorova, E. *Fragmented Mythologies: Soviet TV Mini-Series of the 1970s*, Unpublished Ph.D., University of Pittsburgh (2003), 230.
13 *TV in the Russian Federation*, European Audiovisual Observatory (March 2006), 89.
14 "Smotrim televizor: Bum televizionnykh serialov," *Radio Svoboda*, 11 October (2004): www.svoboda.org/programs/tv/2004/tv.101104.asp.
15 "Mylovary: Rossiiskikh zritelei zastaviat poliubit' otechestvennye serialy," *Samara segodnia*, 16 October (2004).
16 For more on these statistics, see *TV in the Russian Federation*, European Audiovisual Observatory (March 2006).
17 "Vnutrennii geroi i natsional'nyi geroi," *Komsomol'skaia pravda*, 6 November (2004).
18 This idea is fully developed in Brady, B. *Principles of Adaptation for Film and Television*, Austin: University of Texas Press (1994).
19 Zizek, S. *The Puppet and the Dwarf: The Perverse Core of Christianity*, Cambridge: MIT Press, (2003), 70.
20 Inglis, F. "*Brideshead Revisited* Revisited," in Giddings, R. and Sheen, E. (eds.) *The Classic Novel from Page to Screen*, Manchester and New York: Manchester University Press (2000), 195.
21 Afron, C. *Cinema and Sentiment*, Chicago and London: University of Chicago Press (1982), 8.
22 Tan, E. and Frijda, N. "Sentiment in Film Viewing"; and Eitzen, D. "The Emotional Basis of Film Comedy," in Plantinga, C. and Smith, G.M. *Passionate Views: Film, Cognition and Emotion*, Baltimore: Johns Hopkins University Press (1999), 85–6, 129 and 144.
23 "Derrida and Deconstruction," 130.179.92.25/Arnason_DE/Derrida.html.
24 Gurko, E. *Teksty dekonstruktsii: Zhak Derrida – Différence*, Tomsk: Vodolei (1999), 4.
25 Derrida, Zh. *O pochtovoi otkrytke ot Sokrata do Freida i ne tol'ko*, Minsk: Sovremennyi literator (1999), 828–9.
26 Derrida, J. and Stiegler, B. *Echographies of Television*, Cambridge: Polity (2002), 9–10.

228 *Notes*

27 Barker, J. *Alain Badiou: A Critical Introduction*, London: Pluto Press (2002), 4.
28 Badiou, A. *Manifesto for Philosophy*, Albany: SUNY Press (1992), 91, 95 and 103.
29 Ibid., 106–7.
30 Badiou, *Ethics: An Essay on the Understanding of Evil*, London: Verso (2001), 25.
31 Ibid., 43.
32 Ibid., 135.
33 Badiou, A. *Deleuze: The Clamor of Being*, Minneapolis: University of Minneapolis Press (2000), 25.
34 Ibid., 102.
35 "Barukh Spinoza i burzhuaziia," *Iubilei*, Moscow: Khudozhestvennaia literatura (1934), 43.
36 Toporkov, A. "Predislovie," *Spinoza: Ètika*, Moscow: Gosudarstvennoe sotsial'no-èkonomicheskoe izdatel'stvo (1933), xix.
37 Vandek, V. and Timosko, V. *Ocherk filosofii B. Spinozy*, Moscow: Partiinoe izdatel'stvo (1932), 37–8 and 79.
38 Syromlia, Iu. and Petrovich, V. *Russkaia literatura vtoroi poloviny XX veka*, Arkhangel'sk: BshiA (1993), 33.
39 Mickiewicz, E. *Changing Channels: Television and the Struggle for Power in Russia*, Durham and London: Duke University Press (1999), 236.
40 Dingley, J. "Soviet Television and *Glasnost*'" in Graffy, J. and Hosking, G. (eds.) *Culture and the Media in the USSR Today*, London: Macmillan (1989), 7.
41 Paasilinna, R. *Glasnost and Soviet Television*, Ylesradio: Research Report 5 (1995), 186.
42 Mickiewicz, E. *Media and the Russian Public*, New York: Praeger (1981), 199.
43 Stites, R. *Russian Popular Culture: Entertainment and Society since 1900*, Cambridge: Cambridge University Press (1992), 191.
44 Borenstein, E. "MMM and the Marketing of Melodrama," in Barker, A.M. (ed.) *Consuming Russia: Popular Culture, Sex, and Society since Gorbachev*, Durham and London: Duke University Press (1999), 66.
45 Zassoursky, I. *Media and Power in Post-Soviet Russia*, New York and London: M.E. Sharpe (2004), 123–4.
46 *TV in the Russian Federation*, 46–51.
47 "Mass Media 2000–2004," *Kommersant*, 9 August (2004).
48 Elliott, K. *Rethinking the Novel/Film Debate*, Cambridge: Cambridge University Press (2003), 125.
49 Ibid., 121 and 189.
50 Introduction to Jones, M. and Miller, R. *The Cambridge Companion to the Classic Russian Novel*, Cambridge: Cambridge University Press (1998).
51 Bortnes, J. "Religion," in Jones and Miller, 112.
52 Ibid., 127.
53 Belknap, R. "Novelistic Technique," in Jones and Miller, 234.

2 Adaptations

1 Kozhnikov, V. *Russkaia literatura XX veka*, Moscow: Russkoe slovo (1999), 555.
2 "Evgenii Mironov stanet Aleshei Karamazovym?," *RuVideo Forums*, 10 March (2006).
3 "Serial po Dostoevskomu – bezuslovno proval'nyi," *Rossiia telekanal (forum)*, 2 June (2003).
4 "10 maia na kanale NTV startuet serial 'Doktor Zhivago,'" *Parnas*, 17 April (2006).
5 "Serial 'Doktor Zhivago' na Pervom natsional'nom telekanale Respubliki Belarus' pomsotrelo 44.9% gorodskogo naseleniia," *Media Online*, 19 April (2006); and "Chego pilit' budem? Baryshniu," *Gazeta.ru*, 23 March (2006).
6 "Zhivagoloty," *Ogonek*, #15 (2006).

7 "Polugeroi, polupoèt," *Kommersant*, 17 April (2006).
8 "V zhertvu Pechorinu prinesti dvukh piatigorskikh kurits," *Komsomol'skaia pravda*, 6 October (2005).
9 "Pechorin otpravilsia v Botanicheskii sad," *Komsomol'skaia pravda*, 19 September (2005).
10 "Geroi nashego vremeni," *Rossiia telekanal*, 27 May (2005).
11 "Skandal na s"emkakh fil'ma 'Anna Karenina,'" *Komsomol'skaia pravda*, 22 March (2005).
12 "Èkranizatsii, èkranizatsii ... ," *Retranslator*, 25 November (2004).
13 "Doctor's Plot," *Moscow Times*, 6 August (2004).
14 "Idi i chitai," *Rossiiskaia gazeta*, 31 January (2006).
15 "Pavel Basinskii: 'Anna Karenina' v gorazdo bol'shei stepeni neischerpaemyi tekst, chem 'Master i Margarita,'" *Polit.ru*, 26 December (2005).
16 "Anna Karenina vozvrashchaetsia na èkran," *News Moldova*, 1 March (2004).
17 "Mironov idet po ètapu," *Moskovskie novosti*, 23 February (2006); "Tri dnia sharashki Solzhenitsyna. V 10 seriiakh," *Komsomol'skaia pravda*, 19 January (2006); and "Pochemu 'V kruge pervom,'" *Komsomol'skaia pravda*, 2 February (2006).
18 "Razgovorchiki v adu," *Kommersant*, 31 January (2006).
19 "V kruge pervom na kanale Rossiia," www.vkrugepervom.ru/content.html?cid = 8.
20 "Avtor i ego kniga," www.vkrugepervom.ru/content.html?cid = 46.
21 "Sozdateli fil'ma," www.vkrugepervom.ru/content.html?cid = 22.
22 "Solzhenitsyna èkraniziruiut," *Vesti nedeli*, 11 December (2005).
23 "Solzhenitsyn pobedil Terminatora," *Strana.ru*, 31 January (2006).
24 "Evgenii Mironov ne nashel u Solzhenitsyna iz'ianov," *Gazeta*, 19 January (2006).
25 "Stsenarist 'Zolotogo telenka': 'Zolotoi telenok – deshevyi, bezdarnyi balagan,'" *Polit.ru*, 7 February (2006).
26 "Zolotoi telenok val'siruet v kruge pervom," *Komsomol'skaia pravda*, 26 January (2006).
27 "Antipriz 'Abzats' poluchila rezhisser seriala 'Zolotoi telenok,'" *Newsru.com*, 16 March (2006).
28 "Ostap Bender poluchit svoi million?," *Komsomol'skaia pravda*, 24 January (2006).
29 "Voina serialov – èto khorosho," *Grani*, 21 December (2001).
30 "Serial kak natsional'naia ideia," *Iskusstvo kino* #2 (2000).
31 "Sezon okhoty na Zolushkov," *Nezavisimaia gazeta*, 21 October (2000).
32 "Serialy ia delaiu s udovol'stviem," *Molodezhnaia gazeta*, 1 January (2005).
33 "O serialakh i natsional'noi idee," *TV-kolonka/Nezavisimaia izdatel'skaia gruppa*, 13 May (2002).
34 "Pogovorim o serialakh," www.braziliada.ru/artciles/rest/prozorovsky1.shtml.
35 "Zhizn' – na mylo," *TVIN Product Placement*: www.productplacement.ru/publication/arhiv/publication_25.shtml.
36 Vernitskaia, A. "Post-Soviet Film Adaptations of the Russian Classics: Tradition and Innovation," in Hutchings, S. and Vernitskaia, A. (eds.) *Screening the Word: Russian and Soviet Film Adaptations of Literature*, London: Routledge-Curzon (2004).
37 "Idiota mozhno sniat' tol'ko na televidenii," *Izvestiia*, 1 September (2001).
38 "Dolgoigraiushchii Idiot," *Rossiikie vesti*, 23 April (2003).
39 "Idiot – teleprem'era goda," *Slovo*, 23 May (2003).
40 Klioutchkine, K. "Fedor Mikhailovich Lucked Out with Vladimir Vladimirovich," *Kinokultura*, July (2005).
41 "Daniil Dondurei: Nashi serialy predlagaiut zhit' vchera," *Ogonek* #45, November (2004).
42 Hayward, J. *Consuming Pleasures: Active Audiences and Serial Fictions from Dickens to Soap Opera*, Lexington: University Press of Kentucky (1997), 155–6.

43 Prokhorova, E. "Fragmented Mythologies: Soviet TV Mini-Series of the 1970s," unpublished Ph.D., University of Pittsburgh (2003), 230.
44 Merezhinskaia, E. *Russkaia literatura*, Kiev: Radians'ka shkola (1966), 331.
45 "Kakuiu Rossiiu stroit Putin?" *Komsomol'skaia pravda*, 16 December (2004).
46 "Moloduiu gvardiiu' snimaiut ne po Fadeevu," *Komsomol'skaia Pravda*, 24 March (2005).
47 Blagoveshchenskii, F. *Tvorcheskaia istoriia romana "Molodaia gvardiia,"* Moscow: MOPI (1958), 6.
48 Zhukov, I. *Fadeev*, Moscow: Molodaia gvardiia (1989), 328.
49 Boborykin, V. *Aleksandr Fadeev: Pisatel'skaia sud'ba*, Moscow: Sovetskii pisatel' (1991), 343–4.
50 Fedin, K. *Sobranie sochinenii*, Moscow: Khudozhestvennaia literatura (1986 [vol. 11]), 257.
51 Kogan, L. "V.V. Maiakovskii i A.A. Fadeev," in *Roman "Molodaia gvardiia,"* Moscow: Ministerstvo kul'tury SSSR (1973), 3.
52 Red'ko, Z. *Problema voploshcheniia zhivogo geroia v khudozhestvennyi obraz*, Moscow: MGPI (1956), 11.
53 Knipovich, E. *Romany A. Fadeeva "Razgrom" i "Molodaia gvardiia,"* Moscow: Khudozhestvennaia literatura (1973), 94.
54 Kolpakova, E. *Russkaia sovetskaia literatura*, Kaunas: Šviesa (1970), 86.
55 Boltenkova, N. *Sistema prilagatel'nykh v iazyke romana A. Fadeeva "Molodaia gvardiia,"* Leningrad: LGU (1968), 18.
56 Panfilov, O. *Putin and the Press: The Revival of Soviet-Style Propaganda*, London: Foreign Policy Center (2005), 16, 18 and 30–1.
57 "Voina za smysl," *Kinoart* #9 (2004).
58 Ibid.
59 Hill, F. and Gaddy, C., *The Siberian Curse: How Communist Planners Left Russia Out in the Cold*, Brookings Institute: Washington, D.C. (2003), 25.
60 "Kakim uvidelo Putina televidenie na minuvshei nedele?," *Radio Svoboda*, 14 November (2002).
61 "Margarita letaet kruche Garri Pottera," *Komsomol'skaia pravda*, 20 June (2005).
62 "Iudu kaznili v Krymu," *Komsomol'skaia pravda*, 15 October (2004).
63 "Master i kinolenta," *Itogi*, 1 August (2005).
64 "Tainy Mastera i Margarity," *Dni.ru,* 15 October (2004).
65 "Master i kinolenta."
66 "RPTs vystupaet protiv ėkranizatsii romana Bulgakova 'Master i Margarita,'" *Kinokadr* #3, November (2004).
67 "Sergei Bezrukov: pod ruku s muzoi," *Rossiiskaia gazeta*, 26 November (2004).
68 "RTR Planeta: Okhotniki za ikonami," *RTR Planeta*: www.rtr-planeta.com/prog?rubric_id = 939&brand_id = 60288.
69 "Dmitrii Diuzhev voruet obraza," *Komsomol'skaia pravda*, 25 February (2005).
70 "Pravila novye. Litsa te zhe," *Trud*, 21 July (2005).
71 "Okhotniki za ikonami," *Interlinks*: www.serials.interlinks.ru/russianserials/ohotniki_za_ikonami.
72 "Mozhet li byt' blagorodnym okhotnikom za ikonami?" *Komsomol'skaia pravda*, 4 March (2005).
73 "Ia ubival Esenina – posle ėtogo strana menia dolzhna voznenavidet'," *Izvestiia*, 10 March (2005).
74 "Konets revoliutsii," *Segodniashniaia gazeta*, 16 June (2005).
75 "Le Kremlin, inquiet des révolutions périphériques, cultive une nostalgie pour la stabilité de l'ère Brejnev," *Le Monde*, 8 April (2005).
76 "Leonid Il'ich ne byl seksual'no ozabochen!," *Ėkspress gazeta*, 15 April (2005).
77 "Sergei Shakurov: Mne pereteselovat' stol'ko muzhikov!," *Komsomol'skaia pravda*, 20 March (2005).

78 "Nam ne pokazali, kak Brezhnev ulozhil medsestru v postel'," *Komsomol'skaia pravda*, 2 April (2005).
79 "Dva Brezhneva," *Rodnaia gazeta*, 8 April (2005).
80 "Nam ne pokazali ... "
81 *Sotsialisticheskii realizm i sovremennyi kinematograficheskii protsess*, Moscow: Soiuz kinematografistov SSSR (1976), 369.
82 "Rossiiskoe televidenie: propaganda vmesto svobody slova," *Prava cheloveka v Rossii*, 17 February (2004).

3 Soaps

1 "Voina za smysl," *Kinoart* #9 (2004).
2 Prokhorov, A. "Size Matters: The Ideological Functions of the Length of Soviet Feature Films and Television Mini-Series in the 1950s and 1960s," *Kinokultura*, January (2006).
3 The extremely long, mild-mannered 2006 "telesaga" of family affairs *Liubov' kak liubov'* (*A Love Like Any* Other), directed for Channel One by Aleksandr Nazarov, is based upon an original Polish screenplay.
4 Razzakov, F. *Dos'e na zvezd: Tainy televideniia*, Moscow: KSMO Press (2000), 159–60.
5 "Znatoki vozvrashchaiutsia," *Izvestiia*, 26 September (2001).
6 Nepomnyashchy, C. "Imperially, My Dear Watson: Sherlock Holmes and the Decline of Soviet Empire," in Hutchings, S. and Vernitskaia, A. (eds.) *Screening the Word: Russian and Soviet Film Adaptations of Literature*, London: Routledge-Curzon (2004), 171.
7 "Otechestvennyi serial – pribyl'noe lekarstvo," *Russkii fokus*: slav.kubanol.ru/newsr_f.html.
8 "Vlastelin serialov," *Ezhenedel'nyi zhurnal* #87, 15 September (2003).
9 "Televizionnye serialy: Made in Russia," *Kriticheskaia massa* #3 (2003).
10 *Mir teleserialov* (undated): teleserials.narod.ru/Veron/Vercast.htm.
11 "Vechnyi zov russkoi dushi/Mnogoseriinye stradaniia," *Literaturnaia gazeta* #43 (2003).
12 "Tsitiruia Genseka," *Nezavisimaia gazeta*, 23 September (2000).
13 "Vremia, kotoroe okhotisia za nami," *Nezavisimaia gazeta*, 20 October (2001); and "Tushite svet, chtob bylo svetlo!," *Nezavisimaia gazeta*, 27 October (2001).
14 "Rabynia Izaura vernulas' na teleėkrany v 120 seriiakh," *Regions Online*, 19 October (2004): www.regions-online.ru/index.php3?id = 2010.
15 "Khronika brazil'skikh telenovell v Rossii": braziliada.ru/other/chronicle.shtml.
16 "Serial po-russki," *Znamia* #3 (1999).
17 "Ia liru posviashchu zakazu tvoemu!," *Nezavisimaia gazeta*, 15 February (2002).
18 *Television in the Russian Federation: Organizational Structure, Programme Production and Audience* (2003), Strasbourg: European Audiovisual Observatory.
19 "Dokhodnoe mylo," *Iskusstvo kino* #3 (2001).
20 "Industrial'nye itogi i soderzhatel'nye tendentsii," *Radio Svoboda*, 5 July (2004).
21 "Moskovskaia saga: chto ostalos' za kadrom," *Argumenty i fakty* #16, November (2004).
22 "Moskovskaia saga: Bezrukov pokhudel na 15kg," *Komsomol'skaia pravda*, 5 November (2004).
23 Graffy, J. "Film Adaptations of Aksenov: The Young Prose and the Cinema of the Thaw," in Hutchings, S. and Vernitskaia, A. (eds.) *Screening the Word: Russian and Soviet Film Adaptations of Literature*, London: Routledge-Curzon (2004).
24 "Saga o kal'mare," *Kino*: http://kino.br.by/review240.html.
25 "A Small Window onto a Shadowed Past," *Washington Post*, 14 November (2004).

26 "Moskovskaia saga: istoriia s istoriei," *Argumenty i fakty* #10 November (2004).
27 "Moskovskaia saga – èto nasha 'Santa Barbara' stalinskoi èpokhi," *Komsomol'skaia pravda*, 20 November (2004).
28 "Homing Instinct," *Moscow Times*, 17 December (2004).
29 "Moskovskaia saga: TV-serial," *Kino*: http://kino.br.by/film3429.html.
30 "Shpionskie igry," *Komsomol'skaia pravda*, 28 March (2005).
31 "Kagèbèshnikov priniali za mafiiu," *Komsomol'skaia pravda*, 20 July (2005).
32 "Shtrafbat," *Interlinks*: www.serials.interlinks.ru/russianserials/shtrafbat/.
33 "Akter Iurii Stepanov: My posadili derevo u bratskoi mogily shrafbatchikov ... ," *Komsomol'skaia pravda*, 7 October (2004).
34 "Shtrafbat pobedil konkurentov," *Izvestiia*, 15 August (2004).
35 Ognev, A. "Nravstvennyi ideal semeinoi zhizni v russkoi sovetskoi klassike," in Buznik, V. and Vakhitova, T. (eds.) *Russkaia sovetskaia klassika*, Leningrad: Nauka (1989), 9.
36 Anninskii, L. *"Kak zakalialas' stal'" Nikolaia Ostrovskogo*, Moscow: Khudozhestvennaia literatura (1988), 37.
37 Valunaite, I. *Analiz romana N. Ostrovskogo "Kak zakalialas' stal'" v VII klasse litovskoi shkoly*, Vilnius (1976), 23–4.
38 Dostupova, T. *Vtoraia zhizn' Pavla Korchagina*, Moscow: Kniga (1978), 29.
39 Skripnik, V. *Nemerknushie stranitsy – 50 let*, Kiev: Molod' (1983), 17.
40 "Kursanty," *Interlinks*: www.serials.interlinks.ru/russianserials/kursanty.
41 "Ivan Stebunov: Akter," *Ruskino*: www.ruskino.ru/person.php?folder = stebunov.
42 "Fabrika obrazov: Televidenie osnovnoi instrument sozdaniia politicheskikh mifov," *Professiia – zhurnalist* #1 (2000).
43 "Prezident vystupil s poslaniem k Federal'nomu sobraniiu," *Bre.ru*, April (2005): www.bre.ru/news/24360.html.
44 Brooks, J. "Studies of the Reader in the 1920s," *Russian History* 9/2–3 (1982), 202.
45 Walker, G., "Soviet Publishing since the October Revolution," in Remnek, M. (ed.) *Books in Russia and the Soviet Union: Past and Present*, Wiesbaden: Otto Harrassowitz (1991), 80.
46 Ibid., 87.
47 Lovell, S. *The Russian Reading Revolution: Print Culture in the Soviet and Post-Soviet Eras*, Basingstoke: Macmillan (2000), 20.
48 Ibid., 43.
49 Dobrenko, E. *The Making of the State Reader: Social and Aesthetic Contexts of the Reception of Soviet Literature*, Stanford: Stanford University Press (1997), 50 and 57.
50 Ibid., 105–6.
51 "Oppozitsii nadoel serial 'Putin,'" *Agentstvo politicheskikh novostei*, 23 May (2005).

4 Costume drama

1 "Inna Churikova: Russkii miss Marpl – èto smeshno!," *Komsomol'skaia pravda*, 13 January (2005).
2 "Aktrisa Inna Churikova: Obsuzhdenie": http://www.ruskino.ru/acter/forum.php?class = ros&aid = 54&lit = %D0%A7&category = w.
3 "Smotrim televizor: Bum televizionnykh serialov," *Radio Svoboda*, 11 October (2004): www.svoboda.org/programs/tv/2004/tv.101104.asp.
4 "Tsifry govoriat za sebia," www.bednayanastya.ru/figures.htm.
5 "Medovyi mesiats Eleny Korikovoi," *Ėkspress gazeta* #44, November (2003).
6 "O fil'me": www.bednayanastya.ru/synopsis.htm.

7 "Kto zhe èta Nastia?" *Moskovskaia pravda*, 14 November (2003).
8 "Rabynia Izaura po-russki," *Èkspress gazeta* #44, November (2003).
9 "Kakaia zhizn' byla pod kryl'iami dvuglavogo orla," *Antenna* #12, 15–21 March (2004).
10 "Pravdivaia skazka o Bednoi Naste," *Moskovskaia Pravda*, 19 March (2004).
11 "Obratnaia sviaz'," *Tsvetnoi televizor* #2, 5–11 January (2004).
12 "Bednaia Nastia," *Serial* #48, November (2003); and #4, January (2004).
13 "Nebednaia Nastia," *Novaia gazeta*, 3 November (2003).
14 "Anna Gorshkova: dobroe slovo i zlodeike priatno," *Antenna* #3, 12–18 January (2004).
15 "Rokovoi muzhchina," *TV-Park* #48, November (2003).
16 "V Rossii – myl'nyi bum," *Otvet'!* #3, 12–18 January (2004).
17 "Chut' pomedlenee, koni!," *Tsvetnoi televizor* #5, January (2004).
18 "Ia protiv liubovnoi chekhardy," *Èkspress-gazeta* #12, 23 March (2004).
19 "Instinkt okhotnika," *Serial* #11, March (2004).
20 "Liubov' na troikh," *Serial* #7, February (2004).
21 "Moia Natasha – plod fantazii," *Èkspress-gazeta* #9, March (2004).
22 "Sila inogo," *Novoe vremia* #52, 26 December (2004).
23 "Dva nadoia s odnogo 'Vozvrashcheniia,'" *Gazeta.ru*, 3 October (2003): www.gazeta.ru/print/2003/10/03/dvanadoasodn.shtml.
24 "Narodnyi èkran," *Izvestiia*, 28 August (2003).
25 "Stanislav Govorukhin," *Novye izvestiia*, 25 August (2003).
26 "Bol'shaia sovetskaia melodrama," *Kul'tura-portal* #34, 4–10 September (2003).
27 "Khudozhestvennyi fil'm: 'Blagoslovite zhenshchinu.' Obsuzhdenie": www.ruskino.ru/movie/forum.
28 Dobrenko, E. *Aesthetics of Alienation*, Evanston: Northwestern University Press (2005), 120.
29 "Putin byl oderzhim TV," *Sibir' forum*, 1 July (2001).
30 "Mama aktera Il'ina schitaet ego novym Shtirlitsem," *Komsomol'skaia pravda*, 22 October (2004).
31 "Dmitrii Nazarov stal sekretnym agentom," *Komsomol'skaia pravda*, 11 August (2003).
32 "Udacha mesiatsa: Krasnaia kapella," *Ogonek* #39 (2004).
33 "Na rossiiskie teleèkrany vozvrashchaetsia kino pro razvedchikov," *Rossiia: Vesti nedeli*, 12 October (2003): www.vesti7.ru/archive/news?id = 3143.
34 "Krasnaia kapella," *Women.lux*, 15 September (2004): www.women.lux.co.il/hollywood/62.php.
35 "Sredi nas ne bylo predatelei," *Izvestiia*, 24 September (2004).
36 "Kapella krasnaia," *Itogi* #36 (2004).
37 "Zavershilsia pokaz teleseriala 'Krasnaia kapella,'" *Rossiiskaia gazeta*, 5 November (2004).
38 "Pravda o Krasnoi kapelle," *Sluzhba vneshnei razvedki Rossii*: www.svr.gov.ru/smi/2004/rosgaz20041105.htm.
39 "Shestnadtsat' let spustia," *Rossiiskaia gazeta*, 9 February (2004).
40 "Zavershena èkranizatsiia romana 'Deti Arbata,'" *Podrobnosti.ua*, 23 April (2004).
41 "Prodiussery serialov liubiat fast-fud," *TV-Park*, 25 November (2004).
42 "Na s"emkakh u akterov nachalis' romany," *Women.lux*, 13 December (2004).
43 "Istoriia liubvi, vernosti i predatel'stva," *Moskvichka*, 5 December (2004).
44 "Marsh primireniia i soglasiia: 'Moskovskaia saga' kak istoriia dlia bydla," *Novaia gazeta* #88, 29 November (2004).
45 "Istselenie liubov'iu": forum.topkino.ru/viewtopic/t/20/view/next.
46 "Forum Pervogo kanala: Deti Arbata," 23 November, (2004).
47 "Chulpan Khamatova stala blondinkoi," *Komsomol'skaia pravda*, 17 September (2003).

48 "Vo vremia seriala 'Dve sud'by' pod Minskom sgoreli dva doma," *Komsomol'skaia pravda v Belorussii*, 4 October (2003).
49 "Dve sud'by – 2," *TVIN Product Placement*: www.productplacement.ru/project/synopsis_90.shtml.
50 "Na teleėkrany vykhodit novyi serial," *Grani.ru*, 14 October (2002).
51 "Ogovorki po Freidu," *Respublika.ru*, 7 October (2003): www.respublika.ru/docs/respublika/191/5008.html.
52 "Myl'nyi navar," *Kommersant-Daily (Den'gi)*, 17 December (2003).
53 "Protiv techeniia," *Rossiiskaia gazeta*, 22 September (2003).
54 "Takie raznye serii," *Literaturnaia gazeta* #11, 24–30 March (2003).
55 "Nikakaia ia ne sterva," *Argumenty i fakty*, 15 October (2003).
56 Viewers' forum, 23 December 2004.

5 Melodrama

1 Kramov, I. *Aleksandr Malyshkin: Ocherk tvorchestva*, Moscow: Sovetskii pisatel' (1965), 213.
2 McLean, H. "The Countryside," in Jones, M. and Miller, R. *The Cambridge Companion to the Classic Russian Novel*, Cambridge: Cambridge University Press (1998), 59.
3 Weiner, D.R. *Models of Nature: Ecology, Conservation and Cultural Revolution in Soviet Russia*, Bloomington: Indiana University Press (1988), 80.
4 Ibid., 36.
5 Nemilov, A. "Zametki uchenogo," *Varnitso* #6 (1930), 64.
6 "Putin trebuet ubrat' ubogikh personazhei s televideniia," *Gazeta.ru*, 3 May (2005).
7 "Alena Babenko: V kino ia vse ravno riskuiu," *Ėkpress gazeta*, 10 March (2005).
8 "Moskva slezam ne verit. Uzhe 25 let," *Argumenty i fakty*, 16 February (2005).
9 "My snimaem istoriiu novykh russkikh Rastin'iakov," *Izvestiia*, 26 July (2002).
10 "Forum," 25 June (2004): www.ruskino.ru.
11 "Na STS 'Nadezhda ukhodit poslednei,'" *Moskovskii komsomolets*, 9 September (2004).
12 Hallward, P. *Badiou: A Subject to Truth*, Minneapolis: University of Minnesota Press (2003), 32.
13 "Ideal'naia para," Forum: www.ruskino.ru.
14 "Aleksandr Baluev – orel!," *TV-Park* #41, October (2000).
15 "Chetvert' veka nazad – imenno v den' vsekh vliublennykh – kak raz i v liubvi mne i otkazali!," *Fakty i kommentarii*, 13 February (2002).
16 "Sladkie parochki," *Sankt-Peterburgskie vedomosti* #49, 20 March (2001).
17 "Ostanovka po trebovaniiu," *REN-TV*, March (2002): www.ren-tv.com/article.asp?id = 8112.
18 "Serialy," *Telesem'*, 25 December (2004)–2 January (2005).
19 "Mylo i borshch s pampushkami," *Izvestiia*, 9 December (2003).
20 "Marina Aleksandrova izbila militsionera tuflei," *Komsomol'skaia pravda*, 13 February (2004).
21 "U bednoi Nasti budet 'Nebo v goroshek,'" 21 February (2004): www.russia.org.ua/reviews/403a2d32263eb/view_print.
22 "Gorokh nebesnyi – ne manna," *Kievskii telegraf* #201 (2003).
23 "Pervyi pobeditel' konkursa 'Khochesh' sniat'sia v kino?!'" *Dorogaia Masha Berezina: Novosti*, 3 August (2004): www.mashaberezina.ru/news.shtml.
24 "Serial: Dorogaia Masha Berezina" (Forum), 22 September 2004: www.theforum.ru/serial.
25 "Skoraia prem'era seriala," *Kleo*, 28 May (2004): www.kleo.ru/items/news/2004-05-28.shtml.

26 "Dorogaia Anna Azarova," *Vash Dosug*: www.vashdosug.ru/article_page/3839.
27 "Reiting serialov," *Interfaks-zapad*, 4 February (2005).
28 "Supermegaproekt 'Dorogaia Masha Berezina'": ctc-serial/narod.ru/press-a_4.html.
29 "Dorogovizna VO VSEM ... ," *Khar'kovskie okna* #28, 15 July (2004).
30 "Govorit i pokazyvaet 'Bednaia Masha!,'" *Pravda*, 15 July (2004).
31 *TV in the Russian Federation*, European Audiovisual Observatory (March 2006), 55.
32 "Reality-shou vmesto real'nosti," *Kompaniia*, 30 June (2003).
33 "Russia Is Watching Big Brother," *BBC News*, 29 October (2001).
34 "Are We Becoming Dozy Electrical Appliances?," *Moscow Times*, 28 November (2001).
35 "Russian Big Brother Bares All," *BBC News*, 12 November (2001).
36 "Shocking Our Russian Brothers," *BBC News*, 25 November (2001).
37 "Row over Russian 'Big Brother,'" *CNN*, 23 November (2001).
38 "Going Hungry for Russian Reality TV," *Gothamist*, 6 November (2005).
39 "Realiti-shou: chuzhaia zhizn' kak narkotik," *Mednovosti.ru*, 16 April (2005).
40 "Fabrika zvezd." Promotional materials at: www.tv1.ru.

6 Heroines

1 "Serial 'Zhelannaia'": allstars.pp.ru/lenta/index16/s4.html.
2 "Liubovniki Marii," *TV-Park*, 11 December (2003).
3 "Informatsiia kanala," *Moia Udmutriia*, 14 January (2005).
4 "Il'ia Avramenko, Evgenii Kostiuchenko: 'Nina,'" *KM.ru*, 3 October (2003).
5 "Kremlevskii serial," *Nezavisimaia gazeta*, 6 April (2002).
6 "Na Minskom vokzale sniali kino i nashli 8,5 tysiach dollarov," *Komsomol'skaia pravda v Belorussii*, 5 March (2004).
7 "Ona tozhe napisala ubiistvo," *Mir novostei*, 16 September (2003).
8 "Mezhdu nebom i zemlei," *Rossiiskaia gazeta*, 12 March (2004).
9 "Ekaterina Guseva poimala trekh zaitsev," *Rossiiskaia gazeta*, 23 April (2004).
10 "Tam, za oblakami," *TV-Park*, 19 March (2004).
11 "Krasivaia skazka o zhizni pilotov?," *Komsomol'skaia pravda*, 31 March (2004).
12 "Katia Guseva nauchilas' igrat' paralich," *Komsomol'skaia pravda*, 24 March (2004).
13 Beumers, B. "Pop-Sots, or the Popularization of History in the Musical *Nord-Ost*," *SEEJ*, 48.3 (2004).
14 Lipovetsky, M. "Post-Sots: Transformations of Socialist Realism in the Popular Culture of the Recent Period," *SEEJ* 48.3 (2004).
15 Olcott, A. *Russian Pulp: The Detektiv and the Russian Way of Crime*, Lanham and Boulder: Rowman and Littlefield (2001), 114–15.
16 Ibid., 149.
17 "Andrei Sokolov zaputalsia v bliznetsakh," *Komsomol'skaia pravda*, 15 January (2005).
18 "Èlia Bolgova edva li ne utonula na s"emkakh Bliznetsov," *Èkspress gazeta*, 1 February (2005).
19 "Khoroshuiu siuzhetinu pridumali indusy," *Komsomol'skaia pravda*, 5 February (2005).
20 "Mnogie geroi Bliznetsov real'ny!," *Komsomol'skaia pravda*, 10 February (2005).
21 "O seriale," *News.ntv.ru*, 20 April (2006).
22 "Na tom kontse vozdushnogo mosta," *NTV.ru*, 26 April (2006).
23 "Aèroport: 30 serii sploshnogo èkstrima!," *NTV.ru* and "Chto modno, to i dokhodno," *Belarus' segodnia*, both 22 April (2006).

24 Ivanova, T. *Vsevolod Ivanov: Pisatel' i chelovek*, Moscow: Sovetskii pisatel' (1975), 6–7.
25 *TV in the Russian Federation*, European Audiovisual Observatory (March 2006), 96.
26 "Only Skin Deep," *Moscow Times*, 2 December (2005). The worldwide success of the original Colombian show is documented in "Ugly Never Looked So Good," *Los Angeles Times*, 16 September (2006).
27 "Niania i Liuba smeiutsia strogo po formule?," *Telesem'*: http://www.telesem.ru/serials/serials.php?publication = 2423.
28 "Scientists Reveal Formula for Perfect Sitcom," *Daily Telegraph*, 6 June (2005).
29 "Bednaia Nastia khorosheet s kazhdym povtorom," *Antenna*, 31 January – 6 February (2005).
30 "Niania sobiraetsia zamuzh," *Komsomol'skaia pravda*, 28 January (2005).
31 "Telekanaly voiuiut parami," *Izvestiia*, 14 January (2005).
32 "Zdravstvuite, ia Vasha niania!," *Itogi*, 8 February (2005).
33 "Sostoitsia li svad'ba Shatalina i Viki?," *Antenna*, 31 January–6 February (2005).
34 "Skazhi-ka, niania, ved' nedarom!," *Tribuna*, 29 December (2004).
35 "Anastasiia Zavorotniuk: Mama v zhizni, niania – na èkrane," *Vse kanaly TV*, 27 September (2004).
36 "Anastasiia Zavorotniuk: V detstve mne ne povezlo s nianei!," *Èkspress-gazeta*, 15 February (2005).
37 "Dvadtsat' voprosov," *Domashnii ochag*, July (2005).
38 "Sam sebe reality-shou," *Nezavisimaia gazeta*, 18 June (2004).
39 "RIAA preduprezhdaet": www.egitara.ru.
40 "Amerika khochet polozhit' konets rossiiskomu piratstvu," www.security.complementa.ru.
41 "Tsentral'nyi podkast-terminal," www.russianpodcasting.ru.
42 "V Rossiiu prishel 'Podcasting,'" *Internet.ru*, 29 April (2005).
43 "Liudi govoriat," *Computerra.ru*, 23 November (2005).

7 Comedy

1 "Pobeda bessil'noi sily," *Novoe literaturnoe obozrenie* #4/12 (2000).
2 "Rossiia v litse svoego prezidenta," *Radio svoboda*, 25 October (2003).
3 Kordova, N. *Vopros i otvet: Pisateli XX veka*, Voronezh: Rodnaia rech' (1994), 74 and 76.
4 Stepanov, V. *Mnogoobrazie tvorcheskikh iskanii v russkoi literature XX veka*, Cheboksary: ChRIO (1994), 108.
5 Bykov, L. (ed.) *Russkaia literatura XX veka: Problemy i imena*, Ekaterinburg: UGU (1994), 99.
6 Chalmaev, V. (ed.) *Russkaia literatura XX veka*, Moscow: Prosveshchenie (1994), 122.
7 Polukhina, A. *Sovremennaia literatura*, Tol'iatti: Sovremennik (1995), 44.
8 Bikkulova, I. *Sovremennyi literaturnyi protsess*, Moscow: MORF (1995), 5.
9 Pronina, E. (ed.) *Russkaia literatura XX veka*, Moscow: Prosveshchenie (2001 [vol. 2]), 19.
10 Ibid., vol. 1, 3.
11 Shrom, N. *Noveishaia russkaia literatura 1987–1999*, Riga: Retorika "A" (2000), 10.
12 "Sto tomov na bezuprechno chistom russkom iazyke," *Rossiiskaia gazeta*, 18 February (2003).
13 "Nestandartnaia 'Kat'enka,'" *Russkaia Germaniia* #48, 2–8 December (2002).
14 "Anonsy: Agentstvo NLS": tnt.perm.ru/film/?id = 5.

15 "My s priiatelem vdvoem ... ," *TV-Park*, 12 February (2003).
16 "Iz Laptiuga v zvezdy," *Prem'er* #4/230, 30 January (2002).
17 "Uznal o sekse v detskom sadu," *Èkspress gazeta*, 5 March (2002).
18 "Gertsoginiu Iorkskuiu zashchishchal parikmakher," *Smena*, 24 August (2003).
19 "Net alibi v igre bez pravil," *Rossiiskaia gazeta*, 27 February (2004).
20 "Zhenskie serialy: Press-konferentsiia," *The Forum.ru*, 9 May (2004).
21 "Na s"emkakh 'Bal'zakovskogo vozrasta' aktery razdevalis' bez priglasheniia!," *Komsomol'skaia pravda*, 1 June (2004).
22 "Proval seriala 'Bal'zakovskii vozrast ... ,'" *Vazhno.ru*, 28 May (2004): vazhno.ru/society/223.html.
23 "Chto delat' v bol'shom gorode, esli vse muzhiki svo ... ?," *Kleo.ru*: www.kleo.ru/items/about_you/serialy.shtml.
24 "Vot tebe, babushka, i seks v bol'shom go ... ," *Argumenty i fakty*, 24 June (2004).
25 "Klon nezrelogo vozrasta," *Literaturnaia gazeta* #22 (2004).
26 "A seksa vse net, ili vse baby du ... ," *Krokodil* #18, May (2004).
27 "Zhenshchina bal'zakovskogo vozrasta sozdana dlia seksa, kak ptitsa – dlia poleta," *Ogonek* #23, June (2004).
28 "Forum," 14 November (2004): www.ruskino.ru/movie.
29 "Aleksei Maklakov: v armii, v nariade eli my olad'i," *Telesem'*, 7 April (2005).
30 "Liubov' zagnala Pevtsova v kletku," *Sem' dnei*, 18–24 October (2004).
31 "Nekotorye zheniatsia, a nekotorye tak ... ," *Argumenty i fakty*, 20 October (2004).
32 "Marat Basharov: Zhena s docher'iu stali musl'mankami," *Argumenty i fakty*, 14 January (2005).
33 "Oleg Fomin – kholostiak po prikolu," *Èkspress gazeta*, 24 November (2004).
34 "Marat Basharov: Vsegda igraiu samogo sebia v predlagaemykh obstoiatel'stvakh," *Olo*, http://10-04.olo.ru/news/culture/25221.html.
35 "Muzhskie bredni. Serial 'Kholostiaki' snova v èfire," *Izvestiia*, 11 January (2005).
36 "NEXT-2: Sleduiushchii": http://ruserials.narod.ru/archive/next-2.html.
37 Sawka, R. *Putin: Russia's Choice*, London: Routledge (2004), 107.
38 "Na rossiiskom televidenii plokho s ètikoi," *SMI.ru*, 29 March (2000).
39 "Mediatormoz," *Otechestvennye zapiski* #4/13 (2003).
40 "O televidenii, Putine i prognozakh," *Kommunisticheskaia partiia Rossiiskoi federatsii* (kprf.ru), 30 May (2003).
41 Thomson, B. "The Russian Forest," in Cornwell, N. (ed.) *Reference Guide to Russian Literature*, London: Fitzroy and Dearborn (1998), 491.
42 Lapchenko, A. *Chelovek i zemlia v russkoi sotsial'no-filosofskoi proze 70-kh godov*, Leningrad: LGU (1985), 136.
43 Lobanov, M. *Roman L. Leonova "Russkii les,"* Moscow: Sovetskii pisatel' (1958), 112, 156 and 214.
44 Starikova, E. (1954) *Tvorchestvo L.M. Leonova*, Moskva: Znanie (1954), 213.
45 Galanov, A. *Problema sozdaniia kharakterov v romanakh L. Leonova*, Moscow: AON (1959), 14.
46 Zubareva, E. "Mir detstva v 'Russkom lese,'" in Vlasov, F. (ed.) *Bol'shoi mir: Stat'i o tvorchestve Leonida Leonova* (1972), 262–3.
47 Zhuravlev, V. (ed.) *Russkaia literatura XX veka*. Moscow: Prosveshchenie (1997), 249.
48 Porman, R. "Iz opyta chteniia spets-kursa *Tvorchestvo L. Leonova*," in Krylov, V. (ed.) *Problemy izucheniia tvorchestva Leonida Leonova v VUZe*. Leningrad: LGPI (1986), 130.

8 Law and order

1 "Mikhail Porechenkov potreboval za rol' Lekhi bol'shie den'gi," *Komsomol'skaia pravda*, 25 March (2005).

2 "Mikhail Porechenkov: Chto v muzhchine samoe glavnoe," *Megapolis-Èkspress* #2, February (2005).
3 "Lekha Nikolaev ne zhenitsia nikogda!," *Komsomol'skaia pravda*, 18 February (2005).
4 "Bel'giiskuiu ovcharku nataskivali na krotov i sharikovye ruchki," *Telesem'*, 6 July (2005).
5 "Demon poldnia," *Mir TV i kino* #8/236 (2005).
6 "Dal'nii potomok grafa Monte-Kristo," *Rossiiskaia gazeta*, 24 September (2004).
7 "Aleksandr Baluev stal grafom Monte-Kristo," *Èkspress gazeta*, 24 August (2004).
8 Ibid.
9 "Kino bez finala," *Novye izvestiia*, 3 September (2004).
10 "Muzhchiny ne plachut. Tem bolee – sledovateli," *Komsomol'skaia pravda*, 14 March (2005).
11 "Sarmat," Forum: www.levdurov.ru.
12 Ibid.
13 "Belyi kloun," *Moskovskii komsomolets*, 25 July (2005).
14 "Anatolii Belyi: V tom, chto ia ne slomalsia, zasluga Mariny," *Trud*, 26 May (2005).
15 "U Dar'i Moroz roman s frantsuzskim polismenom," *Èkspress gazeta*, 16 February (2005).
16 Miasnikov, A. "M. Gor'kii i voprosy sovremennoi èstetiki," in Shcherbina, V. (ed.) *Gor'kii i sovremennost'* (1970), 211.
17 Belen'skii, E. *Gor'kii i Sibir'*, Omsk: Omskoe oblastnoe izdatel'stvo (1956), 60.
18 "Serial 'Kosvennye uliki'": www.forumy.ru/rtvi/view.php?dat = 20050131225931.
19 "Putin i Gor'kii," *Nezavisimaia gazeta*, 2 September (2000).
20 "Russkii kharakter: voiny i plaksy," *Utro.ru*, 30 May (2005).

9 Criminal series

1 "Ne v pervom kruge," *Belarus' segodnia*, 4 February (2006).
2 "Televidenie chasto kritikuiut za pokaz nasiliia," *Èkho Moskvy*, 8 February (2006).
3 "O t'iurme i o sume," *Moskovskii komsomolets*, 12 January (2006).
4 "Chtoby ne brosalo ten'," *Argumenty i fakty*, 11 January; and "Serial o t'iurme ... nachinaet pokazyvat' kanal NTV," *Èkspress gazeta*, #3 January (both 2006).
5 "Aleksandr Sidorov: 'Zona': Ètot film – smes' militseiskikh i zekovskikh istorii," *Komsomol'skaia pravda*, 2 February (2006).
6 "Ot 'Nasti' Shteina brosilo na nary. NTV pokazhet 'Zonu,'" *Sobesednik*, 18 January (2006).
7 "Zona nesvobody," *Èkspress gazeta*, 27 January (2006).
8 "Vek voli ne vidat'!," *Trud*, 19 January (2006).
9 "Telelidery," *Kommersant*, 8 February (2006).
10 "Blatnye kartinki," *Trud*, 10 February (2006).
11 "Pozhaleite nashikh rodnykh," *Trud*, 26 January (2006).
12 "Na televizionnoi zone i nakolki risuiut sharikovoi ruchkoi," *Komsomol'skaia pravda*, 26 January (2006).
13 "O proekte," www.zona.tv/main_chapter/1.html.
14 "Zona NTV," *Nezavisimaia gazeta*, 8 February; and "Zona v tebe i vo mne," *Gazeta*, 24 January (both 2006).
15 "Moda na kriminal i zhestokost' na rossiiskom televidenii," *Radio Svoboda*, 23 March (2006).
16 "Ulitsy razbitykh fonarei: Kontseptsiia," *Iskusstvo kino* #1 (2003).
17 "Na 'Ulitsakh razbitykh fonarei' nastoiashchie prestupniki pereputalis' s kinoshnymi!," *Komsomol'skaia pravda*, 3 September (2003).

18 "Mozhem pomoch' s ideiami," *Segodnia* #43, 26 February (2000).
19 "Menty prigovoreny k trem godam strogogo rezhima" (undated), http://zapiski-rep.sitecity.ru/ltext_1112152723.phtml.
20 "Nasiliia na teleèkranakh stalo gorazdo bol'she," *Dagestanskaia pravda*, 4 September (2003).
21 "Kamenskoi mogli stat' Drozdova i Glagoleva," *Komsomol'skaia pravda*, 5 December (2003).
22 "Klevyi ment Nastia," *Podmoskovnye izvestiia*, 10 November (2000).
23 "Kamenskikh mnogo ... ," *Shchit i mech*, 19 September (2002).
24 "Svoi serial blizhe k tele," *Moskovskie novosti* #36 (2002).
25 "Voshel v seriiu – 'vyshel v tirazh,'" *Argumenty i fakty: Moskva*, 11 June (2003).
26 "Intelligentsiia v rossiiskom detektive," *Neprikosnovennyi zapas* #4 (2001).
27 Lipaeva, T. "Ideino-kompozitsionnaia rol' pesen i 'muzykal'nykh stsen' v *Chapaeve*," in Kuprianovskii, P. (ed.) *Tvorchestvo pisatelia i literaturnyi protsess*, Ivanovo: Ivanovskii gosudarstvennyi universitet (1984), 100.
28 "Marsh Turetskogo: Novyi supergeroi ne vooruzhen, no ochen' opasen!," *NetTV*, October (2000): www.nettv.ru/tv/article/102000/marsh.shtml.
29 "Marsh Turetskogo privel Domogarova v bol'nitsu," *Komsomol'skaia pravda*, 4 January (2003).
30 "Krizis realista," *Nezavisimaia gazeta*, 11 November (2000).
31 "Brigada postkommunisticheskogo truda," *Izvestiia*, 21 October (2002).
32 "V 'Brigade' vmesto Bezrukova mog sygrat' Mashkov," *Komsomol'skaia pravda*, 4 June (2004).
33 "Brigady-2 ne budet!," *Komsomol'skaia pravda*, 8 January (2003).
34 "Vtoroi 'Brigady' ne budet?," *Argumenty i fakty*, 17 March (2004).
35 "Sergei Bezrukov znaet kak nado liubit'," 22 November (2002).
36 "Sekrety seriala 'Brigada,'" *Dni.ru*, 21 October (2002): www.dni.ru/news/society/2002/10/21/15153.html.
37 "TV ustroilo razborki so zriteliami?," *Komsomol'skaia pravda*, 13 February (2003).
38 "Brigada – luchshii russkii serial?," *Websoft* (undated): www.websoft.net/article618.html.
39 "Kaskadery Rossii obliubovali Zarechnyi," *Molodoi Leninets* #12, 20 March (2001).
40 "Myl'nye puzyri," *WomenClub.ru*, 2 October (2002).
41 "Khoroshie bandity?," *Mesto vstrechi* #50, 9–15 December (2002).
42 "Skazka pro belogo byka," *Moskovskii komsomolets*, 27 October (2002).
43 "Bandit-prodakshn," *Novaia gazeta* #78, 21 October (2002).
44 "*Brigada*: forum," 2 March (2004): www.ruskino.ru/movie.
45 "Teni izmenit' nel'zia," *Itogi* #2, 12 January (2001).
46 "Russia Downgraded to 'Not Free,'" *Freedom House Press Releases*, 20 December (2004): www.freedomhouse.org/media/pressrel/122004.htm.
47 "Uchastok stal samym reitingovym rossiiskim serialom poslednikh let," *Izvestiia*, 31 December (2003).
48 "Opiat' pro nas," *Vremia*, 10 June (2004).
49 "Nepakhannyi uchastok," *Ogonek* #7, January (2004).
50 "Khot' pokhozhe na Rossiiu – tol'ko vse zhe ne Rossiia ... ," *Izvestiia*, 26 December (2003).
51 "Uchastkovyi Bezrukov chut' ne umer ot SPIDa," *Komsomol'skaia pravda*, 24 December (2003).
52 "Bezrukovu podsunuli nepravil'nogo psa," *Komsomol'skaia pravda*, 9 December (2003).
53 "Rossiian perekormili serialami," *RosBiznesKonsalting*, 10 December (2003).
54 "Forum," 9 September–9 November (2004): www.ruskino.ru/movie.
55 "Zelenyi 'Uchastok,'" *Argumenty i fakty*, 3 December (2003).

10 Conclusion

1 Manes, C. "Nature and Silence"; and Evernden, N. "Beyond Ecology: Self, Place and the Pathetic Fallacy," both in Glotfelty, C. and Fromm, H. (eds.) *The Ecocriticism Reader: Landmarks in Literary Ecology*, University of Georgia Press (1996), 25 and 95, respectively.
2 Agenosov, V. (ed.) *Russkaia literatura XX veka (Chast' 1)*, Moscow: Drofa (2001), 156.
3 Von Geldern, J. and Stites, R. *Mass Culture in Soviet Russia: Tales, Poems, Songs, Movies Plays and Folklore: 1917–1953*, Bloomington: Indiana University Press (1995), 22.

Index

72 metra 60, 73

Abdulov, A. 51, 112, 161
Adaptations: and the cost of fantasy 51–54; and prestige issues 32–36, 42–44; and Solzhenitsyn 36–39; and the Soviet heritage 39–42, 44–48
Advokat 210–11
Aèroport 136–40
Agent natsional'noi bezopasnosti 170–71, 178
Agentstvo NLS 152–53, 194
Amedia 68, 86, 143–44
Animated cinema 5–6, 40, 73, 161, 183, 192
Anna Karenina 35–37, 200

Badiou, A. 24–26
Baiazet 84–85
Bal'zakovskii vozrast 155–59, 162, 209
Baluev, A. 69, 108, 131–32, 173–74, 211
Banditskii Peterburg 130, 171
Bednaia Nastia 32–33, 85–88, 90, 92, 115, 136
Bekmambetov, T. 14, 51, 89
Berezovskii, B. 16–17, 28–30, 117
Bez kompleksov 121–22
Bezrukov, S. 35–37, 51–58, 69, 174–75, 198–208
Bliznetsy 60, 135–36, 141
Bol'shaia stirka 117
Bomba dlia nevesty 111–12
Bortko, V. 42–43, 51–54
Brezhnev, L.: and depiction on TV, 58–61, 70; and nostalgia, 5–8, 41, 45, 141, 212–13; and rhetoric, 45, 151; and stability, 20–21, 74, 212
Brigada 55, 101–2, 132, 174–75, 198–203, 209–10
Bukhta Filippa 187

Chto skazal pokoinik? 169
Churikova, I. 37, 69, 85
Cinema: and the 1930s 141–43; and the 1940s 184–86, 206–8; and the 1950s 165–67; and the 1970s–1980s 60–62, 122–24; and relationship with television 13–19; 48–51
Comedy: and city life 155–59; and irony 152–55, 162–65; and loss of stability 149–52; and male experience 159–62; and sitcom formats 143–48
Costume drama: and the 19th Century 84–88; and the 1930s 88–91; and WWII 91–98; and the Thaw 98–102
Crime dramas: and the mafia 198–202; and police work 193–96; and provincial disorder 203–8; and prisons 187–93; and stately arrogance, 196–98

Dal'noboishchiki 175–76
Dasha Vasil'eva 133–34, 143,152
Deviat' mesiatsev 105
Delo o mertvykh dushakh 213–14
Demon poldnia 173
Den' rozhdeniia Burzhuia 170–71
Derrida, J. 24–26, 30, 50
Deti Arbata 60, 70, 91 98, 125, 141
Deti Vaniukhina 105
Deti, Liuba i zavod 143–44
Diuzhev, D. 54–57, 134–35, 174–76, 198–203
Dnevnik ubiitsy 185
Dobrenko, E. 4–5, 8, 83, 90, 163
Doktor Zhivago 32–36, 68, 138
Dom 2 117–19
Domogarov, A. 51
Dorogaia Masha Berezina 114–16, 194
Dos'e detektiva Dubrovskogo, 169–70

Dostoevskii, F. 18, 30–32, 35, 38, 42–44, 161, 200, 205, 211–13
Drugaia zhizn' 110–11
Dubrovka theater siege 16, 29, 131–32
Durov, L. 175, 178
Dve sud'by 60, 98–102, 125, 204

Epstein, M. 3–6, 12, 25, 30, 63, 213–14
Esenin 57–58, 200, 212–13
Eshpai, A. 70, 94–97

Fabrika zvezd 69, 120–21
Fadeev, A. 4–6, 45–51, 53, 75, 94
Finance: and MMM, 27–28, 40; and rising costs, 21–22, 32, 51–54, 86,115; and profits, 68–69, 100–101

Galkin, V. 5, 102, 113, 119–20, 211
Garmash, S. 106–7, 187, 196
Geroi nashego vremeni 34–35
Gibel' imperii 211–12
Gladkov, F. 4–6, 98
Gogol', N. 3–4, 18, 30–31, 35, 213–14
Golod 118–19
Gor'kii, M. 46, 85, 104–5, 150–51, 161, 166, 181–83, 186, 210–13
Govorukhin, S. 88–90, 95
Grace under Fire 143–44
Graf Krestovskii 173–74
Granitsa 202–3
Grazhdanin nachal'nik, 171
Gromovy 62
Gusinskii, V. 29

Heroes: active, 13–18; passive, 9–13
Heroines: and fate, 126–29; and "organic" social ideals, 136–40; and social instabilities, 129–36
Hollywood 14–16, 21–22, 44, 87, 89, 114, 155–59

Ia tebia liubliu 112, 128
Ideal'naia para 108–9
Idiot 42–44, 52, 87, 127, 200
Igra na vybyvanie 174–75

Kafe Klubnichka 144
Kamenskaia 115, 155, 187, 193–98, 209
KGB v smokinge 73–74, 181
Khamatova, Ch. 34, 96–97, 211
Kharat'ian, D. 69, 134–35, 175
Khiromant 149, 198
Khodorkovskii, M. 13, 61, 71–72, 181–82
Kholostiaki 159–61

Kluichi ot bezdny 79–80
Kontora 168
Kosvennye uliki 183
Krasnaia kapella 91–94
Krasnaia ploshchad' 60
Krot 172–73
Kto khochet stat' millionerom? 162
Kursanty 78–79, 213
Kursk submarine disaster 2, 29, 90–91

Lacan, J. 6, 25–26
Lahusen, T. 3, 6, 12
Lednikovyi period 27
Leningradets 60
Leonov, L. 110, 121, 152, 163–65, 167
Lermontov, M. 10, 32, 34, 87, 175
Linii sud'by 105–7, 125, 196
Literature: and competition with television 1, 30–32, 36, 68; and "realism" 8, 47–48, 174–75; and TV adaptations 22–26, 32–63; and Soviet readers 67, 81–83, 149–52
Lynch, D. 36, 95

Maikov, P. 79, 159, 173–75, 198–203
Marsh Turetskogo 196–98, 200–202, 209
Master i Margarita 33, 35–37, 39, 51–54, 200
Men'shikov, O. 34, 36, 40
Mikhalkov, N. 37, 88–89, 145
Moia prekrasniaia niania 145–47
Molodaia gvardiia 44–51, 53, 78, 213
Moskovskaia saga 60, 69–72, 141, 178
Moskva slezam ne verit, 41, 89, 105–6, 201
Music: and cinema, 33, 50–51, 55, 97, 122–23, 142; and documentary/ "reality" aesthetic, 39, 120–21, 191; and metaphors of kinship, 50, 63, 74, 77, 142, 150, 161
Muzhchiny ne plachut 175

Na uglu u Patriarshikh 168–69
Nadezhda ukhodit poslednei 107
Nagiev, D. 51, 116, 162, 172
Namedni 162
Nanny, The 145–47
Navazhdenie 173
Ne rodis' krasivoi 143–44
Nebo i zemlia 130–33, 183–84
Nebo v goroshek 113–14
Next 161–62

Nina 100, 128–29, 134
Nostalgia: and the 1930s 88–91, 146; and the 1950s 165–66; and the 1970s 7–8, 22, 41, 61, 122–24, 141, 205; and WWII 71, 74–75
NTV 21, 29, 60, 68, 115, 158, 189, 194

Ofitsery 170
Ognebortsy 175
Okhota na iziubria 84
Okhota na Zolushku 185
Okhotniki za ikonami 54–57, 75, 124
Okna 116, 162, 172
Orbakaite, K. 69–70, 209–10
ORT (Channel One) 14–15, 21, 28, 42, 48–49, 60, 68, 72, 83, 88–89, 194
Ostanovka po trebovaniiu 41, 108–10
Ostrov iskushenii 119–20

Panfilov, G. 38–39, 72
Parallel'no liubvi 18–20, 23, 112–13
Passazhir bez bagazha 130
Pevtsov, D. 37, 110, 159–60, 171, 209–11
Peyton Place 44
Piatyi angel 172
Piracy 33–34, 138, 147
Po imeni Baron 171
Po tu storonu volkov 42, 102, 196
Pod nebom Verony 60
Porechenkov, M. 79, 170–72
Poslednii geroi 119–20
Prokhorova, E. 20–21, 30, 44
Proshkin, A. 33, 35–36
Protiv techeniia 172
Pugacheva, A 120–23, 206
Pushkin, A. 10, 30–32, 53, 64, 208, 213
Putin, V.: and centralization 44–45; and KGB stereotypes 28; and the law 127, 181, 197, 209; and media 12, 15, 22, 36, 81, 91, 162; and nationalism 1–3, 13, 176; and nostalgia 59; and rhetoric 6, 51, 149–50; and WWII 48–49; and youth movements 30

Reality TV 116–21
Riazanov, È. 8, 41, 52
Rodina zhdet 176
Rodnianskii, A. 49, 116, 145
Rodstvennyi obmen, 209–10
Rostov-Papa 9–13, 23, 26, 183
RTR (Rossiia) 28–29, 38, 42, 48–49, 51–53, 60, 66–68

Ruffo, V. 27–29, 85

Samara-gorodok 134–35
Santa Barbara 21, 68, 71, 86–88
Sarmat 176–79
Sasha + Masha 144–45
Semnadtsat' mgnovenii vesny 28–29, 35–36, 41–43, 65, 91, 95
Sestry 153–55
Sex and the City 155–59
Shakhnazarov, K. 12, 33, 123
Shtrafbat 60, 74–77, 79
Shukshin, V. 18, 62, 123–24
Shukshina, M. 59–60, 112
Slapovskii, A. 41–42, 108–10, 124–25, 205
Soap operas: and debt to Latin America, 64–69, 81–83; and ethos, 69–78; versus story arcs, 43–44
Sokolov, A. 135–36, 210–11
Soldaty 159
Solov'ev, S. 35–37
Sorokin, V. 30
Spas pod berezami, 212
Spinoza, B. 4–5, 26, 181–82, 213
Stalin, J. 7, 30, 39, 45–46, 61, 94–96, 141, 149, 163–65
Starye pesni o glavnom 49, 206
Stilet 171–72
STS 29, 42, 115–16, 143–44
Svetskie khroniki 113
Syshchiki 171

Tarkovskii, A. 33, 72, 187–88
Telenovela 13–14, 36, 42–44, 63–69, 83, 113, 212
Todorovskii, V. 42, 91–93, 95, 106, 153, 195
Tolstoi, A. 18, 90–91, 152
Tolstoi, L. 30–31, 38, 42–43, 50, 86–87, 193, 213
Tri tsveta liubvi 180

Uboinaia sila 194
Uchastok 49, 69, 203–8
Ulitsy razbitykh fonarei 158–59, 178, 193–95
Umnozhaiushchii pechal' 13, 179–83
Utesov: Pesnia dlinoiu v zhizn' 165–66

V kruge pervom 36–39
V ritme tango 83
Vdovichenkov, V. 79, 130–32, 174–75, 198–203

Videocasting 147–48
Viewers: and age, 41; and forums, 114–15; and rhetoric, 49, 51; and station ownership, 27–28
Vintovaia lestnitsa 85–86, 175, 183
Vokzal 129–30
Vsegda govori vsegda 134

X-Files, The 168

Yeltsin, B. 27–30, 41, 61, 177

Za steklom 116–17
Zakoldovannyi uchastok 124–25
Zhelannaia 126–28
Zhenshchiny v igre bez pravil 155
Zolotoi telenok 33, 37–42
Zona 187–97, 197

For Product Safety Concerns and Information please contact our EU
representative GPSR@taylorandfrancis.com
Taylor & Francis Verlag GmbH, Kaufingerstraße 24, 80331 München, Germany

www.ingramcontent.com/pod-product-compliance
Lightning Source LLC
Chambersburg PA
CBHW060559230426
43670CB00011B/1897